Ideologies and National Identities

Ideologies
and National Identities

The Case of Twentieth-Century
Southeastern Europe

Edited by

JOHN R. LAMPE and MARK MAZOWER

Central European University Press

Budapest   New York

English edition published in 2004 by
Central European University Press

An imprint of the
Central European University Share Company
Nádor utca 11, H-1051 Budapest, Hungary
Tel: +36-1-327-3138 or 327-3000
Fax: +36-1-327-3183
E-mail: ceupress@ceu.hu
Website: www.ceupress.com

400 West 59th Street, New York NY 10019, USA
Tel: +1-212-547-6932
Fax: +1-212-548-4607
E-mail: mgreenwald@sorosny.org

ISBN 963-9241-72-5   cloth
ISBN 963-9241-82-2   paperback

Library of Congress Cataloging-in-Publication Data

Ideologies and national identities: the case of twentieth-century
Southeastern Europe / edited by John Lampe and Mark Mazower.
p. cm.
Includes bibliographical references and index.
ISBN
1. Balkan Peninsula—Politics and government—20th century. 2.
Nationalism—Balkan Peninsula. I. Lampe, John R. II. Mazower, Mark.
III. Title.
DR45.I33 2003
949.6'05—dc22
2003017937

PRINTED IN HUNGARY BY
AKAPRINT, Martonvásár

TABLE OF CONTENTS

PREFACE

This volume is the end result of a year-long project of the Open Society Institute to examine the ideas and identities whose representation connects the twentieth-century history of Southeastern Europe to the European mainstream. We brought together a select group of younger scholars, primarily from the region, to proceed from an interdisciplinary perspective and to prepare the chapters that follow. Our reasons remain as compelling as they were when Institute Director István Rév, himself approached by some younger scholars, first approached me about the project in the first year of a new century. The previous century had scarred the region with three separate decades of international and civil war, forced migration and wrenching systemic change, the last convulsions spanning the 1990s. There had been a flood of recent publications, both scholarly and popular, but these concentrated on the most recent decade and on the former Yugoslavia. A large part of the scholarly publications, and almost all of the popular accounts, have further narrowed their focus to the suffering and injustice endured or inflicted by a particular ethnic group. This limitation applies to established historians from the region as much as to those from outside it. And we have seen Western social scientists, often approaching the region for the first time, read its history back from the end of the century to the beginning, rather than the reverse as historians are rightly wont to do.

We were therefore attracted to the possibility of bringing together a cohort of younger scholars primarily from the historical disciplines but also from the social sciences and comparative literature. All were asked to draw on transnational approaches and interdisciplinary perspectives while concentrating on a single country's experience. This comparative approach has been central to the philosophy and programs of Budapest's new Central European University (CEU) during its first decade. The project also provided the opportunity to stimulate our young contributors, as well as interested CEU students, by bringing a series of senior Western scholars specializing in the region to a series of seven sessions that we convened at the university from September 2001 to June 2002. After a presentation from, and a discussion session with, the respective senior scholar, each session devoted the rest of its time to the discussion of outlines and then drafts of chapters by our young contributors. We assumed, correctly I believe, that these periodic gatherings would allow a closer critique and coordination of the individual contributions than is usually the case with multi-authored volumes. In this regard a valuable contribution was provided by the suggestions for the editing of the authors' final drafts that came from CEU students who read them for my January 2003 course on twentieth-century Southeastern Europe, and again from a workshop of scholars from the region to appraise the volume's potential usefulness in their university courses, in English or in translation. I thank both the students and the workshop members—Christina Koulouri from Athens, Nikola Jordanovski from Skopje, Sonja Dujmović from Sarajevo, and Andrei Pippidi from Bucharest.

Already at the initial session our authors had readily recognized the need for such a volume within the region. We expanded and yet sharpened this focus. A review of recently published country histories from Yugoslavia's successor states revealed old nationalist assumptions of native virtue confounded by intervention from near or far, relieved for Bulgaria only by the positivist legacy of actions described without motives. Our discussion of the subjects that should and could be covered by our working group concluded that the project's original title was both too broad and too confining. So "Nationalism, War and Communism: Reappraising the Twentieth-Century History of Southeastern Europe" gave way to "Ideologies and National Identities: The Case of Twentieth-Century Southeastern Europe." We could thereby abjure the full regional reappraisal of the past century that none of this group was prepared to undertake and instead broaden the ideological purview of their country-based studies. Beyond nationalism and communism, appropriate attention could now be paid to fascism, liberalism, and religion *per se*. We could also join in the recent approach across several disciplines, led by anthropology, to consider national or ethnic identities as case studies of popular memory and its political manipulation. And while most of our contributors would deal with war, they would not be treating the course of war itself but rather the role of the remembrance of war as represented in ideology or national identity. My own presentation to this initial session emphasized the recent concern with collective memory in wider Western scholarship on nationalism.

Our next two sessions asked the members of the working group to find four or five brief selections from primary sources that would illustrate the range of local opinion on the particular issue of ideology or national identity or both that they wished to examine. Their inclusion following the text of each chapter would imitate the pattern pioneered by the late Peter Sugar in the volume of country chapters in *Eastern European Nationalism in the 20th Century,* which he edited for American University Press in 1995. His intention, like ours, was that university students in particular needed to compare and contrast these original sources if they are to understand contested issues too often presented within, but also outside, the region as uncontested. Dennison Rusinow, Emeritus Professor of History from the University of Pittsburgh, discussed his own chapter and selected readings on Yugoslavia in the Sugar volume with the working group in November. Lenard Cohen, Professor of Political Science at Simon Fraser University in British Columbia, then joined us in January to share his experiences in addressing heavily contested issues and sources during the writing of his *Serpent in the Bosom: The Rise and Fall of Slobodan Milošević,* just published by Westview Press.

Our last four sessions allowed members of our working group to present drafts of the papers published here. In the first, Mark Mazower, Professor of History at London University's Birkbeck College, drew on insights from *After the War Was Over: Reconstructing the Family, Nation and State in Greece, 1943–1946,* which he edited and introduced for Princeton University Press in 1999. In addition to providing the project with a much desired perspective on the region including the Greek experience, his interest in our interdisciplinary papers in particular prompted him to accept responsibility for co-editing this volume. His suggestions inform the present chapters by Maja Brkljačić, Ildiko Erdei, Rossitza Gencheva, Constantin Iordachi and Sandra Prlenda. Mine were offered to Robert Austin, Mark Biondich, Marko Bulatović, James Frusetta, Dejan Jović, and Andrew Baruch Wachtel. One of our subsequent three sessions concentrated entirely on the revision of the first drafts. In another, Stefan Troebst, Professor of East European Cultural Studies at the University of Leipzig, focused on recent work on the longstanding Macedonian question both from the region and also from German scholarship, which has now returned to the forefront in the study of Southeastern Europe. Maria Todorova, Professor of History at the University of Illinois, Urbana-Champaign, used our final session to suggest a broader comparative approach to the region as a whole, in time as well as space.

Some final words of appreciation are due to a number of particular individuals and institutions. My thanks to István Rév extend beyond his initiative in launching the project to his efforts in securing the necessary funding both from the Open Society Institute and also from the EU's European Commission under an appropriation from the Stability Pact for Southeastern

Europe. Let me also thank the History Department of the Central European University, its Chair László Kontler and Administrative Assistant Zsuzsanna Macht for organizing the concurrent participation of a group of CEU students in our sessions and for convening the subsequent course and workshop. We benefited from the participation in our sessions of two other younger historians from the region, Gabriella Etmeksoglu of Australia's Latrobe University and Predrag Marković of Belgrade's Institute for Contemporary History. And without the remarkable initiative and relentless organizational effort from start to finish from one of our group, Maja Brkljačić, this project and this volume would quite simply not have been possible.

John R. Lampe
University of Maryland, College Park
February, 2003

INTRODUCTION

John R. Lampe

RECONNECTING THE TWENTIETH-CENTURY HISTORIES OF SOUTHEASTERN EUROPE

- most authors from the region (handwritten annotation)

"Only connect," advised the English writer E. M. Forster in a famous phrase, leaving the reader to decide who or what should be connected. Readers seeing "Southeastern Europe" in our title may be tempted to expect that our cohort of younger authors, most of them from the region, will be connecting the burgeoning European and American study of social identity with the uniquely confrontational ethnic nationalism that is often assumed to set this region apart from Europe as "the Balkans." Prior to the twentieth century, of course, there are other reasons to differentiate this region, isolated by its upland geography and distinguished by its Ottoman legacy of military domination, political corruption, and religious tolerance, from Northwestern Europe with its Atlantic connections, political advantages, and religious intolerance. The region took early modern shape as a collection of imperial borderlands, disconnected from each other and too far from the Ottoman or Habsburg cores for a single administrative regime on either side. This better defines the Balkan legacy than does a single Ottoman stereotype. And if the early modern histories of the English, French, and Dutch states are rightly seen as the exceptional cases, then the fragmented empires, fragile polities, and still weaker civil societies that were the rule across the rest of Europe into the nineteenth century do not set the Balkans so far apart.[1]

Our region's history as Southeastern Europe begins with the First World War. As a result of this conflict, five new or expanded states emerged to incorporate all of the Ottoman and Habsburg territories that had surrounded the small but independent Balkan states dating from the nineteenth century. Yugoslavia, or the Kingdom of Serbs, Croats, and Slovenes as it was called until 1929, and Romania were the largest in size and population (12 and

15.6 million in 1920), followed by Greece and Bulgaria with five million each, and Albania with less than one million. All of them began with greater ethnic variety, real or perceived, within their new borders than had been the model for a nation-state in nineteenth-century Europe or the experience of the pre-war Balkan states. The same overall demographic proportions, if not the same ethnic divisions, would endure within borders that remained largely unchanged during the interwar period and again from 1945 to the dissolution of Yugoslavia in 1991. Our volume explores how such neighboring states with a comparable earlier history contested or changed national identities in close connection with eminently European political or religious ideologies. These ideas and identities justify calling this set of states Southeastern Europe, without the customary apology for using a designation picked up and thereby brought into discredit by Nazi geopoliticians in the 1930s. Indeed, the struggle of those states to establish common national identities in the face of ethnic diversity invites comparison with the post-colonial case of Western Europe and its new multi-ethnic and multi-racial makeup during recent decades.

Let us acknowledge that the two world wars and parts played in them by the major combatants still appear to many in the region as its major connection to Europe, a dependent or subordinate position still justifying separate designation as the Balkans. And yet, during the bulk of the interwar period, say from 1923 to 1939, and again from the early 1950s forward, the region's evolution owed more to internal dynamics than to foreign intervention. Those dynamics were nonetheless European in nature, beginning with a commitment to the creation of a nation-state. Like France, the state was to represent the native or assimilated ethnic nation. Charles Maier has identified this "ordered political space" and its prized identification of ethnicity with territory as the principal distinction of the modern European state, spreading from the northwest by the mid-nineteenth century to replace the confederal structures of the early modern empires.[2] He ticks off four features that distinguish its "structural narrative":

(1) strong central government institutions, mainly ministries with growing administrative authority and larger staffs, all at the expense of regional or local authority and on the basis of a common language and loyalty;

(2) a continually mobilized internal military and police as a "resource for governance" and as a complement to a military force to provide internal security;

(3) co-option into the ruling establishment of leaders in finance, industry, and the professions, education in particular;

(4) a growing industrial infrastructure based on coal and iron technology and a railway network, all on the assumption that efficiency was proportional to size and central control, with enterprise headquarters preferably in the capital city.

All of our region's interwar states pursued the first three, and all save non-Communist Greece the fourth, after the Second World War. We are not accustomed to think of these centralizing imperatives, for all their continuity between the interwar and post-1945 periods, as constituting a political ideology in themselves. But before the First World War, they already represented the nation-state's main mechanisms for liberal modernization under the elected representatives that were to provide popular sovereignty. Majority rule was assumed, at first for voters enfranchised on a class basis and then for all citizens to vote in multi-party elections for a powerful legislature. At the same time, this liberal nationalism assumed a single language and a common national loyalty. Other national ideologies would emerge after the First and Second World Wars, other "moral narratives" in Maier's phrase, to inform the rationale for a centralizing state structure. In Southeastern Europe, a range of recognizably European political and religious ideologies combined with a matrix of wartime memories to produce the narratives whose construction, contest, or representation are considered in the following chapters.

I.

Western and regional attention to ideology has flagged following the collapse of Communist regimes from Eastern Europe to the Soviet Union. In American as well as European scholarship, a precipitous fall in the study of Communism as a set of ideas stands out in the midst of a general decline in intellectual history (in favor of social and cultural history). Departments of political science and economics have also turned away from courses in comparative ideas or systems. Richard Pipes's recent survey volume, *Communism* (New York: Modern Library, 2000), observes that the Harvard University library alone lists some 2,000 titles dealing with that subject, but his extensive bibliography reflects the dearth of new scholarship since 1991. While the Western inquiry into fascism's variants, primarily in Germany and Italy, remains extensive, the scholarship from and about Southeastern Europe has paid little attention to the region's ideologies of the right as well as the left in the twentieth century.

Across the formerly Communist countries of the region, this has been an understandable reaction to the ideological constraints of the obligatory Marxist–Leninist approach to left and right before 1989. One result, according to an instructive survey of new textbooks, *Clio in the Balkans: The Politics of History Education*, edited by Christina Koulouri (Thessaloniki: Center for Democracy and Reconciliation in Southeastern Europe, 2002, pp. 39, 193), has been a retreat everywhere except in Macedonia from apply-

ing any sort of Marxist ideology to the political history of the twentieth century. Another variant, evident for instance in Bulgarian textbooks, is the
absence of any ideological perspective but residual reliance on the factual
positivism that was also part of the Marxist heritage. Events are recounted
in the passive voice, with little attention to the actors or the ideas that lay
behind them. The successor states to the former Yugoslavia, Slovenia and
Macedonia excepted, have turned in a different direction. Some scholarly
works and too many school textbooks readily use ideological labels for their
recent adversaries (Serbian forces seen as fascist in Sarajevo and Bolshevik
in Zagreb, Croatian forces as fascists and Bosnian Muslims as Islamic fun-
damentalists in Belgrade).[3]

Also crowding out attention to local actors and ideas across the entire
region is the continuing concentration on the role of the Great Powers during and after the two world wars. The two wars are assumed to be the major
events influencing modern history, and equally important for the region,
determining its fate not just during but also long after the wars. History
textbooks in the successor states to the former Yugoslavia typically allocate
a quarter to a third of their coverage of the twentieth century to the wars
themselves.[4] Published scholarship throughout the region and elsewhere
continues to pay more attention to the world wars than to any other subject
in modern history. The assumption remains widespread within Southeastern
Europe that the primary consequence of the Second World War within their
own countries was to allow the two superpowers to determine the shape of
their domestic evolution long after peace had returned. Its scholarly presence
has been strongest in Greece, free from the sort of long post-1945 restrictions
in Communist regimes to the north whose scholarship minimized Soviet
influence after the Second World War and concentrated instead on the bourgeois failings of their own interwar governments. Until 1974, the bulk of
Greek publications presented the country's postwar history as a justifiable
defense against the Soviet-led threat from the north. From the demise of the
colonels' military regime that year through the PASOK regime of the 1980s,
a revisionist majority focused critically and with considerable documenta-
tion on the Anglo-American intervention that helped to defeat the Communist-led resistance movement of the war in 1944 and again in 1946–49. The
indictment often extended, less persuasively, to the subsequent exclusion of
the left from Greek politics until the 1980s.[5]

The chapters that follow do not seek to add to the enormous literature
linking the world wars and foreign intervention. Our focus is on another
connection, between ideology and the national identity it sought to provide
as the "cement" in the social formation of the modern state.[6] This was the
focus of the volume that inspired the present one. *Eastern European Nationalism in the 20th Century* was a coordinated set of country chapters written

by younger scholars, edited by a senior historian, Peter Sugar, and each accompanied by a set of primary sources, documents that would allow the reader to judge domestic views firsthand.[7] That volume addressed only nationalism, what Sugar called in his concluding chapter "the victorious ideology." Our chapters are still confined within countries but look beyond nationalism alone to consider its connection to other European ideas—socialist, religious, or liberal more than narrowly Communist or fascist—that have contended across Southeastern Europe since the First World War.

We also look beyond the traditional disciplinary boundaries of history to anthropology, sociology, and literary criticism for approaches to the construction of national identity or the representation of ideology they have come to provide. Much scholarship has recently addressed social or cultural identity as a separate but interdisciplinary subject. The journal simply titled *Identities* is now in its eighth year of publication; book titles featuring the word are too numerous to mention. Their most common concern, and surely the one most relevant to our region, is the role of collective memory. Efforts by Communist regimes to replace memory entirely with ideology after the Second World War were quickly abandoned. The collapse of these regimes since 1989 has left such memories to return full force. They feed primarily off the violence and distress of the twentieth century. We join the majority of anthropologists and sociologists in accepting reliance on symbolic events passed on from distant centuries, such as the Serbian defeat at Kosovo Polje in 1389, as collective myths capable of constructing or sustaining an ethnic identity only when connected to living memory of real events.[8]

The two world wars, and for parts of our region attendant civil war, stretched over longer periods than for the rest of Europe. Their memories, real or mythical, personal or official, do indeed register in national identity. The wars of Yugoslavia's dissolution served to revive the trauma of wartime memories across all of Southeastern Europe. Its postwar Communist regimes and Greece's anti-Communist regime as well promoted a selective official memory from the top down but discouraged public or personal memory from the ground up. The latter is what Jay Winter has called "collective remembrance," drawing more on individual and family memories than on any independent scholarly inquiry to accept, mix with, or reject the account presented in schools and through the media.[9]

Winter acknowledges the difficulties of determining exactly how such social learning proceeds but rightly warns against any notion of hereditary memory, passing from one generation to another. What we might call "cultural eugenics" has no more scientific standing than the biological eugenics discredited after its racist and Nazi application from the 1930s into the Second World War. The notion would of course surface again, early in the wars and forced migrations of Yugoslavia's dissolution, and not just with Serbian

accusations against "genocidal Croats" or Croatian characterizations of
"barbarian Serbs." It appears as well in Western presumptions of "ancient
ethnic hatreds" as the root cause of conflict.

II

We set our chapters instead against the background of the twentieth century
and the states that emerged after 1918. Their modern institutional frame-
works were the arenas in which advocates of political or religious ideologies advanced or contested national identities with reduced or transplanted
ethnic majorities and new minorities. Let us briefly review domestic origins, foreign influences, and structural evolution in these institutional arenas during the interwar period and still more briefly for the more familiar
period of Communist, or, for Greece, anti-Communist regimes established
after the Second World War.

The new Kingdom of Serbs, Croats, and Slovenes was proclaimed in
Belgrade on December 1, 1918, under the aegis of previously independent
Serbia's Regent Aleksandar. Whatever the popular support for the new state
in the former Habsburg territory to the west or in formerly Ottoman Kosovo
and Macedonia to the south, an issue still in dispute for the Croatian and
Bosnian Muslim populations, only Serbia's army and French diplomatic
support could guarantee these broad borders against hostile neighbors. And
that guarantee was in place. Serbia survived defeat in 1915 and made its
troops the largest contingent in the French-led forces that broke through the
Salonika front with decisive results in 1918.

In the newly constituted state, Serbs with Montenegrins accounted for
only 39 percent of the population according to the 1921 census. Yet the
Serbian-dominated ministries in Belgrade led the way in expanding the
number of state employees, the army aside, to half again the per capita figure from prewar Serbia. Contesting their authority under the parliamentary
regime of the 1920s was a united Croatian opposition and, weakening it, a
divided Serb political spectrum. When King Aleksandar abolished the parliament and the parties as well in 1929, the power of the Interior Ministry in
particular became greater. Throughout the interwar period, moreover, both
Vardar Macedonia and Kosovo, with their respective ethnic Macedonian
and Albanian majorities, remained under comprehensive ministerial administration from Belgrade. Comparable controls could not be extended to the
former Habsburg lands to the west. Among the Croat and Slovene populations in particular, economic leverage was limited to disparate taxation and
control of the central bank. In education, Belgrade tried to create a unified
national system at the start of the 1920s and the 1930s but did not succeed.[10]

Romania's leaders abandoned neutrality in 1916 and entered the First World War on the side of the Entente powers, a decision which proved costly while the German army was still in the field but paid a handsome territorial dividend after the collapse of the Central Powers in 1918. Under the terms of peace settlements with Austria and then Hungary, the prewar kingdom expanded from Wallachia and Moldavia to include Bukovina and Transylvania. Nor could the new Bolshevik regime in Russia prevent the incorporation of Bessarabia. In each of the three additions, the ethnic Romanian share of the population was less than 60 percent, reducing the overall share to the same 70 percent for which Serbs, Croats, and Slovenes combined accounted in the new Yugoslav state. (Hungarians, Germans, and Jews were the largest minorities in Romania, while in the latter, Bosnian Muslims, Macedonians, and Germans accounted for the same combined 16 percent, with Albanians and Hungarians comprising another 8 percent.)

In Romania, the National Liberal Party of the old kingdom took full advantage of the rival Conservatives having backed the Central Powers in the First World War and thereby vanishing as a political force afterwards. A more comprehensive land reform and financial consolidation, the nationalization of German and Austrian oil assets included, than was possible for the Serbian ministries in Belgrade helped primarily Liberal regimes to preempt regional opposition until 1928. Then the Transylvanian-based National Party, unified with the Peasant Party in 1926, won election to attempt a series of decentralizing reforms. The Depression combined with the reassertion of royal authority under the wayward monarch Carol II in 1930 to sweep them aside. What followed for the rest of the decade was a more decisive expansion of ministerial authority and police powers outside any party framework. Through the entire interwar period, the Ministry of Education pressed ahead with a campaign to spread literacy in the Romanian language in a fashion that Yugoslavia's initial minister of education, the unitarist Svetozar Pribićević, would have envied. The aim was to inculcate through primary schools and adult education a single Romanian cultural identity in the minorities as well as in the ethnic majority.[11]

The Kingdom of Greece had expelled Ottoman rule from Aegean Macedonia and Thrace in the First Balkan War of 1912, thereupon making them the northern third of its territory. In 1918 its nominally Liberal government was concerned with retaking from Bulgaria Thracian areas to the east. (Vardar Macedonia to the north was left for its Entente ally in Belgrade to reclaim from Bulgaria after first winning it in the same 1912 war against the Ottoman Empire). Then came the Greek army's disastrous campaign, initially encouraged by the British prime minister, David Lloyd George, to move deep into Anatolia from the largely Greek port of Smyrna. It collapsed in 1922 under the Kemalist counteroffensive that created modern Turkey from the ruins of the Ottoman Empire. For Greece, the catastrophe forced the British-backed king from the throne but left a divide between royalists and republicans, and between the capital Athens and the north, that would not be resolved until the last quarter of the twentieth century. The flight from Anatolia also brought 1.5 million Anatolian refugees to Greece, mainly to the new northern lands where Macedonian Slav- and Turkish-speaking residents of long standing were now unwelcome unless assimilated. The Venezelist Republic of 1924–36 would pursue that assimilation through the educational system as assiduously as Romania's interwar regime. The Metaxas dictatorship ruled under a restored monarchy until the Second World War. It would distinguish itself by mobilizing the internal military and police for political repression and also by banning the public use of any language other than Greek.[12]

The Bulgarian kingdom but not its king survived the ill-fated alliance with the losing Central Powers in the First World War. Tsar Ferdinand's obsession with capturing Istanbul from the Ottoman Empire in the First Balkan War had contributed to the initial loss of Vardar Macedonia to Serbia, 1912–15. Now, after receiving it from Germany as a prize for joining the Central Powers, it was gone again, along with wartime gains in Thrace and a prewar part of Dobrudja in the northeast. Some 220,000 refugees crowded into the interwar state of five million. By 1923, the young Tsar Boris, members of the prewar elite, and Macedonian irredentists had joined forces to put down the two largest political parties, the larger Bulgarian Agrarian National Union (BZNS) of Aleksandar Stamboliiski and the smaller but Moscow-backed Bulgarian Communist Party (BKP). The assassination of Stamboliiski and the bloody suppression of a belated Communist coup a few months later left the smaller surviving parties, the tsar, and their internationally friendless regime to deal with economic recovery and Macedonian irredentism. The non-party regime that finally emerged under royal auspices would be common to all five of these interwar states during the 1930s, helping in four and almost in Greece as well to set the stage for one-party Communist governments after the Second World War. By 1935, Tsar Boris and his ministers in Sofia were strong enough to push aside the brief military regime that had already ended the virtual autonomy carved out by the Macedonian IMRO organization for itself in the southwestern corner of Bulgaria.[13]

An uncertain Albanian state had first emerged in 1913 under hasty Austro-Hungarian auspices tendered to deny Adriatic access to victorious Serbia. There were no political parties in place even from the late Ottoman period of Young Turk reforms. The state struggled to reemerge after the First World War. Neither ally nor adversary of the victorious powers, Albania had seen a long list of foreign governments dispatch troops to occupy their strategic coastal location. France, Austria–Hungary, and Italy were joined by Greece and Serbia in controlling various parts at various times. The most able and ruthless of the local leaders seeking to consolidate national power, Ahmed Zogu, was able to do so by 1924, but only with initial assistance from Belgrade, and then to hold onto it from 1926 to 1939 only by making first economic and then diplomatic concessions to Rome. He was, however, successful in making himself president of a belatedly constituted republic in 1925 and in crowning himself king of what now became a monarchy in 1928. In the process, he kept Italy, Greece and Yugoslavia from the internal political leverage they sought, at least until the Italian invasion of 1939 swept him and Albanian independence away.[14] At the same time, Albania's interwar pursuit of the centralizing imperatives that would provide the structural framework of a European nation-state was the least successful in Southeastern Europe. Zog's effort in 1933–34 to "nationalize" primary education, for instance, closed Greek- and Italian-sponsored Catholic schools but failed to open many new state schools to take their place.

The Second World War displaced or compromised the established political, ministerial, and military elites across Southeastern Europe. State linkages to economic elites and state systems of education were similarly disrupted. But the centralizing imperatives of the state framework grew under German if not Italian occupation or urging. Centralization only grew stronger in the postwar efforts for recovery. Communist-led resistance movements took power in Yugoslavia and Albania, and tried to do so in Greece. Romania's small Communist Party and Bulgaria's large one relied on Soviet support in inverse proportion to their size to take power as well. By the early 1950s, the Soviet effort to keep Tito's Yugoslavia within its bloc of satellites had failed. Still, the effort helped to solidify a faithful regime in Bulgaria and to keep a weaker one in place in Romania, albeit at the cost of the minority representation for Hungarians and others that had helped to put the Romanian Communist Party in power in 1945–46. The Albanian regime had used the Tito–Stalin split of 1948 to start down the road to isolation by turning to the Soviet Union for support against Yugoslavia. First Soviet and then Chinese rapprochement with Yugoslavia would leave Albania no other large sponsor in the Communist world by the mid-1970s. In Greece, new anti-Communist and old anti-republican forces combined to restore the monarchy by 1946 and to win the civil war against the Communist-led northern core of the wartime resistance. First British and then American support was as decisive as was Soviet support for the Bulgarian Communists, if less so than in Romania.[15]

III

The chapters that follow do not pursue Great Power influence beyond attraction to or rejection of the Soviet model of socialism in the Communist
regimes of Bulgaria and Yugoslavia. We regret the absence of a chapter on
Greece because it could have provided instructive comparison of anti-
Communist with Communist representation. The omission may be justified
in part because of the flowering of domestic and foreign scholarship during
the past decade, a prospect hoped for but not yet realized in the former Communist states of the region. Our chapters concentrate on the domestic efforts
in those states, before and after the Second World War, to foster a self-sus-
taining national identity by combining cultural memory and wartime experience with political or religious ideology.

For interwar Europe as a whole, the youth that survived the First World
War or grew up in its aftermath were attracted to radical or religious movements and charismatic leadership that promised a more distinctive identity
than that offered by their state's typically aged leadership. And in Belgium
and the Netherlands, as in the Croatian and Romanian cases, such movements could connect with fascism before or during the Second World
War.[16]

In Chapters 1 and 2, Constantin Iordachi and Mark Biondich take fresh
looks at the region's two ideologies most often associated with fascism—
those of Romania's interwar Legion of the Archangel Michael and of the
Croat Ustaša movement that came to power in the Second World War. For
the Legion, Iordachi explores the link between its "integral nationalism," on
the French pattern of Charles Maurras, to exclude all foreign influence in
favor of the ethnic majority's cultural hegemony, and its emphasis on the
Romanian Orthodox religion. Long regarded as a unique feature across the
fascist spectrum, the Legion's religious center makes more sense when we
consider, as Iordachi does, Orthodoxy's loss of overwhelming predominance in the greatly expanded territory of interwar Romania.

More familiar to interwar fascism was the reliance of both the Legion
from the start and the Croatian Ustaša from the 1930s on individual charismatic leadership and its attraction to the youth of the post-1918 generation.
Biondich shows how the Croatian movement sought Catholic support but
did not proceed from the same religious grounds. Unlike the Legion's
Corneliu Codreanu with his personal sense of a mystical and purifying mission, Ante Pavelić took his charismatic authority from his devotion to the
idea of an exclusively Croat state. He led his militarized movement into the
exclusionary nationalism of ethnic cleansing during a wartime regime whose
fascist identity is hard to deny. Its post-1945 survival outside of Communist
Yugoslavia would rely on selective historical memory to justify the idea of

an anti-Communist Croatian state on the basis of the dubious existence of the independent Croatia of the Second World War.

In Chapters 3 and 4, Sandra Prlenda and James Frusetta treat two rivalries for ethnic leadership. Prlenda shows us how radical Catholic Croat youth of the 1930s, in multi-confessional Bosnia in particular, were attracted not to Pavelić's Ustaša but instead to the church's own Crusaders organization. Its young leadership and the religion itself, rather than its clerical hierarchy, generated charismatic attraction. Many members were, however, pulled into the Ustaša ranks, or at least into its supposedly separate army, during the Second World War. Frusetta takes us away from religion and the right to show that charismatic leadership was not their sole province. The Communist left also wanted heroes to embody national identity and did not rely solely on the current party leader, as it sometimes appeared. The charisma of an early and dramatic death drew the ideological histories of both Bulgaria and Yugoslavia's Macedonia to Gotse Delchev and several other past leaders of the pre-1914 Internal Macedonian Revolutionary Organization. Frusetta considers the course of conflicting claims to these same figures as representatives of Bulgarian or Macedonian identity.

Our region's postwar Communist regimes took positive steps, beyond their familiar political and religious restrictions, to create a national identity grounded in socialist ideology. Their efforts to train teenage youth, to appropriate classic national literature, to use popular culture, and to monitor everyday life are the respective subjects of the next four chapters. The subsequent collapse of all these Communist regimes has not left much of this socialist nation-building in the public mind. Instead, the contested memories not just of the Second World War but also of earlier nationalist movements such as the Internal Macedonian Revolutionary Organization, as explored in Chapter 4, have come into open conflict.

These Communist efforts sought to represent and widely disseminate a pan-ethnic identity. In Chapter 5, Andrew Baruch Wachtel traces the appropriation of the classic nineteenth-century poem, *The Mountain Wreath*, and its Montenegrin author Petar Petrović Njegoš, from interwar Yugoslavia into the postwar Communist period. The Tito regime tried to make its anti-Ottoman defiance stand for a common Yugoslav identity against separate Serbian or Montenegrin claims and Croatian or Bosnian Muslim protests. Both have returned to the fore, as he notes, since 1991. In Chapters 6 and 7, Ildiko Erdei and Maja Brkljačić bring us back to the socialist identity on which, as Dejan Jović argues in Chapter 11, Communist Yugoslavia would rely. Antropologist Erdei finds the ideology behind Serbia's Pioneer youth organization flexible in the same fashion that we associate with the famous shift from Soviet-style central planning to workers' self-management. By the early 1950s, the training for adult party tasks as well as membership that came from the Second World War and partisan necessity were replaced by an anti-Soviet emphasis on childhood fun. At the same time, the Pioneers would remain tightly tied to the reverent memory of partisan heroics. These efforts, however, did not implant the necessary mass consciousness to preserve "brotherhood and unity" after 1989. Brkljačić finds a stronger link to a deeper, historically familiar, myth-related identity in the regime's initial rejection and eventual acceptance of folk songs composed as epic poems by common people outside the party framework. They glorified the partisan struggle and Tito's subsequent defiance of Stalin, but only as a continuation of the heroic resistance to invaders or oppressors from Ottoman times. Their continued commercial success helped historical remembrance, as defined by Winter for popular rather than official culture, to link first the Communist regime with a deeper national identity, for Serbs in particular, and then to sustain post-1989 Serbia.

In Chapter 8, Rossitza Guencheva takes us into the new field of material culture to show how Bulgaria's more doctrinaire Communist regime sought to advance a socialist identity on the Soviet model through its policy regarding public and private noise in an increasingly crowded urban environment. At first, the noise of machines turning, construction proceeding, and vehicles moving was celebrated as the sound of revolutionary change. But by the 1970s, the Bulgarian party leadership turned to the sort of campaigns already under way in the Soviet Union to deaden sound in apartment blocs, curtain off balconies, and hold private noise-making, including the playing of Western music, accountable. The primary concern was, however, to secure the identity of Bulgarians as efficient labor for socialist enterprise, keeping the campaign as separate from historical memory as the initial celebration of modern sound. This concern deserves as much attention as the regime's representation of its Bulgarian national identity.[17]

We end our volume with chapters on ideological efforts to establish the national identity of Southeast European states within the borders and governments as they existed. In Chapter 9, Robert Austin tackles the controversial question of Albania's interest in and policy toward adding Kosovo to its territory. He does not hesitate to identify the weakness of Albania's interwar state structure and its postwar Communist isolation as partly cause and partly result of a national identity too uncertain or contested to include Kosovo. Although the interwar autonomy of local clans would not survive the imposition of Communist rule, ethnic division between northern Gegs and southern Tosks discouraged inclusion of the Greater Albanian claim to largely Geg Kosovo so often presumed elsewhere in the region. In chapter 10, Marko Bulatović takes us through the interwar travails of Serb intellectual and political leaders as they sought to find enough ethnic convergence at least among the South Slav majority of the first Yugoslavia to promise a common national identity. By the 1930s, some would seemingly abandon this prospect and justify the state's existence solely on the grounds of defending an existing structure vulnerable in the face of hostile neighbors and international uncertainty. But the temptation to turn back to the pre-1914 Serbian identity would leave them with a dilemma that they could not resolve before war came.

In Chapter 11, Dejan Jović critiques the efforts of Tito's Yugoslavia, and its leading ideologist Edvard Kardelj in particular, to overcome internal divisions in the fashion of Enver Hoxha's Albanian regime by identifying the state as guardian against hostile external "others." As for all the East European Communist parties, the "bourgeois regime" of interwar Yugoslavia was one such "other," with class origins held responsible for Serbian centralism. But after the Tito–Stalin split of 1948, the Soviet Union quickly became the more prominent "other," according to Jović. Kardelj legitimized the Communists' continuing one-party regime as necessary in order to stay independent and pursue socialism at the same time. The demise of other Communist regimes and then the Soviet Union in 1991 removed this justification. Interwar dilemmas returned, and the uncertain national identity of Yugoslavia was left to stand or fall on its own.

Notes

1 Significant differences in natural resources and urban development remained to combine with warfare and forced migration. This combination accounted for the considerable economic gap between the Balkans and Central as well as Northwestern Europe by 1800. See John R. Lampe and Marvin R. Jackson, *Balkan Economic History, 1550–1950: From Imperial Borderlands to Developing Nations* (Bloomington: Indiana University Press, 1982), 1–49. On Western presumptions of comprehensive, virtually civilizational differences in the nineteenth and twentieth centuries, the path-breaking, provocative study is Maria Todorova, *Imagining the Balkans* (New York: Oxford University Press, 1997). For an historical overview persuasively arguing the absence of such comprehensive differences before the nineteenth century, see Mark Mazower, *The Balkans* (New York: Modern Library, 2001), 1–76.

2 Charles S. Maier, "Consigning the Twentieth Century to History: Alternative Narratives for the Modern Era," *American Historical Review* 195 (June 2000): 807–31.

3 Falk Pegel, ed., *The European Home: Representatives of 20th-Century Europe in History Textbooks* (Council of Europe Publishers, 2000), 85–193.

4 Ibid., 75.

5 See Alexander Kitroeff, "Continuity and Change in Contemporary Greek Historiography," *European History Quarterly* 19 (1989): 283–88. On the greater attention of Greek scholarship to domestic social history since then, see Mark Mazower's introduction

to his edited volume, *After the War Was Over: Reconstructing the Family, Nation and State in Greece, 1943–1946* (Princeton, N. J.: Princeton University Press, 1999), 3–23.

6 Stuart Hall, as cited by Katherine Verdery, *National Ideology under Socialism: Identity and Cultural Politics in Ceausescu's Romania* (Berkeley: University of California Press, 1991), 10.

7 Peter Sugar, *Eastern European Nationalism in the 20th Century* (Washington, D. C.: American University Press, 1995).

8 Even that leading constructionist Benedict Anderson argued for the primacy of "imagined communities" beyond any face-to-face group but not "imaginary communities," as co-editors Cora Govers and Hans Vermeulen remind us in their introductory chapter to *The Politics of Ethnic Consciousness* (New York: St. Martin's, 1998), 21–22.

9 See his introductory chapter with co-editor Immanuel Sivan to their *War and Remembrance in the Twentieth Century* (Cambridge: Cambridge University Press, 1999), 6–39. For a review of the extensive recent attention to memory, see Peter Fritzsche, "The Case of Modern Memory," *The Journal of Modern History* 73 (March 2001), 87–117.

10 John R. Lampe, *Yugoslavia as History: Twice There Was a Country*, 2nd ed. (Cambridge: Cambridge University Press, 2000), 101–62.

11 See Irena Livizeanu, *Cultural Politics in Greater Romania: Regionalism, Nation-Building, and Ethnic Struggle, 1918–1930* (Ithaca, N. Y.: Cornell University Press, 1995).

12 Anastasia Karakasidou, *Fields of Wheat, Hills of Blood: Passages to Nationhood in Greek Macedonia, 1870–1990* (Chicago: University of Chicago Press, 1997), 141–189. On the period of the republic, see George Mavrogordatos, *Stillborn Republic: Social Coalitions and Party Strategies in Greece, 1922–1936* (Berkeley: University of California Press, 1983).

13 R. J. Crampton, *A Short History of Modern Bulgaria* (Cambridge: Cambridge University Press, 1987), 82–144.

14 Bernd Fischer, *King Zog and the Struggle for Stability in Albania* (New York: Columbia University Press, East European Monographs, 1984).

15 The range of increasingly convergent regional and Western scholarship may be seen in John O. Iatrides and Linda Wrigley, eds., *Greece at the Crossroads: The Civil War and Its Legacy* (University Park: Pennsylvania State University Press, 1995), and in Norman Naimark and Leonid Gibianski, eds., *The Establishment of Communist Regimes in Eastern Europe, 1944–1949* (Boulder, Col.: Westview Press, 1997).

16 See the currently definitive survey of Stanley G. Payne, *A History of Fascism, 1914–1945* (Madison: University of Wisconsin Press, 1995), 276–302, 391–411.

17 This representation is well described in Maria Todorova's chapter on Bulgaria in Sugar, ed., *Eastern European Nationalism*, 55–102.

A GUIDE TO FURTHER READING

The limited citations and brief comments that follow are intended to provide the general reader as well as students and non-specialist scholars with a guide to broader country studies or disciplinary approaches in which each of our volume's chapters may prompt interest. A complete set of annotated bibliographies by country, beginning with Bulgaria in 1989 and proceeding with revised editions for Yugoslavia (1990), Albania (1997), Romania and Greece (1998), with new ones for Slovenia and Croatia added in 1996 and 1999, has fortunately been published for books and journal articles in English by Clio Press of Oxford and Santa Barbara, California. The one comprehensive regional bibliography of publications in all languages is from the Südosteuropa Institut, *Bibliographisches Handbuch der ethnischen Gruppen Südosteuropas,* ed. Gerhard Seewan and Petar Dippold, 2 vols. (Munich: R. Oldenbourg Verlag, 1997).

Let me first supplement my own Introduction by noting several regional surveys that offer an accessible overview to the non-specialist reader and a reference book for the student or course instructor. For political and diplomatic history in particular, Stevan K. Pavlowitch, *A History of the Balkans, 1804–1945* (London: Longmans, 1997) and R. C. Crampton, *The Balkans since the Second World War* (London: Pearson Education, 2002) provide the much needed new set of authoritative surveys. Mark Mazower, *The Balkans* (N.Y.: Modern Library, 2001) is a brief but wide-ranging introduction that emphasizes both the legacies of Ottoman domination and the European nation-state, both for good and ill. The recent evolution of respective national identities receives attention in the essays assembled in F. W. Carter and H. W. Norris, eds., *The Changing Shape of the Balkans* (Boulder, Colo.: Westview Press,

1996), while the longer sociological history of the respective nationalisms is well surveyed and the scholarship well referenced in Victor Roudometof, *Nationalism, Globalization and Orthodoxy: The Social Origins of Class Conflict in the Balkans* (Westport, Conn.: Greenwood Press, 2001). For a theoritically instructive approach to the issue of ideology in the Yugoslav case, see Siniša Malešević, *Ideology, Legitimacy and the New State, Yugoslavia, Serbia a Croatia* (London: Frank Cass, 2003).

For Chapter 1, on interwar and wartime Romania generally, see the model survey volume by Keith Hitchins, *Rumania, 1866–1947* (Oxford: Clarendon Press, 1994), especially Ch. 7, "The Great Debate," pp. 292–334, on national ideology. On interwar identity politics, see Irina Livizeanu, *Cultural Politics in Greater Romania: Regionalism, Nation-Building and Ethnic Struggle, 1918–1930* (Ithaca, N.Y.: Cornell University Press, 1995). A relevant work from recent Romanian scholarship is Z. Ornea, *The Romanian Extreme Right, The Nineteen Thirties* (N.Y.: Columbia University Press, East European Monographs, 1999).

For Chapter 2, on twentieth-century Croatian political ideology, see Mark Biondich, *Stjepan Radić, the Croat Peasant Party, and the Politics of Mass Mobilization, 1904–1928* (Toronto: University of Toronto Press, 2000) and Jill A. Irvine, *The Croat Question, Partisan Politics in the Formation of the Yugoslavia Socialist State* (Boulder, Colo.: Westview Press, 1993). On the Ustaša regime during the Second World War, Jozo Tomasevich, *War and Revolution in Yugoslavia, 1941–1945: Occupation and Collaboration* (Stanford, Calif.: Stanford University Press, 2001), pp. 233–510, is the one detailed study in English.

For Chapter 3, on the Croatian Catholic Church before, during, and after the Second World War, see Stella Alexander, *Church and State in Yugoslavia since 1945* (Cambridge: Cambridge University Press, 1979) and her *The Triple Myth: A Life of Archbishop Alojzije Stepinac* (N.Y.: Columbia University Press, East European Monographs, 1987). A more critical view appears in Vjekoslav Perica, *Balkan Idols, Religion and Nationalism in Yugoslav States* (Oxford: Oxford University Press, 2001), pp. 17–42.

For Chapter 4, informed but varied recent views on this mother of Balkan identity issues appear in Victor Roudometof, ed., *The Macedonian Question: Culture, Historiography and Politics* (N.Y.: Columbia University Press, East European Monographs, 2000), and Jane Cowan, ed., *Macedonia, The Politics of Identity and Difference* (London: Pluto Press, 2001). For recent approaches to the Greek experience, see Peter Mackridge and Eleni Yanakakis, eds., *The Development of Greek Macedonian Identity since 1912* (Oxford: Berg, 1997).

Chapter 5 deals with the political struggle to appropriate literary figures, rather than vanquished heroes as in Chapter 4. For more on Njegoš, see author Andrew Baruch Wachtel's own *Making a Nation, Breaking a Nation: Literature and Cultural Politics in Yugoslavia* (Stanford, Calif.: Stanford University Press, 1998). On the role of other writers from the former Yugoslavia, see David. A. Norris, *In the Wake of the Balkan Myth: Questions of Identity and Modernity* (N.Y.: St. Martin's Press, 1998), and for a comparative perspective, Robert B. Prysant, ed., *The Literature of Nationalism, Essays on East European Identity* (N.Y.: St. Martin's Press, 1998).

For Chapter 6, on the role of folk epics in national poetry, see Milne Holton and Vasa D. Mihailovich, eds., *Serbian Poetry From the Beginning to the Present* (Columbus, Ohio: Slavica Publications for Yale Russian and East European Publications, 1988). The wider variety of repositories for folk or national memory across the region is treated in Maria Bucur and Nancy M. Wingfield, eds., *Staging the Past: The Politics of Commemoration in Habsburg Central Europe, 1848 to the Present* (West Lafayette, Ind.: Purdue University Press, 2001).

For Chapter 7, on the political mobilization of youth and other social groups, see Melissa K. Bokovoy, Jill A. Irvine, and Carol S. Lilly, eds., *State-Society Relations in Yugoslavia, 1945–1992* (N.Y.: St. Martin's, 1997); and on the original Soviet model, Peter Kenez, *The Birth of the Propaganda State: Soviet Methods of Mass Mobilization, 1917–1929* (Cambridge: Cambridge University Press, 1985).

For Chapter 8, on the evolution of Communist ideology, see John D. Bell, *The Bulgarian Communist Party from Blagoev to Zhivkov* (Stanford, Calif.: Hoover Institution Press, 1986). On social change since 1960, current Bulgarian scholarship has provided Nikolai Genov and Anna Krasteva, eds., *Recent Social Trends in Bulgaria, 1960–1995* (Montreal: McGill-Queen's University Press, 2001).

For Chapter 9, Miranda Vickers, *The Albanians, A Modern History* (London: I. B. Tauris, 1997) affords a good readable survey. For well-researched detail on interwar and wartime Albanian politics, see Bernd J. Fischer, *King Zog and the Struggle for Stability in Albania* (N.Y.: Columbia University Press, East European Monographs, 1984) and his *Albania at War, 1939–1945* (London: Hurst & Co., 1999). An international range of authors explore national identity in Stephanie Schwandner-Sievers and Bernd J. Fischer, eds., *Albanian Identities, Myths and History* (Bloomington, Ind.: Indiana University Press, 2002).

For Chapter 10, Joseph Rothschild's chapter on Yugoslavia in his *East Central Europe Between the Wars* (Seattle, Washington, 1974), pp. 201–80, remains the best introduction to its interwar politics. For a sympathetic account of the leading Serbian political thinker, see Aleksandar Pavković, *Slobodan Jovanović: An Unsentimental Approach to Politics* (N.Y.: Columbia University Press, 1993). Useful for comparative purposes is the classic study of interwar Greece's politics, George Mavrogordatos, *Stillborn Republic: Social Conditions and Party Strategies in Greece, 1922–1936* (Berkeley, Calif.: University of California Press, 1983).

For Chapter 11, a perceptive Yugoslav analysis of the Communist regime's theory and practice, with emphasis on the role of Edvard Kardelj, is Laszlo Sekelj, *Yugoslavia: The Process of Disintegration* (N.Y.: Columbia University Press, East European Monographs, 1993). Kardelj's own version is in Edvard Kardelj, *Reminiscences* (London: Blond and Biggs, 1982). On the internal dynamics of the ideologically decisive Tito–Stalin split, see Ivo Banac, *With Stalin, against Tito: Cominformist Splits in Yugoslav Communism* (Ithaca, N.Y.: Cornell University Press, 1988) and Wayne S. Vucinich, ed., *At the brink of war and peace: the Tito–Stalin split in historic perspective* (Brooklyn, N.Y.: Brooklyn College Press, 1982).

CHAPTER 1

Constantin Iordachi

CHARISMA, RELIGION, AND IDEOLOGY:
Romania's Interwar Legion of the Archangel Michael

The Legion of the Archangel Michael has been generally considered an unusual "variety of fascism" mostly because of its mysticism and religious ritualism.[1] Building on Max Weber's theory of charismatic legitimacy and on its numerous reformulations since it was first put forward by the leading German founder of modern sociology, this chapter aims at reinterpreting the Legion as a reactive regional movement of change based on the violent counterculture of a radical segment of the "new generation." It argues that Legionary ideology combined, in a heterogeneous but powerful synthesis, three main strategies of political mobilization: namely, a charismatic type of legitimacy, based on the millennialist cult of the Archangel Michael and the leadership of Corneliu Zelea Codreanu; the messianic mission of the post-war "new generation"; and integral nationalism, including calls for "cultural purification" and "national regeneration" modeled on the pre-1914 French pattern of Charles Maurras, coupled with virulent anti-Semitism.[2] Among these elements, the charismatic component of Legionary ideology was the most integrative, shaping its message and accounting for its genesis, structure, and political evolution.[3]

Weber's perspective on charisma illuminates a pivotal feature of the Legion, which has remained to date under-researched.[4] To be sure, although there seems to be an implicit consensus among students of Romanian fascism that Codreanu was a charismatic leader, no scholarly work has yet attempted to link the study of his leadership to Weber's theory on charismatic authority, or to extend the concept to the study of the movement itself and its structure and organization. This chapter argues that the concept of charisma illuminates the relationship between religion, politics, and violence in the

Legion's ideology and practice.[5] It offers a conceptual umbrella in order to connect two major features of Legionary ideology that stood in apparent contradiction to each other, and have consequently so far been analyzed separately: its alleged Christian character, and its inherent violence and criminality. By exposing the built-in violent character of the movement, this perspective also confronts later Legionary propaganda, which emphasizes the religious character of the Legion but plays down its crimes as accidental or foreign to its spirit.[6]

Charismatic Leadership: Theoretical Mapping

Max Weber theorized, even before the outbreak of war in 1914, that charismatic authority was one part of a triadic typology of political legitimacy, along with legal-rational authority and traditional authority. He defined it as devotion to an exceptional leader and to the normative rules ordained by him.[7] Central to this type of authority is the concept of charisma ("gift of grace"), described by Weber as "a certain quality of an individual personality by virtue of which he is set apart from ordinary men and treated as endowed with supernatural, superhuman, or at least specifically exceptional powers or qualities."[8]

Unlike the other two types of legitimacy, the charismatic bond has, in Weber's view, an exceptional, highly intense, and emotional nature. It arises "out of suffering, conflict," and out of "enthusiasm, or of despair and hope," "in times of psychic, physical, economic, ethical, religious, or political distress."[9] The authority of a charismatic leader is based on an emotional commitment, as well as on a belief in the leader's extraordinary personal qualities. Charisma also involves a social structure: a staff and an apparatus of services and means adapted to the mission of the leader. Those who have a share in charisma form a personal staff, a charismatic aristocracy composed of a group of adherents who are united by loyalty and selected according to personal charismatic qualification. Charisma has a revolutionary nature: being based on the "genuine glorification of the mentality of the prophet and hero," it rejects all external orders and transforms all values, breaks all traditional and rational norms. That is why Weber considered bureaucracy and charisma as opposites. While bureaucracy first changes the social and material order of the society and—*through them*—the people, charisma changes the people *from within*, through a transformation, a mutation in the proselytes' attitude.[10] Consequently, Weber regarded charisma as a necessarily non-economic power, one which is endangered when daily economic interests become predominant. Charisma is therefore transitory and "naturally unstable." It continues only as long as the leader can effectively prove that he is "the master willed by God."[11] Moreover, as a personal quality, it ceases to exist with the disappearance of its bearer. This poses the problem of succession or, as Weber calls it, the routinization of charisma.

Charismatic leadership has been generally called a feature of "generic fascism."[12] Yet its application has been confined until now almost exclusively to the case study of Hitler and the Nazi Party.[13] Studies of what has been generally called "peripheral" or "minor" fascisms in East Central Europe have proven more receptive to viewing fascism as a millenarian movement.[14] Eugen Weber described the Legion as a "cargo cult" triggered by a reaction to sudden modernization. For Zeer Barbu it represented "in a highly compressed yet well differentiated form what is normally known as a two-phase phenomenon, that is, the transition from a religious to a political movement in a developing country."[15] The current study dissociates itself from the approach that regards charismatic movements as "pre-political" manifestations in peripheral economies or post-colonial states. Instead, it draws on sociological and political science approaches which—building largely on Weber's theory—have attempted an "independent reformulation" of the concept of charisma in order to preserve its universality and to offer a more feasible methodology for its application to politics. In a rare application of the concept of charisma to the history of the Balkans, George Th. Mavrogordatos combined charisma with the concepts of clientelist patronage and social cleavage to frame his study of mass politics in interwar Greece.[16] The following analysis applies Weber's conceptual framework and related theories to the study of the Legionary movement.

Charismatizing Nationalism: From Student Rebellion to Generational Messianism

The origins of Codreanu's charismatic cult are to be found in the nationalist student movements that swept Romanian universities in the period 1919–23.[17] To be sure, student rebellion was not a Romanian peculiarity in post-1918 Europe.[18] Yet beyond some general European features, student rebellion in Romania exhibited certain peculiarities due mainly to local social and ethnopolitical cleavages. Romania emerged from the Great War as a winner. The incorporation of the historic provinces of Transylvania, of the Banat and Bukovina from Austria–Hungary, and of Bessarabia from Russia doubled the Old Kingdom's size and population, and considerably strengthened its economic potential. In addition, comprehensive reforms such as universal male suffrage (1919), massive land redistribution (1921), and a new liberal constitution (1923) remodeled it into a parliamentary democracy, and granted full citizenship rights to Jews and other ethno-religious minorities.

At first glance, the prospects for the young generation thus looked brighter than ever. While universal male suffrage abolished class barriers to political participation, the administrative imperatives of the unified Romanian state also required an expansion of the state apparatus with young cadres. However, the new state was dominated by numerous sociopolitical cleavages. Although numerically dominated by ethnic Romanians, Greater Romania also encompassed a relatively high ratio of ethnic minorities—making up 28 percent of the total population in 1930, mainly Hungarians, Jews, Germans, and Bulgarians. Moreover, privileged under the former imperial order, these ethnic minorities in the new territories belonged to the category of "high-status minorities" and were still dominant in the urban population, the liberal professions, and regional bureaucracy.[19] Romanian political elites perceived the domination of socioeconomic life by ethnic minorities as a major stumbling block in the process of national consolidation, a situation that brought the "nationalizing nationalism" of the Romanian ethnic majority to the forefront.[20] In the first postwar decade, the process of "nationalizing the state" by the Romanian ethnic majority was shaped by the vision put forward by the National Liberal Party of the Old Kingdom. In order to compensate for the lack of a substantive Romanian middle class in the new provinces, the Liberal Party launched a strong cultural offensive that would rapidly produce a unified national elite. A central component of this process was building a national educational system. An unprecedented expansion in educational facilities increased the number of students to a record level. Students became the presumed allies of the Romanian political elites in their efforts at nationalizing the state, since they represented the "agents" of the state in the cities.[21]

But the prospective alliance soon turned against the ruling elites, generating an additional political cleavage between traditional politicians and the "new generation." Students were the first compact "Romanian contingent" sent from the rural world, still accounting for over 80 percent of the population, into the hostile and still "foreign" urban environment.[22] They sought to use the unprecedented educational opportunities for upward social mobility. They regarded their diplomas as "certificates" of social success, expecting positions in the bureaucratic apparatus. However, the state administration had a limited capacity for absorption, which shank even more under the impact of postwar economic hardship. Material deprivation and job scarcity caused frustration and alienation, encouraging protest movements. Student discontent was soon turned against the ethnic minorities, whose superior social status was felt responsible for the poverty of Romanian students. Moreover, while prior to 1918 the superior urban status of Jews was "compensated" by their exclusion from state citizenship and substantive econom-

The Văcărești. The founding members of the Legion, generically called the "Văcărești," soon after their acquittal by the Turnu Severin jury in 1924 following their participation in a student plot. Later named "The Knights of the Annunciation," they formed the charismatic nucleus of the movement, preserved their influence on the decision-making process, and were held in high esteem by the Legionaries. In the center is Corneliu Zelea Codreanu, with Tudose Popescu at his right and Corneliu Georgescu at his left. In the upper row, Ilie Gârneață on the left, Radu Mironovici center, and Ion I. Moța on the right.

ic and political rights, nationalists claimed that the civil emancipation of ethnic minorities required by the 1919 Minority Convention granted Jews potential access to state jobs and resources, thus making possible their political domination as well.[23] Radical student organizations blamed the international community for the "forced" and "premature" citizenship given to ethnic minorities in Greater Romania, and disapproved of the slow pace of nationalizing the state promoted by the ruling elite. They agitated for the implementation of a *numerus clausus* in higher education, restricting Jewish admission to their small share of total population and thus curbing job competition from their intellectual elites.

Charisma as Counterculture

The nucleus of the nationalist student movement was located in regional universities, where the new "Romanian order" was unconsolidated and the student body still dominated by ethnic minorities. Its main centers were Iaşi —the old capital of Moldova, Czernowitz—the capital of Bukovina, and Cluj—where the former Hungarian university had just been Romanianized. The most combative leaders were Ion I. Moţa, the son of a Romanian priest who had been active in the national movement in Austro-Hungarian Transylvania, and a law student at the University of Cluj; and Corneliu Zelea Codreanu, a law student at the University of Iaşi, and the son of a highly nationalist secondary school teacher from Bukovina. In contrast to those leaders who wanted to confine student protest to the university campus, Moţa and Codreanu intended to transform the student movement into a radical–nationalist organization. By 1923, when student mobilization began to fall off, Moţa initiated a desperate plot, urging his comrades "to finish the movement in a beautiful way by sacrificing ourselves, while taking with us all those whom we find guilty of betrayal of the Romanian interests," such as corrupt politicians and Jewish bankers.[24] His proposal received enthusiastic support from a half dozen close collaborators, including Codreanu. But the group was arrested before turning their criminal plans into action, and imprisoned in the Văcăreşti Monastery. Following a wave of public sympathy and media support, they were soon released, except for Moţa. He remained in jail for an additional six months for shooting his comrade Vernicescu for alleged betrayal.

Although unmasked, the plot was ultimately instrumental in transforming the student movement into a radical nationalist organization. Benefiting from national press coverage, the group of nationalist leaders, subsequently called the *Văcăreşteni*, became notorious and served as the nucleus of the future movement. As Codreanu later recalled, the mystical atmosphere of the monastery inspired their first common plans for creating an "army of youngsters educated in love for the country and fatherland," following the example of the *Action Française*. The new organization had to fulfill three roles: "1. To educate the entire Romanian youth in a military spirit. 2. To be an army of propagandists of the Legion. 3. To be the fanatical element of sacrifice for the national movement, toward the solving of the Jewish Question! This army was to be dedicated to the Archangel Michael—the one with the fiery sword."[25]

The events following the student trial also established the basis of Codreanu's cult, projecting him as the leader of this integral nationalism. On 25 October 1924, several months after his acquittal for participation in the plot, Codreanu assassinated Constantin Manciu, the police prefect of Iaşi, as revenge for his acts of repression against the student movement. After another controversial trial, Codreanu was yet again discharged. Moreover, his "heroic" gesture, as well as his acquittal, assured him an immediate popularity, transforming him from a regional into a national leader. In July 1925 his wedding ceremony took the form of a mass celebration, paving the way for his charismatic cult. A month later, Codreanu became the godfather to more than one hundred children born on the day of his marriage.[26]

In sum, the process of nationalizing the state in Greater Romania generated as a side effect a confrontation between the hegemonic official culture and a radicalized student counterculture, working by its own rules for its own radical aims. The main promoter of this counterculture was the *Văcăreşteni*, formed by plans of criminal plots, the common experience of prison, and assassinations. Its creators were Corneliu Zelea Codreanu and Ion Moţa; they spelled out students' frustrations and put forward a mystical sublimation of their experience. In his fictitious spiritual autobiography, Moţa voiced the feelings of social inadequacy experienced by Romanian students of rural extraction, portraying himself as being suspended between "the Old World" of the idyllic village life and "the New World, alienated from ancient mores and invaded by pagans." (See Document 1.) His hero, Nuţu Doncii, was forced to sever his ties with the village community and to relocate to the city: "I found somewhere else another youth and plunged into another life. ... I became a city dweller." This experience was a source of great frustration and alienation: "I could not find peace in this world; I hated it and, in its turn, it hated me deadly." Moţa thus underwent a process of self-stigmatization, by dramatizing the students' situation through victimization. The tension between self-stigmatization and the sense of guilt generated by their violent and unlawful response gave birth to charismatic claims.[27] In the process of charismatization, negative features were sublimated and declared as positive: students' material misery was portrayed as emblematic of the state of the Romanian nation, while their marginality was recompensed by their belief in being the "chosen ones," making up an alternative elite.

After a brief affiliation with the anti-Semitic League of the National Christian Defense, the *Văcăreşteni* decided in 1927 to establish its own organization, called the Legion of the Archangel Michael. In this way, they distanced themselves from the moderate nationalism of the previous generation and put forward a messianic call to generational solidarity under the banner of charismatic nationalism. We now turn to the charismatic genesis and nature of Legionary ideology and its success in channeling youth protest and appropriating the discourse of the "new generation."

The Legion of Archangel Michael as a Charismatic Organization

The Legion of the Archangel Michael was founded on 10 July 1927 by the nucleus of activists led by Corneliu Zelea Codreanu. Its genesis was typical for a charismatic movement. (See Document 2.) According to Codreanu, the creation of the Legion was the fulfillment of a charismatic vision he had had in November 1923, while in prison. He professed that the Archangel Michael had appeared to him and urged him to dedicate his life to God. In the spirit of his vision, Codreanu proclaimed Saint Michael as patron of the new movement, one of the seven archangels who defeated Lucifer and his followers, expelling them to hell. The Archangel Michael became the object of a fanatic Legionary cult: the religious commemoration of his name-day on 10 November was proclaimed the official holiday of the movement. The icon of the Archangel on the wall of Codreanu's prison cell, which allegedly inspired his vision, became the sacred relic of the Legion and was permanently guarded by a Legionary team.

The main source of Legionary ideology was thus the avenging figure of Saint Michael. Legionaries adopted an apocalyptic, dual vision of the world, portraying themselves as an earthly Christian army, as knights of the light in perpetual combat with the devil. Their writings were therefore dominated by the effort of defining and fighting the enemy. In their view, the main threat to Romania's national security was posed by the socioeconomic domination of ethnic minorities. In his analysis of the minority question in Romania, Ion I. Moţa established a hierarchy among the country's ethnic minorities according to their attitude toward Greater Romania. In the first category, he placed revisionist ethnic groups—such as Bulgarians, Russians, and Hungarians—who advocated the dismemberment of the Romanian national state. In the second category, he placed those minority groups that were not motivated by competing nationalist projects but were open to collaboration with the Romanian state, such as Germans, Slovaks, and Poles. The third category posed the main danger to Romania's national security. It was represented by Jews, who occupied "a special position" within Greater Romania, due to their tendency to monopolize liberal professions and to gain control of the country's political leadership.[28] Codreanu's and Moţa's writings, as well as the main Legionary journals, such as *Pămîntul Strămoşesc*, *Biruinţa*, and *Sfarmă Piatră*, were dominated by virulent anti-Semitic manifestos. In their articles, the imminent "Jewish danger" that allegedly threatened the national community was transformed into an apocalyptic image and closely associated with an alleged universal conspiracy. In an analysis of the "conspiracy theory of history," Franz Neumann distinguished among five main variations: the Jesuit conspiracy, the Freemason conspiracy, the Communist conspiracy, the capitalist conspiracy, and the Jewish conspiracy.[29] Significantly,

The cover of the official journal of the Legion, Pământul Strămoşesc (*The Fatherland*), is illustrative of Legionary symbolism. In the middle of the page is the venerated image of Saint Michael. Under this is a map of Greater Romania indicating major Romanian cities; the black spots show the proportion of the Jews out of the total population of each city, in an attempt to document the alleged "Jewish invasion" of Greater Romania. On the left is a quotation from the Bible attributed to Saint Michael and written on his icon in the Cathedral of the Coronation in Alba Iulia (where Greater Romania was proclaimed): "Against unclean hearts who come into the immaculate house of God I mercilessly direct my sword." On the right side there is a quotation from the Romanian poet George Coşbuc, glorifying sacrifice: "Gods if we were descended from / A death we are still owing / It makes no difference if you die / Young men or hunch-backed old / But it is not the same to die / A lion or a chained slave."

the salvationist formula proposed by the Legion was based on a "double" conspiracy theory, since it joined the Jewish and the Communist danger— in the formula of "Judeo-Communism"—thus adding to its proselytizing power. The Legion's anti-Semitism built on a local tradition represented by prominent Romanian intellectuals and politicians. Its apocalyptic component was an influence from the *Protocols of the Elders of Zion*. Translated into Romanian by Ion I. Moţa, and published in 1923, the book fit firmly into Legionary ideology as comprising "the concrete plans devised over centuries by Jews, for achieving their dream of conquering the world." Moreover, in the postwar political environment, Communism was the concrete form taken by the Jewish danger, seen as "the work of Lucifer" and "a new attempt to destroy the kingdom of God."[30]

As a charismatic movement, the Legion put forward a salvational formula, based on the imminence of the apocalypse and encompassing strong messianic overtones. In July 1927 Codreanu defined the leading principles of the Legion: (1) "faith in God"; (2) "faith in our mission"; (3) "love for each other"; and (4) "songs as the chief manifestation of our state of mind." Unlike a political party, the Legion had no program: "The country is dying because of lack of men, not programs." Instead, the Legion defined as its goal the salvation of the Romanian nation: "The final aim is not the life, but the resurrection. The resurrection of people in the name of our savior Jesus Christ." Significantly, while Jews were the satanic enemy, Romanians were portrayed—according to a symbolic substitution—as a chosen people: "God granted us, Romanians, a mission, conferred on us a historical destiny." This destiny could be fulfilled only through the efforts of the Legion. In his article "La Icoană" (To the Icon), Moţa suggestively spelled out the Legion's goal as the national salvation of the Romanian people, under the charismatic leadership of Codreanu, and through the sacrifice of the Legionaries, as the "recipients of the rescuing force." (See Document 3.) The emphasis on salvation was defined as peculiar to the Legion, differentiating it from both Italian fascism and German Nazism. In a 1933 article in the journal *Axa*, the leading Legionary ideologue Mihail Polihroniade pointed out that "fascism venerates the state, Nazism the race and the nation. Our movement strives to fulfill the destiny of the Romanian people through salvation."

While sharing most of the features of a millenarian prophecy, the Legion's salvational formula reinterpreted them through Romanian national symbols and the country's specific sociopolitical context.[31] In the Legionary textbook *Cărtica şefului de cuib*, (Booklet of the Nest's Chief) Codreanu spelled out a code of conduct and a set of ideological commandments on the manner in which Legionary salvation was to be achieved. The code of conduct combined military discipline with religious asceticism. It contained nine Legionary commands (referring to faith in God, self-discipline, dedication,

and love of Legionary death), along with six fundamental laws "of discipline," "of work," "of silence," "of education," "of reciprocal help," and "of
honor" (Point 3 in Cãrtica). Proper Legionary conduct was to lead to salvation by spiritual rebirth from within—through creation of the new man—
and through sacrifice. In Codreanu's view, "the new man, or the renewed
nation, presupposes a great rebirth of the soul, a great spiritual revolution of
the whole people, in other words a fight against the spiritual direction of
today" (Point 69). Through a significant mutation, spiritual rebirth and messianic salvation became the nation itself: "All the virtues of the Romanian
soul should rejuvenate the new man. All the qualities of our race. In the new
man, we should kill off all the faults or tendencies toward evil" (Points 69–
70). The fundamental feature of the new man was his capacity for spiritual
renewal through sacrifice. In order to attain the superior rank of a Legionary,
a member of the Legion had to pass a series of initiations, as part of a sacrile-
gious version of *Imitatio Christi*: the would-be Legionary had to "receive on
his shoulder the yoke of our savior Jesus Christ" (Point 56). The experience
of suffering was thus central to the training of Legionaries. In Codreanu's
view, without "the exam of pain, the exam of bravery, and that of faith, one
cannot be a capable man, cannot be a Legionary" (Point 60). The propensity
of sacrifice led to the cult of Legionary death, glorified as "the most sacred
death among deaths." The political value that Ion I. Moţa attached to life-sac-
rifice accounts for the self-destructive character of the Legion: "The spirit of
sacrifice is essential! We all dispose of the most formidable dynamite, the
most irresistible instrument of fight, more powerful than tanks and rifle-guns:
our own flesh and blood."[32] Legionary fanaticism led to the creation of "death
teams" whose members carried out revenge missions at all costs, thus giving a terrorist character to the Legion. As a charismatic community, the
Legionaries thus committed to a peculiar way of life and adopted a distinct
mode of "want satisfaction," marked by salvation through violent revenge.

Corneliu Zelea Codreanu as a Charismatic Leader

The foundation of the Legionary ideology was the charismatic cult of
Codreanu, proclaimed by Legionary propaganda as "a new messiah," the
instrument sent by the Archangel to fulfill his commandments in order to
bring salvation to the Romanian people. Ion I. Moţa, the second in rank in
the Legion and its "gray eminence," spelled out the messianic scenario by
way of which Codreanu became a main protagonist—namely, his divine
mission, the revelation, the recognition of his charismatic authority over his
followers, and the reverence for his leadership. Codreanu's charismatic claims
were later synthesized by Ion Banea in his hagiographic work *Cãpitanul*,

published for the first time in 1936. Banea portrayed Codreanu in multiple charismatic roles, as a religious prophet, spiritual reformer, predestined hero, and political innovator.[33] As a hero-fighter, Codreanu was represented as belonging to the local panoply of heroic figures, as the end result of a teleological line of the Romanians' historical development.[34] He was compared to great historical figures such as Moldavia's Prince Stephen the Great, and was addressed with the title of "Captain," inspired by the mythology of the *haiducs,* popular outcasts fighting for social justice. Legionary propaganda also emphasized Codreanu's exceptional personal gifts, particularly his physical appearance and power of attraction, regarded as a confirmation of his charismatic qualification. Horia Sima, the later wartime leader of the Legion, elaborated on Codreanu's physical charisma: „What was most impressive, on first contact with Codreanu, was his physical appearance. Nobody could pass him by without noticing him, without being attracted by his look, without asking who he was. His public appearance provoked curiosity. This young man seemed a god descended among mortals. Evaluating him according to the artistic canons of our civilization, one could say he was a synthesis between the beauty of the northern type and the ideal of beauty of ancient Greece. Looking at him, you felt dazed. His face exercised an irresistible fascination. He was a 'living manifesto,' as the Legionaries used to call him."[35]

Was Codreanu a "genuinely" charismatic leader? In order to distinguish between genuinely charismatic leaders and mere "frauds," Robert Tucker has proposed a set of subjective and objective criteria for identifying charismatic leaders. Codreanu's self-identification fulfills all the subjective criteria of Tucker's test: namely, power of vision, sense of mission, confidence in the movement and in himself as the chosen one, and faith in the possibility of deliverance. The portrait of the leader put forward by Codreanu in his autobiographical work *Pentru Legionari* strongly resembled the archetype of a charismatic leader, focusing on power of attraction, courage, and "capacity for love." While the portrait fulfilled an obvious propagandistic function, Codreanu's fanaticism suggests, however, the internalization of the charismatic behavioral model. According to numerous firsthand accounts, Codreanu used religious language, practiced ascetic rituals such as fasting and praying, and imposed severe personal discipline upon himself. He constantly legitimated his leadership by way of his charismatic vision:

"From the first moment I have had the clear vision of the final victory. I have assumed the full responsibility of the leadership. From that time I have suffered many difficulties, dangers and innumerable risks, but this vision of victory has never left me."[36]

Codreanu's leadership also fulfills the objective criteria put forward by Tucker. Although a mediocre speaker, lacking Hitler's mobilizing oratorical abilities, he was an "action hero," distinguished by his nonconformist and counter-normative behavior. Educated by his father, Ion Zelea Codreanu, in a highly militant nationalist spirit, Codreanu proved to have a remarkably combative attitude at an early age.[37] During his student years, Codreanu was the source of continuous trouble, being expelled by the university senate and readmitted to classes only at the insistence of his godfather, the influential anti-Semitic professor and politician A. C. Cuza. Moreover, although he never held an official position in the state apparatus, Codreanu succeeded in building a voluntary nucleus of faithful followers, becoming the object of a fanatic cult of personality.

How can one account for the mass response to Codreanu's charismatic claims? Many historians have tried to explain it from the narrow perspective of Codreanu's personal qualities, or—in apologetic terms—through his alleged "exceptional" personality. Significantly, while Codreanu was seen by his loyal followers as "exceptional," other collaborators such as Nichifor Crainic and Mihai Stelescu portrayed him as a mediocre and violent personality. Codreanu's charisma was not due to his personal qualities but was a combination between a "situational charisma"—due to the "charisma hunger" of Romanian society—and a charismatic agency responsible for its dispersion in innovative forms of political propaganda. The following section therefore turns our analysis from the alleged "exceptional qualities" of the charismatic leader to his "followers and their needs."

Charisma and Politics in Interwar Romania

In accounting for the emergence of charismatic bonding, Erik H. Erikson pointed out that "charisma hunger" is generally due to an "identity vacuum" triggered by a combination of sociopolitical upheaval and decline of traditional forms of religion, on the one hand, and psychological trends such as "fear" and "anxiety," on the other.[38] The sociopolitical upheaval of Greater Romania favored the emergence of charismatic types of authority on both grounds. Although Romania developed after 1918 as a "rationalized" mass parliamentary democracy, based on a liberal constitution and a multiparty system, the lack of democratic experience favored the emergence of personalized movements. A relevant example of postwar charismatic leadership may be seen in the political odyssey of General Alexandru Averescu in the early 1920s. Emerging from the war as a military hero, Averescu was venerated by the peasantry as a messianic savior. His tours in the countryside raised "waves of pagan mysticism."[39] But his charisma was short-lived: after a sweeping electoral victory as leader of the People's Party, Averescu proved unable to manage his popularity and evolved in a clientelist direction, becoming a pawn of the dominant Liberal Party.

Codreanu was the most successful charismatic leader from the plethora of "saviors" that mushroomed in postwar Romania. His success can be explained by the fact that, unlike Averescu, Codreanu placed charisma at the very center of his political propaganda. He directed his efforts at building a movement of devoted followers and specifically targeted certain age or socio-professional categories, such as students. Moreover, Codreanu developed his charismatic claims in an anti-establishment and anti-democratic direction, thus directly benefiting from the crisis of the parliamentary system. Last but not least, his counter-ideology united two central dimensions of Romanian national ideology, religion and nationalism. This combination accounts for the Legion's proselytizing power and social composition.

Upon its establishment, the Legion functioned as a small religious confraternity of young males, having in 1929 an estimated number of roughly 400 to 1,000 members, the great majority young people between twenty and twenty-five.[40] They were based in two rooms in the Iaşi Cultural House, and in a chapel where they venerated the icon of the Archangel Michael. The warlike charismatic sect was often mocked for its religious bigotry, Legionaries being pejoratively named "Christians of the wood" due to their cult of the icon.

Starting in 1929, Codreanu set as the Legion's main task its "going to the masses," mostly through electoral contests organized in Moldova and Bessarabia. During these contests, Codreanu exploited an elaborated charismatic message and imagery, usually appearing to peasants on a white horse and wearing a white shirt with a black sign of the cross. His short speeches announced a new era for the righteous believers: "The hour of resurrection and of the Romanian's salvation is at hand. He who has faith, who struggles and suffers, he will be recompensed and blessed by his people." In addition, Legionary propaganda skillfully manipulated religious sensibilities, at a time when traditional forms of religiosity were waning. In 1928, eleven students imprisoned in Cluj claimed that Jesus Christ visited them in their prison cell.[41] Their claim was endorsed by Moţa, who proclaimed it to be "the beginning of a capital phase in the fate of our people and of humankind," namely, "the active intervention of the Divinity in the problem of the defense of humankind, in the question of the earth's liberation from Satan's rule."[42] Later, during the 1930s, Romanian media reported numerous religious "visions," such as the "miracle" of Maglavit (1935), where the peasant Petrache Lupu claimed he saw God, or the "vision" of Maria Rusu, who claimed to have spoken to the Virgin Mary. As a result, as the Marxist intellectual Lucretiu Pătrăşcanu recalled, "a wave of religious exaltation swept over the whole country, from one end to the other."[43] These events were integrated by the Legionary press into their millennial message, as proof of divine signs.

Electoral gains were modest, however, due mainly to the hostile attitude of the state administration. Beginning in 1932–1933, the Legion took advantage of the pauperization of social life generated by the great economic depression and became a mass party, now assuming political prominence. First, the Legion expanded its regional basis. Its original nucleus originated in northern Moldova, an area that acquired a peripheral status following the 1859 political union between Moldova and Wallachia, and a steady economic pauperization allegedly due to the "Jewish invasion." Significantly, in his early manifestos, Codreanu appealed to Moldovans as "the poorest and most oppressed of all Romanians," urging them to unite "wherever they live in the Romanian lands."[44] Gradually, the Legion penetrated other historic regions as well. Building on partial electoral data, Eugen Weber argued in a pioneering article that the mass base of the Legion was recruited predominantly from the impoverished, overwhelmingly rural, and geographically isolated regions of Romania, such as northern and southern Moldova, southern Bessarabia, and the center of Transylvania.[45] His conclusions were challenged by Armin Heinen, who pointed out that the Legion was in fact

Corneliu Zelea Codreanu among relics of Romanian soldiers who died in World War One, excavated by a Legionary team in 1937 at Predeal. The image is illustrative of the cult of the dead—and of the skull—that characterized Legionary ideology. The setting of the picture, as well as the lonely, contemplative and focused pose of Codreanu, is meant to suggest his charismatic "responsibility" and qualification.

more successful in regions exposed to sudden modernization, "advancing by means of industrialization, trade and communication, as well as more widely spread literacy."[46] It attracted active middle social categories, such as lawyers, priests, teachers, and students, who felt restricted in their upward social mobility. The Legion could penetrate these social categories using innovative political methods, among which charismatic propaganda figured predominantly.

Codreanu's charismatic image-building was further consolidated by the right-wing intellectuals joining the Legion in the period 1932–1934, most notably those grouped around the journal *Axa*. As the journalist and theologian Nichifor Crainic recalled, the merger between Codreanu's nucleus and the *Axa* group, which occurred at his own initiative, was at first a difficult enterprise, since those intellectuals portrayed Codreanu as "criminal and ignorant." However, in a short time "they all embraced him and opened the large gate through which were to enter tens of thousands of young intellectuals."[47]

The animator of a religious–nationalist trend generically called Orthodoxism, Crainic intended to channel Codreanu's movement into a nationalist party under his own direction. His association with the Legionaries was, however, short-lived, giving way to another recognized guru of the new generation, the journalist and Bucharest University professor Nae Ionescu. Under Ionescu's spiritual patronage, the Legion benefited from a new wave of intellectual sympathizers, followers of the controversial but admired professor. This intellectual input marked a turning point in the history of the Legion. Attracted by the spiritual renewal preached by the movement, new intellectual members or sympathizers further developed Codreanu's charismatic claims into a highly polished and effective propaganda offensive.

The testimony of Nicholas Nagy-Talavera, a historian of Jewish–Hungarian extraction from Transylvania, is relevant in this respect. (See Document 5.) He recounts the emotional memory of an eight-year-old child confronted with the skillfully choreographed appearance of Codreanu at the peak of his political popularity in 1937, when propagandistic methods made his "charismatic aura" seem stronger than ever. The document first records the strong repulsion Codreanu exercised among certain groups of people, alluding to what Tucker called "counter-charisma." Moreover, Codreanu's appearance, as well as the entire Legionary performance, emphasized Orthodox religious rituals and biblical imagery, while the repression of the prefect gave it an extra aura of virtuous political resistance.[48]

The Legion and the Orthodox Church

Talavera's recollection pointed out the similarities between the Legion's rituals and several Orthodox religious practices. The core of Legionary ideology was based on religious themes, such as their proclaimed belief in God and in salvation. Legionary ceremonies centered on religious symbols, most importantly the cross and the icon, and took place according to a religious ritual, always starting with a liturgy officiated by an Orthodox priest. The charismatic nature of the Legion and its pseudo-religious practices thus account for its ambivalent relationship with the Orthodox Church, oscillating between periods of collaboration and stiff conflict.

The religious rituals and message of the Legion attracted numerous Orthodox priests, especially of lower ranks. Veiga estimated that in 1937, out of approximately 10,000 Orthodox priests, 2,000 converted to or sympathized with the Legion.[49] Consequently, in their propaganda, Legionary ideologues often identified Orthodox priests with the Legion: "A true priest will consequently be a Legionary through the very nature of things, exactly as, and again through the nature of things, a Legionary is the best son of the church."[50] Nevertheless, Legionary ideology was ultimately not only different from but even opposed to the official theology of the church. This was underlined by Codreanu himself, who stated that "we make a great distinction between the line we are following and the line of the Christian church. The line of the church is a thousand meters above us. It reaches the perfect and the sublime. We cannot pull down this line for explaining our deeds."[51] The distinction served to justify the usage of a millenarian message for accomplishing worldly, and secular aims through violent political action. Codreanu believed that this type of action was permitted only to laymen, since priests could not use or encourage the use of arms.

On several occasions the Orthodox leadership showed sympathy for the anti-democratic and anti-Semitic message of the Legion, and put forward attempts at political collaboration. This temporary cooperation was directly linked to the institutional crisis of the Orthodox Church. The establishment of Greater Romania had changed the country's religious configuration, challenging the fragile equilibrium between the Orthodox Church and the state. The inclusion into Greater Romania of a large number of Roman Catholics, Greek Catholics, Protestants, and Jews added to religious pluralism, posing the dilemma of interconfessional relations. Although declared a "dominant" church by the 1923 constitution, the Orthodox Church felt underprivileged, chiefly as compared to the material power and political influence of the Roman Catholic Church. In striving to defend their institutional interests, Orthodox officials intensified their political lobbying and looked for potential political allies, such as the Legion. In spite of occasional collaboration,

higher Orthodox hierarchs were nevertheless concerned by the active participation of clergy in Codreanu's movement. On 4 October 1935, the Holy
Synod portrayed the Legionary working camps in the countryside as a hidden agency for attracting Orthodox believers and refused their voluntary
assistance for church repairs. Reacting to the hostility shown by the Orthodox
hierarchy, leading Legionary theologians, such as Gheorghe Racoveanu,
argued instead for a natural alliance between the Legion and parochial priests:
"It is surprising the lack of understanding from the upper hierarchy of the
Orthodox Church. But communal priests know who is their real ally, and
they support Codreanu's efforts, despite unavoidable risks."[52]

The divergence between the Orthodox establishment and the Legion is
not surprising. As a charismatic movement, the Legion blended religious and
secular elements. Although its message of theological inspiration attracted
numerous lower-rank prelates, from the point of view of the established
church the Legion was ultimately a heretical movement. At certain moments,
the Orthodox leadership tried to use the Legion for pressuring the politicians. In the long run, this collaboration was harmful to church interests: the
charismatic legitimization of the Legion was ultimately in competition with
and subversive of the charismatic monopoly of the church. Later, therefore,
the Orthodox Church acted as a pillar of the personal regime of Carol II
(1938–1940) and supported his repression of the Legion.

Charismatic Leadership versus Party Organization

The charismatic nature of the Legion also shaped its organizational structure. In the Nazi Party, the *Führerprinzip* fused with a bureaucratic party
organization, resulting in a peculiar syncretism called by Orlow "bureaucratic romanticism."[53] The Legion had a less structured organization, shaped
by the spontaneity of the charismatic leadership. Initially, the Legion was
dominated by the inner group of the *Văcărești*, who made up a charismatic
elite and commonly endorsed major decisions. In August 1927 the Legion
announced its first structural framework, made up of four sections: the first
—and most important one—was "the youth section," having as a subsection
the teenaged "Blood Brotherhood"; the second, "protecting" section was
composed of "mature men"; the third, "assisting" section encompassed
women; and the fourth, "international" section was made up of Romanians
living abroad.[54] The leadership of the Legion was to be commonly exercised by a council composed of former or current student leaders, the latter
being granted only a consultative vote; and by a senate made up of elected
personalities over fifty years of age.

Despite its collective guiding forums, the Legion had in fact an authoritarian structure, based on the undisputed leadership of "the Captain"—also named the Chief of the Legion (*șeful Legiunii*)—and on a hierarchical line of charismatic commanders. The organizational basis of the Legion comprised grass-root cells made up of three to thirteen members (subsequently called "cuiburi"—"nests"). Several nests made up garrisons, which were further organized into sectors, counties, and regions. While nests and garrisons were led by charismatic leaders emerging spontaneously, the political leadership of regional and central structures was appointed by Codreanu and was directly responsible to him, in an effort to prevent rival exploitation of charisma that could result in defections. Codreanu added a military wing in 1930, whose name, the Iron Guard (*Garda de Fier*), became synonymous with the entire Legion.

The growing membership of the Legion challenged its initial organization, necessitating an expansion of the Legion's line of command, the tightening of organizational discipline, and an increased role for ritual socialization. First, in order to cope with this development, starting in 1934 Codreanu put greater emphasis on the process of selection: in order to become "Legionaries," new members were subject to a probation period of up to three years. They had to pass a series of initiating tests, allegorically described by Codreanu as "the mountain of suffering, the forest with wild beasts, and the marsh of desperation."[55] In addition to regular screening of membership, Legionaries were subject to extended practical training and participated in a process of community socialization following detailed rituals centered on the cult of "the Captain" and aimed at emulating his personality (see Document 4). Second, new ranks of command were established, such as "Legionary instructor" and "deputy commander." In order to prevent their autonomous consolidation, Legionary leaders could retain their posts for a maximum of two years. Deviant behavior was punished with a warning, temporary suspension, or even assassination. Most importantly, the circle of charismatic aristocracy composed initially of the *Văcărești* was considerably enlarged, so that in 1933 Codreanu established the rank of "Legionary commander," awarded to prominent Legionaries such as Moța, Ion Banea, and Mihai Stelescu. In 1936 Codreanu further enlarged the charismatic aristocracy by establishing the "Knights of the Annunciation," a corpus of Legionary commanders selected on the basis of their combat merit, trust and loyalty.

The reorganization necessitated by the political growth of the Legion brought into question the power and influence of the founding group, resulting in factional competition and reciprocal accusations of deviation from the original charismatic goal. Reportedly, in 1934 four main factions were jostling for prominence: one led by Ion I. Moța, another led by Mihai Stelescu, a third one led by Ion Dumitrescu, and last but not least, the intellectuals grouped around the journal *Axa*.[56] The balance among these factions was kept by Codreanu in a deliberate policy of divide and rule. The first defection from the Legion was that of Mihai Stelescu. Accusing Codreanu of political opportunism, Stelescu founded a rival organization in 1936 called *Cruciada Românismului*. For his "treason," he was soon executed in a "ritual murder" by a Legionary squad. The balance among rival factions was further changed in 1937, when prominent Legionary cadres assembled a team for fighting in the Spanish civil war on Franco's side. After taking part in several battles, on 13 January 1937 Ion I. Moţa and Vasile Marin were killed in action near Majadahonda. Moţa's gesture was subject to conflicting interpretations. Based on his "testament," Legionary propaganda portrayed it as a Christian sacrifice. More neutral contemporary analysis regarded it as a desperate attempt of the *Văcăreşteni* to restore the idealism of the movement, though a spectacular action. Indeed, the dead Moţa shaped yet again the evolution of the Legion. The two "martyrs" were buried with national funerals, the impressive ceremony being attended by numerous politicians, religious officials, and foreign diplomats. The death of Moţa and Marin inhibited the political reorganization of the Legion, provoking instead "a pietist turn."[57] The cult of the two martyrs became a central feature of the Legion, closely related to that of the Captain.

Taking advantage of this propaganda boost, and in the absence of credible political alternatives, the Legion became a significant political player. Consequently, Carol II started to regard it as a potential partner in establishing his personal regime. Secret negotiations for political collaboration with Codreanu were conducted in February 1937 but proved fruitless. Codreanu's account of the meeting with King Carol II illustrates his understanding of his leadership as charismatic. To the king's request to be proclaimed "the Captain" of the Legion, Codreanu replied that "as the Legionaries had sworn their faith to me and not to another person, this faith, this attachment cannot be a political object."[58]

This refusal led to open confrontation. In the 1937 parliamentary elections, Codreanu joined an anti-Carlist political alliance and won a major electoral success: his party, All for the Fatherland, received 437,378 votes, representing 15.6 percent of the total number of the electorate, and 66 parliamentary mandates. But the Legion was unable to take advantage of this success. On 10 February 1938, Carol II staged a coup d'état and assumed authoritarian powers. The Legion's position rapidly deteriorated. On 17–19 April, Codreanu was arrested. After two consecutive summary trials, he was sentenced to ten years of forced labor. Moreover, fearing his political resurrection with German help, Carol II ordered the assassination of Codreanu. On the night of 29–30 November 1938, Codreanu was strangled together with thirteen other Legionaries. His body was buried in the courtyard of the Jilava prison, burned with acid, and covered with a thick layer of cement.

Despite this desperate attempt to eradicate Codreanu's charisma, the spirit of "the Captain" obsessed his followers more than ever. Revenge was quick to follow. On 21 September 1939, a Legionary "death team" assassinated Prime Minister Armand Călinescu in a public square in Bucharest. After that, they stormed the national radio, publicly announced the avenging of their captain, and gave themselves up to the police. They were carried back to the public square and executed. Their bodies were displayed for several days for public opprobrium. During the next several days, the symbolic violence of the state was abandoned in favor of mass repression: all over the country, 253 Legionary leaders were executed without trial. The confrontation between the two "systems of belief" had reached its peak. Unable to tame or use them for his own purpose, Carol II had the Legionaries killed by their own lawless methods as the only effective way to counter their fanatical terrorism.

Factionalism and the Routinization of Charisma

Codreanu's death opened the question of succession to charismatic leadership. On the one hand, there were no rules of succession, and Codreanu had not designated anyone as a legitimate successor. On the other hand, the waves of repression against the Legion in 1938–39 almost completely eliminated its original leadership, promoting second-rank Legionaries to the forefront and generating factionalism. In a secret report, the Hungarian political secretary in Bucharest judged that in late 1940 the Iron Guard was divided among three main factions: the group gathered around Horia Sima, a dynamic local leader from the Banat, which was the most pragmatic and least Orthodox in its orientation; the group composed of Corneliu Zelea Codreanu's family, namely his father, Ion Zelea Codreanu, and his brothers; and "the Moța-Marin" group, which wanted to strengthen the religious character of the movement.[59] In this context, several options appeared for the routinization of Codreanu's charisma. The first one lay, unsurprisingly, in the selection of a new charismatic leader. After a long period of confusion, Horia Sima, representing the less radical wing of the Legion, overcame all competition and assumed leadership. Unable to put forward claims of charismatic legitimacy, Sima was invested as the leader of the Legion on 6 September 1940 by a body created *ad hoc* at his own initiative, the Legionary Forum.[60] His legitimacy was soon contested by a second option for the routinization of charisma: its transfer to a kin of Codreanu. Asserting that he was "the Captain's father and his earthly representative," on 28 September Ion Zelea Codreanu and his followers stormed the Legionary Green House in Bucharest, in an unsuccessful attempt to install "charisma by kinship."[61]

After the loss of much of Transylvania to Hungary and of Bessarabia to the Soviet Union forced Carol II to abdicate, General Ion Antonescu stepped in to fill the political vacuum on 6 September 1940. This change opened the Legion's way to power. On 14 September Antonescu proclaimed the "National–Legionary state" that lasted until January 1941. The Legion became the ruling party but had to share executive power with the army. Upon the Legion's accession to power, its propaganda exploited a third option for the routinization of charisma: the cult of the dead leader and of the Legionary martyrs. The ritual basis of the new political regime was the exhumation, public burial, and rehabilitation of the Legionary "martyrs," retrospectively regarded by Sima as the most important task justifying the Legion's accession to power.[62] The exhumation of Codreanu's remains, and those of the two groups charged with political assassinations, the "Decemvirs" and the "Nicadors," on 21–23 November 1940, occasioned a strong reaffirmation of Codreanu's charisma, as the foundation of Legionary ideology. On the day of the reburial, *Cuvîntul*, the leading Legionary newspaper, wrote: "It is the day of the Captain's resurrection. He is resurrected, as he promised, according to the Gospel. He is resurrected, rising from the grave to present to us again Romania itself, buried by this sinful age." In a radio interview, philosopher Emil Cioran, at the time a youngster in his twenties, provided a powerful endorsement of Codreanu's charismatic cult: "With the exception of Jesus, no other dead being has been so present among the living. Has anybody even thought about forgetting him? 'From this moment on, our country is being led by a dead man,' a friend was telling me on the bank of the Seine. This dead man spread a perfume of eternity over our human dung and brought back the sky over Romania."[63]

Codreanu's reburial prompted a terrifying orgy of Legionary vendettas: on the night of 25–26 November, sixty-five former dignitaries considered guilty of persecutions against the Legion were executed without trial. The Legion had thus finally succeeded in its goals. The old order collapsed under its blows, and with it all the enemies of the Legion were punished. But it was the triumph of nihilism, criminal revenge, and self-destruction. The subsequent rule of the Legion was characterized by tension between its charismatic nature and the need for a pragmatic political orientation. Internal contradictions aggravated the conflict of interest between the Legion, as the political basis of the new regime, and General Ion Antonescu, as its executive head, paving the way for the Legion's political elimination. On 21–23 January 1941, after the failure of a chaotic Legionary rebellion that was meant to transfer full governing power into their hands, the Legion was disbanded and its leaders exiled. According to Sima's own appraisal, the Legion had thus proved itself incapable of "moving from the revolutionary phase to the governing phase." The political ineffectiveness of the Legion was direct-

The exhumation of the corpses of Codreanu and the members of the Legionary terrorist groups called the "Decemvirs" and the "Nicadors," killed at the order of King Carol II in November 1938 and buried in the courtyard of the Jilava prison under a thick layer of cement. The ceremony, which took place in November 1940 under the "National-Legionary Regime," was attended by high state representatives and Orthodox clerics, and is illustrative of the cult of the dead leader as a form of routinization of his charisma.

ly linked to its charismatic nature. As Weber pointed out, "all charisma is on the road from a turbulently emotional life that knows no economic rationality to a slow death by suffocation under the weight of material interests. Every hour of its existence brings it nearer to the end."[64]

Conclusions

This chapter proposes a reinterpretation of the ideology and practice of the Legion of the Archangel Michael, following Weber's theoretical and methodological perspective on the charismatic type of authority. It also places the Legion within the larger sociopolitical context of interwar Romania. In so doing, it redirects the study of the Legion toward the conflict of values between the official hegemonic culture and a resistant youth counterculture. While students of the Legion have so far explained Codreanu's charisma by his personal magnetism, this essay asserts that Codreanu put forward claims for charismatic leadership based on belief in his messianic call for a divine mission and his promise of salvation. In analyzing Codreanu's leadership, the analysis draws on the test of charismatic leadership developed by Robert

Tucker, based on such criteria as sense of mission, capacity for mobilization, and consistency of leadership.

In addition, the chapter addresses the relationship between Codreanu's leadership and the charismatic movement it generated. Codreanu's charismatic claims emerged in the context of the nationalist student movements, which provided him both with a political cause of national importance and with a favorable environment for proselytizing that generated a nucleus of close followers. In analyzing the transformation of a regional student organization into a messianic nationalist movement of the "young generation," the argument here rejects a "modernizing" perspective on charisma, according to which the appeal of Codreanu's leadership was due to the existence of a "primitive mentality" in a developing country. Instead, it asserts that Codreanu's leadership exhibited a conjunction between a "situational charisma," generated by the sociopolitical upheaval of Greater Romania, and a charismatic agency, based on his own self-identification and Moţa's ideological creativity.

The chapter also points out the responsibility of members of the Romanian political elite, who supported the Legion with the intention of manipulating it for their own political purposes, and of those intellectuals who paid lip service to Codreanu's leadership, actively contributing to the merger between the new nationalism of the young generation and Codreanu's charismatic cult. This alliance resulted in a complex ideological syncretism among transcendental charismatic calls, local cultural codes—such as Orthodox ritualism and traditional nationalist symbols—and the messianic discourse of the young generation.

Its charismatic ideology shaped the organization of the Legion. It was structured around Codreanu's leadership and personality, and dominated by a circle of close followers, as well as by a hierarchical line of charismatic leaders emerging at the local level. In the long run, the evolution of the Legion exhibited underlying tensions between its charismatic nature and the need for a more bureaucratic party organization, accounting for factional competition, experiments in the "routinization" of Codreanu's charisma, its inefficient rule and rapid fall from power. The theory of charisma thus proves an essential analytical tool in the study of the Legion of the Archangel Michael in interwar Romania. On a more general level, this case study asserts that, instead of adding to the stalemated debate concerning the "true" nature of universalized concepts such as "fascism," students of interwar right-wing political movements might benefit more from a broader theoretical approach in order to identify the specifics of their ideologies.

Sources

Document 1:

I do not know how it happened but it seems that I broke loose from that cradle of humanity and strain, of bravery and peace that dominated the village of the Balşeni. And, as this book proves, although it seems hardly believable, I have found myself another youth somewhere else, and I have plunged into another life. (It indeed proves true the story about the seven lives of the Romanian.) I have thus become a city-dweller, I have taken another name, and I have entered the whirlpool of today's life. Here, I struggled into a world alienated from the old customs and invaded by pagans. I wrestled against it and against all its kikes and scoundrels, in the same way as I jumped to the very heart of the danger during the time I used to prop up oxen on the slopes of the mountain gaps. Quietness and contentment in this world I could not find, I hated it and it hated me back deadly. It is clear that the fate of the rebellious—but ultimately triumphant—slave was predestined to me, too, as to my forerunners.

In this fight I used the pen as well. As such, mostly at random, for the needs of the battle, and not at all for giving Romanian writing unforgettable charm. It is only for the benefit of the fighters that I include here some of the articles from these years of youthful struggle from 1922 until today... Not even a clean Romanian language should be sought for here. I know that it will not be found, and this is the only criticism that I cannot take with a light heart. But it is I myself who first make this criticism here, openly, because reading again articles written fourteen years ago, and even the later ones, before handing them to the printer, I was saddened by the multitude of foreign words ("cranii" ... [skulls]) and of the foreign forms of writing, which had overwhelmed me as they had all the others, almost my entire generation. This alienation against which we are fighting, the calamity to which we react, penetrated even us, the "nationalists": in spirit, in faith, in our way of thinking, in mores, in language, and in customs. The fortunate thing is that it did not terminate everything and that it still retains so much strength in us as to overcome the obstacles of this century of confusion and alienation, and allow us to be able to return to our origins, and, once returned there, to resume the broken line of our life in the Romanian house, community and spirit, and to elevate this people to the material and spiritual power and fruitfulness it deserves.

This is how it should be understood and received, this book to which I have given the title of that article which evokes one of the most intense feelings of a fighting army: the burial of its comrade dead in battle.

Let me now abandon the aristocratic language and return to myself. I was saying that I hated the world of this second life of mine. And it hated me back mortally, as it hated all my Legionary comrades, and my Captain. The old world, that of Nuțu Doncii, in which are rooted all our feelings and longings, we do not find anywhere anymore. It was terminated by this new century with its politics and discord, with its denial of God and love for foreigners and for all that comes from others, the century which tramples under its foot our way of life, with its strengths, its qualities, and its beauty.

As such, our soul, tied to another world, strolls around today in a life which is not ours. Facing today's world, we feel strangers, we cannot find in it any other sense except that of terminating it in order to revive the old times and to increase their beauty, their strength, and rightful Romanian order.

It would thus seem that I and my comrades are a kind of strange being with two lives, a kind of zombie risen in an extinguished world to bear the spirit of fear in today's world. This is exactly the way we are. We are uprooted souls who, carrying their restlessness over a ruined life, will not find peace in any grave until we elevate again what others have scattered, wasted, and cursed.

The people of today's century should stop for a moment their lives of ease and indifference and listen to the strange noises that rack mysterious depths and yell like the night winds. And this is to be heard and known: the terrible rule of the zombies is approaching.

Source: Ion I. Moța, "Autobiografie (în loc de introducere)," in *Cranii de Lemn. Articole 1922–1936*, 4th ed. (Bucharest, 1940), 9–11.

Document 2:

Confronted with the situation described above, I decided to go together with none of the parties. Not that I wanted to renounce [the fight], but to start the organization of the youth on my own responsibility, by my own head and soul, to continue the fight, and not to capitulate.

During these hours of agitation and dilemma, we remembered the icon that protected us in the Văcărești prison. We decided to sit closer and to continue the fight under the protection of the same Holy Icon. To this end, it was transported from the shrine of Saint Spiridon where I had left it three years ago, to our center in Iași.

The Văcărești group joined immediately in these thoughts. After several days, I called the *Văcărești* and the few students who remained tied to us for a meeting in Iaşi, on Friday 24 June 1927 at ten o'clock, in my room on Florilor Street, No. 20. Several minutes before the meeting, I wrote in a chronicle the following order, registered as Number One:

"Today, Friday 24 June 1927 (Saint John the Baptist), 10 p.m. 'The Legion of Archangel Michael' was established under my leadership. Let him come here who has an unlimited faith. Let him stay aside who has doubts. I name Radu Mironovici as chief of the guard at the Icon.

This first meeting lasted one minute, as long as it took me to read the above order, after which the participants withdrew in order to decide if they felt determined enough and spiritually strong enough to enter such an organization, which had no program, the only program being my previous life of fighting and the prison life of my comrades.

Even for the members of the Văcăreşti group I left time for reflection and inspection of their consciences, to see if they had any doubts or reservations, since once starting on this path they had to continue it during their entire lives without any hesitation.

This was our intimate state of mind that gave birth to the Legion: we were not interested if we would survive, if we would fall exhausted, or if we would die. Our aim was different: to go ahead, united. Going together, united, along with God and with the justice of the Romanian people, no matter what fate this would give us, defeat or death, it would be blessed and would bear fruit for the Romanian people. There are defeats and deaths that resurrect a people to life, as well as certain kinds of victories that weaken it, Professor Iorga once said.

We were now alone as in a desert, and we had to find a way in life by our own power. We gathered together even closer around the Icon. And the more the hardship of life overwhelmed us and the blows of the world hit us, the more we would stay under the shield of Archangel Saint Michael, and under the protection of his sword. For us he was not a photograph on an icon anymore, but we felt him alive. There, at the Icon, we guarded day and night, with a lit candle."

Source: Corneliu Zelea Codreanu, *Pentru Legionari*, 3rd ed. (Bucharest, 1940), 1: 276–77.

Document 3:

We therefore want to build, and—with God's help—we will build, a cell of shining light, which will act, in other words it will save, of its own accord. We are not creators of light. That is to be found only in

God. We are thus not the creators of the desired salvation, but we want to be the recipients of this saving force, which we seek in a different place, in the only place where it is to be found: in God. Therefore: to the Icon!

This house is—naturally—a system. It already exists. And, like every living system, it is moved by a force. In the system of human societies, this force can be captured only through an organization. Therefore, our system has to have an organization, and it has it. Our organization cannot be born and developed in a healthy way without order, hierarchy, or, especially, a Leader (*Conducător*). Thus our organization has a leader whom no one elected but who has the consensus of all those who, seduced by a mysterious force, have come to constitute, under the leader's direction, the disciplined nests of the organization. Our leader is Corneliu Zelea Codreanu.

Our system, with its own order and leadership, gathered around the pillar of its faith in God (its only supporting pillar), starts today, in front of the world, its work, its effort, to which is linked our only hope of salvation. We have the creed that, this time, we go straight to the target, and victory is assured. People will be served and saved, because we do not intend to deviate a single moment from the Icon and its order. It is not our work anymore, but it is its own, and that is invincible.

As an ending we imprint here a confession: we firmly believe, and see on the horizon, in the line of our path, unknown victories and divine wonders. We do not announce them here, to be believed at once (we know that even the contrary can happen), but because tomorrow, when they will be fulfilled, when there will be poured on us the unbelievable gifts of the divine mercy bearing salvation, we should have proof that we have foreseen it, and that we have judged well.

Until then, to those who are strong enough in their souls to understand us, grant us your approval, and go together with us from now on. We send our call: to the Icon! The others, the multitudes, will come later, but they will surely come.

Source: Ion I. Moța, "La Icoană," *Pământul Strămoşesc* 1 (August 1927) 1: 9–10.

Document 4:

For Ismet's sake, the boys established complete order in prison life. The engineer Clime took command of the several hundred prisoners, combined Legionary discipline with that of the military, formed teams for kitchen duty and cleaning, and divided the day into hours of instruction, songs, discussions, and entertainment. Nobody from the prison's personnel interfered anymore. In the first days, it turned out that one [prisoner] was missing: he jumped out of the truck on the way to Jilava and disappeared. The boys sent word to the city asking for a volunteer prisoner from among the free Legionaries, so that the commander of the prison did not get into trouble with the superior authority! The immense cellar seemed an oven on fire: it vibrated with Legionary songs. I was hearing most of them for the first time. It was the time when those glorifying assassinations did not yet appear. What heroic, seducing songs! And what words animated by love of the country and of the Romanian people! It was difficult for a soul to resist this wave of creator enthusiasm, no matter how dry it was. The personnel of the prison knew them by heart. The song was the great dynamic force of the Legionary movement—this bizarre mixture of sublime moral and of abjection. In stormy, innovating upsurges of unlimited sacrifice and of demonic criminality! These boys were all wearing the icon of Jesus Christ or of the Virgin Mary, prayed regularly in the morning and evening, and still spoke with infinite tenderness of the "heroes" who killed! If later years revealed to me the creative will and impulse toward sacrifice of this youth, prison revealed to me its most intimate elements, the black and white mixture of its good and bad instincts, unfortunately all equally disciplined, within their own line. "The Captain's" way of being lived in every boy. "The Captain" was a dogma, a god, a supernatural existence. In that particular moment, nobody knew where he was or what he was doing. It was not possible that "the Captain" was not well where he was! He was working, he did not sleep. He would arrange it in such a way that on a happy day we would all get out of prison victoriously. In their burning feelings, some felt offended that I called him Corneliu instead of "the Captain" and that I did not take part in his deification. Then I realized that his entire character, in a strange phenomenon of osmosis, was absorbed in the marrow of the movement itself and constituted its fatality, which nothing could change anymore. During this time, "the Captain" was safe in Bucharest. For four and a half months the vigilant police of the capital could not discover him, because he was protected by Elena Lupescu herself, as he and nobody else told me on the night when he appeared at the trial! He did not suspect, poor him, that this refined protection was to lead him in several years to the same fate as I. G. Duca, assassination.

Source: Nichifor Crainic, *Zile albe, zile negre* (Bucharest, 1991), 257–58.

Document 5:

Though very young at the time, this writer remembers well the turbulent days of the autumn of 1937, when the most hotly contested elections of the interwar period were being fought in Transylvania. As a child of eight, I visited with my parents some relatives and family friends in a village deep in the Apuseni Mountains, the heart of Romanian Transylvania, home of the moți and the birthplace of the legendary Avram Iancu. In the evening, when the intelligentsia gathered in the salon of the owner of the local saw mill (a Hungarian Jew), the venerable dowager duchesses of village society discussed but one thing, the visit of Codreanu, the dreaded Captain of the Iron Guard, the next day. There was simply no limit to the abuse these ladies and gentleman, Hungarians of the Christian and Jewish faith, heaped on him.

One of the ladies who had seen him in Târgu Mureş the year before spoke of him as if she had seen the monster's head, but dared not describe it. Something of an adventurer by nature, I decided I must take a closer look at this fabulous being, whatever the cost. The next day, I proceeded to carry out this decision. My best friend, the son of the local Orthodox priest, older than I by four years, provided some pieces of peasant costume, and two conspirators [us] headed toward the church yard, where the Legionary meeting was to take place.

The little square before the church teemed with peasants dressed in their colorful Sunday best. Many of them had walked dozens of miles to get there, and there were many, too many gendarmes from the local gendarme station. The prefect of the district of Turda had, as officials of corrupt regimes often do, administered a pin-prick to exasperate rather than a blow to crush. He had forbidden Codreanu to speak, but had not outlawed the meeting itself. And a crowd of simple miserable peasants swelled until the churchyard could hold no more.

There was suddenly a hush in the crowd. A tall, darkly handsome man, dressed in the white costume of a Romanian peasant, rode into the yard on a white horse. He halted close to me, and I could see nothing monstrous or evil about him. On the contrary, his childlike, sincere smile radiated over the miserable crowd, and he seemed to be with it, yet mysteriously apart from it. Charisma is an inadequate word to define the strange force that emanated from this man. He was more aptly part of the forest, of the mountains, of the storms on the snow-covered peak of the Carpathians, and of the lakes and rivers. And so he stood amid the crowd. He had no need to speak; his silence was eloquent. It seemed to be stronger than me, stronger than the order of the prefect who denied him speech. An old whitehaired peasant woman made the sign of the cross on her breast and whispered to us, "The Emissary of the Archangel Michael." Then the sad little church bell began to toll, and the service, which invariably preceded Legionary meetings, began. Deep impressions, created in the soul of the child, die hard. In more than half a century, I have never forgotten my meeting with Corneliu Zelea Codreanu.

Source: Nicholas M. Nagy-Talavera, *Nicolae Iorga: A Biography*, 2nd ed. (Jassy, Portland, Oxford: Center for Romanian Studies, 1998), 343–345.

Notes

1 See Eugen Weber, "Romania," in idem, ed., *Varieties of Fascism* (Princeton, N.: Princeton University Press, 1964), 96–105. Stanley G. Payne also judged that the Legion was "the most unusual mass movement of interwar Europe" in *Fascism: Comparison and Definition* (Madison: University of Wisconsin Press, 1980), 115.

2 On interwar movements of "cultural purification," with direct reference to the Legion, see Anthony D. Smith, "Culture, Community, and Territory: The Politics of Ethnicity and Nationalism," *International Affairs* 72 (July 1996): 445–58.

3 The usage of the term "ideology" in reference to Legionary propaganda may seem intriguing, given its heterogeneous nature, its contradictions, and its numerous intellectual borrowings. This essay does not define Legionary ideology as an "ism" comparable to other, more coherent and elaborated "isms," such as communism or nationalism, but uses the term "ideology" for describing the Legionary "world-view," based on the writings of the main ideologues of the movement, Corneliu Zelea Codreanu, Ion I. Moţa, and Horia Sima, and of other Legionary intellectuals such as Ion Banea, Ilie Imbrescu, Mihail Polihroniade, and Nicolae Roşu. For minimal versus enlarged definitions of the Legionary "doctrine," see Dan Pavel, "Legionarismul," in Alina Mungiu-Pippidi, ed., *Doctrine politice: Concepte universale şi realităţi româneşti* (Iaşi: Polirom, 1998), 212–28. For an attempt to grant fascism "full ideological status," see Roger Griffin, "General Introduction," in *Fascism* (Oxford: Oxford University Press, 1995), 1–12.

4 In the 1960s there began a wave of scholarly interest in the study of the Legion. See Eugen Weber, "Romania," in Hans Rogger and Eugen Weber, eds., *The European Right: A Historical Profile* (London: Weidenfeld & Nicholson, 1965), 501–74; idem, "The Men of the Archangel," *Journal of Contemporary History* 1 (1966): 101–26; Stephen Fischer-Galati, "Fascism in Romania," in Peter F. Sugar, ed., *Native Fascism in the Successor States*, 1918–1945 (Santa Barbara: ABC-Clio, 1971), 112–22; Francis L. Carsten, "Anti-Semitism and Anti-Communism: The Iron Guard," in *The Rise of Fascism* (Berkeley: University of California Press, 1967), 181–93; Z. Barbu, "Psycho-Historical and Sociological Perspectives on the Iron Guard, the Fascist Movement of Romania," in Stein Ugelvik Larsen, Bernt Hagtvet, and Jan Petter Myklebust, eds., *Who Were the Fascists: Social Roots of European Fascism* (Bergen: Scandinavian University Press, 1980), 379–394; and Radu Ioanid, *The Sword of the Archangel: Fascist Ideology in Romania* (Boulder, Col.: East European Monographs, 1990). For a comparative view of fascism in Romania

and Hungary, see Nicholas Nagy-Talavera, *The Green Shirts and Others: A History of Fascism in Hungary and Rumania* (Berkeley: University of California Press, 1967). For the most complete monograph to date, see Armin Heinen, *Die Legion "Erzengel Michael"*, in *Rumänien: Soziale Bewegung und politische Organisation: Ein Beitrag zum Problem des internationalen Faschismus* (Munich: Oldenbourg, 1986). Quotations in this chapter are from the Romanian translation, *Legiunea "Arhanghelului Mihail." Mişcare socialǎ şi organizaţie politicǎ* (Bucharest, 1998).

5 I use the generic name of the Legion for the whole range of successive political movements based on Codreanu's leadership, namely the Legion of the Archangel Michael established in 1927; the Iron Guard, created in 1931 as a political section and subsequently identified with the Legion itself; and the All for the Fatherland party, established in 1933. The movement was also known under the generic name of the "Legionary Movement" (*Mişcarea Legionarǎ*).

6 Current attempts at reviving the Iron Guard heavily exploit the messianic "hero-image" of Codreanu. See the writings of the Legionary émigré Faust Brǎdescu, *Corneliu-Zelea Codreanu: Erou Neo-Cosmogon* (Madrid: Editura Carpaţi, 1987), in which he refers to Codreanu as "the symbol of the Divine Will, the metha-human." Other émigré Legionaries, such as Constantin Papanace and Ştefan Palaghiţǎ, claim the virtuous charismatic "purity" of the Legion's initial leadership, represented by the duo Codreanu-Moţa, denouncing the leadership of Horia Sima as an illegitimate succession which distorted the spirit of the Legion and was responsible for its abominable crimes. See Constantin Papanace, *Destinul unei Generaţii* (Rome: Biblioteca Verde, 1952); and Ştefan Palaghiţǎ, *Garda de Fier: Spre reinvierea României* (Buenos Aires: S. Palaghiţǎ, 1951).

7 Max Weber, "The Pure Types of Legitimate Authority" in S. N. Eisenstadt, ed., *Max Weber on Charisma and Institution Building* (Chicago and London: Chicago University Press, 1968), 46.

8 Max Weber, "The Nature of Charismatic Authority and Its Routinization" in S. N. Eisenstadt, ed., *Max Weber on Charisma*, 48.

9 Max Weber, "Charisma and Its Transformation," in *Economy and Society: An Outline of Interpretative Sociology* (Berkeley: University of California Press, 1978), 2:1116.

10 Max Weber, "Sociology of Charismatic Authority," and "The Nature of Charismatic Authorithy," in Eisenstadt, ed., *Max Weber on Charisma*, 18, 49.

11 Max Weber, "Charisma and Its Transformation," 1114.

12 A recent typology of fascism was elaborated by Stanley Payne, who argued that fascist movements in Europe were united by the following common features: "a new functional relationship for the social and economic systems, eliminating the autonomy … of large scale capitalism," "a new order in foreign affairs," and "highly ethnicist as well as extremely nationalist" priorities. A second set of characteristics is represented by the fascist negations: anti-fascism, anti-communism, and anti-conservatism. Finally, fascist movements also exhibited certain features of style and organization, such as charismatic leadership. See Payne, *A History of Fascism, 1914–1945* (Madison: University of Wisconsin Press, 1995). The existence of universal features of fascism remains, however, a matter of academic controversy. For a refutation of the concept of "generic fascism," see Gilbert Allardyce, "What Fascism Is Not: Thoughts on the Deflation of a Concept," *American Historical Review* 84 (1979): 367–88.

13 See Joseph Nyomarkay, *Charisma and Factionalism in the Nazi Party* (Minneapolis: University of Minnesota Press, 1967); Dietrich Orlow, *The History of the Nazi Party: 1919–1933* (Pittsburgh: University of Pittsburgh Press, 1969); and Hans Gerth, "The Nazi Party: Its Leadership and Composition," *American Journal of Sociology* 45 (January 1940): 517–41.

14 This view is mainly represented by Norman Cohn, *The Pursuit of the Millennium: Revolutionary Millenarians and Mystical Anarchists of the Middle Ages* (London: Pimlico, 1993). Cohn concluded that totalitarian ideologies of the twentieth century, such as fascism and communism, were millennial movements of the poor, the deprived, and the déclassé.

15 Barbu, "Psycho-Historical and Sociological Perspectives," 393.

16 George Th. Mavrogordatos, *Stillborn Republic: Social Coalitions and Party Strategies in Greece, 1922–1936* (Berkeley: University of California Press, 1983).

17 Cf. Irina Livezeanu, *Cultural Politics in Greater Romania. Regionalism, Nation Building and Ethnic Struggle, 1918–1930* (Ithaca: Cornell University Press, 1995). Livezeanu focuses on the genesis of the Legion in the 1920s, placing it in the context of the nation-building process within Greater Romania and linking it with inter-ethnic and rural-urban social cleavages, most manifest in the educational system. This section builds on her perspective, and highlights the intrinsic relationship between the social position and charismatic ideological view of the main legionary ideologues.

18 See Robert Wohl, *The Generation of 1914* (Cambridge: Harvard University Press, 1979), 203. Wohl distinguishes between "the notion of generation as thirty-year intervals of genealogical time" and "historical generations" encompassing people united by common beliefs and historical destiny. Unfortunately, his analysis of discourses on the "new generation" in postwar Europe is missing a chapter on Romania.

19 Livezeanu, *Cultural Politics*.

20 On the concept of "nationalizing nationalsim," see Rogers W. Brubaker, *Nationalism reframed: nationhood and the national question in the New Europe* (Cambridge: Cambridge University Press, 1996) 4–5.

21 Livezeanu, *Cultural Politics*, 234, 300–301.

22 Ibid., chapter 6, esp. 235–43.

23 For a comprehensive analysis of citizenship legislation in the Old Kingdom, see Constantin Iordachi, "The Unyielding Boundaries of Citizenship: The Emancipation of 'Non-Citizens' in Romania, 1866–1918," *European Review of History* 8 (August 2001): 157–86.

24 Codreanu, *Pentru legionari*, 3rd. ed. (Bucharest, 1940), 1: 58.

25 Corneliu Zelea Codreanu, *Pământul Strămoşesc* (Iaşi) 2 (15 May 1928), 10: 4.

26 As Max Weber pointed out, the practice of lay/political patronizing of religious ceremonies such as baptisms and weddings originates directly from a charismatic type of authority. The practice has a long tradition in Romanian political life. It also held a central role in Legionary ritualism. According to the statutes of the Legion, each male member had an obligation to become, within a maximum of five months after his enrollment, the godfather of five young couples, and to subsequently attract them into the Legion. See "Organizarea Legiunii 'Arhanghelul Mihail'" *Pământul Strămoşesc* (Iaşi) I (15 September 1927), 4: 1.

27 For the main stages of the process of charismatization, see Guenther Roth, "Socio-Historical Model and Developmental Theory: Charismatic Community, Charisma of Reason, and the Counterculture," *American Sociological Review* 40 (April 1975): 148–57.

28 See Ion I. Moța (alias Zyrax), "Problema minoritară în România," *Axa* 2 (22 January 1933), 5: 2.

29 Franz Neumann, "Anxiety and Politics," in *The Democratic and the Authoritarian State: An Essay in Political and Legal Theory* (Glencoe, Ill.: Free Press 1957), 279.

30 Horia Sima, quoted in Crăcea, ed., *Dezvăluiri Legionare*, (Bucharest, 1955) 2: 209. Legionary anti-Semitism thus resembled the type of "demonologic anti-Semitism" analyzed by Norman Cohn in *Histoire d'un mythe: La "conspiration" juive et les Protocoles des Sages de Sion* (Paris: Gallimard, 1967).

31 As Norman Cohn pointed out in *The Pursuit of the Millennium*, proponents of millenarianism interpret biblical texts in a personal manner, by regarding religious salvation as collective, terrestrial, total, and miraculous, through the intervention of supernatural agents.

32 Ion I. Moța, "The Spasm and Its Conclusion," in *Almanahul Societății "Petru Maior"* (Cluj: Cartea Românească, 1929), 207.

33 See Ion Banea, *Capitanul* (Sibiu, n.d.).

34 Cf. *Pămîntul Strămoșesc*, 4 (10 March 1930), 1.

35 Horia Sima, quoted in Crăcea, *Dezvăluiri Legionare*, 2: 210.

36 Codreanu, *Cărtica șefului de cuib*, 42. On Tucker's criteria, see Robert C. Tucker, "The Theory of Charismatic Leadership," *Daedalus* 97 (1998): 731–56.

37 In 1916, when Romania entered the world war, the young Codreanu wanted to join the regiment of his father in the military campaign against Austria–Hungary and could barely be forced to return back home. In 1917, at the age of nineteen, he attempted to set up a clandestine organization for fighting an "imminent" Soviet invasion. See Codreanu, *Pentru legionari*.

38 Erik H. Erikson, *Young Man Luther: A Study in Psychoanalysis and History* (London: Faber, 1959).

39 Constantin Argetoianu, *Memorii* (Bucharest: Machiavelli, 1996), 6 [1919–1922]: 46.

40 Heinen, *Legiunea "Arhanghelului Mihail"*, 139.

41 "Minunea cerească întimplată zilele trecute în închisoarea Clujului. Cu cine e Isus!" *Pămîntul Strămoșesc*, 2 (1 February 1928), 3: 3–4.

42 Ion I. Moța, "... Isus apare în închisori!" *Pămîntul Strămoșesc* 2 (15 February 1928), 4: 8–9.

43 Lucretiu Pătrășcanu, *Sub trei dictaturi* (Bucharest: 1970), 56; see also Nichifor Crainic, "Vizită la Maglavit," *Sfarmă Piatră* 1 (1936): 8.

44 Codreanu, *Scrisori studențești din închisoare* (Iași, 1925), 7–8.

45 Weber, "Men of the Archangel," 110–113. He concluded that the Legion was a populist movement developed in areas where there was a political vacuum which could be exploited (118).

46 Heinen, *Legiunea "Arhanghelului Mihail,"* 470.

47 Nichifor Crainic, *Zile albe, zile negre* (Bucharest, 1994), 237.

48 Talavera's recollection of his childhood fascination with Codreanu is very striking, especially since it comes from a Hungarian Jew from Transylvania who suffered "every Nazi persecution, except death." In fact, other quotations reveal Talavera's open admiration of Codreanu. "More than half a century later, if one ignores the Legion's later actions, it is not easy to condemn the Legion's ideas. If only all Legionaries had been like Codreanu, Moța, or the Transylvanian Ion Banea!" See Nicholas M. Nagy-Talavera, *Nicolae Iorga. A Biography,* 2nd ed. (Iași, Portland, Oxford: The Center for Romanian Studies, 1998), 348.

49 Francisco Veiga, *La Mística del Ultranacionalismo: Historia de la Guardia de Hierron. Rumania, 1919–1941* (Bellaterra: Universitat Autònoma de Barcelona, 1989). Published in Romanian as *Istoria Grăzii de Fier, 1919–1941: Mistica ultranationalismului,* 2nd ed. (Bucharest, 1995), 231.

50 Ilie Imbrescu, *Biserica și mișcarea legionară* (Bucharest, 1939), 201.

51 Corneliu Zelea Codreanu, "Mișcarea legionară și Biserica" in Nicu Crăcea, *Dezvăluiri Legionare* (Bucharest, 1995), 2: 31.

52 Gheorghe Racoveanu, "Mișcarea legionară și Biserica", in Crăcea, *Dezvaluiri*, 57.

53 Orlow, *History of the Nazi Party*, 80.

54 "Legiunea Arhanghelul Mihail," *Pămîntul Strămoșesc* 1 (15 August 1927), 2: 3–4; and "Organizarea Legiunii Arhanghelul Mihail," *Pămîntul Strămoșesc* 1 (1 October 1927), 5: 3–4.

55 Codreanu, *Cărticica*, Part IX, Points 56–60.

56 Dragoș Zamfirescu, *Legiunea Arhangelului Mihail: De la mit la realitate* (Bucharest, 1997), 206.

57 Francisco Vega, *Istoria Gărzii de Fier*, 211–36.

58 Quoted in Kurt Treptow, "Populism in Twentieth-Century Romanian Politics," in J. Held, ed., *Populism in Eastern Europe* (Boulder, Col.: Westview Press, 1991), 208.

59 Hungarian National Archives, Foreign Ministry, Diplomatic Reports, Bucharest, File K63, (10 November 1940), 66–67

60 Heinen, *Legiunea "Arhanghelului Mihail"*, 416.

61 Ion Zelea Codreanu, *O mărturie* (Iași, 1941), 13, 15. The Ion Zelea Codreanu and the Sima factions are giving conflicting accounts of this event.

62 Horia Sima, *Doctrina legionară* (Bucharest, 1995).

63 Emil Cioran, "Profilul interior al Căpitanului," *Glasul strămoșesc* 3 (25 December 1940), 10.

64 Weber, "Charisma and Its Transformation," 1120.

CHAPTER 2

Mark Biondich

"WE WERE DEFENDING THE STATE":
Nationalism, Myth, and Memory in Twentieth-Century Croatia

Since the collapse of Communism in 1989, Central and Southeast Europeans have experienced a "revival of memory" and been involved in a painstaking revision of their national pasts.[1] This is both understandable and necessary, given the Communist domination of historical "truth" since the 1940s. New historical interpretations, often of a markedly nationalist hue, have formed a new orthodoxy. The transition from ideological, party-sponsored history to a more dispassionate and professional history has not been simple or uniformly successful in the region. The demystification of the past on a popular level has been even harder to achieve. What was once uncritically regarded as absolute truth in the Communist era has now often been replaced by new and equally uncritical nationalist absolutes. In some countries, the outcome of this transition still remains uncertain to this day. It has been most problematic in the countries of former Yugoslavia. Since nearly all the Yugoslav successor states were born in conflict, in wars of brutal dimensions, the utilization of memory and nationalist mythology for political objectives and mobilization has been of great importance. Politics, history, and collective memory have been intimately intertwined and seem hopelessly inseparable.

In the Croatian case, the politics of collective memory have arguably been more problematic than in any other former Yugoslav republic. After 1989 the leader of the non-Communist Croat opposition, the historian and former general in the Yugoslav National Army, Franjo Tuđman, led the drive for Croatian sovereignty and under his auspices the recasting of the Croatian past took place. Central to this reassessment was the Croat experience in the Second World War, for between 1941 and 1945 Croats had achieved "independent" statehood for the first time in modern history. The reassessment occurred, however, without a public discussion of many controversial issues, not least of all the wartime Croatian state's policy toward Serbs, Jews, and Roma. An honest and sincere discourse was immensely complicated by the reality of a brutal conflict waged in Croatia and neighboring Bosnia–Herzegovina between 1991 and 1995.

There is definitely a need in Croatia and Southeastern Europe to cut through popular myth, to separate fact from fiction, and to end the repeated utilization of history for political ends. In a recent interview the widely respected historian Mirjana Gross, bemoaning the use of the past for contemporary political purposes, legitimately asked, "When will our history finally pass away?"[2] In order to understand the function of postwar myth and memory in Croatia, one first must understand the nature and history of Croat nationalism through the Second World War. To that end the first part of this chapter analyzes the evolution of Croat nationalism, and in particular the nationalist ideology of the Croat political right, to the end of the Second World War. Among the themes addressed are defining nationality, identity, and the limits of Croat national space, and the interwar political right's cult of Croatian statehood and the integral role of history in its political program. The second part will chart the post-1945 evolution of a divided Croat memory and the myths surrounding Croatian history in the modern period.

The History of Croat Nationalism to 1941

The most significant factor shaping modern Croat nationalist ideology has been the concept of historical rights, that is, the belief that the medieval Croatian kingdom had never completely lost its independence, despite the union first with Hungary (1102) and then with the Habsburgs (1527). Like their counterparts in Hungary, the Croatian nobility (the "political nation") defended their social privileges, identity, and political rights by associating them with the institutions of the Kingdom of Croatia–Slavonia. Whether we are dealing with nationalists of a South Slavic (e.g., Ljudevit Gaj, Josip Juraj Strossmayer, Franjo Rački) or purely Croat (e.g., Ante Starčević) orientation, all operated within a framework of historic state rights. The second factor shaping Croat identity and nationalism was the identification with other (Southern) Slavs, which was, as in the case of Czechs and Slovaks, essentially a reflection of Croat numerical inferiority in relation to the Habsburg monarchy's dominant nations, the Magyars and the Germans. It also stemmed from the fact that there was a numerically significant Serb minority in Croatia.

Both factors, the state-oriented, historically rooted perception of nationalism and the emphasis on Slavic solidarity, were evident in the first stage of modern Croat nationalism, Ljudevit Gaj's Illyrian movement of 1836–48.[3] The Illyrian movement gave way to two competing national programs in Croatia after the 1848 revolutions. The first was associated with Ante Starčević and the other with Josip Juraj Strossmayer. Basing their program on historic state rights, Starčević and his Party of (Croatian State) Right claimed that the Croatian kingdom had throughout its long existence been *de jure* an independent entity.[4] In practice, its independence had been undermined by the despotic Habsburg dynasty, which had repeatedly violated its "contract" with the Croat political nation, and more recently by the Magyar ruling oligarchy. Under these circumstances, they opposed collaboration with either Vienna or Budapest and refused to become involved in constructive political action. Starčević believed that his role and that of his followers in the Croatian *Sabor* (Diet) was simply to draw attention to and rail against "foreign" hegemony and its native "collaborators." Thus the seeds of a purely Great Croatian national orientation were planted. Starčević defined historic Great Croatia as present-day Croatia, Bosnia–Herzegovina, and Slovenia, and adopted a political concept of nationality, inherited from the old notion of a noble "political nation," thus defining Croats as all people residing in Great Croatia, be they Catholic, Muslim, or Orthodox Christian. His party refused to recognize the existence of "political" Serbs in those lands regarded as historically Croatian, for there could only be one nation on the territory of the Croatian state. Thus the Serbs and Bosnian Muslims of the Habsburg lands remained, in the minds of the Party of Right, Orthodox and Muslim "Croats," respectively.

Starčević's political program reflected a sense of weakness then prevalent in Croat intellectual circles *vis-à-vis* the dominant "historic" German and Magyar nations. But it also revealed the powerful hold of historical state rights on the thinking of Croatia's nineteenth-century intellectuals. It is worth noting that even Josip Juraj Strossmayer's National Party, which supported a policy of cultural Yugoslavism and recognized the "genetic" distinctiveness of Serbs in Croatia, refused to recognize Serbs as a "political nation" in Croatia.[5] To do so would have meant opening the door to separate Serb rights in, or even demands for territorial autonomy within, Croatia. The thinking of the Croat political elite, whether of the Starčevićist or Strossmayerist school, thus fit the Central European pattern of conceptualizing the region as being inhabited by "historic" and "non-historic" nations, with the Croats falling into the former category.

By the turn of the twentieth century, the proponents of the Croat national movement increasingly believed that the Croat nationality and Croatian political rights were threatened, either by their traditional foes within the Habsburg monarchy (i.e., Habsburg absolutism, the Magyar ruling oligarchy) or by nascent Serb nationalist ideology, which claimed that all the speakers of the

Štokavian form of language, be they Orthodox, Catholic, or Muslim, were Serbs. Most Croat nationalists continued to claim that Croats alone possessed a historic right to statehood, but in fact they were themselves painfully incapable of altering Croatia's subordinate status within the Habsburg monarchy. Because of these political frustrations, some Croat intellectuals turned in the immediate antebellum period (1905–1914) to unitarist Yugoslavism,[6] while the nationalism of one segment of the Starčevićist current acquired increasingly powerful defensive–hegemonic tendencies. Though Starčević's movement splintered after 1895 into a number of factions,[7] all remained committed to the idea of one Croat nation in Great Croatia and the negation of Serbs and others as distinct peoples. However, by 1918 some of his followers supported the creation of Yugoslavia. After 1918 only the Frankists, now known formally as the Croat Party of Right, remained ostensibly committed to Starčević's original program. In the 1930s they would form the nucleus of Ante Pavelić's Ustaša movement.

The formation in December 1918 of the Kingdom of Serbs, Croats, and Slovenes ("Yugoslavia") represented a challenge to the very *raison d'être* of the Frankists, who now regarded themselves as the only "true" Croat party and defender of Croat rights.[8] The prevailing theory of Yugoslavist trinomialism, and its concomitant *narodno jedinstvo* (national oneness), asserted that Serbs, Croats, and Slovenes, were "tribes" of one and the same "nation." In the 1920s all nationalities and political parties were forced once again to revisit, albeit in a new political setting, the problem of identity. Were all South Slavs really one people, as the proponents of Yugoslavist unitarism argued? Would they, over time, assimilate to a new hybrid Yugoslav "nationality"? Or had they always been, and would they remain, distinct nationalities?

In 1918 the ideology of Yugoslavism was an abstraction, alien to the peasant masses of all nationalities and nurtured only by a segment of the intelligentsia. In Croatia, opposition to the new state did not translate immediately into dislike or hatred of Serbs, however. In 1918 the Croat masses generally knew little of Serbs, except in those areas where they lived intermingled. They were simply preoccupied with their own difficult postwar lives. The political situation in Croatia, and with it Croat-Serb relations, began to deteriorate when Svetozar Pribićević, the leader of Croatia's Serbs and a prominent Yugoslav unitarist, implemented a rigid centralism and, in his capacity as minister of internal affairs, began enforcing it through a variety of strong-arm tactics. These heavy-handed policies—pejoratively termed *politika batine* ("the policy of the cudgel") in Croatia—gradually fomented resentment of Serbs generally, who were collectively identified with the oppressive new Yugoslav state and the political parties that supported centralism, just as many Serbs began to nurture a distrust of Croats for suppos-

edly undermining the unity of the new state, viewed by Serbs as the culmi-
nation of the nineteenth-century struggle for Serb unification.

In the post-1918 circumstances, Croat nationalism generally took two
forms: on the one hand, that of the mainstream Croat Peasant Party (HSS,
Hrvatska seljačka stranka) of Stjepan Radić,[9] and, on the other, the nation-
alism of everyone to the right, which meant the Croat Party of Right and the
Catholic clericalist Croat People's Party. The political divide between the
HSS and the Croat nationalist right only widened in the interwar era. The
Croat political right believed that it was engaged in a struggle against a Great
Serbian policy "which with unbending consistency is working to destroy
Croatdom."[10] It believed Belgrade's intention was "to conquer and absorb
the other South Slavic nations and to establish its own greatness and power
on the ruins of neighboring countries."[11] Radić's role in mobilizing peasants
to the Croat national cause was hailed, but his political capabilities and
pacifist policy were summarily dismissed as ineffectual and utopian. The
Frankists saw their program and theirs alone as being sufficiently rooted in
an affirmation of Croatian historic right. They stood for the historic Croat
nation, a nation "with remembrance and strong memory," and, to use Milan
Šufflay's expression, "with strong egoism." For Šufflay, who emerged in the
1920s as an intellectual luminary of the Croat right, the new Yugoslav state
was a modern Serbian empire that aspired to "the balkanization of the Croat
nation."[12] (See Document 1.) For the Croat political right, Croatia had in
1918 become "an occupied land,"[13] and it now believed that a new movement was needed to serve as "the bearer of an uncompromising and revolutionary struggle [against Belgrade]."[14]

Such a struggle seemed unlikely in the 1920s, when the politically dominant HSS, whose strength lay in Croatia's socially dominant countryside,
repeatedly marginalized its Croat opponents. The Croat Party of Right's
followers were drawn almost entirely from the Croat petite bourgeoisie of
Zagreb and the provincial towns. In the November 1920 elections to the
Constituent Assembly, the Croat Party of Right won only 10,880 votes
(2 percent of the vote), almost one-third of which came from the city of
Zagreb, and 2 of 93 seats in prewar Croatia–Slavonia. And it proved to be
the party's best performance. In the September 1927 elections, the last
before the royal dictatorship of 1929 and arguably the last truly democratic
elections of the interwar period, the Croat Party of Right won only one
seat.[15] The party's leadership, comprised of a small group of lawyers and
intellectuals, was itself drawn for the most part from the same social milieu.
In Zagreb the Croat petite bourgeoisie, long obsessed with the defense of its
endangered socioeconomic and national *pravice* ("rights"), was centered,
ironically enough, in a district whose name was their synonym for Serbs,
Vlaška ulica. This obsession with "rights" kept the petite bourgeoisie firmly

in the ranks of the Croat Party of Right, which had since Starčević's day stood for principled and stubborn opposition to foreign rule and native "collaborators."[16] Those in power were always "traitors," be it in the days of the corrupt Károly Khuen-Héderváry (governor of Croatia, 1883–1903) or under Svetozar Pribićević, the Croatian–Serb leader of the Independent Radicals, who was minister of education in the Pašić government in Belgrade until 1925. He was popularly viewed in Croatia as a latter-day Khuen. Here, too, lay the origins of the Croat petit bourgeois's animosity toward the Serb, whom he always referred to as the "Vlach." In the days of the Habsburg "Military Frontier," which was incorporated into Croatia in 1881, the Orthodox "Vlach" was a synonym for the soldier and frontiersman; he was a lackey, an instrument of Habsburg tyranny, without any "rights."[17] He was, in short, a threat to the "rights" of the free man, which is how the Croat petit bourgeois saw himself. When these "Vlachs" began acquiring a Serb consciousness in the second half of the nineteenth century, and were later used by Khuen to serve Hungarian interests in Croatia, this animosity toward the Vlach-Serb intensified immensely. It matured under Pribićević in the 1920s, when the "treasonable" Vlach seemingly became an agent of Great Serbian rule.[18] And thus the act of Yugoslav unification of December 1918, to borrow Josip Horvat's apt description, "demolished the psychological balance of the Croat petit bourgeois." His "rights" had been violated yet again, this time by another "foreigner" who seemed far worse than his predecessor. The Magyar had at least permitted the ancient *Sabor* in Zagreb and an autonomous status to Croatia, but the Serb tolerated neither. In 1868 Ferenc Deák and the Magyar ruling oligarchy had recognized the Croats as a political nation and granted them autonomy. In 1918 Nikola Pašić of the National Radical Party and Ljubomir Davidović of the Democratic Party recognized Croats only as a liberated "tribe" of either the Serb or Yugoslav nationality, respectively.

In 1918 a number of the Croat Party of Right's most prominent leaders emigrated to Budapest and Vienna, where in 1919 they formed the Croat Comité to fight for Croatian independence. Marginalized in the 1920s, as Stjepan Radić's peasant movement became a mass national party, the Comité's expectations were seemingly dashed. However, Radić's assassination in 1928 revived their hopes and ultimately set the stage for "Ustašism." In January 1929, when King Aleksandar Karadjordjević established a royal dictatorship in Yugoslavia, the moribund Comité was led by Vladimir Sachs and Manko Gagliardi, neither of whom could be expected to lead the Croat struggle against Belgrade, as the former was an assimilated Croatian Jew and the latter a son of Italian immigrants. They turned instead to the Zagreb lawyer Ante Pavelić, the leader of the Croat Party of Right and, after 1930, "Poglavnik" (leader) of the Ustaša movement.[19]

The defining characteristics of the Ustaša movement were anti-Serbianism, anti-Communism, and its cult of Croatian statehood. Croatian independence was the goal and was to be achieved at any cost. But how was the problem of identity treated and what was to become of the non-Croats of Great Croatia? Croat nationalism in the late nineteenth century, in both its Starčevićist and Strossmayerist forms, had been an ideology of inclusion. After 1918 it became, at least in the form nurtured by the Croat Party of Right, a far more exclud-ing and intolerant ideology. In the interwar period the Croat political right continued to deny the existence of Serb and Bosnian Muslim nationalities in Great Croatia, although its attitude toward the latter remained relatively benign. The denial of Serb existence was normally expressed in one of two ways. On the one hand, some Croat intellectuals claimed that the Orthodox of Great Croatia were in actual fact "Croats" who had adopted a Serb con-sciousness in the nineteenth century because of the assimilationist work of the Serbian Orthodox Church.[20] The theory of Serbs as Orthodox "Croats" had one of two origins. For some Croat intellectuals, it represented continu-ity with Starčević's theory of Croat political nationality. Others believed that the Orthodox of Great Croatia were descended from the native, pre-Ottoman Catholic (and thus supposedly Croat) population, which had con-verted under Ottoman rule to Orthodoxy.[21] On the other hand, some Croat intellectuals saw the Serbs as foreign to Great Croatia. Even in this case, however, they were often not regarded as Serbs *per se* but of Vlach origin. Serb identity was viewed as being derived through the agency of the Serbian Orthodox Church, but Serbs were also seen as different by blood, a foreign element distinct from the autochthonous "Croat" (i.e., Catholic-Muslim) population. A racial or racist subtext is discernible but more often than not implied rather than explicit; the Ustaše never formulated a coherently racist ideology.[22]

Having denied the existence or distinct identity of Serbs in historic Great Croatia, the political right naturally denied their entitlement to any special political status. If there were no "real" Serbs in Great Croatia, then they could claim neither a legitimate historical nor natural right to these lands, nor a special status to the detriment of the Croat population.[23] They were "guests" and "colonists"[24] in a foreign land, and had to submit to the historically dominant Croat nation. Those persons in Great Croatia who chose to call themselves Serbs were in actual fact making a hostile, anti-Croat political declaration. They were, quite simply, "a tumor in a foreign body."[25]

It is hardly surprising that the Croat political right condemned the August 1939 "Agreement" (*Sporazum*) negotiated by the HSS leader Vladko Maček and Yugoslav premier Dragiša Cvetković, which created an autonomous Croatian province (*banovina*) within Yugoslavia. The borders of the autonomous Croatian *banovina* did not include all the territories deemed to be historically Croatian, and in the opinion of the political right left hundreds of thousands of "Croats" outside Croatia.[26] Moreover, autonomous Croatia had only a limited internal administrative autonomy, which was far less than what Croatia had possessed before 1918. As such, Maček's policy was not "an interpretation of the will of the Croat nation, but an attempt to save Yugoslavia at any cost."[27] In the mind of the political right, the *Sporazum* was simply "too far from the realization of the demands of the Croat people."[28]

At that point the two currents of interwar Croat nationalism, represented by the HSS and the political right, parted company for good. The HSS, which had dominated Croatian politics since 1918, now reluctantly committed itself to the preservation of Yugoslavia at a time of growing international crisis. The Croat political right, although ideologically still quite diverse, was slowly coalescing around Pavelić's Ustaša movement, and committed itself to independence by exploiting the international crisis. While the HSS often alternated between recognizing Yugoslavia and seeking Croatian independence, and had in the meantime recognized the existence of a Serb people in Croatia and Bosnia–Herzegovina, the Croat political right was by 1939 unyielding on these questions. It wanted nothing short of independence, and the tradition of historic state right and its ongoing fear of assimilation powerfully influenced its treatment of identity. In the interwar era Belgrade had replaced Vienna and Budapest as the main perceived threat to Croatdom. The Starčevićist legacy was important in helping the political right conceptualize the nature of the post-1918 struggle against Belgrade, by imparting to it a sense of historical hubris. In the political conditions of interwar Yugoslavia and Europe, hubris turned to malice as the political right (and later the Ustaše) distorted Starčević's integrative or inclusive ideology, which had never questioned the place of Orthodox or Muslim within the ranks of the Croat nation even as it denied their distinct identity. Ustaša ideology vacillated between exclusionist and assimilationist tendencies. In actual fact, the former tendency was the stronger of the two as Croat nationalist ideology in general became more exclusive after 1918. During the Second World War, the Serbs of Great Croatia were for the most part seen as an alien element, a view that manifested itself in the murderous practices of the Ustaša regime.

The Second World War: The Croatian State, 1941–1945

In April 1941 Croats finally achieved statehood in the form of the Independent State of Croatia (hereafter NDH, *Nezavisna Država Hrvatska*), in reality an Italo-German condominium and brutal *ad hoc* creation. The Ustaša regime lacked enough popular support to have seized power on its own, although one segment of the HSS's right wing now sided with Pavelić because it was elated at the creation of a Croatian state. After so many years of foreign rule the desire for independence was undoubtedly overwhelming, both psychologically and politically. In the heady days of April 1941 many Croats, even those who had little or no sympathy for the Ustaše, must have seen Pavelić as "the hero of the day, the new and only program ... [and] the avenger of a martyred past." To his loyal followers Pavelić was in 1941 "practically a mythical being, a little 'demi-god,' the greatest Croat of all time."[29] In the event, for the Ustaša movement an opportunity was presented at long last to settle a range of scores under the not-so-benevolent tutelage of the Axis. It enthusiastically exploited the advantage afforded by German conquest to launch a brutal campaign to rid the NDH of all "undesirable" elements, the most prominent of whom were the Serbs, all in an attempt to safeguard Croatia's recently obtained "independence."[30] The Ustaše had sworn themselves to independence at all cost, and now they were determined to preserve it by all available methods. In the process, the Ustaše left a painful legacy for the peoples of Croatia and Bosnia–Herzegovina.

The "Serb Question" was certainly not the only important question of the day, but the Ustaše were determined to force its resolution. Indeed, from its inception in 1930, anti-Serbianism had been "the quintessence of the Ustaša doctrine, its *raison d'être*."[31] How did the Ustaše intend to solve the "Serb Question"? In the interwar era, the Croat political right had vacillated between exclusionist and assimilationist tendencies. During the war, both tendencies were at work in Ustaša rhetoric and policy toward the Serbs, which evolved through three phases. The first phase, from April to August 1941, may be termed the most radical, during which Ustaša leaders heralded in rhetoric and deed a newly cleansed Great Croatian state. Anti-Serb measures in this period largely took the form of legislation and the arrest of the Serb intelligentsia. On 4 June 1941, the Croatian and German governments agreed to a massive population exchange, involving Slovenes and Serbs.[32] Two days later, Pavelić met with Adolf Hitler at Salzburg, where discussion invariably turned to the nationality composition of the new Croatian state. Hitler pointedly remarked that, "if the Croatian State was to be really stable, a nationally intolerant policy had to be pursued for fifty years."[33] Pavelić must have concluded that the German authorities would not interfere, as far as the Serb question was concerned, in Croatian affairs. At that point, the Ustaša authorities turned to a more systematic "cleansing" of the predominantly Serb-populated regions of the NDH. At the same time, the first large-scale Ustaša massacres of Serbs were committed; from late July 1941, Ustaša massacres became widespread. The thrust of Ustaša policy toward Serbs in the spring and summer of 1941 was deportation and mass murder. When the deportations were halted indefinitely in September 1941, the German military command in Belgrade estimated that at least 118,110 Serbs had been deported to Serbia from the NDH.[34] In this same period, policy toward Serbs was matched by an equally exclusionist official rhetoric which characterized Serbs as Croat enemies, as a predatory and alien element in Great Croatia that aspired to the destruction of all Croats.[35]

In September 1941 a range of new problems confronted the Ustaša regime and called into question its Serb policy. Faced with armed Communist insurrection, the Italian decision to occupy large parts of the NDH, ostensibly to suppress the insurrection, where Croatian authority was then neutralized, and, finally, with the German decision to halt deportations to Serbia and pressure to moderate their Serb policy, Pavelić and the Ustaša leadership were forced to back away from their earlier exclusionist rhetoric and policy toward the Serbs. This they never did entirely, but a tactical shift was nonetheless informally announced in September 1941 in rhetoric and deed. At that point the Ustaša authorities turned to a policy of forced conversion to Catholicism.[36] Both the rhetoric and extant archival material indicate that a large-scale, centrally driven policy of forced conversion was initiated only in the fall of 1941.[37] Ustaša rhetoric also changed abruptly. The Serbs were now described as former Catholics who, under Ottoman Turkish rule, had supposedly converted to Orthodoxy. In the minds of some, though not necessarily all or most Ustaša leaders, catholicizing the Orthodox meant assimilating or croatizing them. Although the policy of forced conversion had its origins in the assimilationist tendency found in the prewar thinking of the Croat political right, the decision to implement it was largely functional, a response to the dire circumstances confronting the Ustaša authorities.

By February 1942, however, the Ustaše were forced to abandon the policy of forced conversion. Although it had been pursued zealously in some quarters, ultimately the Ustaše themselves undermined the policy. Since regional variations were highly pronounced, the policy of forced conversion could not serve as an adequate solution to the "Serb Question," and thus failed. Failure stemmed from many sources. In large parts of the NDH the Italian military had effectively neutralized the local Ustaša civilian and military authorities. Armed insurrection against the Ustaša authorities was yet another important factor, for by late 1941 the Croatian authorities controlled probably not more than one-third of the NDH's territory. But perhaps most important, from the perspective of Ustaša national ideology and policy, was continued persecution of Serbs by the Ustaša authorities, sometimes after conversion had occurred.

By early 1942 it seemed clear to the Ustaša authorities that their Serb policy had "arrived at a blind alley."[38] The authorities needed to deal urgently with the Communist insurrection, which in its early phase relied heavily on recruits from the persecuted Serb population, and desperately sought to establish some kind of legitimacy. To that end, in February 1942 Pavelić convoked a gerrymandered parliament. When he addressed that body on 28 February, Pavelić acknowledged the existence of Orthodoxy in Croatia. There was now evidently room for Orthodoxy, but not for the Serbian Orthodox Church. His speech has been interpreted as the Ustaša regime's first step toward creating the Croatian Orthodox Church, as a means of "pacifying" the remaining Serb population.[39] In early April 1942 Pavelić ordered the creation of the Croatian Orthodox Church.

With the formation of the Croatian Orthodox Church, Ustaša policy toward the Serbs entered its third and final phase. From April 1942 to the end of the war, Orthodoxy was recognized as a state religion, along with Roman Catholicism, Lutheranism, and Islam, and the Orthodox were regarded as "Croats."[40] If the Orthodox had become Serbs through propaganda, then it was simply a matter of time and proper nurturing, according to Ustaša rhetoric, before they acquired a Croat consciousness.[41] Viewed in this context, the Croatian Orthodox Church was supposed to serve as an instrument of assimilation. And, by extension, official Ustaša policy toward the Serbs was assimilationist, although in a very perverse way.

That is not meant to suggest, however, that Ustaša leaders necessarily regarded most of the Orthodox to have been Croat in the distant past, or believed they could become Croat in the future. A careful reading of Ustaša rhetoric prompts suspicion of their official policy. Even after April 1942, there are numerous references in Ustaša rhetoric to the Croat nation, comprised only of Catholics and Muslims, which would tend to support the view that the Ustaše never really accepted their rhetoric or official policy with due conviction.[42] Perhaps even more important, Ustaša leaders continued to make implicit reference to the Orthodox as hostile outsiders. For example, Matija Kovačić, who in 1942–43 served as the "main director of propaganda" of the Ustaša regime, repeatedly differentiated in his speeches between "Croat Catholics and Muslims," on the one hand, and "the Orthodox," on the other.[43] Other prominent Ustaša officials echoed this sentiment.[44] A rhetorical distinction was repeatedly made between the indigenous Catholic-Muslim population ("Croat nation") and the Orthodox "other." These contradictory rhetorical premises (the Orthodox both as "Croats" and as "outsiders") were never completely resolved. In actual fact, however, the preferred solution to "the Orthodox question" was through exclusion rather than assimilation. Nevertheless, the official Ustaša line, that the Orthodox were largely of Croat nationality and that the Croatian Orthodox Church would assist in the task of returning the Orthodox to their true identity, remained unchanged to the end of the war.[45]

It seems evident that after February 1942 there was a willingness on the part of the Croatian authorities to adopt a more tolerant policy toward the Serb population, if only for political and military reasons. In fact, as the tide of war turned against the Axis, the Ustaše gradually trimmed their earlier radicalism and tried to recast their movement as the program of Croatian statehood, which all Croats should support. (See Document 2.) Were the NDH to disappear, the Croat nation, too, might meet its demise. However, with respect to the "Serb Question," the Ustaša authorities still had to contend with their own deeply instilled prejudices and the fact that much of the Serb population had taken up arms and was supporting the Communist resistance or Chetnik movement. The only appreciable change in Ustaša policy in 1942, apart from the creation of the Croatian Orthodox Church, was its willingness to collaborate with some Chetnik leaders in Bosnia in the name of "pacification."[46] On the ground, however, Ustaša forces continued to operate a blanket policy toward Serbs, whom they suspected, whether Orthodox or Catholic converts, of hostility toward the NDH. For example, in early July 1942 the prefect of Gora county (Petrinja), reporting on local anti-partisan operations, confirmed that one of the objectives of "the last cleansing operation," as he called it, had in fact been "evacuating the entire Orthodox population and even converts [to Catholicism] from the above-mentioned endangered regions."[47] The Serbs of Bosanska Dubica suffered the same fate: virtually all of them were deported in late May 1942 to the Jasenovac camp system. The town's Muslim mayor, himself an Ustaša official, opposed the deportations; he had been appalled by the fact that these Serbs had committed no anti-Croatian acts, "nor did they participate in any kind of anti-state or anti-national work."[48] In May 1943 the Croatian government's liaison with the Italian military command in the NDH, David Sinčić, urged the central Croatian authorities to adopt a more tolerant attitude toward the Orthodox, now that the Italians were withdrawing from the country. He implored the Ministry of Internal Affairs to realize that it was necessary "precisely at this moment to treat the Orthodox population ... lawfully and tactfully."[49] That he made this urgent suggestion at all indicates that, as late as May 1943, Ustaša policy toward the Serbs was anything but lawful or tactful. As later reports testify, the language of the Ustaša party-military bureaucracy betrayed a deep distrust of the Orthodox population to the bitter end. Indeed, in late 1943 the Ustaša propaganda official Vilko Rieger allegedly remarked to the exiled Ustaša police chief Dido Kvaternik that the Serbs "are the main problem," and that they "should be surrounded and all slaughtered."[50]

In the end, wartime Ustaša rhetoric and policy toward the Serbs proved complex and contradictory in nature, as they vacillated between annihilationist and assimilationist impulses. The contradictory rhetoric (and action), which certainly predated the war, was never resolved in a coherent manner.

In practice, however, the exclusionist tendency was the stronger of the two. What can be said with some deal of certainty is that the premises underlying the integral nationalist Ustaša ideology were historicist. Indeed, history was their hubris. The Ustaše were committed to Croat state rights and their concomitant, one Croat political nation in historic Great Croatia. Their refusal to tolerate the existence of "political" Serbs in Great Croatia was amply borne out by wartime practice. But whatever the complexities of Ustaša nationalist ideology, their wartime rule left brutal scars on the peoples of Bosnia–Herzegovina and Croatia and helped poison mutual relations between the country's nationalities. Of the approximately one million dead in all of Yugoslavia, roughly 60 percent died on the territory of the NDH. And of the total number killed in the NDH, it is now believed that approximately 100,000 (or 17 percent), three-quarters of whom were Serbs, Jews, and Roma, died in the Jasenovac camp system alone.[51]

The Postwar Era: Divided Memory, 1945–1990

In the aftermath of the Second World War, one can certainly speak of a divided Croat memory. In Communist Yugoslavia the new authorities faced the task of governing a multinational society torn by complex divisions that had been exacerbated by horrifying wartime atrocities. Tito's regime had its own version of the war in which all peoples of Yugoslavia, including Croats, participated in the heroic struggle against fascism. In Croatia, as elsewhere, only a small criminal minority had opted for collaboration. This official version of the war was reinforced by state authority, which suppressed competing memories just as it suppressed manifestations of Croat, Serb, and other nationalisms. Outside the country, the Croat political emigration cultivated a very different memory of the war. In Croat émigré circles of the Cold War era, the prewar Croat political right's ideology seemed validated because of its radical opposition to communism. Over time, this memory became intertwined with a number of wartime myths that served to explain the "Croatian" defeat and the victory of the supposedly Great Serbian Communist movement.[52] This divided postwar Croat memory was built on ideological extremes, between which no dialogue was possible and in which a democratic discourse was naturally absent and impossible.

One of the fundamental postwar myths of the Croat political emigration involved the very nature of the conflict that had been fought in the former Yugoslavia during the Second World War. The political emigration claimed that ideological considerations were ultimately of secondary importance. This had been a war waged by Great Serbian ideology, whether in its Communist or royalist form, against the Croat nation and its newly independent state. Although some postwar Croat émigré writers readily acknowledged that many regrettable "excesses" had been committed against the Serb population, they insisted that the scale of these excesses had been grossly exaggerated. More importantly, since the war had been fought on historic Croatian territory, every act, however seemingly brutal, undertaken by the Ustaša government represented "a legitimate self-defense against the [Serb] enemy," who aspired to "the annihilation of the Croat nation and Croatian homeland."[53] Or, to quote the Ustaša émigré Vjekoslav Vrančić, "We were defending the State."[54] Since it was a state that allegedly represented the legitimate realization of Croat national aspirations, the wartime authorities had a right to defend this state, which was under assault, using all means at their disposal.[55]

If the behavior of the Croatian authorities could thus be ascribed to defensive motives, then the wartime orgy of horrors that was the NDH really had little to do with Ustaša intent. This was a conflict that had been forced on the Croatian state by a resolute and implacable foe. The Ustaša movement had simply fought for national self-determination using all methods available to it at the time.[56] Croat self-determination had been achieved, but Serbs, regardless of their political affiliation, rose against the Croatian state. They wanted the NDH destroyed and "aimed at the biological extermination of the Croats."[57] The wartime Serb resistance, be it Chetnik or partisan, was anti-Croatian and would have revolted against the NDH regardless of Zagreb's policy toward the Serbs. In this context, the "excesses" of the Croatian regime were in retaliation for Serb killings of Croats. Although massacres of Serbs occurred, Serbs always gave as good as they got.[58]

The inability to take responsibility for wartime crimes extended to many fronts. The Croatian role in the Holocaust was minimized and a myth was nurtured that anti-Semitic legislation and other measures had originated with, and were enforced solely by, the Germans, while the Croat side had implemented these measures reluctantly and had done what it could to assist Jews.[59] Ivo Rojnica, who in 1941 had served as Ustaša party boss in Dubrovnik, would later baldly claim, and he was hardly alone, that "Croats are not guilty for the fate of the Jews," whose fate the Nazis ultimately did dictate. In his opinion, and that of much of the Croat political emigration, no "Jewish Question" had existed in Croatia before 1941.[60]

Because of the cultivation and acceptance of these myths by a large segment of the postwar Croat political emigration, there was no apparent need to confront some central moral issues stemming from the wartime experience. Even members of the democratic emigration, who were linked to the HSS and had distanced themselves from the Ustaša emigration, failed explicitly to condemn the wartime practices of the regime, although they readily condemned its leadership. The case of Branko Pešelj, a prewar HSS activist who had been jailed by the Ustaše in 1941 and later immigrated to the United States, is indicative. Neither he nor any other member of the HSS emigration condemned Ustaša atrocities against Serbs, as much as they had clearly seen such a policy as morally repugnant. In part that was because, as Pešelj observed, it seemed best "to forget the sad events of that time." Resurrecting the crimes of the Second World War served no positive purpose. More importantly, he relativized those atrocities. He claimed that he would denounce Ustaša massacres of innocent Serbs only when the democratic Serb emigration denounced Chetnik massacres of innocent Croat civilians. The Ustaše had murdered Serbs, Jews, and Roma, but also Croats who opposed their rule. And thus, although Ustaša crimes could in no way be minimized, the Croats' right to a state and their own wartime suffering could not be minimized, either.[61]

In the Croat memory of war, Bleiburg was synonymous with Croat suffering and held a far more prominent place than did Jasenovac. While themselves dismissing as exaggerated the postwar official estimates of wartime Serb losses, as deliberately designed, at least in part, to smear the Croat name, Croat émigrés perpetrated their own myth—the Bleiburg myth—according to which hundreds of thousands of Croats, most of them innocent civilians, were murdered by Tito's forces in May 1945.[62] That the massacre occurred and that tens of thousands of lives were lost is beyond dispute, but the number of victims was grossly exaggerated and the meaning of the tragedy mythologized. For the Croat emigration, Bleiburg was the Croat Jasenovac. And while Jasenovac had only existed for four years, Bleiburg was but a gateway to a Great Serbian and Communist gulag called Yugoslavia.

It is hardly surprising that, among politically active Croats outside Yugoslavia after 1945, the Second World War would be commemorated through Bleiburg and not Jasenovac. The dead who were remembered were Croat dead, and it was the loss of Croatian statehood that was mourned. The Croat political emigration commemorated 10 April as "Croatian Independence Day," venerating in this way the day of the NDH's proclamation in 1941 and hence the memory of statehood. Insofar as Croat responsibility for any crimes was acknowledged, it was in the context of political errors committed by a criminal element within the regime or relative to crimes perpetrated by the Serb royalist Chetniks or Tito's Communist partisans, both of which were seen as ideological variations on a Great Serbian theme.[63] Moral culpability was thus avoided and Croat nationalism in its radical manifestation was vindicated and assessed to be healthy.

Accordingly, Ustašism came to be viewed in postwar émigré-nationalist mythology as the apotheosis of Croat nationalism. It had been a movement for statehood at any price; its basic postulate had been "the idea of the state and the struggle to the end for the state."[64] And in this respect, the political emigration would contend, since the vast majority of Croats wanted their own state, *ipso facto*, the overwhelming majority of Croats had adopted Ustašism. Whatever its wartime political shortcomings, or the failings of its individual leaders, Ustašism was recast as anything but a party-political idea. By stripping Ustašism of ideological accoutrements, it could be presented not as a fascist movement but simply as the ideology of Croatian statehood.[65] The NDH was the result, the Croat emigration claimed, "of a national revolution led by the Ustaša movement."[66] Croat collaboration with the Third Reich was purely functional, resulting from the failure of repeated Croat attempts, beginning with Radić in 1919, to win the support of the League of Nations, France, Britain, and the United States, for legitimate Croat national aspirations. That Croats had to turn to the Axis was the fault of the democratic Western states, which were unwilling to address the Croats' plight in Yugoslavia. Croats could not be blamed for the West's callous indifference.[67]

If the Ustaša movement were to be judged at all, it would have to be assessed in relation to its one true objective: statehood. Despite the NDH's disappearance, the movement had to be assessed positively in the larger framework of Croatian history since it had achieved statehood for the first time in modern history.[68] And the Ustaša "revolution" of 1941, which created that state, could not be interpreted simply through the prism of policy toward Serbs or Jews. The Croat nation was not the first nation to experience, after a prolonged struggle for its national freedom, "a revolutionary period." Just as the French Revolution could not be interpreted only through the Terror, the Croatian revolution of 1941 could hardly be interpreted only through its violent nature or any crimes that may have been perpetrated in its name.[69]

Over time, more sophisticated attempts were made to relativize the wartime experience. One prominent émigré historian, Jere Jareb, admitted that the Ustaša movement's policy toward the Serbs was both morally deplorable and politically incomprehensible. He also readily dismissed the notion, perpetuated by Ustaša propagandists since 1941, that Serbs had launched an insurrection and war of extermination in 1941 against Croats. But whatever the crimes and errors of the Ustaše, the fact was that they had for the first time in modern history spearheaded the creation of an independent state. This was an attempt to rehabilitate the NDH *without* Pavelić and the "totalitarian" Ustaša regime.[70] The state was an entity unto itself, desired by all Croats, and had to be divorced from the atrocities perpetrated by the Ustaše.[71] Or, as another writer put it more recently, it was necessary "to separate the fact that the Croats finally obtained [in 1941] their own state from the individuals who ... created out of this state a synonym for crime and suffering."[72] In the final analysis, neither the undemocratic nature of Pavelić's

regime nor the limited sovereignty of the NDH was denied. Nor was the
existence of concentration camps or race laws disputed. These facts were
acknowledged but often perfunctorily condemned. What mattered was the
reality of Croatia's independent existence, which was proof of the desire of
the Croat nation to live in its own state. And ultimately the wartime Croatian
state was held to be no worse than interwar Yugoslavia, which for the better
part of its existence had an expressly undemocratic government, enacted
anti-Jewish decrees, and established its own camps for political prisoners.
"In spite of all its difficult imperfections," one commentator alleged, "Croats
largely experienced the NDH as Croatian. Even when they were opponents
of the Ustaša regime, they knew that the NDH had no Croatian alternative."[73]
(See Document 3.)

And thus the Croat nationalist movement, stigmatized internationally
after the Second World War because of its association with the Third Reich,
continued to view the wartime experience as a legitimate political experiment and defense of Croat national rights. The fact that the wartime Croatian
regime lacked popular support and therefore political legitimacy was simply
denied. So, too, was the fact that a substantial number of Croats had participated in the Communist resistance. Well after 1945, the Croat nationalist
memory of the Second World War continued to be nurtured on the perception that Croats had since 1918 repeatedly been victimized by Serbs, whether
in royalist or Communist Yugoslavia. The brief and bloody wartime inter-
lude was seen as no exception. The myth of victimization prevented many
Croats in the democratic West from coming to terms with the Ustaša past
and the horrendous nature of their crimes.

Post-Communist Croatia: Myth and Memory

In 1990, at the First General Congress of the Croat Democratic Union (HDZ,
Hrvatska demokratska zajednica), the party's founder and president, Franjo
Tuđman, claimed that the NDH was not simply a quisling entity but "an
expression of the political desires of the Croat nation for its own independent state."[74] The comment was significant on many levels, coming as it did
not just from a historian and former participant in the wartime Communist
resistance, but from the future president of the Croatian state. In the event,
it represented the first step in Tuđman's effort to reconcile and synthesize
Croats' divided and competing memories, and culminated six years later in
his proposal to transform the Jasenovac memorial into a collective monument for all Croat victims of the war in addition to non-Croat victims of
the Ustaše. The proposal was inordinately insensitive, but it represented
Tuđman's attempt at a "historic reconciliation" between Croats in Ustaša

and partisan ranks. To that end, contemporary Croatia's wartime partisan resistance roots were emphasized and Tito's role still acclaimed, while at the same time the Ustaša state was gradually rehabilitated as the incarnation of the Croats' desire for statehood.

This "revival of memory" was publicly manifested through the renaming of academies, institutes, and boulevards. The most poignant moment in this revival came in September 1990, when Zagreb's city council, acting with the tacit approval of President Tuđman, renamed the city's "Square of the Victims of Fascism" as the "Square of Great Croats." The original name was restored in 1999. This was a moment of great symbolic importance. During the Second World War, the Square (then known as Square "N") had been home to the Zagreb offices of the Gestapo and the Ustaša security police. The Rubicon had been crossed. With this act numerous other name changes were initiated, monuments commemorating the Communist resistance were defaced, and a general remodeling of history took place. Shortly thereafter, one could begin publicly to hear in Croatia a number of absurd theories, such as that fascism had not existed at all in the NDH and that the victims of the Ustaša regime, whose criminal nature was now largely denied, deserved their fate because the Croatian state was simply defending itself. The Jasenovac camp virtually disappeared from Croatian school textbooks and was replaced by stories of Bleiburg and the Communist-organized death marches.[75] All this occurred either at the instigation of the authorities or with their toleration.

Why was this historical revisionism and revival of memory possible in the first place? After all, in 1990 the memory of the Second World War and the NDH was not particularly vivid in the minds of most Croats. People tend to nurture memories that possess some meaning in the present, but in socialist Croatia (1945–90) there was arguably no meaningful reason for most Croats to remember the NDH. Nor was it politically possible for them to remember it in the way the Croat emigration did. All that changed in 1990–91, however. As the political crisis in Yugoslavia deepened, contemporary events made possible a retelling of the history of the NDH in a new light. At that time the views of the political emigration were transplanted to Croatia and the events of 1990–91 were reinterpreted through the prism of Croatia's previous attempt at statehood, in 1941. In the interpretation of many Croat nationalists, the drive toward independence and the nascent conflict with Belgrade and the Croatian Serbs paralleled the events of 1941. The Croat public was told that in both these periods Croats only wanted an independent Croatian state but Serbs were opposed to this legitimate aspiration. At that particular point, the "revisionist" interpretation of the NDH became meaningful for many Croats in Croatia since it appeared to correspond to what they saw unfolding before their own eyes.

The revival of memory occurred in the context of Croatia's war of independence from 1991 to 1995. Unlike the Second World War, the "Homeland War" (*Domovinski rat*) was not an ideological affair but produced, or so it seemed at the time, a remarkable unity within national ranks against the perceived threat of Great Serbian expansionism. All Croats were now on the same side, regardless of the political histories of their fathers and grandfathers. However, the war only forestalled an honest discussion of the past and even made possible a reinterpretation of the NDH in a positive light. The popular sense of victimization at Serbia's hands in the 1990s played into the Croat nationalist right's long-nurtured belief of historical Croat victimization. As one journalist noted in May 1993, "For Croats the memory of Bleiburg is not only the memory of yesterday, but also the memory of today and tomorrow. The same mental framework which in 1945 killed [at Bleiburg] ... today kills in Vukovar, Zadar, Šibenik, Srebrenica, Žepa, Tuzla. ... The executioner, yesterday like today, is the Yugoslav Army. ... The state, for whose creation is necessary the blood of innocents, was yesterday called Yugoslavia, today Great Serbia."[76] The widely accepted belief in Croatia of the defensive nature of the Croat struggle against Belgrade left no room for an acknowledgement of the possible existence of Croat perpetrators of war crimes. Relatively few people in Croatia were prepared to acknowledge that Croatian forces between 1991 and 1995 might have committed any crimes, either in Croatia or in Bosnia–Herzegovina. For the Croat nationalist right and its cult of Croatian statehood, the very notion that Croats could have perpetrated war crimes while waging a defensive war was illegitimate. After all, this war was fought on historic Croatian territory; it was a legitimate and "just" war as wars go. In this respect, *Vergangenheitsbewältigung* will in all likelihood not be possible in Croatia until such time as a new history of the "Homeland War" is found.

Unfortunately, neither the Croatian political opposition nor the historical profession has helped matters. The major political opposition parties for the most part passively tolerated the historical revisionism of the 1990s, while much of the historical profession participated in its articulation. In October 1995 the Croatian Institute for History commemorated the fiftieth anniversary of the end of the Second World War with a symposium on "Croats in the Second World War." The symposium lent the unfortunate impression that the NDH and Ustaše were a legitimate option for Croats in 1941. Few truly controversial themes were addressed.[77] Croatia's new nationalist historiography has for the most part nurtured the view that Croats have, since 1918, been forced to wage an on-going defensive conflict against Great Serbian ideology. Even the 1999 trial of Dinko Šakić, who served for eight months in 1944 as commander of the Jasenovac camp, and his resulting conviction for war crimes—the issue of genocide was avoided in the courtroom and media generally—did little to sway public attitudes, one way or another.[78] Although a public discourse was initiated, the trial failed to force a genuine reassessment of this inglorious and contested part of the Croatian past. Significantly, not a single major political figure in Croatia attended the trial. The Croat intellectual elite was hardly represented at all.[79]

It is thus virtually impossible to speak of *Vergangenheitsbewältigung* in post-Communist Croatia. That is hardly surprising, however: coming to terms with the past is not simple. The process has hardly been initiated in Southeastern Europe, took decades to initiate in postwar Western Europe, and has been complicated immensely by the recent war in former Yugoslavia. One can only hope that, as memories of Communism and the recent war gradually fade from the popular imagination, they will be replaced by a collective memory forged in a democratic political discourse. Today, more than at any other point in the past century, the prospects for democracy in Croatia and Southeastern Europe appear genuinely strong. Ultimately, it is a thriving democratic environment and the political discourse that such a milieu enables which will ensure that the taboos and myths of the past are addressed. It was precisely the absence of such an environment over the last half-century, held back by the ideological extremes of the Cold War, that enabled the proliferation of myths and their use to justify Communist and later nationalist policies. The future may not bring "the passing away of history," as some would like, but one can hope that at the very least it will bring history's relegation from the political arena to professional academia, where it properly belongs.

Sources

Document 1:

> Yes, [Benito] Mussolini is the dictator of Italy. Yes, [Count István] Bethlen is a politician of the old school. But both men are living exponents of their nations, ... historic nations with remembrance and strong memory, and because of that, with strong egoism. Because there can be no egoism without memory, nor nations without history. And precisely because Mussolini and Bethlen are like that, they are renowned and respected in the entire West. ...
>
> Mussolini sits atop the old Roman imperialism and medieval Papism. Bethlen operates from the historic Holy Crown [of St. Stephen], and in this abstract fiction, because it is a symbol of national memory, he finds living power of the first order. And [Nikola] Pašić is an exponent of the historic Serb nation; in the slogan "Dušan's empire" lies his immense power.

And whosoever today wants his nation to be fresh and powerful must not destroy national memory, because thereby he destroys its egoism. Then, and only then, can he make it the rapine of egotistical neighbors. ...

The mind of the American politician, the mind of the English philosopher may see in blood the bearer of dumb history, the difficult burden of heredity. The mind of the enlightened Christian can hope for that distant time when there will no longer be the idea of nationalism, which divides humanity into hostile groups, and in particular creates a barracks out of Europe, declares man to be a foreigner, turns Christian love for one's neighbor into wild hatred. But the mind of the most enlightened Croat must, out of ethical motives, which are higher than nationalism, listen to the voice of his Croat blood. Because, at the edge of the Balkans, on the frontier of West and East, Catholicism and Orthodoxy, European culture and barbarism, the Croat name, Croat blood does not simply mean the nation! Croat blood here means civilization. Croatdom is here a synonym for everything nice and good that was formed by the European West. ...

The HSP [Croat Party of Right] places no hopes in Mussolini and [Hungarian regent, Miklós] Horthy. But in Dušan's empire, in which it finds itself today, it sees something that is worse than death itself; it sees the balkanization of the Croat nation. ...

The Western Catholic Croats have nothing to look for in the Orthodox Balkans. Today it is the domain of the Serbs, who are adapted to this region through numerous generations. Even were Dušan's empire to break apart and a federation to be formed, it would be a purely Balkan creation. In it the Croats would lose that which is best about them, in the opinion of the Party of Right. ... They would lose a sense for Western civilization and for—humaneness."

Source: Milan Šufflay, "Radić, Bethlen i Mussolini," *Hrvatska misao*, 24 April 1924.

Document 2:

In the question of preserving the Croatian State, we cannot at all entertain a discussion, even if many around us would like this matter to be discussed. From the time of the rule of imperial Vienna to this day, the same question has always arisen from the side of various interested parties, whose idea it is to raise doubts about the ability of the Croatian State to exist on Croatian ethnic and historic territory. Our current generation has answered this question in the affirmative by the very creation of the Croatian State, which was formed in the most difficult of times, solely by the will of the Croat nation, regardless of how other factors behaved toward this fact [contributed to this achievement]. On 10 April 1941, the Croatian State was formed, as an expression of the will of the Croat nation. On that day there were no differences among Croats, and today there is no difference among us with respect to this fundamental fact. It is even more necessary to emphasize this, since today many point to the supposed divisions among the Croats with respect to this basic question.

Regardless of the social and cultural orientation of individuals and groups in the Croat nation, there is no discussion among us about the very fact of the existence and the need for the continued survival of the Croatian State. ... In the present decisive phase of the war, ideological questions are not in any case of the first order. Indeed, it may seem otherwise to the uncritical observer of today's events, but that is by virtue of the fact that today ideology has become the exclusive instrument of politics. Today's phase of the war is a struggle for survival, and every member of the Croat national community must keep this in mind. The only ideology which we can and may follow is that ideology which was represented through the centuries by the Croat political elites, which is the preservation of Croat national individuality, for whose survival today one's own national state is the only guarantee.

Source: Milivoj Magdić, "Hrvatski egoizam," *Spremnost*, no. 106, 5 March 1944.

Document 3:

No one will deny the undemocratic nature of [Ante] Pavelić's regime, the limited sovereignty of the NDH, the existence of collection (concentration) camps, the so-called race legislation, or that a significant number not only of its military and political enemies, but innocent civilians too, died in the name of the Croatian State of the time. These are things which merit condemnation and of which, as members of the Croat nation, we cannot be proud. They can be explained and described, they can be analyzed and judged, but they cannot be denied, just as they must not be exaggerated and used as an instrument against the natural right and desire of the Croat nation to live in its own state. ...

It does no good to ignore [the fact] that autonomous Croatia, within the structure of the Kingdom of Yugoslavia, was also under an expressly undemocratic administration. In this structure ... the first anti-Jewish decrees were issued, the work of Freemasons was banned, the vote was limited, election results were illegally annulled, and the first collection camps were opened for Communists (which has been written about for fifty years), and for Croat nationalists, too (which was ignored for half a century, even by academics). Men were thrown into these camps without trial, which is also useful to know. It could be said that this was the spirit of the time. ...

In spite of all its difficult imperfections, Croats largely experienced the NDH as Croatian. Even when they were opponents of the Ustaša regime, they knew that the NDH had no Croatian alternative. The alternative was Yugoslavia: monarchist (Karadjordjevićist) or Communist (Tito's). ... The statement by Archbishop Stepinac is clear and comprehensible precisely in light of this alternative: "The Croat nation expressed itself by plebiscite for a Croatian state and I would have been a worthless man had I not felt the pulse of my nation, which was a slave in the former Yugoslavia."

Source: Tomislav Jonjić, "Je li bilo hrvatske alternative ustaškoj Hrvatskoj?" *Vjesnik*, 17 July 2001.

Notes

1 For studies of myths, collective memory, and different mythologized histories, be they Communist or other, in East Central Europe, see Lucian Boia, *History and Myth in Romanian Consciousness* (Budapest: Central European University Press, 2001); Mark Mazower, "The Cold War and the Appropriation of Memory: Greece After Liberation," in *The Politics of Retribution in Europe: World War II and Its Aftermath*, ed. István Deák, Jan T. Gross, and Tony Judt (Princeton: Princeton University Press, 2000), 212–32; Stevan Weine, *When History Is a Nightmare: Lives and Memories of Ethnic Cleansing in Bosnia–Herzegovina* (New Brunswick, N.J.: Rutgers University Press, 1999); Noel Malcolm, *Kosovo: A Short History* (New York: New York University Press, 1998); and Christoph Reinprecht, *Nostalgie und Amnesie: Bewertungen von Vergangenheit in der Tschechischen Republik und in Ungarn* (Vienna, 1996).

2 "Kad će nam proći prošlost?" *Feral Tribune*, no. 810 (2001).

3 For studies of Gaj and Illyrianism, see Elinor M. Despalatović, *Ljudevit Gaj and the Illyrian Movement* (New York: East European Monographs, 1975); and, Josip Horvat, *Ljudevit Gaj: Njegov život, njegovo doba* (Zagreb, 1975).

4 On Starčević and the Party of Right, see Mirjana Gross, *Povijest pravaške ideologije* (Zagreb, 1973); and Josip Horvat, *Ante Starčević: Kulturno-povjesna slika* (Zagreb, 1940).

5 On Strossmayer and his cultural Yugoslavism, see Josip Juraj Strossmayer and Franjo Rački, *Politički spisi*, comp. by Vladimir Košćak (Zagreb, 1971).

6 Unlike Strossmayer's cultural Yugoslavism, the unitarist Yugoslavism of this period was a revolutionary political ideology, which claimed that all South Slavs, sometimes including Bulgarians, were "tribes" of one and the same "nation." On the different

currents of Yugoslavist ideology in Croatia in this period, see Mirjana Gross, "Nacionalne ideje studentske omladine u Hrvatskoj uoči i svjetskog rata," *Historijski zbornik* 21–22 (1968– 1969): 75–144.

7 On the various Starčevićist factions, see Gross, *Povijest pravaške ideologije*, 331f. Eventually the most important of these factions were the Frankists, who derived their name from Josip Frank, Starčević's successor and leader of the "Pure Party of Right" from 1895 to 1911.

8 On the Kingdom of Serbs, Croats, and Slovenes, see Ivo Banac, *The National Question in Yugoslavia: Origins, History, Politics* (Ithaca: Cornell University Press, 1984); the relevant sections of John Lampe, *Yugoslavia as History: Twice There Was a Country* 2nd ed. (Cambridge: Cambridge University Press, 2000); Ferdo Čulinović, *Jugoslavija izmedju dva rata*, 2 vols. (Zagreb, 1961); and Branislav Gligorijević, *Parlament i političke stranke u Jugoslaviji 1919–1929* (Belgrade, 1979).

9 On Radić and the HSS, see Mark Biondich, *Stjepan Radić, the Croat Peasant Party and the Politics of Mass Mobilization, 1904–1928* (Toronto: University of Toronto Press, 2000); and Ljubo Boban, *Maček i politika HSS, 1928–1941*, 2 vols. (Zagreb, 1974).

10 Stjepan Sarkotić, *Radićevo izdajstvo* (Vienna, 1925), 27.

11 L. von Südland (pseud. of Ivo Pilar), *Južnoslavensko pitanje: Prikaz cjelokupnog pitanja*, trans. by Fedor Pucek (1943; reprint, Zagreb, 1990), 215. Originally published as *Die Südslawische Frage und der Weltkrieg* (Vienna, 1918).

12 Milan Šufflay, "Radić, Bethlen i Mussolini," *Hrvatska misao*, 24 April 1924. For Šufflay, see Ivo Banac, "Zarathustra in Red Croatia: Milan Šufflay and His Theory of Nationhood," in *National Character and National Ideology in Interwar Eastern Europe*, ed. by Ivo Banac and Katherine Verdery (New Haven: Yale University Press, 1995), 181–93.

13 Nikola Rušinović, *Moja sjećanja na Hrvatsku*, comp. by Božo Rude (Zagreb, 1996), 287.

14 Eugen Dido Kvaternik, *Sjećanja i zapažanja, 1929–1945: Prilozi za hrvatsku povijest*, comp. by Jere Jareb (Zagreb, 1995), 271. The need for such a struggle was buttressed by the belief that Croats were demographically in decline *vis-à-vis* Serbs in Great Croatia. See Mladen Lorković, *Narod i zemlja Hrvata* (Zagreb, 1939), 164–65; and Pilar, *Južnoslavensko pitanje*, 402–05.

15 By contrast, in November 1920 the HSS (at that time, the HPSS) gained 37 percent of the popular vote and 50 of 93 seats in prewar Croatia–Slavonia. In September 1927, the HSS won 53 of 84 seats in prewar Croatia–Slavonia and Dalmatia, compared to the one seat (held by Ante Pavelić) of the Croat Party of Right. See Čulinović, *Jugoslavija izmedju dva rata*, 1:312–13, 500–01.

16 Josip Horvat, *Živjeti u Hrvatskoj: Zapisci iz nepovrata 1900–1941* (Zagreb, 1984), 146–47.

17 On Croatia's Serbs, see Nicholas J. Miller, *Between Nation and State: Serbian Politics in Croatia before the First World War* (Pittsburgh: University of Pittsburgh Press, 1997).

18 Horvat, *Živjeti u Hrvatskoj*, 147.

19 Ibid., 306–07.

20 M. S., "Srpski apetit," *Nezavisna Hrvatska Država*, 24 December 1938, 4; and Mirko Puk, "Ante Starčević i Muslimani," *Hrvatski narod*, 9 February 1939, 3.

21 On Catholic conversions to Orthodoxy in the Ottoman era, see the works of Krunoslav Draganović, *Katolička crkva u Bosni i Hercegovini nekad i danas* (Zagreb, 1934), and *Masenübertritte von Katholiken zur "Orthodoxie" im kroatischen Sprachgebiet zur Zeit der Türkenherrschaft* (Rome, 1937). Although Pilar made reference to these conversions in his study, he emphasized the Vlach origin of the Serbs of Great Croatia and the role of the Serbian Orthodox Church in assimilating them. See Pilar, *Južnoslavensko pitanje*, 112–17.

22 For example, see "Ne damo Bosnu!" *Nezavisna Hrvatska Država*, 3 June 1939, 2; Luka Grbić, "Još o Srbo-Cincaro-Vlasima," *Nezavisna Hrvatska Država*, 4 November 1939, 4; "Hrvatska politika u Bosni," *Hrvatski narod*, 28 July 1939, 6; M. O., "Vlasi a ne Srbi," *Nezavisna Hrvatska Država*, 1 June 1940, 2; "Doseljenje Srba u Hrvatsku i turska politika Svetozara Pribićevića," *Hrvatski narod*, 13 October 1939, 1; and, M. G., "O Hrvatstvu," *Hrvatski narod*, 7 July 1939, 7.

23 a.r.b., "Frankovci," *Hrvatski narod*, 29 September 1939, 1.

24 "Smiješna akcija 'narodnih srpskih novina'," *Hrvatski narod*, 8 December 1939, 1; "'Nove žrtve' nezadovoljnih hegemonista," *Hrvatski narod*, 15 December 1939, 1; "Uzaludni napori 'samostalaca'," *Hrvatski narod*, 15 December 1939, 6.

25 "Zahtjevi nekih doseljenika vukovarskog kotara," *Hrvatski narod*, 17 November 1939, 1.

26 That was the critique made by Mladen Lorković, who alleged that the 26 August 1939 Agreement left nearly 800,000 Bosnian "Croats" (by which he meant Bosnian Muslims) outside autonomous Croatia's borders. Lorković, *Narod i zemlja Hrvata*, 225. See also Matija Kovačić, *Od Radića do Pavelića: Hrvatska u borbi za svoju samostalnost* (Munich, 1970).

27 Ivo Rojnica, *Susreti i doživljaji, 1938–1945* (Munich, 1969), 28.

28 Stjepan Hefer, *Croatian Struggle for Freedom and Statehood* (Buenos Aires, 1959), 128.

29 Dragutin Kamber, *Slom NDH: Kako sam ga ja proživio*, comp. by Božica Ercegovac Jambrović (Zagreb, 1993), 5.

30 On the Ustaše and NDH, see Jozo Tomasevich, *War and Revolution in Yugoslavia, 1941–1945: Occupation and Collaboration* (Stanford: Stanford University Press, 2001); M. Broszat and L. Hory, *Der kroatische Ustascha-Staat, 1941–1945* (Stuttgart, 1964); Aleksa Djilas, *The Contested Country: Yugoslav Unity and Communist Revolution, 1919–1953* (Cambridge: Cambridge University Press, 1991); Bogdan Krizman, *Pavelić i ustaše* (Zagreb, 1978), *Pavelić izmedju Hitlera i Mussolinija* (Zagreb, 1980), and *Ustaše i Treći Reich*, 2 vols. (Zagreb, 1982); and Fikreta Jelić-Butić, *Ustaše i NDH* (Zagreb, 1977).

31 Kvaternik, *Sjećanja i zapažanja*, 285.

32 *Documents on German Foreign Policy, 1918–1945* (hereafter, DGFP), series D, vol. 12 (Washington, D.C.: U.S. Government Printing Office, 1962), Doc. 589, 957–958.

33 DGFP, D/12, Doc. 603, 977–981.

34 DGFP, D/12, Doc. 350, 552–555.

35 The salient theme in Ustaša rhetoric of this period was that the Serbs of Great Croatia were an alien element. For example, see "Sav je narod uz Poglavnika," *Hrvatski narod*, 27 May 1941, 1, 3; "U svim krajevima Hrvatske neograničena ljubav i odanost prema Poglavniku i NDH," *Hrvatski narod*, 3 June 1941, 2; and "Poglavnik je uvijek imao pravo," *Hrvatski narod*, 16 June 1941, 16.

36 The literature on forced conversions in the NDH is extensive but polemical. A comprehensive and dispassionate study of conversions and the role of the Croat Catholic clergy in the NDH has yet to be written. See Viktor Novak, *Magnum crimen: Pola vijeka klerikalizma u Hrvatskoj* (Zagreb, 1948), 527f.; Sima Simić, *Prekrštavanje Srba za vreme Drugog svetskog rata* (Titograd, 1958); Veljko Đ. Đuric, *Prekrštavanje Srba u Nezavisnoj Državi Hrvatskoj: Prilozi za istoriju verskog genocida* (Belgrade, 1991); and Jure Krišto, *Katolička crkva i Nezavisna Država Hrvatska, 1941–1945*, 2 vols. (Zagreb, 1998). The most balanced Western studies are Stella Alexander, *Church and State in Yugoslavia since 1945* (Cambridge: Cambridge University Press, 1979), and *The Triple Myth: A Life of Archbishop Alojzije Stepinac* (Boulder, Col.: East European Monographs, 1987).

37 On 15 September 1941, the Ustaša regime decreed the formation of a "Religious Section" within the State Directorate for Renewal, which was supposed to conduct the policy. An original copy of this decree may be found in Hrvatski državni arhiv (hereafter HDA), Ministarstvo pravosudja i bogoštovlja, Odjel za bogoštovlje, Box 11: Broj 3049-B-1 ("Okružnica u pogledu postupka kod prelaza sa grčko-istočne vjere na druge priznate vjere"), 12 December 1941.

38 Kvaternik, *Sjećanja i zapažanja*, 285.

39 The text of Pavelić's speech can be found in "Velike smjernice hrvatske državne politike," *Hrvatski narod*, 1 March 1942, 3.

40 Pavelić himself affirmed the new Ustaša policy in an article on Bosnia's place in Croatian history, where he addressed, *inter alia*, the question of Orthodox identity. One thing was above dispute, Pavelić argued: the Orthodox of Great Croatia were not Serbs. Some were of Vlach origin, and the others were descended from the native Catholic population, which had converted to Orthodoxy in the Ottoman era. See Ante Pavelić, "Pojam Bosne kroz stolječa," *Hrvatski narod*, 28 February 1942, 2.

41 Franjo Perše, "Dvojaka kriza Srbstva," *Hrvatski narod*, 22 August 1942, 2.

42 For example, see H. Dubravić, "Sloga Hrvata muslimana i katolika," *Hrvatski narod*, 6 November 1942, 3; and Mile Starčević, "Mi hoćemo da na svom području slobodno i nesmetano stvaramo svoja dobra," *Hrvatski narod*, 17 November 1942, 4.

43 For example, see "Radi se na konačnom sređenju u državi," *Hrvatski narod*, 24 November 1942, 1–3; and "Odmetnici, njihovo lice i naličje," *Nova Hrvatska*, 15 January 1943, 2. See also Kovačić's remarks at the Croatian Foreign Ministry's official promotion of its "Grey Book" about Chetnik and Partisan atrocities against Croats: "'Siva knjiga' predana hrvatskoj javnosti," *Nova Hrvatska*, 24 January 1943, 2; and Matija Kovačić, *Odmetnička zvjerstva i pustošenja u Nezavisnoj Državi Hrvatskoj u prvm mjesecima života hrvatske narodne države* (Zagreb, 1942), 8–9.

44 For example, see the remarks of the Ustaša officials Ljudevit Šolc and Alija Šuljak, "Ustaški pokret otvara vrata cielom hrvatskom narodu," *Hrvatski narod*, 1 December 1942, 1 & 3; "Putem žrtava dolazi se boljim danima – dolazi se slobodi," *Nova Hrvatska*,

9 January 1943, 4; and "Hrvatskom je narodu osigurana velika i sretna budušnost jedino u NDH," *Nova Hrvatska*, 27 January 1943, 4.

45 Verus, "Pravoslavlje u Hrvatskoj," *Spremnost*, 13 February 1944, 1.

46 On the guidelines that were to be followed in all future Croatian–Chetnik negotiations, see HDA, fond 223, Ministarstvo unutarnjih poslova, Box 300: Broj 9–X–1942 ("Okružnica"), 7 December 1942.

47 HDA, fond 211, Fond Hrvatskog državnog sabora, Box 1: Broj 103 ("Velika župa Gora - prilike," Taj. Broj 274-1942), 9 July 1942. The prefect's report was not, however, an endorsement of this policy. He expressed concern that such tactics only strengthened the partisan movement. Moreover, he noted that most local Serbs had behaved loyally toward the Croatian authorities and had not taken up arms against the state.

48 HDA, fond 211, Fond HDS, Box 1: Broj 82 ("Zapisnik"), 1 June 1942.

49 HDA, fond 227, Ministarstvo vanjskih poslova, Box 4: Broj 162 Tajno ("Pravoslavno pučanstvo, postupak"), 31 May 1943.

50 Cited in Kvaternik, *Sjećanja i zapažanja*, 300.

51 On wartime population losses, see Bogoljub Kočević, *Žrtve Drugog svetskog rata u Jugoslaviji* (London, 1985); and Vladimir Žerjaviž, *Gubici stanovništva Jugoslavije u Drugom svjetskom ratu* (Zagreb, 1989).

52 The Great Serbian nature of Tito's Communist movement was another wartime Ustaša myth that was nurtured after 1945 by the political emigration. See Fran Nikolić, *Novo pokoljenje i komunizam* (Zagreb, 1942), for an early version of this genre.

53 Kvaternik, *Sjećanja i zapažanja*, 285–286.

54 *Branili smo državu: Uspomene, osvrti, doživljaji*, 2 vols. (Barcelona and Munich, 1985). The myth of a defensive war originated during the Second World War. See *Uzori Draže Mihajlovića i partizana* (Zagreb, 1943); *Odmetnici u pravoj slici* (Zagreb, 1943); and Mladen Lorković, *Hrvatska u borbi protiv Boljševizma* (Zagreb, 1944).

55 Hefer, *Croatian Struggle for Freedom and Statehood*, 13–14, 131.

56 Ibid., 105.

57 Ibid., 135–36, 160, 191.

58 Kamber, *Slom NDH*, 14–15, 23–24.

59 Rušinović, *Moja sjećanja na Hrvatsku*, 120, 289.

60 Rojnica, *Susreti i doživljaji*, 170–71. See also Rušinović, *Moja sjećanja na Hrvatsku*, 210–11; and Vlado Raić, *Dr. Ante Pavelić: U svjetlu činjenica* (Buenos Aires, 1959), 35.

61 Cited in Kvaternik, *Sjećanja i zapažanja*, 254–55. One finds this sentiment implicitly echoed in the memoirs of Vladko Maček, who mentions Ustaša atrocities but generally devotes more attention to Chetnik and Partisan atrocities against Croats. See *Memoari* (Zagreb, 1992).

62 Bleiburg is located on the Austrian-Slovenian border. In May 1945 British troops at Bleiburg repatriated thousands of mostly Croatian troops and civilians to the Communist partisans, who then murdered many of them. Most of the literature on Bleiburg is tendentious and alleges that as many as half a million Croats were murdered by Tito's forces. I will cite only a few of the better known émigré works: namely, John Prcela and

Stanko Guldescu, eds., *Operation Slaughterhouse: Eyewitness Accounts of Postwar Massacres in Yugoslavia* (Philadelphia: Dorrance, 1970); Vinko Nikolić, *Bleiburška tragedija hrvatskog naroda* (Munich, 1977), and *Bleiburg: Uzroci i posljedice* (Munich, 1988). The topic was first seriously addressed in Croatia in Marko Grčić, ed., *Bleiburg* (Zagreb, 1990). Of the more serious treatments of this subject, see Nikolai Tolstoy, *The Minister and the Massacres* (London: Century Hutchinson, 1986).

63 The Catholic priest Dragutin Kamber, who in 1941 served briefly as a member of the Ustaša commission that ran the Doboj municipality (Bosnia) before moving to Zagreb to write for and edit Ustaša periodicals, claims rather unconvincingly in his posthumously published memoir that he quickly reached the conclusion in 1941 that Ustaša policy in Zagreb was being set by "primitives," and feared that at some future point all Croats would suffer collective guilt for the actions of these men and their criminal policy. Kamber, *Slom NDH*, 12.

64 Ivan Oršanić, *Vizija slobode*, comp. by Kazimir Katalinić (Buenos Aires, 1979), 240.

65 Ibid., 7. See also Branimir Jelić, *Političke uspomene i rad dra. Branimira Jelića*, comp. by Jere Jareb (Cleveland, 1982), 106–07, 215.

66 Bruno Bušić, "Činjenice o hrvatskoj revoluciji i državi," in *Jedino Hrvatska! Sabrani spisi*, comp. by Vinko Lasić (Toronto, 1983), 131. See also Raić, *Dr. Ante Pavelić*, 30.

67 Jeliž, *Političke uspomene*, 221.

68 Oršanić, *Vizija slobode*, 250–51.

69 Ibid., 240, 243.

70 Jere Jareb, *Pola stoljeća hrvatske politike, 1895–1945: Povodom Mačekove autobiografije* (1960; reprint, Zagreb, 1995), 89, 92–93.

71 Ibid., 123.

72 Darko Sagrak, *Zagreb 1941–1945: Suton Banovine Hrvatske – Uskrišenje Nezavisne Države Hrvatske i njezin slom – Prva godina u Titovoj Jugoslaviji* (Zagreb, 1995), 87.

73 Tomislav Jonjić, "Je li bilo hrvatske alternative ustaškoj Hrvatskoj?" *Vjesnik*, 17 July 2001.

74 Cited in Marinko Čulić, *Tuđman: Anatomija neprosvijećenog apsolutizma* (Split, 1999), 20.

75 Slavko Goldstein, "Pogrom i pakao," *Feral Tribune*, no. 713 (May 1999).

76 Edvard Popović, "Polje velike pouke," *Danas*, 14 May 1993, 20.

77 The conference proceedings may be found in *Časopis za suvremenu povijest*, 27 (1995), no. 3.

78 On the trial, see Viktor Ivančić, *Točka na U: Slučaj Šakić: Anatomija jednog skandala* (Split, 2000). In practice the attitude of the democratic, post-Tuđman center-left coalition government toward the Croat extreme right can still be described as ambivalent. See Drago Hedl, "Croatia: Ustasha legacy alive and kicking," *Institute for War and Peace Reporting*, no. 256 (7 March 2002).

79 Vladimir Primorac, " Šakić," *Feral Tribune*, no. 706 (March 1999).

CHAPTER 3

Sandra Prlenda

YOUNG, RELIGIOUS, AND RADICAL:
The Croat Catholic Youth Organizations, 1922–1945

"Everything's getting organized! Freemasons, socialists, and liberals are organizing, so let us organize, too."

Anton Mahnič, bishop of Krk, 1903

This often quoted call to religious youth marks the beginning of what is known as the Croatian Catholic movement. It led to several political and social projects organized by Catholic intellectuals and priests from the turn of the century until the Second World War.[1] They all shared in the belief that rapid social change was endangering the Catholic faith and the church in their position as the supreme arbiter in society. In addition to priests, the majority of these groups included lay intellectuals and students whose activities ranged from editing newspapers and magazines and participating in public polemics with liberals to founding an (unsuccessful) political party. Their most successful initiative was an organization for the upbringing of young Catholics that in its best years assembled more than 40,000 active members and younger children who were trained for the "rechristianization" of public life. Although by no means dominant in Croatian interwar society, the huge amount of energy that its leaders spent to ensure the visible presence of Catholic values in a traditionally Catholic society invites us to try to understand the dynamics of this kind of youth mobilization. Whereas most of its ideological foundation was drawn from the militant Catholicism in contemporary Europe known as Catholic Action,[2] the specific historical context pushed the Croat interpretation beyond the framework of three contending ideologies (Catholicism, liberalism, and Communism). It was nationalism that would explain both the ups and the unhappy downs of organized young Croat Catholics.

This chapter traces Catholic youth mobilization through two organizations, *Hrvatski orlovski savez* (the Croat Eagle Union, 1923–1929) and its successor *Križarska organizacija* (the Crusaders' Organization, 1930–1945).

The former was a Catholic gymnastic society banned by Yugoslavia's King Aleksandar at the beginning of his dictatorship in 1929. The latter inherited all but the name and the gymnastics. Although the Eagles and Crusaders claimed to be outside of daily politics, their program of publicly confronting both liberalism and Communism with radical Catholicism has generated continual accusations of "clericalism" by liberal, leftist, or non-Croat nationalist elements, not just by interwar Croat Peasant Party leader Stjepan Radić and post-1945 Communist historiography. I will argue that the public character of the ideological confrontation with their liberal or leftist adversaries combined with interwar Yugoslavia's challenge to Croat national identity to make these lay youth organizations a major political force in the twentieth-century history of the Catholic Church in Croatia.

Youth and Catholicism in Modern Croatian Politics

Anton Mahnič, bishop of Krk, was one of the most vocal proponents of organized action for both clergy and laity to promote the rechristianization of society. Already in 1903 he had written that "liberalism has taken public life away from Christ and the Church by proclaiming religion a private matter. An individual can believe and pray to God alone, while state, science, arts, legislation, and public schools acknowledge neither God nor Christ, nor do they obey any supreme law. Therefore a human being is divided in two: a private and a public person. A double morality is molded for him, a double consciousness: public and private. ... Public life has to be reconquered for Christ, whom God the Father made King not only of individuals but of peoples and states, and consequently of public life."[3]

These terms defined the struggle of the Catholic Church against the secularization that characterized much of European religious history during the nineteenth century.[4] However, in Croatia liberal clerics such as Bishop Josip Juraj Strossmayer and Franjo Rački, founding fathers of Yugoslavism, were more active as national leaders than as proponents of strict Catholicism. Even more conservative priests gladly involved themselves in politics and were not criticized, as long as the most important political issue was the struggle for national rights in the German- and Magyar-dominated Habsburg monarchy. What finally mobilized the church in Croatia politically and turned religion into a political question, was new legislation proposed by the liberal government in Hungary from 1894 on.[5] But political organizing proved ineffective because of the divisions among the priests. Among the general public, the idea of founding a Catholic political party was seen as unnatural. This was a society where Catholicism was a tradition, not a political option. The main political alternatives to be chosen were Yugoslavism, promoting cooperation with non-Catholic South Slavs, or integral Croat nationalism, which tended to neglect religious differences.[6] Among various new initiatives, newspapers, and associations that advocated social criticism from a Catholic viewpoint, it was the youth movement that managed to create the most durable structure.[7]

A majority of political, social and cultural undertakings in Croatia, as in other Central and East European societies in the nineteenth and beginning of the twentieth century, involved high school and university students. In the early period of national integration, prospective intellectuals took their first steps in political organizing for the national cause at provincial theological seminaries and at the law faculty in Vienna, and from 1874 in Zagreb. Towards the end of the century, the student groups tried to emancipate themselves from the often disappointing set of existing political parties and to find their own voices in politics and culture. At first, Zagreb university students supported existing political parties, such as the Party of Right, exhausting their patriotic enthusiasm in celebrations and concerts.[8] Moving beyond that celebratory spirit (*nazdravičarstvo*, or toasting) of the 1880s, the next generation of students sought to further political emancipation, the social and cultural improvement of the population, and their own intellectual and moral edification. Croat students in Prague (the "Progressive Youth"), future national leader Stjepan Radić among them, embraced this new approach under the influence of Professor Tomáš Masaryk.[9] They also brought back criticism from Prague of the role of the Catholic Church in Croatian history and culture. For example, they judged the pope's purported medieval designation of the Croats to be *Antemurale Christianitatis* (the ramparts of Christendom) shameful. Young modernist writers also denounced the large contingent of priests in cultural institutions such as the Academy of Sciences and Arts and the cultural institution *Matica hrvatska*.[10]

In this atmosphere, Catholic students began to organize under the direct influence of Bishop Mahnič. A Slovene by birth, he was not just conservative but intransigent, refusing unconditionally any compromise with liberal ideas.[11] First in Slovene Carinthia, and then in Croatia, he launched an appeal for what he called the "division of spirits."[12] Echoing the papal encyclicals of Leo XIII and Pius X that asked the Catholic laity to engage in social life from a position of radical Catholicism, he urged young laypersons to carry on that struggle: "The Croatian people must opt for God or against God. Croatian youth will follow the banner of Christ or the banner of Lucifer."[13]

The youth of the era were at first reluctant to choose sides. One of the Catholic students described the students' state of mind in these times: "In the lower grades, there was mechanical fulfilling of religious duties, in the higher ones negligence, and at the university contempt for the faith. ...

'Progressivism' was at its peak. Most of the university students, and a considerable number of those in high school, were progressive, antireligious; the rest were indifferent. Religiosity and Catholicism were proclaimed to be enemies of culture, and committed Catholics seen as mentally inferior."[14] The first student Catholic society, *Hrvatska*, was founded in Vienna in 1903 by only five students, three of whom were priests.[15] Three years passed before the Croatian Catholic Academic Club, *Domagoj*, named after a medieval Croat prince, was founded at a meeting of Catholic students at Trsat, again with only five members. Soon, however, these small student groups were entering into genuine newspaper wars with other young intellectuals who were violently attacking clericalism, however they defined it. Nationalistic young Croats considered the church to be the slave of Rome and demanded the establishment of a national church; Yugoslav advocates wanted the role of religion minimized, as it contributed to the separation of the Croats and the Serbs. The Catholics were also divided, as some were more willing than others to support Yugoslav unification. As they finished their studies, the core of the Catholic intellectuals, members of academic clubs such as *Domagoj*, formed the *Seniorat* in 1912. This group proposed to direct the whole Catholic movement and provide ideological guidelines. It was a small élite which nonetheless hoped to realize its program through political participation. The new political cards dealt after the First World War and the creation of the new Yugoslav state gave them their chance. They founded the first and only Croat Catholic political party. This was the Croat People's Party (*Hrvatska pučka stranka*), which in the elections to the Constituent Assembly in Belgrade in 1920 won 46,599 votes and nine seats. It would be their best result—in 1923 the party won no seats, returning to Parliament only in 1927 with one seat.[16]

The Eagles: Physical Culture and Ideological Competition

In contrast to the failed political project of the small *Seniorat*, the supposedly apolitical set of local clubs for Catholic youth would prove much more successful. Their ascent began in 1923 when the existing set of youth and gymnastic organizations, already called *Orlovi* (Eagles), united to form one national Catholic gymnastic association. As already noted, in 1929 King Aleksandar banned all organizations, including gymnastic ones, based on "tribal" (ethnic), religious or regional affiliation. The organization was then transformed into the Great Crusaders' Brotherhood and Sorority, with the same membership, leadership, ideology, and methods of work minus the gymnastics. In 1939, there were 43,100 Crusaders, male and female, in Croatia, Bosnia and Bačka (in the Vojvodina).[17]

A new approach shaped this type of Catholic mobilization. The originator and main ideologist of *Orlovstvo* (Eaglehood) among the Croats, Ivan Merz,[18] enthusiastically embraced the concept of Catholic Action proclaimed by Pope Pius XI in the encyclical *Ubi arcano Dei* in 1922.[19] It invited the laity to "participate in a hierarchical apostolate." Lay organizations had to be strictly apolitical but were expected to include the clergy and act upon their bishops' directions (*nulla sine episcopo*). Those principles marked a sharp break with previous practice in the Catholic movement. Political parties, syndicates, and cooperatives were, as organizations with "worldly goals," left out of the Action. Merz, although himself a Senior, applied the new apolitical approach by borrowing from Czechoslovakia[20] via Slovenia. The vehicle was a youth organization that primarily functioned as a gymnastic society but whose ambition was to nurture, through discipline, spiritual guidance and promotion of group unity, a new generation that would bring victory to Catholicism over liberalism in Croatia. At the great international Eagle assembly (*slet*) in Ljubljana in 1920, 5,000 young Croat Catholics participated in a parade with Czechs, Slovaks and Slovenes, totaling 50,000 people. Existing Croat youth gymnastic sections united in 1923 to form a centralized organization with an elaborate ideology, methodology, structure and paraphernalia such as uniforms, an emblem, a flag, songs, a slogan (Sacrifice, Eucharist, Apostolate) and a salutation (God lives!).[21] Some of this was taken from Czech and Slovene models, some were original additions. The Eagles' membership grew steadily; new

Members of the Croat Catholic Eagles in Prelog, in the Croatian region of Medjumurje (1926)

Public performance of female Eagles in Bosnia

local organizations were founded in small towns and villages all around Croatia and Bosnia.[22] The female branch, *Savez hrvatskih orlica*, was founded in 1925.[23]

Nationalistic gymnastic societies had a considerable tradition in Slavic lands. The most important, *Sokol* (Falcon), was founded in 1862 in Czech lands, and spread in a couple of decades to other Slavic peoples. It combined mass physical exercises in a military spirit with liberal, nationalistic and pan-Slavic ideas, in order to mobilize popular resistance to Germanization in the Habsburg monarchy. The aim was to build healthy and disciplined youth with a developed national consciousness, ready to fight, when the moment came, for national liberation. The Slovene (1863) and Croat (1874) Falcons had similar goals, even more so the Serb Falcons. Serb branches emerged between 1904 and 1909 in Serbia, Bosnia and Herzegovina, Montenegro, Dalmatia, Macedonia, and Croatia, espousing a common nationalistic program for the unification of all Serbs.[24] Eventually, some Falcon leaders began to cooperate with each other and promote Yugoslav unification. In 1918 armed squads of Falcons were therefore engaged by the new political authorities in Zagreb to help establish the Yugoslav state.[25]

As we can see, the link between physical education and political ideas was there from the beginning. A healthy individual was seen as a prerequisite for national liberation, a disciplined body being valued for physical fitness in an eventual armed confrontation. Gymnastic societies were also well suited to organize a large number of people, especially youngsters, around

an idea. A spirit of togetherness emanating from assembled bodies performing the same movement fostered the sense of belonging to a larger community, in this case the nation. The Croat Eagles represented the Catholic response
to the Falcons' pronounced liberalism and religious indifference. At the same
time, the socialists founded similar organizations for workers. Physical education, in the epoch when it gradually entered national systems of education, became a field for ideological competition.[26]

Joining with this trend toward collective physical exercises, the leaders
of the Croat Eaglehood theorized in detail about gymnastics as a tool both
for building a healthy, disciplined generation and for carrying the Catholic
message to the world. The apostolic spirit, the foundation of Catholic Action,
made from disciplined squads of performers not simple sportsmen but
knights of Christ. The rechristianization of public life was the main goal of
the Eaglehood, making it in that respect different from various other intra-
ecclesiastic congregations aiming at spiritual renewal. Of the four demands
for Catholic radicalism in Eagle ideology, three were related to the public
sphere. First, Eaglehood was equated with the division of spirits, as defined
by Mahnič, since the manifest character of their activities enabled clear-cut
ideological differentiation in the local community. Secondly, by the public
confession of faith, religion was to be restored to public life. Thirdly, the
clergy could assume the leading public role it had lost under liberal criticism. The fourth demand was for the radicalization of religious life. One of
the visible signs of strict religious life was the frequent taking of communion, a change from the prevailing practice of receiving the Eucharist only at
Easter and Christmas.[27]

One goal was, therefore, to show a large membership and the strength of
the idea by using public space for group exercises. This would convey both
to the performers and to the public a strong sense of collective identity and
ideological unity. Thus a modern mass organization could use the discipline
of the body as a classical method of disciplining the mind, a fundamental
part of Catholic tradition. So-called simple exercises were purposely preferred as accessible to everyone regardless of physical condition.[28] They
consisted of turning movements of arms, head, and body, executed simultaneously by the whole group. The Eagles' *Organizational Bulletin* theorized
that "through simple exercises we show our strength towards the outside.
Every member can do them, and by this the public may evaluate the work
and progress of the organization. No other type of exercise involves such a
multitude of performers as the simple exercises do."[29] Regular gatherings at
the local, national, or international level,[30] the so-called *slets*, were events
of central importance. There were mass performances of symbolic exercises
such as "We Are Eagles" and the "Dalmatian Boatman," where the movements also conveyed the content of the songs that accompanied them. "The

Eagles training in Gornje Selo on the island of Šolta (1926)

Croats from the Time of Their Arrival until [King] Tomislav" was presented on the occasion of the celebration of the millennium of the Croatian kingdom, as recorded in Document 2.[31]

In practice, Croat Eaglehood competed in the highly politicized realm of physical education with the state-sponsored gymnastic society *Jugoslavenski Sokol* (Yugoslav Falcon) that promoted the national (Yugoslav) spirit. Eagles and Falcons vied for their young public on both ideological and national grounds. Complicating the competition was the separate presence of the nationalistic but anti-clerical *Hrvatski Sokol* (Croat Falcon). Their structural relation was one of mutual exclusiveness, grounded on the Catholic side in a refusal to compromise with what was seen primarily as liberal ideology, a major threat to Catholicism. Membership in both organizations was strictly forbidden, and Catholic membership in scout associations or other sport clubs strongly discouraged, on the ground that their religious indifference presented a moral danger for young persons.[32] The Falcons were labeled from the beginning in Eagles' discourse as "our adversaries" (*naši protivnici*). The Eagles, on the other hand, were denounced as a clerical and political organization not only by the Falcons but even more so by the leader of the preeminent Croat Peasant Party, Stjepan Radić.[33] Likewise, the Croatian Serb leader Svetozar Pribićević, as minister of education in 1922, prohibited all students from being members, condemning them as politically oriented organizations.[34] Schoolteachers, as state employees, and often ethnic Serbs were expected to encourage membership in the Yugoslav Falcon. Sometimes they were very hostile to, or at best ignored, the Eagles' (and later the Crusaders') representations of their pupils.[35]

Crusaders' Brotherhood in Vela Luka on the island of Korčula

Although the Yugoslav Falcon was promoted by the state to eradicate "tribal" differences, Catholics in the 1920s insisted on the ideological divide between liberalism and Catholicism. They denounced the religious indifference of both the Yugoslav and the Croat Falcons. The predominance of the ideological over the national is particularly noticeable in the frequent exchanges between the Eagles and the Croat Falcons.[36] The Croatian nationalist orientation of the Eagles was nonetheless explicit, and they therefore competed in the 1920s at the local level with other Croat nationalists, some of them anti-clerical, such as Radić's Peasant Party, or the Croat Falcons.[37] The animosity was not limited to the press; it occasionally led to verbal and physical violence, as when one organization held a public performance or other gathering.[38] (See Document 1.) In some small towns and villages, several organizations had to share the same building for training and assemblies, pushing the rivalry into open confrontations.[39]

The Crusaders as an Alternative School

Much as the Eagle was, by its athletic nature, an attractive tool for assembling a young crowd, this was not a mere gymnastic club. In the first place it was designed to be an organization for education and upbringing—a kind of alternative school for the Catholic élite.[40] This last dimension became dominant after King Aleksander banned all political parties and all organizations based on tribal, religious, or regional affiliation, including organizations for physical education, in 1929. The state took control of physical culture, regarding it as a tool for the promotion of integral Yugoslavism; hence *Sokol Kraljevine Jugoslavije* (the Falcon of the Kingdom of Yugoslavia) became the first state organization for physical education. Membership was mandatory for all schoolchildren.[41] All local Eagle branches were disbanded, flags and uniforms locked in boxes, to the great regret of many teenagers. The Catholic laity had to find other ways of action in the unfavorable circumstances of a royal dictatorship that outlawed even the use of ethnic names.

This they nonetheless did in a couple of weeks. Ivo Protulipac and his associates quickly sketched the rules of the new organization and submitted them to Zagreb archbishop Antun Bauer and other bishops for confirmation. They found their new niche under the umbrella of the Catholic Church and registered as a religious association, part of the Apostolate of Prayer, under the supervision of the Jesuits. The leadership of the Eagles, Ivo Protulipac and Marica Stanković, were at the head of the "new" organization, the Great Crusader Brotherhood and Sorority, the Crusaders. Even though Protulipac was arrested and questioned by the authorities, the Crusaders were a religious association and therefore remained outside state control.[42] Local organizations were slowly set up anew. The state authorities watched and suppressed any gathering outside church premises. Thus it seemed that the movement was restricted to the sacristy. More than before, the parish priest became a very important figure. If he was willing, he was the one who provided space and time for weekly meetings and Sunday Mass assemblage.[43] Still, a nucleus of lay activists from Zagreb, Ivo Protulipac, Avelin Ćepulić, Marica Stanković and others, remained as active as ever, traveling every weekend to the provincial towns and villages, founding local branches, giving lectures and propagating their ideas.

Although the Eagles were also designed as an organization for upbringing and education, the Crusaders were able to develop this mission to a greater extent. The conceptualization was ambitious, aiming at shaping the totality of the young person's character and at reaching all social classes.[44] Reaffirmation of faith and moral conduct (particularly the physical and spiritual purity of boys and girls in adolescence) made up a large portion of the pedagogical effort. Yet the ultimate goal was to form a disciplined and militant younger generation in order to secure radical Catholicism in many aspects of social life. Instead of training for gymnastics, boys and girls met separately each week to listen to lectures and discuss them. Topics regularly included liturgy and faith, the organization's management, social problems (the church and social questions, anti-Communism), and Croatian history.[45] According to the Crusaders' manual, 90 percent of the members left schooling after primary school. These lectures were therefore seen as crucial to the continuous education of young peasants and workers.

The Crusaders took great care in building up a very centralized organization, with strict procedures for communication between the central office in Zagreb and local organizations. The central office planned and prepared activities, summer courses, brochures, and lectures. Along with anti-liberalism, anti-Communism became another main ideological concern of the Crusaders in the 1930s. Most of the local assemblies and summer courses included at least one lecture on the social question, with a critique of Communism. Their newspapers repeatedly wrote of the dire situation in the Soviet Union, stressing the persecution of religion and the anti-religious upbringing of children and youth. Republican persecution of the Catholic Church in Spain was also highlighted. With the pope leading the anti-Communist campaign, the Crusaders' publications followed suit: "Brethren Crusaders! Vox Papae, Vox Christi! Be apostles of the word: speak out to the people about the horrors of Bolshevist atheism, about deadly misery, about the bestial subjugation under which Russian people now live, into which all the world will plunge if the young Crusader generation doesn't stop it. To make it easier for you, we will say it again: Be *Crusaders*, that is, *defenders and conquerors!*"[46]

The concern for exerting decisive influence on the public thus remained very important, though now approached somewhat differently. Document 3 shows these methods of work. Not allowed to appear in public as a group, the Crusaders kept holding weekly meetings, lectures and debates, but once again with the clear goal of creating committed Catholics, who would themselves act in public. The pedagogical manual "Our Way" was explicit about the objective of the weekly meetings—first, through lectures and discussions the youngsters had to understand actual social issues; and second, through declamations and play-acting they should be encouraged and trained for public speaking, in order to defend Catholic ideas in front of their friends and co-villagers.[47] In villages and small towns, the tavern and the square were the central places of socializing and political life, where all kinds of ideas were put forward and discussed. Before and after the dictatorship, there were activists of the Peasant Party, sympathizers with the Communists, supporters of the government, as well as atheists pure and simple—all of them considered by the Crusaders' mentors as dangerous "demagogues" that poisoned youth. The Crusader was encouraged and trained to speak up confidently, with strong arguments, and passionately defend his beliefs. More than a prayer circle, the Crusaders' organization was a school for public exhortation.

Female Crusaders worked especially hard to fulfill their apostolic program in their environment. Document 4 represents an appeal for a larger participation of girls in the movement. Charity work was carried on in the framework of Christmas Action, when members collected food and clothes for poor worker settlements. There they sought to bring back workers who had deserted religion, partially under Communist influence. Some new methods of work were copied from Belgian Catholics, such as the "Easter Struggle," started in 1937. Participants in this initiative asked people to go to Easter confession and communion by distributing leaflets on the streets, in factories, and at the university.[48] Female Crusaders employed in factories were encouraged to pray loudly during work breaks and to form prayer groups. At the same time, elements of the everyday life for youth were supposed to be remodeled in accordance with Catholic morality: wearing decent clothes and avoiding make-up, dancing in pairs, mixed bathing-places, and short sportswear.[49] Such strict demands were not easily accepted by the young, especially the boys. Nonetheless, a group of Crusaders did manage to disrupt the Zagreb performance of scantily clad Josephine Baker.[50]

Additionally, the Crusaders continued organizing Sunday parades, collective communions, and public meetings for the community, with singing, theater, and oratory. In this fashion, they stayed in the public eye as an important religious and national organization.[51] Eucharistic congresses in big cities were places and times for mass gatherings, when boys and girls traveled to Zagreb or Sarajevo from the greatest distance to demonstrate the magnitude of Catholicism.[52] The celebration of Christ the King was established as a new holiday in 1925, by which the Catholic Church wanted to underline the sovereignty of Christ even in this world. It became one of the most important dates in the Crusaders' calendar, as did the Pope's Day from 1932. On these occasions, the president of the Great Crusaders' Brotherhood, Ivo Protulipac, used his oratorical skill to deliver speeches that landed him in court, accused of political involvement.[53]

Those accusations were largely related to the Crusaders' Croat nationalism. From the beginning, love for the homeland was declared to be a religious duty and one of the principles of the organization. Yet the homeland was not Yugoslavia, but Croatia, imagined in its greater version, as the land where Croat people lived, including Bosnia, Herzegovina, and Bačka. Especially in those areas beyond Croatia proper, the Crusaders' movement fostered a process of national integration and integral Croat national identity. Thus in Sombor, Teslić, and Sarajevo, the Crusaders shared the vision of Holy Croatia, learned about Croatian history, and sang the Croatian anthem at every meeting, just like their fellows in Zagreb or Senj. The movement proceeded within a strictly national framework, so that even contacts with their Slovenian counterparts were not pursued. The Crusaders provided young people with an alternative way of life through which the leadership sought to separate them from both non-Catholic and Yugoslav influences.

In all the texts produced by and for the Eagles and Crusaders, the name of the state, Yugoslavia, was rarely if ever mentioned. "In this state" was the usual way of identifying the entity containing the "homeland," which was always understood as Greater Croatia. Nor was there any mention of non-Catholic citizens and neighbors, of Orthodox Christians or Muslims.[54] The past they related to was the narrative of Croatian kings, freedom fighters, and Croatian relations with the papacy throughout history.

By the late 1930s, the nation was gaining equal importance with God in the Crusaders' agenda. More than before, the catchwords "God, Church, Homeland" appeared in their discourse. Membership grew along with the Croat national movement for political emancipation from Belgrade. Protulipac approached Vladko Maček, Radić's successor as head of the dominant and expanding Croatian Peasant Party, who had cut back on his predecessor's anti-clericalism. This approach prompted internal dissension inside the Catholic movement against Protulipac.[55] The hierarchy decided to intervene in the longstanding rivalry between the Crusaders and the *Domagoj* (Seniors), over which it did not have enough control. The attempt to put all Catholic organizations under one authority was, however, unsuccessful. In 1936 Protulipac was first appointed to the position of the president of Catholic Action, the umbrella organization, but soon resigned under pressure from his opponents. They now came from two directions, not just from the rival

The first public performance of the Little Crusaders' brass band in Dubrovnik (1939)

Domagoj but also from an increasingly assertive Archbishop Stepinac. Stepinac then founded the so-called neutral Catholic Action, a set of class-based organizations for Catholic peasants, workers and students, in which the Seniors held leading positions.[56]

After Protulipac was dismissed by Stepinac in 1938, he weakened the Crusaders' organization further the next year when he formed a new youth organization, *Hrvatski Junak* (Croat Hero). He did so in cooperation with several leading figures from the Croat Peasant Party, former active members of the Croat Falcon, and some former Crusaders. After fifteen years at the head of the Catholic movement, Protulipac now created a militant, exclusive nationalist organization that, by some accounts, advocated fascist ways of mobilizing the young.[57] Apparently, many Crusaders joined the Croat Hero, which was supported by the newly permissive Maček administration of the enlarged and explicitly Croatian *banovina*.[58] The outbreak of war in 1941 deepened the crisis for any separate Catholic movement. The Crusaders enthusiastically welcomed the proclamation of Croatian independence as the final coming of the New Holy Croatia for which they had fought over the past two decades. Four days after the invasion of Yugoslavia and the bombing of Belgrade, on 10 April, German troops entered Zagreb and made it possible for leaders of the Fascist Ustaša party, (see chapter 2) to proclaim the Independent State of Croatia. The Crusaders' newspaper cheered the "resurrection of the Croatian state" as the most beautiful Easter in all Croat history. The accomplishment of their dreams about the state, expressed in Document 5, was even seen by some as a fulfillment of the Crusaders' mission and the end of their *raison d'être*.

There was, however, no special place for Crusaders within the Ustaša state apparatus. The regime demanded mandatory participation in the "Ustaša Youth" for all children and young people. Its leader, Ivan Oršanić, had been an active member of the Eagles' administration in the 1920s (as was his good friend Dušan Žanko, now intendant of the Croatian National Theater). During his reception of twenty-nine Crusader leaders on 19 June 1941, Ustaša chief Ante Pavelić expressed his desire to cooperate with the Crusaders, but it seems that not much happened after that. Other Crusader leaders soon took high-ranking positions within the Ustaša Youth.[59] When a group of Crusader leaders visited the influential canon of the Sarajevo archdiocese, Čedomil Čekada, he sharply criticized the participation of Crusaders in the Ustaša movement as "intolerable politicization." Marica Stanković justified the inclusion of her colleagues in the leadership of Ustaša Youth on the grounds that they had to prevent the dominance of liberals and anti-Catholics in the only official youth organization.[60]

By the end of 1941, internal discussions prompted another effort to depoliticize the Crusaders' organization. It was proclaimed in an official resolution

of December 1941 that members who had already entered the Ustaša movement or the state administration must leave the Crusaders. Consequently,
the president of the Great Crusader Brotherhood, Felix Niedzielsky, left the
Crusaders in 1942. The Crusaders' newspaper *Nedjelja* stopped putting pan-
egyrics to Ante Pavelić on its front page. Favorable news about the Ustaša
movement, plus anti-Semitic and anti-Communist articles that had appeared
during the first six months after the proclamation of the new state, now vanished. Besides traditional religious topics, it covered news about Crusaders
who died in the Ustaša and regular army ranks fighting against the "bandits." Letters were printed from Crusaders on the Eastern front in Ukraine
who wrote of their pride in fighting against the bestial Reds. As Živko
Kustić put it later, "If I had been a few years older, I would have definitely
volunteered for the Eastern front against the Bolsheviks."[61]

With this wider war, the activities of the Crusaders' organization declined.
Male members volunteered or were recruited into the regular army. Female
Crusaders provided food and lodging for refugee members, as well as continued education for refugee school children.[62] They continued such activities after the Communist assumption of power in May 1945. In an agreement with the Crusader leadership, Archbishop Stepinac disbanded the formal Crusader organization. Yet some groups continued to work. Marica
Stanković, the restless activist, pursued her apostolic vocation in these new
circumstances. Some female Crusaders helped captured soldiers of defeated
armies in the partisan POW camps by providing them with food, underwear
or medicine.[63] They met secretly in churches. But Marica Stanković also
continued to promote what was the essence of the Crusaders' ideology—
publicly defending the church and Catholicism. As a teacher, she attended
the great meeting of teachers convoked by the Communists on 2 July 1945,
at which the speakers attacked Archbishop Stepinac. She and a colleague
publicly voiced their disagreement and disgust with what they regarded as
defamation of their shepherd. She was arrested in September 1947, accused
of conspiracy and anti-state activities, and sentenced to five years' impris-
onment, together with seven other (mainly female) Crusaders. She spent
five years in harsh postwar detention, along with female Crusaders who were
active Ustašas and nationalists, opposed to her more religious orientation.[64]

Conclusion

Marked by the "clericalist" stigma in the Communist period, the Eagles and
the Crusaders still remain in the shadow of contemporary Croatian historiography's interest in the controversial figure of Archbishop Stepinac. Yet
the role of the Catholic Church in shaping modern Croat identity cannot be

properly assessed without further research into grassroots Catholic organizing. The same could be said of interwar Croatian political history, often too narrowly focused on the Croat Peasant Party and its success in elections. A brief glance, offered by this study, at the political landscape in smaller communities shows that irreconcilable political differences were to be found even among teenagers. This invites us to further study of the political orientation and influence of the Catholic Church in interwar and wartime Croatia and Yugoslavia.

As for Catholic grassroots mobilization, whether in the form of gymnastics or as an alternative educational initiative, the principle message sent to the youngsters was always the same: be Catholic and speak out. Their leaders, mainly young laypersons themselves, were selling an old idea on the market of historically new competing ideologies: liberalism, Communism, nationalism, Yugoslavism. Not least of the sources of their appeal was the method of mobilization they used. Collective participation in parades, processions or gymnastic performances, with all participants dressed as one, together with confidence in the world dimension of Catholicism affirmed through mass celebrations with thousands taking part, fostered the process of identity-building among receptive adolescents. The merging of religious and national identity with particular efforts to ensure its presence in the public realm were, in a multi-religious and multi-national country such as Yugoslavia was,[65] necessarily perceived as a strong political choice. Its cultural and social consequences survived the twentieth century.

Sources

Document 1:

Here we are in Sinj, a nice squad of male and female Eagles, but our adversaries are always nagging us because to them we are a constant pain in the neck. The other day (the 21st of the current month) they proved the full extent of their hatred. Our whole Eagle society undertook an excursion to a nearby village close to the Cetina River. There we held our assembly and the whole program in nature. You can imagine how wonderful we felt. We all started parading from Sinj as early as half past seven, accompanied by our marching band, and arrived at the destination of the excursion around nine o'clock. It was more delightful there than at any promenade. We had fun all day long and in the evening, at around six-thirty, we arrived at the market place in Sinj, where we were met by Falcon bandits. But God was with us. We were informed by their party that Falcons were getting ready and that we should be prepared. We were marching without

fear in our most imposing stride to the sound of our band, playing the
Eagle's march, when all of a sudden their people rushed and started
slapping our people. But ours yelled "hurrah," charged, and pounded
them good. They got what they asked for. And so, my dear friend,
they are only making us stronger with these attacks, and are even disregarded by their own smarter party members. This is what I really
wanted to describe to you in detail.

Source: A letter written by Fileta Franjić from Sinj, 1922, published in: Marica
Stanković, *Mladost vedrine* (Zagreb: Veliko Križarsko Sestrinstvo, 1944), 25.

Document 2:

At the beginning of August this year, all Croat Eagles should gather
in this old Croatian city in Dalmatia—*first* because the importance of
the *slet* about to be held demands it, and *secondly* because with that
slet the Croat Eaglehood is celebrating the thousandth anniversary of
our kingdom.

The *slet* is by itself a very powerful tool of our work. During the
slet we become aware of our forces and strengthen our brotherhood.
We put forth much propaganda for Eaglehood and through public
manifestos assert to the public the strength and magnitude of our
principles. We become visible to the world with all our values, present ourselves to the people with one complete performance, and
announce our final victory to the liberal intelligentsia.

Yes, all of this is waiting for us in Šibenik. The consciousness of
our Eagles' duty is calling us there, because a young Eagles' army is
about to be shown there for the first time in all its present strength
that it has among the Croats.

But our ardent patriotic love is also calling us there. The consciousness of Croatianhood and nationality. Šibenik is placed in the
middle of the Croatian kingdom's cradle, on the rugged Dalmatian
coast, where the Croatian national crown sprouted and developed its
activities throughout the centuries—from great Tomislav to the last
one, Peter.

It is the best place to celebrate the millennium, where the Croat
Eaglehood needs to perform with the utmost dignity and thus express
its patriotic feelings. To the sounds of the Eagles' anthem, thousands
of Eagles' voices should shout to the first king: Glory!

Therefore, brethren Eagles, get busy!

Prepare your Eagle uniforms, so that we can show ourselves in all
our beauty and shine as the knights of Christ. ...

Particular attention should be given to the special exercise, "The

Croats from Their Time of Arrival until Tomislav," which every
Eagle should know. ...

Once again I shout, **brethren Eagles, let's go to Šibenik, so that
we can repay our debt to mighty Tomislav with our Eagles' strength
and prove to the world that**

we are still a strong Croat race.

God lives!

(*Note:* emphasis and display of the text as in the original form, except for the word
"slet.")

Source: Dušan Žanko, "Let's go to Šibenik!", *Organizacijski vjesnik* 3, no. 3, 1 May
1925, 1.

Document 3:

To accomplish their goal, the Crusaders will:

1. endeavor that all member Crusaders be Catholic in their lives, full
   of faith and God's spirit. Therefore, all members will:
   a) participate in church meetings, at least once a month, when the
   chaplain determines;
   b) live by the principles of the Catholic faith and collectively
   receive Holy Communion every month;
   c) attend to spiritual exercises at least every other year. If it is not
   possible to observe closed spiritual exercises (especially in the
   Home of Spiritual Exercises), the exercises will be organized
   for the whole membership in a local church;
   d) collectively participate in religious celebrations, everyone with
   his own society, according to the decisions of the council of the
   Crusader Brotherhood or superior units. Participation in the
   Easter and Corpus Christi processions is always collective;
   e) celebrate together special Crusader holidays;
   f) be active in liturgical life and spread the liturgical movement.
2. endeavor that all members receive the right education, suffused
   with religious truths, and are ready in their knowledge, inspired by
   the spirit of togetherness in their lifework. Therefore, they will:
   a) organize Crusader meetings, instructors' lectures, and courses of
   study on religious, cultural, social, and general issues;
   b) establish libraries and reading rooms, rehearse and give performances, recitations, etc.;
   c) foster music and singing, especially liturgical;
   d) nourish the fellowship by collective games, excursions, etc.

3. spread Catholic consciousness, determination, and instruction among Catholic population, especially through:

    a) fighting against cursing and swearing, our national evil;

    b) working for devoting the family to the Holy Heart of Jesus, working on the mobilization of the masses in religious associations, spreading the Catholic press, etc.;

    c) organization of manifestations, special religiously instructive lectures for the common people, meetings, conventions, entertainment in the Catholic spirit, our society's papers and publications;

    d) helping the ecclesiastical authorities in pastoralization, particularly by participating in the catechistic education of believers as catechism instructors, as well as by working for the missions in missionary sections of their own.

4. In order to facilitate their work, the Crusaders will collect material funds from membership fees, contributions, donations, and manifestations.

5. For female Crusaders, special regulations are to be decreed.

Source: "The means of social work," from the *Manual of the Crusaders' Organization* (1930), published in: Božidar Nagy, *Hrvatsko Križarstvo: Pregled osnivanja, razvoja i obnove Križarske katoličke organizacije u Hrvatskoj* (Zagreb: Križarska organizacija—Postulatura za beatifikaciju Ivana Merza, 1995), 108

Document 4:

Yes, if we want all our people to be reborn in Christ, if we want the former religious ardor of the Croats to return to the hearts of our children, our youth, families, and public life, it is impossible to accomplish this without a woman, a mother, and a girl. She makes the basis of the family, she has children's education in her hands, her influence on public life is constantly growing stronger and larger. ...

Liberal organizations have well noticed the importance of the woman and her influence on the family and public life, and therefore are making efforts to conquer the woman's world, especially female youth. Only among us, the Catholics, do many still question whether it is necessary to organize female youth in Catholic associations. ... Girls are good by their nature, they are pious, so at this moment they don't need any association. The most important task is to organize young men. ... This is the wisdom of some who, in the end, don't organize either of them, because the liberal organizations have already taken the youth away.

The Female Crusaders' Organization clearly and openly announces:

We want a strong, firm, solid movement of Croatian Catholic female youth. We want religiously and eucharistically built units, which will nourish with the richness of their souls everyone with whom woman by her vocation comes in touch. We want thoroughly educated girls, whose life will be completely permeated by Catholic principles, the principles of real truth and devoted love for their fellow men. We want to create a strong army among the girls, always ready to fight for the Kingdom of Christ. ...

Although the Female Crusaders are not the only religious organization among us, none of the others carries out work with children as systematically as we do. The little five-year-old girls are already organized, and by the age of fifteen the delicate child soul must be completely cultivated in the Catholic spirit. Our best members come from the troops of the Little Crusaders.

In this way the Female Crusaders' Organization has organized children, girls, and women, because when a Crusader girl gets married, she becomes a leader and stays in touch with the association. ...

Like no other organization, we develop in a girl a sense of apostleship, apostolate in family and in public. Today we need strong, formed, iron women and girls that will raise their voices everywhere. This is the essential characteristic of the Female Crusaders' Organization. We cannot find it in any other organization. Therefore, we are certain that every friend of Catholic thought will support our organization. There should not be a place without it. Let the Crusaders unite all the noble girls of our villages and towns.

Source: Marica Stanković, "Why the Female Crusaders' Organization?" *Križ* 3, 5 May 1932, 5–6.

Document 5:

The Great Crusader Brotherhood has passed on, through Ustaša military chaplain Dr. Ivo Guberina and Reverends Cvitanović and Vitezić, this salutation to the *Poglavnik*, the regime's leader Ante Pavelić:

"It is our indescribable joy and happiness that, on behalf of the Great Crusader Brotherhood and the whole Crusaders' Organization, we can salute our *Poglavnik*, liberator of the Croat people and founder of the independent State of Croatia. ·

Our members, led by our motto, "Sacrifice, Eucharist, Apostolate," had no fear of difficulties; on their communion bench they sought heavenly solace, and among the people they were the apostles of our religious and national sanctities. Raised in the spirit of Catholic radicalism, which in its principles knows no compromise, they had no knowledge of yielding in the Croat nationalist program, either.

Today, when the sun of freedom has shone, we remember all the events and mishaps of our long-lasting activities. We remember how gendarmes and mercenaries of former regimes battered our members, stamped on our flags, tore off Croatian colors and badges from our chests, restricted our work in church and sacristy, until our members among the Senj victims and in other places testified to their idealism with blood and their own lives. But at the same time we remember our meetings and camping, when young men inscribed the letters "ŽAP" [acronym for "Long live Ante Pavelić"] onto the tree barks, and when at night, around the campfires, reverberated the song, "Come back, Ante, Croatia is calling you!"

Dear *Poglavnik*, the Crusaders salute you and declare their deep love and loyalty to you. Let the Almighty bless you and our state! And the Crusaders will keep on building immortal souls for God, and unbreakable characters for the Croat nation.

God lives! For homeland prepared!
Chaplain-General Dr. Milan Beluhan
President Dr. Felix Niedzielski
Secretary Ivica Kribić

Source: "Crusaders Greet the State of Croatia and the *Poglavnik*," *Nedjelja*, 27 April 1941, 2.

Notes

1 Any involvement of priests and commited Catholics in politics, including those referred to in this chapter, was simply labeled by its opponents and post-1945 Communist historiography as "clericalism." Post-Communist historiography prefers to speak of "organized Catholicism," "political Catholicism," even "Catholic Croatism" and "Catholic Yugoslavism," their respective national programs. The most detailed monographs are Jure Krišto, *Prešućena povijest: Katolička crkva u hrvatskoj politici, 1850–1918* (Zagreb: Hrvatska sveučilišna naklada, 1994); Mario Strecha, *Katoličko hrvatstvo: Počeci političkog katolicizma u banskoj Hrvatskoj, 1897–1904* (Zagreb: Barbat, 1997); and Zlatko Matijević, *Slom politike katoličkog jugoslavenstva: Hrvatska pučka stranka u političkom životu Kraljevine SHS, 1919–1929* (Zagreb: Hrvatski institut za povijest, 1998). There is no comprehensive nor analytical historiographic account of the professedly apolitical youth organizations examined in this chapter, except for an uncritical book by Božidar Nagy, *Hrvatsko križarstvo: Pregled osnivanja, razvoja i obnove Križarske*

katoličke organizacije u Hrvatskoj (Zagreb: Križarska organizacija—Postulatura za beatifikaciju Ivana Merza, 1995).

2 See Martin Conway, *Catholic Politics in Europe, 1918–1945* (London: Routledge, 1997), 40–44.

3 Anton Mahnič, *Knjiga života. Izvatci iz govora i članaka Biskupa Antuna Mahniča*, 149, as quoted in Nagy, 14.

4 See Herbert Jedin, ed., *Velika povijest crkve*, vol. 6, part 2 (Zagreb: Kršćanska sadašnjost, 1981).

5 Until then, according to the Concordat that had regulated the position of the church in the Habsburg monarchy since 1855, the church in Croatia had suffered only the loss of the direct control of public schools. Strecha, *Katoličko hrvatstvo*, 57–60. The defense of Catholic principles as fundamental collective values of the Croat nation was used for the first time in the election campaign of 1897, with a large participation of priests. Strecha, *Katoličko hrvatstvo*, 64. In 1900 the first forum of organized Catholics, the Croatian Catholic Congress, took place in Zagreb.

6 See Mark Biondich's preceding chapter on the evolution of Croat nationalism.

7 For detailed accounts of the Catholic movement until 1918, see Strecha, *Katoličko hrvatstvo*, and Krišto, *Prešućena povijest*.

8 Mirjana Gross, "Studentski pokret 1875–1914," in *Spomenica u povodu proslave 300-godišnjice Sveučilišta u Zagrebu* (Zagreb: Sveučilište u Zagrebu, 1969), 456.

9 They were forbidden to study in Zagreb after they had burnt the Hungarian flag during Emperor Francis Joseph's visit to Zagreb in 1895.

10 See Mile Vidović, *Povijest Crkve u Hrvata* (Split: Crkva u svijetu, 1996), 355–59.

11 He was influenced by Spanish Catholic writer F. Sardà y Salvany, who in the 1880s in his book *Liberalism Is a Sin* demanded that the Catholic Church formally condemn liberalism and all modern ideas born after the French Revolution, as Pope Pius IX had done in his 1864 *Syllabus of Errors*. Strecha, *Katoličko hrvatstvo*, 218.

12 As Anton Bozanić explains, the division of spirits (in Slovenian *ločitev duhov*, in Croatian *dioba duhova*) was "the cultural struggle that was supposed to result not only in drawing the line between conservative Catholic and liberal intellectuals, but also in the gradual elimination from public life of all ideas that contradicted in any way the Catholic interpretation of reality." Quoted in Strecha, *Katoličko hrvatstvo*, 219. Cf. the *Kulturkampf* in Germany in the 1870s.

13 "Radical Catholicism" and "Catholic radicalism" were the terms used by the movement's participants themselves. This basically meant consistency in faith and actions. Protulipac defines Catholic radicalism as the public profession of faith. To Mahnič the term is opposed to Catholic liberalism—defined as "Catholic duplicity, compromise of the Catholics with the devil by reason of 'peace, concord, and general unity.'" Such behavior included reading the atheist or anti-Catholic press and supporting anti-Catholic political parties, while at the same time attending church. See Ivo Protulipac, *Hrvatsko Orlovstvo* (Zagreb, 1926), 18–20.

14 Vlado Šrajcer, *Luč* 1912–1913, no. 17–20, as quoted in Krišto, *Prešićena povijest*, 197.

15 Initiator Ivan Butković was a priest from the island of Krk, Mahnič's diocese.

16 See Zlatko Matijević, *Slom politike katoličkog jugoslavenstva*, and idem, "Hrvatska pučka stranka i dr. Ivan Merz," *Obnovljeni život*, 3–4 (1997): 232–33. The majority of Croatian votes was gradually taken over by the Croat Peasant Party, whose leader Stjepan Radić became the incarnation of the Croat national movement in the first decade of life in the common state of the South Slavs.

17 As the archives of the Crusaders' organization were seized by the Communist security service after the Second World War and their whereabouts are still unknown, we have only summary data on membership during the period 1931–1939, as follows: 3,600 (1931), 4,755 (1932), 8,800 (1933), 11,599 (1934), 14,060 (1935), 16,508 (1936), 22,800 (1937), 26,689 (1938). These numbers apply to the Great Crusader Brotherhood, the organization's male branch. It was divided into class-based subgroups. In 1937, there were 1,000 high-school students, 4,610 workers, 8,700 peasants, and 8,490 Little Crusaders (under fifteen years old). As for the Great Crusader Sorority, data for 1938 indicate 15,000 members in 414 sororities—123 for peasant girls, 74 for working girls, 25 for high-school students, 185 for Little Crusaders, and 7 for leaders. Nagy, *Hrvatsko križarstvo*, 158–159. At the same time (1939), there were 590 members of *Domagoj*, 47,000 members of the Yugoslav Falcon in Croatia proper (adults and non-Croats included), and 9,000 members of the Communist Youth (SKOJ) in the whole of Yugoslavia. For membership of the Yugoslav Falcon, see Nikola Žutić, *Sokoli: Ideologija u fizičkoj kulturi Kraljevine Jugoslavije, 1929–1941* (Beograd: Angrotrade, 1991), 167. For the Communist Youth, see *Povijest Saveza komunista Jugoslavije* (Beograd: Izdavački centar Komunist – Narodna knjiga – Rad, 1985), 152. The total population of Croatia in 1931 was 3,430,000, while the ethnic Croats in all of Yugoslavia totaled three million.

18 Ivan Merz (1896–1928) devoted all of his short life to organizing Catholic youth. He studied literature in Paris (1920–1922), where he became acquainted with organizations such as La Croisade eucharistique française, whose slogan "Sacrifice, Eucharist, Apostolate" he borrowed for the Eagles. He was the moving spirit and secretary of the Croatian Eagle Union from its founding until his death. The process of his beatification is currently (2002) in its final phase.

19 URL: http://www.ewtn.com/library/encyc/p11arcan.htm

20 For concise information on the Eagles in Czechoslovakia, see Miloš Trapl, *Political Catholicism and the Czechoslovak People's Party in Czechoslovakia, 1918–1938* (Boulder, Col.: Social Science Monographs, 1995), 35.

21 Compare these to the symbolic apparatus of the Communist Pioneers analyzed in chapter 6 below by Ildiko Erdei. The white cross, cap and uniform were also seen as a constant spur to the member's good behavior.

22 It seems that the geographical distribution of the Eagle branches corresponded to the previous divisions between pro-Yugoslav Seniors and Domagoj, on the one hand, and the uncompromising faction, on the other. Thus, strong centers of Eaglehood, and later Crusaders, were the diocese of Sarajevo (Bosnia), Slavonia, central and northern Croatia, the diocese of Šibenik in Dalmatia, and the Adriatic islands. The bishops that especially supported their work were Antun Bauer (Zagreb), Ivan Ev. Šarić (Sarajevo), Josip Srebrnić (Krk), Jerolim Mileta (Šibenik), Mihovil Pušić (Hvar), Antun Akšamović (Đakovo), Petar Čule (Mostar), and Smiljan Čekada (Skopje, Sarajevo). Nagy, *Hrvatsko*

križarstvo, 68. There were very few branches in Herzegovina, or in ethnically mixed areas of Croatia such as Lika. The Jesuits tended to support the Eagles and Crusaders more than the Franciscans did.

23 The president of the Croatian Eagle Union and of the Great Crusader Brotherhood until 1938 was Ivo Protulipac (1899–1946), a lawyer, and the president of the female Eagles and Great Crusader Sorority until 1945 was Marica Stanković (1900–1957), a teacher.

24 Dušan M. Bogunović, *Pregled telesnog odgoja i Sokolstva* (Zagreb: Hrvatski štamparski zavod, 1925), 66–96. On the unification of ethnic Falcons into one Yugoslav organization, see Dušan M. Bogunović, *Od Ujedinjenja Sokolstva do II. Sokolskog Sabora* (Zagreb, 1924).

25 Engaged by the National Council of Slovenes, Croats and Serbs, the Falcons participated in the armed conflict with the former Austro-Hungarian soldiers who demonstrated in favor of the republic on 5 December 1918. See Ferdo Čulinović, *Jugoslavija između dva rata* (Zagreb: Izdavački zavod JAZU, 1961), 1: 160–68.

26 For instance, Croatian nationalistic authorities in the 1880s enabled the Croatian Falcons to teach Falcon gymnastics in schools. The subsequent oppressive regime of Khuen-Héderváry, in order to suppress Yugoslavism, curricula in 1893, propagated the introduction of the Swedish gymnastic system into school curricula, as it was different from the Slavic and the German systems alike. Žutić, *Sokoli*, 6. Gymnastic systems were considered to be expressions of national spirit.

27 Protulipac, *Hrvatsko Orlovstvo*, 20–26.

28 The Falcon program also included light athletics and exercises with equipment; hence their members participated in European gymnastic competitions. Among the Eagles, such disciplines were recommended for advanced members, if circumstances allowed. The ideal was a healthy, harmonious and beautiful body, without exaggerated muscle size or tone.

29 *Organizacijski vijesnik* 6 (1924): 4–5. See also *Priručnik Orlovske organizacije* (Osijek: Naklada Strossmayerovo orlovsko okružjc Đakovo, 1923), 118–22. Public performance is there presented as an image of success, an agitational tool, and a source of enthusiasm and courage.

30 The first great international Eagle *slet*, in which Croatian Catholics participated, was held in Ljubljana in 1920. In 1922, in Brno (Czechoslovakia), the Croatian flag was carried by the future Zagreb archbishop, young Alojzije Stepinac.

31 See Dušan Žanko, "Two words on symbolic exercises," *Organizacijski vijesnik* 2 (February 1925): 15.

32 "No one can serve two masters!" *Organizacijski vijesnik* 1 (January 1926): 23. The fact that members of those organizations and clubs could also belong to other religions was perceived as a particular problem. In fact, the readers were warned that for that reason "the Church condemns joining those associations."

33 Žutić, *Sokoli*, 23.

34 Ibid. See also Marica Stanković, *Mladost vedrine* (Zagreb: Veliko križarsko sestrinstvo, 1944), 21. The Yugoslav Falcon was temporarily the only organization in which a high-school student could engage.

35 As in the ethnically mixed town of Pakrac. *Nedjelja*, 1940, no. 4, and no. 34: 3.

36 "Falcon is Falcon, whether Croat or Yugoslav. For us, it is a liberal organization we have to suppress every step of the way. The brethren have a duty to distribute our new inexpensive brochure, 'The Croat Falcon from the Catholic point of view,' especially among Catholics who maybe still sympathize with this Falcon. We need to break their ridiculous illusions that this Falcon isn't liberal and atheist."—"Mi i hrvatsko Sokolstvo," *Organizacijski vijesnik* 10/11 (November/December 1924): 7. The paper also invited members to submit reports on activities of both Croatian and Yugoslav Falcons in their towns, with special attention to their attitude toward religion. It was suggested that the leader of the Falcons was an apostate priest and that Catholics only joined the Falcons because they wanted to be good Croats, or for the sake of fun. *Organizacijski vijesnik* 1 (January 1925): 3.

37 Membership of the Eagles in the extremist Croatian Nationalist Youth (*Hanao*) was also strictly forbidden. "Our Eagles are definitely better Croats and will be enormously more useful, and bring more good to our people, than the elements that have elevated nationalism to the altar but serve it with every means." *Organizacijski vijesnik* 10/11 (October/November 1924): 7. However, it is not possible to find a specific political program or standpoint on the Croat national question or the Yugoslav state (e.g., federation vs. a unitary state, separatism, republicanism). Those issues were seen as quintessentially political and therefore avoided.

38 Fights over politics between the memberships of Eagle and Falcon were reported in Imotski (1925), in Cernik (Slavonia, 1926), in Čitluk (Herzegovina, 1927) where weapons were fired, in the village of Bojnikovac near Bjelovar (1928), and in Tuzla (Bosnia, 1929). Stanković, *Mladost vedrine*, 53–54; *Orlovska straža* 5 (1927), 4: 129–30; 6 (1928), 10. In August 1940, in Sombor (Vojvodina), the members of the local soccer team attacked the Crusaders that wore Crusader uniforms, while the following week the Falcons disrupted the Crusaders' assembly in Pag. *Nedjelja* 1940, no. 34: 8 and no. 35: 4. See also Nagy, *Hrvatsko križarstvo*, 202–4, for reports on conflicts with the Communist Youth (SKOJ) and Peasant Concord (*Seljačka sloga*), an educational organization of the Croat Peasant Party.

39 A girl from the village of Rakitovica, in Slavonia, wrote to Zagreb in 1927 how "many think that our organization is political and directed against Radić's movement. The villagers protest and incite the membership to split. Without our own hall, we exercised in our private homes, and when the weather was fine we met outside in the field, where we were exercising and reading. ... " Stanković, *Mladost vedrine*, 50.

40 The Croatian words *prosvjeta* and *odgoj*, used to define the Eaglehood, imply more than education—the former has the connotation of "enlightenment" and "mass education," while the latter means "upbringing," often more precisely defined as of a physical, moral, religious, and patriotic sort.

41 Žutić, *Sokoli*, 40.

42 Nagy, *Hrvatsko križarstvo*, 88–103. The first issue of the new journal, *Križ,* was sequestered, Protulipac imprisoned, and Archbishop Bauer put under pressure to ban the Crusaders, but they persevered in their plans.

43 The role of priests in the organization was defined according to the principles of the Catholic Action, thanks to Ivan Merz. While in Slovenia priests could become members of the Eagle, though not in any special position, in Croatia the members were strictly laypersons; but every organization had one priest as a spiritual guide, the chaplain (*duhovnik*).

44 The Crusaders' organization assembled separate local organizations of peasants, workers, high-school students, leaders and children (Little Crusaders). Separation was grounded on the idea that each class (*stalež*) and gender had its own needs. The brotherhood of all classes and respect for fellow Eagles of different social rank were promoted in the spirit of Christian democracy.

45 Joso Felicinović and Frano Grgić, *Naš put: Nacrt za vjersko-prosvjetni rad omladine* (Zagreb: Veliko Križarsko Bratstvo, 1936), 6–11. As Živko Kustić remembers, "When I was fifteen, I already knew what revelation, dogma, and devout belief were, and what smelled like heresy. We knew all about the persecutions of Christians in Spain, Mexico, Russia; we knew who Hitler and Stalin were, we knew that Nazism, Fascism and Bolshevism were dangerous, negative phenomena." Nagy, *Hrvatsko križarstvo*, 212.

46 Stj. Tomislav Poglajen D. I., "Na *križarsku* vojnu protiv boljševičkog bezboštva," *Križ* 1 (January 1931): 12.

47 Felicinović, *Naš put*, 18–20. Also, "The Crusader has to wear his badge publicly on his chest, because he is sent out to defend God, the church, his nation and society. The Crusader has to be an apostle in the family, in the school, in the workshop, in the field, in the office, in the military barracks, in the parish, so that Christ's spirit is felt ·everywhere. At all times and in all places, Crusaders have to be apostles and soldiers of Christ the King." Ibid., 82.

48 Stanković, *Mladost vedrine*, 219–22.

49 A "resolution on fashion and dance" was passed in 1926 by the Union of Croat (Female) Eagles, under the influence of Ivan Merz. Stanković, *Mladost vedrine*, 35. Archbishop Stepinac later regularly devoted circular letters to issues such as dancing and bathing. For all aspects of desirable behavior, including standpoints on fashion, entertainment, the separate upbringing of boys and girls, and specific exercises for females, see Stanković, *Mladost vedrine*, 120–57.

50 Stanković, *Mladost vedrine*, 121.

51 "Our youth has to learn to openly profess the Catholic beliefs. Hence the collective holy communions, collective participation in processions or pilgrimage, advocacy of Catholic ideas, etc." Felicinović *Naš put*, 98.

52 In May 1932 one such Eucharist celebration took place in Sarajevo. The program included a procession with 15,000 people, a brass band, a parade with torches and lamps (all in red, white, and blue, the colors of the Croat national flag), a serenade under the episcopal building, the singing of patriotic and religious songs such as "To the Croats," "God and Croats," and "We Want God," an assembly in the National Theater, and a high mass. Josip Srebrnić, bishop of Krk, proclaimed the Eucharist congress in Sarajevo to be "the historical foundation for the future of Croat Herceg-Bosna" (i.e., Bosnia and Herzegovina). *Križ* 6 (June 1932): 9. The movement of Eucharist congresses originated in France in the 1880s. See Jedin, *Velika povijest crkve*, 248–49.

53 In 1930 he was accused of inciting religious hatred in his programmatic article in the first issue of the Crusaders' periodical *Križ*, but the charges were dropped. In 1938 he was again on trial, accused of antistate activities, because in his speech at the Eucharistic congress in Bosanski Brod, on 22 August 1937, he allegedly called for an independent Croatian state. See Vladimir Cicak, *Za istin: Nekoliko dokumenata povodom procesa vođenog protiv Dra Ive Protulipca* (Zagreb, 1938).

54 In her book written in 1944, Marica Stanković openly discourages religiously mixed marriages. Stanković, *Mladost vedrine*, 166.

55 See "O stogodišnjici rođenja Ivana Protulipca. Prilog povijesti hrvatskog katoličkog pokreta," *Kolo*, 2 (1999): 501–23. Protulipac (a lawyer) defended Maček in his trial at the Court for Protection of the State in 1933.

56 See Lav Znidarčić, "Organizirano djelovanje katoličkih svjetovnjaka na području Zagrebačke Nadbiskupije (1852–1994)," in *Zagrebačka biskupija i Zagreb, 1094–1994* (Zagreb: Nadbiskupija zagrebačka, 1995), 386–437.

57 The Croat Hero promoted the building of a "new man in a new and better Croatia," while its newspaper wrote sympathetically about militant organized youth in Italy, Germany, Slovakia and Japan. The program treated the youth as "the executor of national, social and cultural-revolutionary enterprises." (For a comparison with Romania's Legion of the Archangel Michael, see Constantin Iordachi's chapter 1 in this volume.) Zdenka Lakić, "Prodor ideologije fašizma u redove omladine. Djelovanje 'Hrvatskog junaka' u razdoblju 1939–1941," *Marksistička misao* 3 (1986): 74. Lakić traces continuity in the activities of some former Crusaders, who became activists in the Croat Hero and later joined the Ustaša movement. Ivo Protulipac was completely passive during the Second World War, but nonetheless in 1945 he fled the country with the Ustaša army and others. He was assassinated in Trieste in January 1946 by an agent of the Communist secret service.

58 A separate entity, *Banovina* Croatia was formed under the *Sporazum* of 1939 with the Belgrade government. In 1940 both the Yugoslav and Maček's (Croatian) administration intensified persecution of Communist and other political opponents, adopting anti-Jewish legislation as well.

59 Just to name a few: the president of the Great Crusader Brotherhood, Felix Niedzielsky, joined the state administration (as *podžupan*) in Tuzla and Banjaluka, and in 1944 became a commander in the Ustaša Youth, a position until then held by Ivan Oršanić, also a former Eagle. Vlasta Arnold joined the Women's Vine of the Ustaša movement and in 1943 became deputy commander. Kaja Pereković was active in the Women's Ustaša Youth.

60 Lav Znidarčić, "Sjećanje živih svjedoka na Čedomila Čekadu," in Marko Josipović and Mato Zorkić, ed., *Život u sužbi riječi. Čedomil Čekada* (Sarajevo: Vrhbosanska katolička teologija, 1997), 112.

61 Nagy, *Hrvatsko križarstvo*, 213.

62 Žarko Brzić, *Nasmijano lice. Tragom životnih putova prof. Marice Stanković* (Đakovački Selci: Župski ured, 1990), 102.

63 Brzić, *Nasmijano lice*, 55.

64 She wrote that only a few of the imprisoned (female) Crusaders were "politicians" (i.e., political activists). The majority were students and intellectuals, girls who idealisti-

cally joined the Ustaša Youth or out of charity helped outlaw Ustaše in the mountains. Marica Stanković, *Godine teške i bolne* (Zagreb: Glas koncila – Suradnice Krista Kralja, 2000), 40. See also Mara Čović, *Sjećanje – svjedočenje: Zvuči kao priča a bila je istina!* (Rijeka: Riječki nakladni zavod, 1996). It should be noted that those Ustaše who continued fighting after May 1945 appropriated the name of Crusaders but were not in any way related to this organization. Marica Stanković also founded the civic order, the Associates of Christ the King (*Zajednica Suradnica Krista Kralja*), which was an old wish of her spiritual teacher Ivan Merz, and devoted herself to this community after her return from prison. Brzić, *Nasmijano lice*, 32. She died in 1957. Lav Znidarčić, president of the Great Crusader Brotherhood from 1942, died in December 2001.

65 With a permanent identity crisis, as chapter 10 by Marko Bulatović in this volume demonstrates.

CHAPTER 4

James Frusetta

COMMON HEROES, DIVIDED CLAIMS:
IMRO Between Macedonia and Bulgaria

Who owns history? In the romantic, primordialist tradition of most national histories there is an assumption that historical events, institutions and individuals "belong" to a nation as part of its history. Modernity-based theories of nationalism on the other hand stress a modern "invention" of national identity based on interpretations and representations of the past: nations define themselves by what they *claim* for their national history. Both traditions intersect at the importance placed on the historical symbols used to define national identity and national history. National heroes, literature, folklore, events and the sites of events in the past—these are some of the symbols utilized to define what it means to be a member of a particular people.[1]

Disputes over history have helped fuel the continuation of the "Macedonian Question"—what is the ethnic identity of the inhabitants of Macedonia at present, and what was it in the past? In the Macedonian case, there are few historical symbols utilized by the Republic of Macedonia that are not disputed by conflicting historical traditions in neighboring states. Those competing claims on key symbols, in turn, are seen as provocative. Under the assumption that such symbols possess a quality of "objective truth," they cannot be shared: rival claims undermine the legitimacy of national identity.[2]

Bulgarian-Macedonian disputes over the identity of "national heroes" from the Internal Macedonian Revolutionary Organization (IMRO) such as Gotse Delchev and Yane Sandanski illustrate this rivalry.[3] During the socialist period the role of national ideology helped shape how each state utilized them as representatives of the nation. Transition from Communist rule after 1989 and the emergence of an independent Macedonian state in 1991 saw the rise of new uses of such symbols, now only partly moderated by the state and by academia as a wider, popular debate in the media, popular press, domestic political elections and other public forums arose. Despite significant internal disagreements within both countries over the "proper role" of these figures in national history, IMRO heroes are nonetheless claimed for one's own country—and denied to the other.[4]

The Lens of Socialist National Ideology: 1945–1989

The Communist regimes in both Yugoslavia and Bulgaria established after the Second World War sponsored history that approached the past in terms of approved ideology. As Dejan Jović notes in chapter 11 in this volume, Yugoslavia's party elites helped to shape new visions of the world. Through their efforts, writers of history served to support such new visions through representations of the past. History, often cast in a presentist framework, was called upon to support the legitimacy of the new socialist states by providing historical precedent.[5] For their part, the party leadership regulated access to state-owned publishing houses, university positions, records, research funding and opportunities for prestige. As the sole "market" for history, the state was correspondingly able to broadly influence the production of history.[6] Beyond academia, the state controlled those forums by which history could be distributed to a wider audience, such as the publication of "popular histories," print and broadcast media and the educational system. This resulted in a conflation of interests between historians and the state, and a certain degree of uniformity in approach.

National heroes were called upon to serve as symbols for the new socialist ideologies—assuming their actions could be reconciled as being properly progressive in nature. The vague populism or anarchism espoused by such IMRO leaders as Gotse Delchev[7] and Yane Sandanski[8] was transformed into overt socialism, of the sort ascribed to them in both Document 1 and Document 2.[9] The Macedonian revolutionary movement as a whole was characterized as a mass-based national liberation movement fighting foreign oppression. As such, it served as a precursor to the movements that established the People's Republic of Bulgaria and the Yugoslav Socialist Republic of Macedonia. In this common approach, the revolutionary nature of IMRO and its struggle against backward, regressive Ottoman rule was tied to the later, pro-socialist left wing of IMRO in the 1920s and its opposition to the repressive monarchist regimes of the period. Both, in turn, were tied to more recent struggles against fascism, against the former "bourgeois" regimes of both states, and against the new, postwar threat of American imperialism.

With broad agreement on the ideological use of Macedonian heroes by both Bulgaria and Macedonia, the potential for conflict was limited to issues of their *national* identity. As long as the Bulgarian Communist Party tacitly acknowledged Belgrade's lead on the recognition of a Macedonian nation, as it did from 1944 to 1948, this was not an issue.[10] Following the Tito-Stalin split of 1948, however, the Bulgarian government was free to change course and challenge the legitimacy of the Macedonian nation. From 1948 to 1989, disputes between the two states over Macedonian history had implicit political overtones and were influenced by the status of Bulgarian-Yugoslav relations.[11] Yet the dispute over the Macedonian nation also took on importance for the national ideology of both states over this period, beyond its "tactical significance" in international diplomacy. The heroes of IMRO would be called upon to serve both Communist regimes.[12]

In Macedonia, the federal government in Belgrade and the republic's government in Skopje fostered an official national ideology centered on a Macedonian national identity. The standardization of the Macedonian language, the creation of an autocephalous Macedonian Orthodox Church and new interpretations of history all reinforced this identity.[13] Macedonian national history was traced to the nineteenth century, with its most prominent expression being the revolutionary struggle for freedom, equality and independence.[14] As the vanguard of this people's movement, IMRO, was thus a consciously ethnically Macedonian and politically socialist organization. Historians made a direct connection between the Ilinden uprising of August 1903 and the Partisan struggle against Bulgarian and German occupation over 1941–1944: "Ilinden 1903 was the first Macedonian Ilinden. It foreshadowed the Second, which took place in 1941. Through these struggles the Macedonian people confirmed the historic existence of the Macedonian nation…"[15] Only through the latter struggle had, indeed, a Macedonian state finally been achieved. Its foundation in 1944 through the auspices of ASNOM in August 1944 (the Anti-fascist Assembly for the National Liberation of Macedonia) was supported by the Yugoslav Communist Party.

The Yugoslav Socialist Republic of Macedonia thus fulfilled the goals of Ilinden as defined by the new national ideology. The development of a Macedonian national history served as a cornerstone of the republic, along with the codification of the Macedonian language and the creation of a Macedonian Orthodox Church in 1958 (autocephalous after 1967).[16] Accordingly, it was crucial to prove that the leaders of IMRO were consciously Macedonian in identity and to enshrine them as part of a pantheon of national heroes.

Both Delchev and Sandanski were not only honored with monuments and publications but were adopted as symbols of the republic, as in Document 3—the Macedonian and their struggles were synonymous. The republic itself was characterized as the natural outgrowth of Delchev's aspirations for an autonomous Macedonian state.[17] During the socialist period both the popular press and academic publications focused on IMRO and its leaders: nearly two-fifths of the articles in the journal *Macedonian Review* over the years 1971 to 1989, for example, center on IMRO members, on the broader organization, or on the Ilinden uprising.[18]

At the same time, there was a tendency to cast "non-progressive" historical elements or factions within IMRO as explicitly Bulgarian in nature: Todor Aleksandrov, for example, was not only a reactionary agent of the bourgeoisie, he was also an agent of "Greater Bulgarianism" and the "chauvinist Bulgarian bourgeoisie."[19] Delchev and Sandanski were not only national heroes for their struggles against the Turks; they had opposed Bulgarian agents of assimilation and reactionary, pro-Bulgarian factions such as the Supreme Macedonian Committee. This reinforced their national identities as Macedonians. Bulgarian claims on Macedonian symbols could thus be portrayed as merely the most recent manifestation of a "chauvinist" attitude of long provenance and as direct attacks on the Macedonian people.[20]

The work of Macedonian historians could actively be used in support of political agendas *vis-à-vis* Bulgaria. For example, academic publications attesting to the Macedonian character of Pirin and Aegean Macedonia (in neighboring Bulgaria and Greece, respectively) bolstered the suggestion of their eventual unification with Yugoslav (Vardar) Macedonia. The legacy and identity put forward regarding Sandanski and other IMRO leaders, for example, supported arguments for the Macedonian character of the inhabitants of the Pirin region of Bulgaria, bolstering Skopje's potential claims on the region.[21]

In Bulgaria, the potential for the history of IMRO to be incorporated into a new Bulgarian socialist national ideology was more problematic. The organization had been associated between 1923 and 1934 with repressive, anti-Communist regimes in Bulgaria. IMRO had taken part in the violent overthrow of the Agrarian government of Aleksandar Stamboliiski in 1923, a regime that was now portrayed as a progressive historical precedent for the new people's republic. IMRO had, moreover, intervened actively against the abortive revolution of Bulgarian Communist Party (BCP) in that same year. The left wing of the movement was embarrassingly small and ineffective compared to the larger, nationalist factions. Finally, IMRO's reputation in Bulgaria in the interwar years had been tarnished by its repeated use of assassinations, its gangsterism and the violence between different factions of the movement. The BCP had in fact repressed the remaining elements of IMRO after taking power.[22]

Most importantly, the BCP's own recognition of a Macedonian nationality in 1944–48, and a more circumspect recognition of such over 1948–1956, restricted any initial incorporation of the Macedonian revolutionary movement into new versions of Bulgarian national history. Pressure from Moscow regarding relations with Belgrade influenced official policy regarding Macedonian history. This official policy of recognizing Macedonian identity was opposed, in turn, both by factions within the BCP and by members of the Macedonian émigré community living within Bulgaria.[23]

The BCP was thus initially ambiguous about drawing on Macedonian heroes in the new national pantheon. On the one hand, Delchev and Sandanski, among others, were honored with monuments and museum exhibits in the 1950s, and with newspaper articles in the regional publications. A further sign of favor was the renaming of towns in the Pirin region after both men; Sveti Vrach was renamed Sandanski in 1949 and Nevrokop as Gotse Delchev in 1950.[24] But unlike other revolutionary figures from Bulgarian history, Delchev and Sandanski were not presented in a systematic fashion. Recognition was piecemeal, and largely limited to the Pirin region. Typical was the Central Committee of the Politburo's decision in May 1953, which noted the fiftieth anniversary of the Ilinden uprising—yet in a related announcement listing the national "revolutionary fighters against Turkish slavery, fascism and imperialism," it included neither Delchev nor Sandanski.[25]

Articles on Macedonian topics in academic journals such as *Istoricheski Pregled* and academic monographs published on the subject were rare in the 1950s and early 1960s, although the subject was never a complete taboo.[26] Responding to the outpouring of material from Skopje, treatments of Macedonian history in the press and in academia seemed reactive. State-owned newspapers retaliated to perceived provocations from Skopje and Belgrade (and, indeed, to other contended issues in history), and the Bulgarian government occasionally protested specific provocations.[27] Still, there was initially no sustained, systematic attempt to integrate specifically Macedonian events as part of Bulgarian history.

By the 1960s, this Bulgarian policy of benign neglect began to change. There were moves to reclaim the Macedonian revolutionary movement as a part of Bulgarian history, encouraged at the highest levels of the Bulgarian Communist Party as seen in Document 4. Beginning in the 1960s, Bulgarian historians sought to prove the Bulgarian credentials of the Macedonian revolutionary movement. In laying claim to its history, Macedonian revolutionaries were portrayed as the inheritors of a tradition stemming from such prominent Bulgarian revolutionaries as Vasil Levski.[28] Academic treatments increased significantly during the period, although the history of the Macedonian movement remained something of a "backwater" and there remained conflict within the ranks of historians over methods of approach.

By the 1980s, the Bulgarian government was increasingly incorporating elements of integral, or ethnically exclusive, nationalism into national ideology. On the one hand, ethnic minorities such as Turks and Pomaks (Muslim ethnic Bulgarians) were encouraged (or forced) to assimilate or to emigrate.[29] Even as those minorities were suppressed, Macedonian historical themes enjoyed a new prominence—a number of articles on Macedonian history were released during the Celebration of 1300 years of the Bulgarian State that took place in 1981. Macedonian heroes were now openly identified as historical symbols for the Bulgarian state. That year, Liudmila Zhivkova (minister of culture, and daughter of party secretary Todor Zhivkov) listed both Delchev and Sandanski as among the "national heroes who fought for the freedom of the Bulgarian nation."[30] Delchev's elevation to an "apostle of freedom" now occasionally reached to the level of Levski:

"It was unlikely there was another personality in the national-liberation struggle of the Bulgarian nation whose life, deeds and exploits were so bright as to bear a resemblance to Vasil Levski, as was Gotse Delchev."[31]

Even Todor Aleksandrov, previously treated as something of a pariah for his role in suppressing agrarianism and the Bulgarian Communist Party in 1923, saw a partial rehabilitation by the mid-1980s by virtue of his professed Bulgarian nationalism and patriotism—not without significant debate among historians and members of the BCP regarding incorporation of a historical figure previously interpreted as a "fascist."[32] By the end of the Communist era, Macedonian history and its symbols were increasingly incorporated into the national ideology of Bulgaria.

After 1989: Fracturing the Lens

For the history of IMRO, the political transition to post-Communism in both Macedonia and Bulgaria proved to be a watershed. In both states, socialist national ideology had served to regulate the writing of history: historical approaches that were unacceptable found it difficult to obtain a public forum. The political transition in Bulgaria in 1989 and the emergence of an independent Macedonian state in 1991 greatly weakened the ability of both government and of professional academia to continue to act as gatekeepers of national history. Neither government was now willing to restrict debates over Macedonian history. The old pressures from Moscow and Belgrade to be circumspect in historical debates vanished—indeed, as emerging democracies both states were instead now pressured by the West to allow more open, public discussion of history. New claims on Macedonian heroes could now be voiced.

Within the Republic of Macedonia, political debates over the Yugoslav and Communist legacies left to the new state were mirrored by debates about what formulation the country's national history should take after independence.[33] Controversy initially centered on whether or not the half-century of

*50 denar stamp
commemorating Gotse
Delchev, issued 1994*

*40 denar outsize stamp
commemorating the 100th
anniversary of the Ilinden
uprising, issued 1993*

Communist historiography had deliberately distorted the historical record. Historians had marginalized or obscured certain figures that were politically unacceptable, such as Boris Sarafov, Metodij Shatorov and Metodij Antonov-Chento.[34] Debate over their contributions to Macedonian independence emerged soon after independence. Historians now argued over the previously exaggerated socialist qualifications of Delchev and Sandanski. The popular press seized on incidents such as the reputed Partisan massacre of Macedonian members in Skopje in December 1944 when they refused to march north and fight on the Srem Front against the retreating German army. From these debates emerged other questions. To what degree had the Communist Party in Belgrade and Skopje "controlled" the formation of a Macedonian national history? To what degree had native Macedonian traditions been obfuscated? The debate over such matters drew in members of the Macedonian National Institute for History and spread to both academic journals and the popular press.[35]

For many Macedonians, such debates were limited by the fact that there were no pre-socialist traditions of national history to which they could turn. The only autocthonic paradigms of Macedonian history were produced in the socialist period and relied on a linkage between IMRO and its hopes for Communist revolution. New alternative theories of national origin that might minimize IMRO and the Ilinden uprising—such as the descent of the modern Macedonian nation from intermarriage between migrating Slavs and remnants of the ancient Macedonian people of Alexander the Great— proved controversial at best among scholars, and met a mixed reception in popular forums. The academic production of history remains largely in the hands of historians trained in the old school of this national ideology, in institutions that remained state-funded and which largely retained their pre-1991 staff and outlook.[36] Although professional historians reassessed aspects of the old paradigm and removed some of its more overtly polemical theses, by and large historiographic traditions continued after the transition and proved slow to change.

New challenges from Greek and Bulgarian historians that Macedonian identity was the product of "Titoist brainwashing" encouraged Macedonian historians to focus on defending the historical legitimacy of that single identity for the population in general and IMRO specifically.[37] Greek foreign policy in the mid-1990s, including an economic embargo of the Republic of Macedonia, highlighted disagreements of portrayals of national history—the Greek government refusing to sanction any use of the term "Macedonia" by the new state since the term was held to be exclusively Greek in historical context.[38]

The political ramifications of independence influenced the shaping of a new national ideology. Coalition governments led by former members of the regional Communist Party of Macedonia and anti-Communist nationalists alike have maintained much of the pantheon of national heroes created under socialism and as such draw on them for symbols of the new state, as noted by the accompanying illustrations. Delchev, the Ilinden uprising and IMRO all adorned postage stamps in the early 1990s. The monument to the

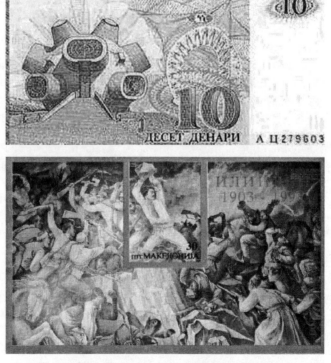

10 denar banknote, illustrated on the reverse with the Krushevo Monument to the Ilinden uprising, issued 1993
30 denar outsize stamp commemorating the 100th anniversary of the Ilinden uprising, issued 1993

Ilinden uprising of 1903 in Krushevo was used on the reverse of lower denomination banknotes issued in 1992, and on the front of the 10 denar note issued in 1993.

Several political parties adopted the legacy of IMRO; a number went so far as to name themselves after the movement.[39] Most ethnic Macedonian political parties saw the utility in portraying themselves as the true heirs of Delchev's ideology, adapting his legacy as appropriate for their agendas. Political leaders continued to link contemporary politics with Ilinden, such as claiming that that Macedonians "live in the time of the dreams of Gotse Delchev."[40] While the division of opinion between the precise nature of the history of IMRO continued, there was broad agreement that it represented something of crucial importance for Macedonian history.[41]

The Macedonian government in the 1990s could perhaps no longer strictly enforce a "standard" national history. But the perception of Macedonia as a state threatened by hostile neighbors, the diplomatic disputes with Greece and Bulgaria over the use of historical symbols, and the perceived threat posed by the ethnic Albanian minority encouraged a sense of cohesiveness. In a time of perceived crisis and with limited alternatives, there was little inclination among ethnic Macedonians as a whole for a radical restructuring of national symbols.

Transition in Bulgaria opened the way for a more pluralistic restructuring. With no credible threat to the existence of a Bulgarian nation there was perhaps more tolerance for public disagreement than in the Republic of Macedonia, and there was less incentive to keep the status quo in national history. Almost immediately after 1989 there were calls to change significantly the approach to the history of Macedonia and the Macedonian revolutionary movement. Particularly significant was the rapid reformation after 1989 of organizations suppressed during the Communist era. Most prominent were the Macedonian Scientific Institute (and its journal *Makedonski Pregled*) and the IMRO-Union of Macedonian Societies, which quickly evolved into a political party, as well as a number of smaller or regional organizations. Many Bulgarians of Macedonian origin, professing resentment of political interference in historical treatments, supported such groups —and were prominent in publishing the subsequent flood of memoirs, academic work and popular histories on the topic.[42] In many cases, these publications represented traditions of oral histories that had been handed down within families or localities and which had never been incorporated into "official" histories.[43] While many of these works were of scholarly merit, a strongly patriotic ethos permeates much of the work in question. This ethos, in turn, on occasion led these groups to criticize as "insufficiently patriotic" those Bulgarian historians who warned of the dangers of nationalism and irredentism.[44]

Some Bulgarian historians, particularly those affiliated with Macedonian organizations, now sought to reaffirm a Bulgarian identity for both the Macedonian revolutionary movement and for the population of Macedonia in general. National history as produced in Skopje was reviewed and rebutted, as was history produced in Bulgaria on the subject during the Communist period. The BCP's policies in the Pirin region during the 1940s and 1950s were particularly criticized—even derided as "national treason"—and a flood of new scholarly publications on the Macedonian question were released.[45] More provocative and less scholarly were tracts intended for a popular audience, such as Bozhidar Dimitrov's *Ten Lies of Macedonian History*.[46] Forays into popular history and newspapers by historians, as in Document 6, tended to blur the distinction between writing history for an academic and for a popular audience. On the other hand, such forays allowed those historians to reach a wider national audience than did the more scholarly work. Although the number of historians actively engaging in this debate is relatively small, they permeate Bulgarian educational institutions.[47] Serious critiques of this kind of history, while made, are aimed at a scholarly audience rather than a popular one—gatekeeping within the historical profession, but not over scholarly works as a whole.[48]

As in Macedonia, the political use of IMRO symbols emerged in the post-Communist period, but in a more limited fashion. Much of the broad debate on Macedonian identity centered on the question of relations with the new Republic of Macedonia, particularly around the Bulgarian government's decision to recognize the state but not necessarily the Macedonian national identity. Language in particular became a sticking point, as Skopje stressed the equality of the Macedonian language to Bulgarian (while Sofia, regarding Macedonian as a "dialect," questioned the need for translators in inter-state meetings, for example). Much of the debate tended to focus on broad issues of the argued "Bulgarian character" of the population of the Republic of Macedonia.

A more specific debate, however, was spurred by the rapid transformation of the IMRO-UMS into a political party in Bulgaria. The party, as Document 6 notes, drew directly on the Macedonian revolutionary movement as its basis and appealed to Bulgarians of Macedonian origin. The organization as a political body stressed conservative national values, and appropriately enough drew on such symbols as IMRO's red-and-black colors and, notably, Todor Aleksandrov.[49] The existence of the rival United Macedonian Organization-Ilinden, comprised of ethnic Macedonians and claiming the legacy of IMRO for itself, touched off a bitter debate over the use of Macedonian symbols. Notable was the furor over Yane Sandanski, now rejected by some in IMRO-UMS due to his leftist leanings but upheld by UMO-Ilinden. Sandanski, problematic for some both due to his opposition to Aleksandrov and his extensive role in Communist-era histories, was now further compromised by his identification as being a symbol for political rivals. UMO-Ilinden's pilgrimages to Sandanski's grave on the anniversary of his death became a focal point in domestic politics and domestic debates surrounding the "appropriation" of national symbols, a debate that spread to the Republic of Macedonia.[50] Legal complications over UMO-Ilinden's ability to register as a political party and to use public monuments in celebrations led to a series of allegations concerning human rights violations and further debate.[51]

On the whole, however, the debate in Bulgaria is far more marginal in its national importance: the incomplete assimilation of Macedonian heroes into the Bulgarian national pantheon means that many Bulgarians lack close identification with them. After all, the modern Bulgarian state never incorporated all of geographic Macedonia; accordingly, Delchev and Sandanski are in many respects of regional rather than national importance. Nonetheless, given that as many as one in eight Bulgarians can claim some Macedonian descent, a large *potential* audience exists. Within this "Bulgaro-Macedonian" community (much of which maintains a strong sense of Macedonian heritage) the debate is no less significant than in the Republic of Macedonia. Moreover, claims within the Republic of Macedonia that IMRO (as well as other historical symbols) is exclusively part of that country's heritage have proven a constant irritant, provoking feelings that Skopje was "stealing" Bulgarian history—and thereby, part of Bulgarian identity.

One new factor in both Bulgaria and Macedonia is the manner in which new technology transformed the way debates over history took place. Not only did the expansion of print and broadcast media provide forums unavailable before 1989, but the advent of the internet transformed the nature of the debate. The internet allowed individuals to reach much wider audiences, and to "self-publish" work on the web; a plethora of "authoritative" websites and e-mail pundits duly appeared. This further weakened the ability of the state and of professional historians to act as gatekeepers of national history (a complaint common to historians in the age of the internet).[52] A number of web pages, many of them in English for an international audience, provided personal and often politically motivated interpretations of Macedonian history and on the provenance of specific individuals like Delchev and Sandanski. On-line discussion groups, both on local bulletin boards in the two countries and in international USENET groups such as alt.soc.macedonia have turned into forums for debate. Increasingly, the internet is used consciously in an attempt to authoritatively distribute rival perspectives on national history to foreign audiences.

Conclusion

Treatments of the contemporary use of history in Southeastern Europe often approach it in cynical terms, stressing the political manipulation of history.[53] The theme of "manipulation" is pertinent, as there has been a clear linkage between political motivations and the way history has been portrayed on the Macedonian question. This should not lead observers, however, to forget that even if national symbols are "invented," they are still widely *perceived* as possessing objective truth by members of the nation in question. The heroes of IMRO have ascribed meanings that have proven important in the creation of a Macedonian national ideology and that have enjoyed resurgence since 1989 in Bulgaria, especially among those Bulgarians of Macedonian descent.[54] In both cases, historical traditions flourish that seek to *prove* that their version of historical truth is the correct one, and that the opposite view is false.

When there are multiple and rival claims to historical symbols of the nation, history becomes a zero-sum game. Any argument advanced by rival tradition threatens the stability of one's own national identity, and encourages a defense that the rival in turn sees as an attack upon their identity. As such, the "objective history" of national symbols becomes unimportant; what is relevant instead is the role ascribed to a given symbol in interpretations of history.[55] The very dynamic of the "use of history" in such cases precludes a common use of common heroes by rivals, at least until their relative importance for the present has faded.

Sources

Document 1:

Today, 35 years have passed since the death of Yane Sandanski, the great Macedonian revolutionary and fighter of our national-liberation struggle; who was killed by agents of Ferdinand II's camarilla because of the following struggle in which he gave his life for the national liberation of the Macedonian people.

Yane Sandanski has a particular place in the history of Macedonian national-liberation activities as the truest follower of the ideals and principles of the pristine IMRO of Gotse Delchev. He is a great progressive figure in our revolutionary past, who did historic service for our Macedonian nation as an uncompromising leader, organizer and strategist of our national-liberation activities. ...

... [Because] the activities of Sandanski were diametrically opposed to the acquisitive aspirations of the Greater-Bulgarian bourgeoisie and clique of Ferdinand, they arranged the physical destruction of Sandanski ... But the deeds and the ideals of Sandanski remained alive in the heart of the Macedonian nation and became a banner in its national struggle for national freedom and independence, a struggle which is complete under the leadership of the CPY.

Source: "Trieset i pet godini ot smrtta na Jane Sandanski," *Nova Makedonija*, 22 April 1950.

Document 2:

...Macedonians had the closest and unbroken historical and cultural past with the Bulgarian people. In Bulgarian progressive society [Gotse Delchev] found a brotherly reception and from them he selected military and intellectual cadres for the Macedonian liberation movement. From Bulgarian progressive society appeared such great Macedonian revolutionaries as Hristo Chernopeev, Krastio Asenov, Petar Yorukov, Parashkev Tsvetkov, Marko Leriiski, Aleksandar Iliev, Luka Ivanov, Todor Panitsa, Aleksandar Bunov, Chudomir Kantardzhiev and still many more who laid down their lives for the freedom of Macedonia.

From the Bulgarian Communist Party ... came the closest comrade of Gotse Delchev and the theorist of Macedonian progressive thought, Dimo Hadzhidimov ...

Therefore, even today, Gotse Delchev is for the Macedonians, wherever they may live, as a banner against the imperialist fomenters of a new war. Therefore, even today, Gotse Delchev is a banner in our war for the triumph of democracy, peace and socialism. For every Macedonian patriot today the deeds of Gotse Delchev have the closest connection with the politics of the socialist progressive powers of peace, democracy and socialism. Under the paternal concern of the Bulgarian Communist Party after 9 September 1944 great material and cultural progress began in our region. ...

The Macedonian inhabitants and every working man in the Pirin region will express their love for the deeds and the legacy of Delchev while working with all their might for the strengthening of our native rule in our People's Republic of Bulgaria, so as to fight for the erection of moral-political unity under the flag of the Fatherland Front at the guidance of the Bulgarian Communist Party, so as to fight for the flowering of our socialist Bulgarian homeland.

Source: "Gotse Delchev," *Pirinsko Delo*, 3 May 1958.

Document 3:

> Today above Macedonia is born
> the new sun of liberty
> The Macedonians fight
> for their own rights!
> The Macedonians fight
> for their own rights!
>
> From now on, the flag flies of the Krushevo Republic
> Gotse Delchev, Pitu Guli
> Dame Gruev, Sandanski!
> Gotse Delchev, Pitu Guli
> Dame Gruev, Sandanski!
>
> The Macedonian forests in one voice sing
> new songs, new news
> that Macedonia is liberated
> and liberated it lives!
> Macedonia is liberated
> and liberated it lives!

Source: "Today over Macedonia," the anthem of the Socialist Republic of Macedonia (also adopted as the national anthem by the independent Republic of Macedonia), written by Vlado Maleski, 1943 or 1944.

Document 4:

When did talk about a Macedonian nationality and Macedonian nation begin? Talk began after Macedonia fell under Serbian slavery. At that time Serb historians, so as to please the Serbian bourgeoisie for the assimilation of this population [of Macedonia], after they couldn't succeed in forcing them to become Serbian through violence, they began to say that these are neither Bulgarians, nor Serbs, but are Macedonians. These are historical facts...

The leaders and founders of the Internal Macedonian-Adrianople Revolutionary Organization never speak about a Macedonian nation and Macedonian national consciousness. For them the struggle of the inhabitants of Macedonia was a struggle for liberation from Turkish slavery. They always emphasized that the Bulgarians in Macedonia were a compact mass, but among them were Greeks, Albanians, Vlachs and other nationalities. They launched the slogan for autonomy—"Macedonia for the Macedonians"—but not as a Macedonian national community but as a slogan for struggle, for equal rights and freedoms for every nationality which inhabited Macedonia. They counted on the incorporation of Macedonia into Bulgaria afterwards. I speak of the left democratic current in the Macedonian revolutionary movement, whose main founder, as is well known, was Gotse Delchev.

Source: Speech by Todor Zhivkov to the Plenum of the Central Committee of the Bulgarian Communist Party, 11–12 March 1963. TsDA fond 1b, op 5, a.e. 567, 1 274–289; here, cited from "Glavno upravlenie na arkhivite pri ministerskiiat suvet," *BKP, Kominternut i Makedonskiiat Vupros* (1917–1946), vol. 2 (Sofia: PK "D. Blagovev," 1999).

Document 5:

I understand the world just as a field of cultural competition of the nations"—this is another thought of the legendary national revolutionary Gotse Delchev, who gave a basis for hope. But in order to have this we have to do everything possible to meet, wherever and on whatever occasion, but freely with Macedonians, and them freely with us.

We will gain nothing if we continue looking through curtains, portals and barriers. The fear of this meeting, which was carefully blocked and could not materialize for more than eighty years, was greatest in Belgrade, Skopje and Athens ... But every day, as more and more people from the two sides of the border communicate they will understand that in fact there is nothing divisive. They will discover that not only the language but also our roots, history, national heroes and enemies are in common. And there is no way to avoid the knowledge or the conviction that almost all "Macedonian heroes" have been predominantly Bulgarians and never Macedonians. That is enough.

Source: Veselin Angelov, "Shte imame li nai-setne edina natsionanlo otgovorna politika po makedonskiia vupros," *Demokratsiia*, 14 August 1997, 16.

Document 6:

In 1893, six Bulgarian intellectuals, striving to obtain civil rights for the Bulgarian population in Macedonia and Thrace—regions cut off from Bulgaria and left under the domination of the Ottoman sultans, founded [in Thessalonika] the Internal Macedonian Revolutionary Organization (IMRO).

After numerous unsuccessful attempts to make the international community solve the problem and in response to the persecutions by the Turkish Ottoman administration, IMRO took the course of armed resistance in order to obtain human rights and liberties for the enslaved nationalities within the empire. ...

After the Balkan Wars and the First World War, only 10% of Macedonia was included in Bulgaria. The remaining 90% were occupied and divided between the Kingdom of Greece and [Yugoslavia] ...

In Greek (Aegean) Macedonia, the Greek authorities set up an inflexible tyrannical regime, so the Organization immediately undertook armed activities; whereas in the Serbian part different ways for legal political activities were sought at first. The ruthless persecution of members and supporters of the Organization as well as the terror imposed on those who declared themselves Bulgarians, forced IMRO to use the methods of armed resistance. ...

Although in 1934 an antidemocratic authoritarian coup in Bulgaria banned all the political parties as well as IMRO. The last fractions of the Organization were abolished as late as in the late 1940s by the newly established Communist dictatorships in Yugoslavia and Bulgaria.

After the Second World War a "Socialist Republic of Macedonia" was created in the framework of Tito's "Federal" Yugoslavia. Belgrade was motivated by its political objective to continue the execution of the old Comintern resolution (adopted in 1934 in Moscow) postulating the creation of a separate "Macedonian" nation. Under the pressure of the Communist regime, the Bulgarian population was obliged to accept the geographical denomination "Macedonian" as a national one. Up to 1990 more than 700 legal trials were held against citizens refusing to adopt the new "Macedonian" national identity ...

Source: IMRO's website, "VMRO: Bulgarsko natsionalno dvizhenie," "VMRO History" (In English) [http://www.vmro.org/stari/index.htm] (Viewed 8 June 2002).

Notes

1 For surveys, see Anthony D. Smith, *Nationalism and Modernism* (London: Routledge, 1998) and Umut Özkirimli, *Theories of Nationalism: A Critical Introduction* (New York: St. Martin's Press, 2000). History is only one area from which symbols are drawn; see chapter 5 by Andrew Wachtel in this volume on the importance of literature as well as his *Making a Nation, Breaking a Nation* (Stanford: Stanford University Press, 1998).

2 Moreover, if one assumes an objective truth in history, if one's own claim is true all other claims *must* be errors at best, lies at worst. Note Keith S. Brown's influential

work, particularly "A Rising to Count On: Ilinden Between Politics and History in Post-Yugoslav Macedonia," in Victor Roudometof, ed., *The Macedonian Question: Culture, Historiography, Politics* (New York: Columbia University Press, 2000), 151–52.

3 The term "IMRO" itself is contested, since the movement was at times known as the "Internal Macedonian–Adrianople Revolutionary Organization" (IMARO) and "Secret Macedonian–Adrianople Revolutionary Organization" (SMARO). Since both names emphasize a Bulgarian nature of the organization by linking the inhabitants of Thrace and Macedonia, the use of the terms can take a political cast. IMRO is used here throughout, however, for simplicity.

4 The "right" to national heroes is similarly at stake in debates over the "ownership" of Sts. Cyril and Methodius and Tsar Samuil. Claims to Alexander the Great and associated symbols (the first Macedonian flag, or indeed the very term "Macedonia") proved a sore point in Macedonian-Greek relations in the mid-1990s.

This should not be misconstrued as a phenomenon limited to Southeastern Europe. Note, for example, the continuing debate within France over what Joan of Arc "stands for" in French history, claimed variously by monarchists, revolutionaries, liberal democrats, socialists, Vichy France, and more recently by both Jean-Marie Le Pen's National Front and its opponents.

With reference to other Bulgarian heroes, Maria Todorova has a forthcoming volume on treatments of Vasil Levski, and her article "'Public memory' and the 'hero': Vasil Levski (1837–1873–1997)," *Nations and Nationalism in East-Central Europe, 1806–1948: A Festschrift in Honor of Peter Sugar*, ed. Sabrina Ramet, et al. (Columbus: Slavica, 1999).

5 E.g., explicitly linking historical events in relation to contemporary socialism in the Balkans. For example, Hristo Andonov-Poljanski, ed., *Documents on the Struggle of the Macedonian People for Independence and a Nation-State*, 2 vols. (Skopje: Kultura, 1985), includes the memorable chapter title "The People's Anti-Feudal Liberation Struggle against Byzantium."

6 On national ideology's relationship to the writing of history, see the seminal work by Katherine Verdery, *National Ideology under Socialism: Identity and Cultural Politics in Ceausescu's Romania* (Berkeley: University of California Press, 1991), particularly 76, 237–39.

7 Georgi (Gotse) Delchev (1872–1903) was born in Aegean Macedonia, finished secondary school and was a student at the military academy in Sofia until expelled for revolutionary activities in 1894. An IMRO founder and its representative in Sofia for 1896– 1901, he then returned to Vardar Macedonia and was preparing for the Ilinden uprising of 2 August 1903, when killed in May during an encounter with Ottoman troops.

8 Yane Sandanski (1872–1915) was born in Vardar Macedonia and rose to prominence in the IMRO for his major role in the kidnapping and ransoming of the American Ellen Stone in 1901. Although doubtful about the wisdom of the brutally suppressed Ilinden uprising of 1903, he established control of the larger, Macedonian-based "internationalist" faction of the IMRO after the Rila Congress of 1905. His implication in the assassination of IMRO founder Damian Gruev in 1906 and continued opposition to the Sofia-based Supremist faction contributed to his own murder in 1915.

9 For a Bulgarian socialist perspective on the relationship of IMRO figures to their

socialist contemporaries, note Veselin Hadzhinikolov, Liubomir Panaiatov et al., eds., *Istoriia na blagoevgradskata okruzhna organizatsiia na BKP* (Sofia: Partizdat, 1979). For a Macedonian view, see Hristo Andonov-Poljanski, "Ilinden 1903," *Macedonian Review* 13:3 (1983) or Michael Radin, *IMRO and the Macedonian Question, 1893–1934* (Skopje: Kultura, 1993). For a critical perspective regarding the revolutionary ideology of IMRO, see Duncan Perry, *The Politics of Terror: The Macedonian Liberation Movements, 1893–1903* (Durham, N. C.: Duke University Press, 1988).

10 The Bulgarian government continued to retain aspects of "Macedonianization" in the Pirin region well into the 1950s, on its own terms. See Veselin Angelov, "Politikata na BKP po makedonskiia vupros, Iuli 1948–1956 g.," *Istoricheski Pregled* 52: 5 (1986), 83–107. A first-hand Bulgarian account of this political maneuvering is Tsola Dragoicheva, *Takava e istinata* (Sofia: Partizdat, 1981).

11 For an overview, see Evangelos Kofos, *Nationalism and Communism in Macedonia: Civil Conflict, Politics of Mutation, National Identity* (New Rochelle, N. Y.: Aristide D. Caratzas, 1993); Stephen Palmer and Robert King, *Yugoslav Communism and the Macedonian Question* (Hamden, Conn.: Archon Press, 1971); and Paul Shoup, *Communism and the Yugoslav National Question* (New York: Columbia University Press, 1968).

12 The best survey, if not covering the entire period, is Stefan Troebst, *Die bulgarisch-jugoslawische Kontroverse um Makedonien, 1967–1982* (Munich: Südost-Institut, 1983); the Macedonian edition (Skopje: Institut za natsionalna istorija, 1997) is used here, 53.

13 King and Palmer, 153–54.

14 Initially, in the 1940s, the nineteenth century served as the starting point for the Macedonian nation, but this was later pushed back in time to encompass the medieval empire of Tsar Samuil, the lives of Sts. Cyril and Methodius, and the Slavic migrations into the Balkans. Stefan Troebst, "IMRO + 100 = FYROM? The politics of Macedonian historiography," in James Pettifer, ed., *The New Macedonian Question* (London: Macmillan Press Ltd., 1999), 63. Also note the first volume of *Documents on the Struggle of the Macedonian People*, which uses the same pattern.

15 Andonov-Poljanski, 241.

16 Kofos, 159.

17 Nikola Minchev, "The Ideals of Gotse Delchev are Built into the Macedonia of Today," *Macedonian Review* 2: 2 (1972), 148–50.

18 James Krapfl provides a statistical analysis of such in "The Ideals of Ilinden: Uses of Memory and Nationalism in Socialist Macedonia," Institute on East Central Europe, Columbia University, *CIAO* web edition.

19 E.g., Ivan Karadzhiev, *Vreme na Zreenje: Makedonskoto natsionalno prashanje megju dvete svetski vojni*, (Skopje: Kultura, 1977), 1: 171–75.

20 The stress on "falsification" is notable. For example, see "Falsifikatite na bugarskite 'kriihari' ne mozhat da go zasenat svetliot lik na Jane Sandanski," *Nova Makedonija*, 11 May 1948, 3.

21 Dimitar Mitrev, *Pirinska Makedonija vo borba za natsionanlo osloboduvanje* (Skopje: Glavniot odbor na Narodniot Front na Makedonija, 1950); Vasil Jotevski,

Natsionalnata afirmatsija na Makedontsite vo Pirinskiot del na Makedonija 1944–1948 (Skopje: Institut za natsionalna istorija, 1966).

22 Naum Kaichev and Ivanka Nedeva, "IMRO Groupings in Bulgaria After the Second World War," in James Pettifer, ed., *The New Macedonian Question* (London: Macmillan Press Ltd., 1999).

23 Shoup, 152.

24 Indeed, placing them on a par with Dimitur Blagoev, for whom Gorna Dzhumaia was renamed as Blagoevgrad in 1950—though Blagoevgrad was both larger and the district capital.

25 Tsentralen Durzhaven Arhiv (TsDA), fond 1b, op. 6, a.e. 1801, l. 15–16 (on Ilinden), 5–13 (list of national heroes). Ilinden was noted on other occasions as well, e.g., a.e. 472, l 10–11; a.e. 5102, l. 73.

26 The regional newspaper *Pirinsko Delo*, for example, regularly published articles on Macedonian history (particularly on Delchev and Sandanski) throughout the 1950s and early 1960s during the period of "taboo." Or, for example, the monograph by Khrum Hristov, *Gotse Delchev* (Sofia, 1955),

27 For example, Petur Georgiev, "Kak se falshifitsira istoriiata," *Pirinsko Delo*, 8 January 1958, 3–4. The Central Committee of the Politburo on rare occasions protested Yugoslav portrayals of history—for example, on treatments of Bulgaria's role in the First World War. TsDA f. 1b, op 6, a.e. 3341

28 Dino Kiosev, ed., *Gotse Delchev: Pisma i drugi materiali* (Sofia: BAN, 1967); Liuben Tolev, "Bulgarskata Istoricheska nauka i patriotichnoto vuspitanie," *Istoricheski Pregled* 26: 1 (1968), 131–83; Iordan Vanchev, *Apostoli na Bulgarskata Svoboda* (Sofia: Narodna Mladezh, 1981); Dimitur Gotsev, *Ideiata za avtonomiia kato taktika v programite na natsionalno-osvoboditelnoto dvizhenie v Makedoniia i Odrinsko, 1893–1941* (Sofia: BAN, 1983).

29 The motivations for this turn to nationalism are unclear, although economic difficulties may have encouraged it. For some suggestions regarding the pressures the BCP felt about Minorities at home, see John D. Bell, "The 'Revival Process': The Turkish and Pomak Minorities in Bulgarian Politics," in Thanasis D. Sfikas and Christopher Williams, eds., *Ethnicity and Nationalism in East Central Europe and the Balkans* (Aldershot: Ashate Publishing Ltd., 1999), 242–245.

30 Liudmila Zhivkova, "Uvereno i dostoino kum budeshteto na Bulgariia," *Istoricheski Pregled* 47: 2 (1981), 16.

31 Iordan Vanchev, *Apostoli na bulgarskata svoboda* (Sofia: Narodna Mladezh, 1981), 64.

32 Ivan Aleksandrov, *Za novo mislene i nov podhod po niakoi vuprosi ot bulgarskata istoriia: protiv oburkvane na poniatiiata po bulgarskiia natsionalen vupros* (Sofia: Kulturen dom "Vladimir Poptomov," 1988).

33 Troebst, ibid.

34 Sarafov was a leader in the Ilinden uprising, but unacceptable for his Bulgarophile views (including the goal of uniting Macedonia with Bulgaria). Metodij Shatorov was the head of the (Vardar) Macedonian Provincial Committee of the Yugoslav Communist Party during the start of the Second World War, but fell out with Tito when he

sought to align Macedonian Communists to the Bulgarian Communist Party. Metodij Antonov-Chento was the president of the presidium of ASNOM; for pushing too strongly for autonomy he fell from power and was for a time erased from official history, although he was later rehabilitated during the Communist period.

35 Brown, 155–62, notes the strength of the debate in the 1990s.

36 Brown, 147–48, 170*n*.

37 Both in new works and in new editions of older ones. For example, Dimitar Dimeski, *Gotse Delchev* (Skopje: Matitsa makedonska, 1994); Ivan Katarjiev, *Istorija na Makedonskiot Narod: Makedonija megu Balkanskite i Vtorata svetska vojna* (Skopje: Institut za natsionalna istorija, 2000), part of a new five-volume history of the Macedonian people; Vasil Jotevski, *Nationalnata afirmatsija na makedontsite vo pirinskiot del na Makedonija, 1944–1948* (Skopje: Institut za natsionalna istorija, 1996).

38 Opposition by the Greek government to the country's name led to the use of the term "the Former Yugoslav Republic of Macedonia" by most governments and international organizations—including both the United States and the United Nations.

39 Given the importance of IMRO in Macedonian history as argued here, the plethora of Macedonian parties that have claimed the name after 1991 should come as no surprise. IMRO: Democratic Party for Macedonian National Unity is the largest, but others have included IMRO: Democratic Party, IMRO: Fatherland Party, IMRO: Macedonian National Democratic League, IMRO: United, IMRO: Movement for Restoration of Macedonian, and IMRO: True Macedonian Reform Option.

40 Speech by president of Macedonia Boris Trajkovski to the émigré United Macedonian Organization of Canada at "Gotse Delchev Night," 5 February 2000. [http://www.unitedmacedonians.org/activities/trajkovski_eng.html] (Viewed 8 June 2002).

41 The continued state use of this Macedonian national ideology, however, was a source of complaint for minorities in the Republic in the 1990s, who saw this as a part of a tendency to a "national" rather than a "civic" state in which all nationalities were equal. The second half of the 1990s saw a partial retreat from the more overt use of IMRO as a national symbol by the state, although its use continued by ethnic Macedonian political parties.

42 As well as work that borders on apologia for less savory actions of IMRO, such as Mitre Stamenov, *Atentatut v Marsiliia* (Sofia: Izdanie na VMRO–SMD, 1993).

43 I am particularly indebted to Angel Angelov for his comments on this point in conversations with the author.

44 Thomas Meininger, "A Troubled Transition: Bulgarian Historiography, 1989–1994," *Contemporary European History* 5: 1 (1996), 113–14.

45 Among them, note the four-volume history produced jointly by the Macedonian National Institute and the Bulgarian Academy of Sciences, *Natsionalno-osvoboditelnoto dvizhenie na makedonskite i trakiiskite bulgari, 1878–1944, v chetiri toma* (Sofia: Akademichno izdatelstvo "Marin Drinov," 1994), and Dimitur Gotsev and Dimitur Michev, eds., *100 godini Vutreshna Makedono-Odrinska revoliutsionna organizatsiia* (Sofia: Makedonski nauchen institut, 1994). More critical are Kostadin Paleshutski, *Makedonskoto osvoboditelno dvizhenie, 1924–1934* (Sofia: Akademichno izdatelstvo "Marin Drinov," 1998); Veselin Angelov, *Khronika na edno natsionalno predatelstvo: Opitite za*

nasilstveno denatsionalizirane na Pirinska Makedoniia (1944–1949 g.) (Blageovgrad: Izd. "Neofit Rilski, 1999); and Dimitur Tiulekov, *Obrecheno rodoliobie: VMRO v Pirinsko 1919–1934* (Blagoevgrad; Universitetsko izdatelstvo "Neofit Rilski," 2001).

Also worth noting are reviews of books released in Macedonia and other countries; for example, the three reviews in *Makedonski Pregled* 24: 1 (2001).

46 Bozhidar Dimitrov, *Desette luzhi na makedonizma* (Sofia: Izdatel "ANIKO," 2000). Although the work is not scholarly in nature—indeed, it seems deliberately inflammatory—Dimitrov himself is the head of the National Museum of History. Most "popular histories" are drier fare: e.g., the three-volume *Makedoniia: Istoria i politicheska sudba*, ed. P. Petrov et. al. (Sofia: Izdatelstvo "Znanie," 1998).

47 As suggested by the Bulgarian Academy of Science's "National Doctrine for the Twenty-First Century" of 1997, which stressed the presence of Bulgarian minorities in all neighboring states—a point seen as provocative in Macedonia.

48 Note, for example, the critical review of *Desette luzhi* by Chavdar Marinov, "Za luzhite na *Makedonizma* i mitovete za *Bulgarshtinata* v Makedoniia," *Kritika i Humanizum* 12: 3 (2001).

49 See the pamphlet by Decho Dobrinov, *Todor Aleksandrov: Legendarniat vodach na VMRO* (Sofia: Znanie, 1994), part of the "Pantheon of the Bulgarian Government and Culture" series. Aleksandrov, viewed as a Bulgarian patriot and anti-Communist of Macedonian origin, perhaps can be drawn upon more easily than Delchev's more ambiguous national and ideological preferences. As a figure suppressed during the Communist period he also can represent a break with that period.

50 The repeated vandalization of the Sandanski monument (reportedly by members of IMRO–UMS) underscores the bitterness of this debate.

51 The Macedonian Information Liaison Service report of 21 April 1995, regarding the decision by the city of Melnik to allow a celebration by Ilinden on the 80th anniversary of Yane Sandanski's death, reported that Bulgarian Public Prosecutor Ivan "Tatarchev, formerly a member of IMRO–UMS, told an A1 Television reporter that the Bulgarian Government is making a wrong move, [sic] as Sandanski is no part of Bulgarian history."

52 Although academia, too, is turning to the internet to state its position. Note the on-line "virtual exhibition" of the State Archive of Macedonia touching on, among other things, IMRO and the Macedonians of the Pirin region. Slava Nikolovska, project leader, "Macedonia through the Centuries," Archive of Macedonia and Open Society Institute of Macedonia, 1998. *http://www.soros.org.mk/archive/index.htm*] (20 March 2002).

53 Note the critique of Western theories of nation formation in Ivelin Sardamov, "Mandate of History: War, Ethnic Conflict and Nationalism in the South Slav Balkans," unpublished dissertation, University of Notre Dame, 1998, 24–25. For that matter, the use of historical symbols in the United States and Western Europe is just as manipulative.

54 Note Anthony Smith's theories about the importance of "myth of descent" in nationalism. As such, Delchev, Sandanski and other figures represent the deeds of grandfathers and great-grandfathers, and are important on a personal level as well. Anthony D. Smith, *The Ethnic Origins of Nations* (Cambridge, Mass.: Blackwell Publishers, Inc., 1995).

55 Or, rather, that "objective proofs" are chiefly significant when they can trigger a Kuhnian shift, and allow for a change in historiography that allows a figure to become a national hero, or allows an existing hero to be removed.

CHAPTER 5

Andrew B. Wachtel

HOW TO USE A CLASSIC:
Petar Petrović Njegoš in the Twentieth Century

"[Njegoš is] the immortal apostle and herald of the unity of our people."
King Aleksandar[1]

"Njegoš is Montenegro and Montenegro is Njegoš."
Josip Vidmar[2]

"Njegoš is a Serbian writer and this emerges logically from his work."
Zora Latinović[3]

It is a truth self-evident that an East European nation in search of its identity must have a national literature and a national poet. Following the model proposed originally by Herder in the early nineteenth century, East European nation-builders have generally conceived their fellows in terms of linguistic communities, and in most cases cultural self-definition preceded and was a precondition for the achievement of political independence. That is to say, language created nations, rather than the other way around. Poets like Sándor Petőfi in Hungary, Adam Mickiewicz in Poland, and Alexander Pushkin in Russia were and still are prized by critics for their exquisite verse. But what eventually earned them large bronze statues in the streets and squares of their respective countries was not so much the quality of their literary output as their ability to express the nation's collective self (or so, at least, claimed the nation-building intellectuals who pushed the candidacy of these "national poets"). The appearance of a national poet was seen as proof that a given people had attained a level of cultural development sufficient for its pretensions to nationhood to be taken seriously.[4] Elites in each country mobilized fellow citizens by using the person and the work of the national poet as a source of pride and a rallying point for future cultural and political development. If high culture had previously been seen as something borrowed from others, now Poles, Hungarians, or Russians could imagine beginning their own tradition, and future generations of writers would inevitably trace their genealogy back to Petőfi, Mickiewicz, or Pushkin rather than to Shakespeare, Homer, Dante, or Goethe.

In the South Slavic lands, the situation was no different. Here, too, with almost miraculous alacrity poets appeared—France Prešeren in Slovenia,

Ivan Mažuranić in Croatia, and Petar Petrović Njegoš in Montenegro—to create literary monuments in the vernacular, helping to codify (and sometimes even to create) the modern literary language in the process. Among the South Slavs, however, the situation was complicated by the fact that it was not clear then, and in some cases it remains unclear today, what nation a given "national" poet's work represented. That is, if Pushkin was unequivocally a Russian writer, Mickiewicz a Pole, and so on, Ivan Mažuranić might well have been not a Croatian national but an Illyrian, proto-Yugoslav writer, and, as we will see in this essay, Njegoš has been considered, at various times, to be the national writer of Serbs, of Yugoslavs, and of Montenegrins.[5] This reflects, of course, the contested nature of national identity in the lands of the former Yugoslavia, just as it points to the arbitrariness of allowing a single poet to stand for the nation as a whole.

Petar Petrović Njegoš was undoubtedly an outstanding figure. He was born in 1813 to the Njegoši tribe in Montenegro, perhaps the most isolated European land of its day. Unlike the other South Slavic lands at the time, however, it did possess an independent political existence, albeit a rather tenuous one, under the rule of a series of prince-bishops who provided both secular and religious leadership to a group of exceptionally fractious clans.

*Photograph of Njegoš as a Montenegrin
mountaineer—1851*

As it happened, Njegoš's uncle had been the previous prince-bishop, and upon his death in 1830 Njegoš was appointed in his stead. Njegoš spent the rest of his short life (he died in 1851) laboring to improve the situation of his homeland. He strengthened the power of central authority, opened Montenegro's first schools, built its first roads, and defended his tiny land against Ottoman onslaughts. Simultaneously, he produced a body of literary work that helped to lay the foundations for modern South Slavic literature (see photograph on page 132 for a typically romantic image of Njegoš).

His epic in dramatic form entitled *Gorski vijenac* (The Mountain Wreath) was published in 1847. It has been hailed as the greatest work of South Slavic literature, and seen as the national epic of Montenegro, of Serbia, and of Yugoslavia (both the first and the second). More recently, it has been reviled as a blueprint for ethnic cleansing and banned in the school curriculum of Bosnia and Herzegovina. Its author has been treated as a secular saint, and his body has been exhumed and inhumed multiple times since his death in 1851 by those who wished to use Njegoš for their own national and political purposes. This essay will concentrate primarily on the ways in which Njegoš and his most famous work were used by nation-building elites to create Yugoslav, Serb, and Montenegrin national identities throughout the twentieth century and to this day, but first we must say a few words about the work itself.

The Mountain Wreath opens with a dedication to Karadjordje, the leader of the first Serbian uprising against Turkish rule in 1804, who is extolled as a military leader of equal stature to Napoleon, Suvorov, and Kutuzov. The attempt to elevate a character from Serbian history to a pan-European pedestal is part of Njegoš's overall strategy for his epic to imbue a relatively minor event in Montenegrin history with universal significance.[6] The introduction closes with an invocation of the legendary Serbian medieval hero of the battle of Kosovo, Miloš Obilić, thereby tying the hoped-for rebirth of Serbia to its legendary demise in 1389.

With the beginning of the main body of the text, Njegoš switches to the ten-syllable line of the folk epic and introduces his central character, the brooding Bishop Danilo. Danilo contemplates and curses the conquests that have been made by Islam, and thinks about how they can be rolled back. True, Montenegro itself is still free, but Danilo believes that this freedom is threatened, not by arms but by slow conversion to Islam. Danilo curses the Slavic apostates: "May God strike you, loathsome degenerates, / why do we need the Turk's faith among us?"[7] However, Danilo's belief that only a "religious cleansing" of his land can effect its eventual rebirth is tempered by his recognition that the Montenegrin Moslems are nevertheless blood relations. It is Danilo's tragedy to be paralyzed by this knowledge.

The other Christian Montenegrins lack any trace of Danilo's hesitation,

as the straightforward response of one of the clan leaders to Danilo's brooding indicates: "Is today not a festive occasion/on which you have gathered
Montenegrins/to rid our land of loathsome infidels?" (Njegoš, 7). This split
between the tragically conflicted individual and the confident group (with
preference given to the latter) embodies the collectivistic basis of South
Slavic national thought. Ultimately, the epic's plot revolves at least as much
around whether Danilo can join himself to the collective will as it does on
the massacre of the converts that forms the work's ostensible subject. The
collectivistic bias of *The Mountain Wreath* is further emphasized by the
intermittent presence of an updated version of a Greek chorus. The role of
the chorus, here called a Kolo (the Serbian national round dance), is to open
up the historical level of the epic by connecting events of the drama with
earlier moments in Serbian history.

When the Montenegrin leaders gather, it is clear that all are in favor of
destroying their Islamicized kin. Yet Danilo still hesitates and calls for talks
with the converts, hoping they can be baptized without violence. These
unproductive talks do not cure Danilo of his inability to act, and the whole
middle section of the work is a long pause during which Njegoš builds tension by moving the central question into the background. He provides in its
stead a series of vignettes of Montenegrin life, a veritable encyclopedia of
folk customs and beliefs.

In the course of the work Danilo's ambivalence is raised to a basic principle of world organization. By far the strongest expression of this philosophy appears in the statements of the old Abbot Stefan. Unlike Danilo, however, Stefan is not paralyzed by his recognition of the world's essential
duality. Instead, he exhorts the Montenegrin Christians to purge the country
of its Islamic element, arguing that resurrection of the Serbian people can
only come through death. Thus, as is the case with many epics, the direction
of this work is circular (like the Kolo that plays such a crucial role here),
with events in the poem's present forging a tie to the medieval Serbian
kingdom. Like the *Odyssey*, *The Mountain Wreath* will end with the hero's
return to the home that had seemingly been lost; in this case, however, the
home is the unity of national life that was lost at Kosovo, and the hero is a
collective rather than an individual. Ultimately, even the wavering Bishop
Danilo is won over, although he never gives an overt order for the massacre.
And when he is informed that, at least in one area, the "Turks" who did not
run away were killed, their houses burned, and their mosques destroyed, he
rejoices with the others.

Before beginning our discussion of the ways in which Njegoš has been
used in creating various national identities, one general comment is in order:
it is neither possible nor productive to make a simple statement about the
relationship between *The Mountain Wreath* and contemporary events in the

former Yugoslavia. I do not say this from the point of view of a relativist who believes that no claim regarding an author or his work is better than any other. Rather, it is because a work of literature as great and complex as this one is ambiguous enough to allow for a wide variety of interpretations. I fully agree with Srdja Pavlović who says that "the long-gone Montenegro that Njegoš wrote about had little in common with the Montenegro of his time, and has nothing to do with contemporary Montenegro."[8] At the same time, it cannot be denied that there is something deeply troubling about a text that implies the absolute inability of members of the same linguistic group who adhere to different religions to live together without brutal conflict and that, with whatever reservations, ultimately does celebrate the massacre of one religion's adherents by the others.

Nineteenth-century interpretations of him and his work were notably uncontroversial. *The Mountain Wreath* was early on treated both as Njegoš's greatest work and as a major if not the major work of South Slavic romanticism. After its first printing in 1847, it was republished a dozen times through 1905, and an authoritative commentary by the Slavist Milan Rešetar was produced in 1890.[9] Rešetar treats the destruction of the Islamicized Montenegrins as both a historical fact and the central theme of the work. He does not consider this theme in its ethical dimension, but neither does he see it as having any relationship to the present. Rešetar simply says that Njegoš saw these events as "the beginning of the Serbian people's battle for liberty" (Rešetar, iii), and it was abundantly clear to the commentator that Njegoš was a Serbian writer. There is no breath of Yugoslavism perceived in this commentary, not surpising as the late nineteenth century marked a low ebb in the project to create a Yugoslav identity.[10]

As the Yugoslav movement picked up steam in the years after 1903, and particularly after the founding of the Kingdom of the Serbs, Croats and Slovenes in 1918, however, it became important for the new "Yugoslav" nation to have a national poet to represent it in the world literary and cultural pantheon. Njegoš was chosen as just such a national poet. *The Mountain Wreath*, despite its Serbianism and its intolerance toward Islamicized Slavs who made up some 10 percent of the new nation's population, was clearly Njegoš's greatest work, and so it was reinterpreted in a Yugoslav vein. Already by 1921, the author of an overtly Yugoslav-oriented literary anthology cum textbook could say that Njegoš "to this day has remained on the highest poetic pinnacle of our people," adding that "well-known passages in *The Mountain Wreath* are the most beautiful and greatest that our artistic literature exhibits."[11]

However, the real work of transforming Njegoš into the Yugoslav national writer par excellence was carried out in 1925 in conjunction with the translation of Njegoš's remains from Cetinje to a mausoleum on top of Mt. Lovćen,

*Two designs from the 1921 competition for the Njegoš
mausoleum*

the highest peak in Montenegro. This was not the first time that the author's
body had been moved. At his death in 1851, Njegoš had asked to be buried
on Lovćen, in a church dedicated to St. Petar Cetinski that he had designed
and erected in 1845. For a number of reasons this desire could not be carried out immediately, and he was first interred at the monastery in Cetinje.
However, in 1855 his mortal remains were transferred to Lovćen and they
remained there until 1916. At that time, the Austrians, who had crushed the
Serbian and Montenegrin armies in the course of 1915, decided to commemorate their victory by raising a monument to Franz Joseph on the top of
Lovćen. Evidently it was felt to be unseemly for the Austrian Emperor to
share this lofty perch with a symbol of South Slavic national feeling, so the
Austrian authorities demanded that Njegoš's remains be removed from

A further design proposed in the 1921 competition for the Njegoš mausoleum

Lovćen and transferred to Cetinje. However, the care and stealth with which the Austrians carried out the exhumation (it was supervised by clergy of the Orthodox Church in order to avoid any accusation of desecration) attests to their recognition that Njegoš's bones carried as much symbolic weight as did his work.[12]

By the end of the war Njegoš's chapel had been severely damaged. Negotiations between Montenegrin authorities and the new government in Belgrade went on for years regarding respectively when, in what building, and at whose expense Njegoš would be reburied. Essentially, Montenegrin authorities favored restoring the original church. Belgrade authorities had mixed feelings on the subject, and at first opened a competition for new designs for Njegoš's mausoleum. Some were quite far from the original

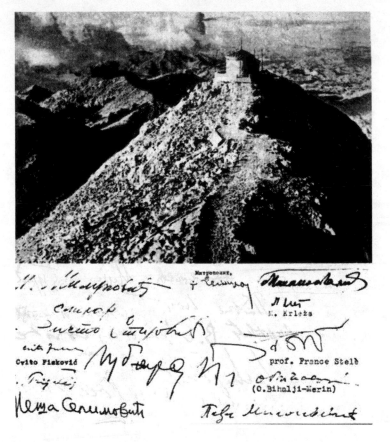

The rebuilt Njegoš mausoleum as it stood on Mt. Lovćen from 1925 until 1970

Byzantinesque building (see photographs on page 136). In the end, however, a combination of Montenegrin wishes and financial reality (it proved much cheaper to reuse the stone from the mostly destroyed church than to bring new materials to the site) won out. The king made funds available from his own purse, and the rebuilt chapel was a replica of the original (photograph on page 137).[13]

The chapel was rededicated and Njegoš's remains were reburied there in September 1925 in the course of a three-day ceremony sponsored and attended by King Aleksandar himself. The tone of the event, which was described extensively in the Yugoslav press, bordered on a piety more appropriate for the treatment of a saint than a writer.[14] Before the transfer, the coffin holding Njegoš's remains was opened to allow the king and queen to have a look. The coffin was again opened on Lovćen in the presence of the entire Orthodox Church hierarchy of Yugoslavia. And the plaque that was placed above his mausoleum by the king officially inscribed Njegoš as the Yugoslav national writer, calling him "the immortal apostle and herald of the unity of our people."[15]

The solemnity of the reburial was enhanced by the simultaneous, albeit coincidental, announcement that the Austrian government was returning to Yugoslavia the original manuscript of *The Mountain Wreath*, which had been in their possession since Njegoš had submitted it to the Habsburg censorship. Like the transfer of Njegoš's remains, the return of the manuscript was hailed as an historic moment; it encouraged the conflation of religious, political, and literary canonization.[16]

Nevertheless, turning Njegoš into an avatar of Yugoslav identity required more than just a pronouncement from the king. Serious literary critics as well as more humble textbook writers needed to find strategies that would make Njegoš and his *Mountain Wreath* acceptable, nay admirable in a Yugoslav context. One widespread method was to concentrate not on the plot of his major work, but rather on more abstract philosophy. As one critic put it: "His *Mountain Wreath* is a hymn to freedom, a rejection of force and tyranny, a glorification of national and human ideals, the affirmation of moral ideas over brute desires."[17] The problem, however, elided by most Yugoslav-inclined commentators, is that the Islamicized Slavs who bear the brunt of the Montenegrins' attempts at "ethnic cleansing" are not identical to the tyrannous Ottomans. It may indeed have been true that only a united Montenegro could have kept the Turks at bay, but it is also true that unity is achieved in *The Mountain Wreath* through fratricidal bloodletting. When the global tyranny of Turk against South Slav is echoed by the local tyranny of Christian Slav against Moslem, the result is tragic. Njegoš seems to have recognized that his "hymn to freedom" was built on blood and to have agonized over it, but interwar commentators ignored this.

Perhaps only Ivo Andrić was able to bring Njegoš into the Yugoslav canon without distorting the essence of his position. In his essay "Njegoš as Tragic Hero of Kosovo Thought," Andrić does not speak directly about *The Mountain Wreath*. Rather he concentrates on its author's personal situation, seeing him as a synecdoche for Yugoslavia (see Document 1 for a fuller exposition of Andrić's position): "The tragedy of this struggle was sharpened and deepened by the unavoidable fratricidal battles that our difficult history has frequently provided. The tragedy was all the greater for Njegoš in that from his high point of view, like all the great and light-bearing souls of our history, he could capture at a glance the totality of our nation, without differentiating between belief or tribe."[18] Njegoš is equated with Danilo and is seen as having been placed in the same position as Prince Lazar, who, according to the oral poems of the Kosovo cycle, was forced to choose between an earthly and a heavenly kingdom. In Andrić's reading, Prince-Bishop Njegoš combined in himself the earthly and heavenly kingdom, but no angel asked him which he would choose. He had, instead, to try to balance the two, and this tragic balancing act is seen to have defined him and his greatest work.

A different tack was to shift attention away from the subject matter of *The Mountain Wreath* and turn readers' attention to extratextual information. This background information was meant to bolster Njegoš's credentials as a proto-Yugoslav and to imply, fairly convincingly in fact, that *The Mountain Wreath* should be seen as an evocation of a distant historical period rather than as a call to similar action in the present. In one oft-quoted letter to Osman-Pasha of Skoplje, for example, Njegoš had said: "I would like more than anything on earth to see accord between brothers in whom a single blood flows and who were nursed with the same milk."[19] Comments like these, in addition to the fact that Njegoš was never a stickler for the external regalia of religion, allowed Yugoslavizing commentators to make extravagant claims, such as those made in Document 2 below by Nikola Skerović, "Led on by the great idea of the liberation of his nation and its amalgamation into a single great, free, and enlightened motherland, Njegoš felt equally close to Belgrade, Zagreb, Travnik, Dubrovnik, Skadar and Mostar. He had the same brotherly feelings toward the rebellious Bosnian Vizir Gradaščević, to Ali-Pasha Rizvanbegović and to Osman-Pasha Skopljak as he did toward Aleksandr Karadjordjević or Ban Jelačić. It was all the same to him whether one or another of them was baptized or not or what their names were; the important thing for him was that they were all sons of the same mother, of a single people, that they were brothers."[20]

Interwar textbooks, especially ones designed for young readers, took a different tack. In the excerpts they presented from the work of the national writer, they avoided entirely passages that might be uncomfortable or difficult to interpret. Given the numerous digressions in *The Mountain Wreath*, this proved rather easy. By far the most popular excerpt for such purposes was the section in which Vojvoda Draško describes his visit to Venice. Of course, it has nothing at all to do with the most problematic action of the work, nor does it touch on the central philosophical message of permanent struggle. It is, however, quite funny, and was deemed to be the safest passage for student consumption.[21]

While the postwar Communist government rejected much of the legacy of interwar Yugoslavia, they decided to continue, and even to enhance the candidacy of Njegoš as Yugoslavia's national poet. Their most intensive effort in this regard can be seen in the celebration of the 100th anniversary of the publication of *The Mountain Wreath* in 1947. There were two major stumbling blocks to the creation of a red Njegoš, however. First of all, his work was overly Serb-oriented. But as this issue had been successfully skirted by their interwar predecessors, postwar Yugoslav critics had home-grown models for dealing with it. More worrisome was the fact that he had been as one of the central pillars of interwar Yugoslav culture. If Njegoš was to be rehabilitated in the Communist context, he would have to be freed from the weight of his previous interpretive history. This required a certain amount of interpretive legerdemain.

One might wonder why the Communists bothered, but in addition to the convenient timing of the jubilee (in the first year that the new government had the energy to put on a big cultural show), the work and its author had a number of advantages. First, he was long dead. As opposed to such still-living interwar advocates of Yugoslavism as the great sculptor Ivan Meštrović, for example, Njegoš could not respond to reinterpretations of his legacy. In addition, Njegoš's ethnic background was an advantage. Since the main lines of cleavage in interwar Yugoslavia had been between Serbs and Croats, it would have been unwise to promote a Serb or Croat as national writer.[22] But as Montenegro was by far the smallest Yugoslav republic and the Montenegrins had never been accused of hegemonic tendencies, Njegoš could be accepted by all; and commentators in 1947 made sure to refer to him as a Montenegrin, rather than as a Serbian writer. It probably did not hurt that Yugoslavia's two leading cultural tsars—Milovan Djilas and Rado-van Zogović—were themselves from Montenegro.[23] The fact that Njegoš had also been a central political figure was also significant, helping to legit-imate the new regime's insistence on a close alliance between politics and culture.[24] Finally, *The Mountain Wreath* was genuinely popular, at least among the semi-literate Serbs and Montenegrins who made up a substantial portion of the population. Because his work is mostly written in the *deseter-ica* (the decasyllabic verse form employed in most Serbian and Croatian oral epic verse), it was easier for them to digest than works written in a more obviously literary style. As the research presented in chapter 7 by Maja Brkljačić indicates, Njegoš was frequently referred to in the epics that were written to commemorate contemporary events in postwar Yugoslavia, an indication that he was indeed a living presence to at least a percentage of the population.

In any event, the 7 June anniversary was celebrated as a national holiday (the front page of the Croatian newspaper *Vjesnik* on 9 June 1947, for exam-ple, displayed a portrait of Njegoš with the headline "The celebration of the hundredth anniversary of 'The Mountain Wreath' is a holiday for all the nations of Yugoslavia"), while Njegoš and *The Mountain Wreath* were transformed into precursors of the most up-to-date Communist thought. New editions of *The Mountain Wreath* were published in Serbia, Croatia, and Bosnia-Herzegovina, a new translation appeared in Slovenia, as did the first-ever Macedonian translation. twenty-five thousand copies were published in Montenegro alone to ensure that "practically every house in Montenegro will have it."[25]

As might be expected, *Pobeda*, the organ of the Montenegrin "People's Front," contained the most lavish press coverage. Seven of this biweekly's eight pages on 7 June and six of eight on the 11th were devoted to the festival. The lead article on 7 June, by Niko Pavić, concentrates in one place all the catchphrases and interpretive moves that were employed to recanonize *The Mountain Wreath* and its creator in a Communist spirit:

"*The Mountain Wreath* has played a gigantic role in the patriotic and martial upbringing of our younger generations over the past 100 years. This role is no smaller today. Quite the reverse. The War for National Liberation, the most difficult and the most glorious period in the history of our peoples, brought it closer to us than it had ever been. Tito's generation embodies, in new conditions and in broader fashion, those very qualities of our people which were the key factor in all their triumphs, those qualities that are sung, with unheard of poetic strength, in *The Mountain Wreath*: self-sacrifice, heroism, the refusal to give in, and the noble hatred of enemies of and traitors to the fatherland, the highest conscience and answerability to the people and history. That is why, during the course of the War of National Liberation, the verses of *The Mountain Wreath* sounded like a password on the lips of our fighters, and they could achieve their heroic feats, which enabled the realization of the ideals of national freedom and a better life. That is why when we read *The Mountain Wreath* today we see in its heroes the same qualities we see in the heroes of our War of National Liberation. Those same people who perfectly developed and completed the struggle for national liberation, fulfilled the ideals and dreams of the great Njegoš and the heroes of *The Mountain Wreath*. That is why *The Mountain Wreath* is today a true textbook of patriotism for today's and future generations. That is why we celebrate its hundredth anniversary not only as the most important cultural event of the new Yugoslavia, not only as a confirmation of a new attitude toward great people and events from our past, but as a true national holiday."

Of primary importance is the idea that the partisans of the Second World War were merely updated versions of the "freedom fighters" Njegoš had described. The uncomfortable fact that Njegoš's work describes, with a fair amount of enthusiasm, the slaughter of a group very similar to that which made up some 12 percent of the nation's population was easily elided by turning what in *The Mountain Wreath* is a homogeneous ethno-religious group (Islamicized Slavs) into the more generalized "traitors." Of equal importance is the claim that the simple folk (i.e., the workers and peasants who officially made up the backbone of Yugoslav Communist society) both knew and appreciated Njegoš (again, Brkljačić's article in this volume indicates that this was not entirely untrue). Thus, despite Njegoš's noble background, he was an honorary man of the people. It is also noteworthy that the ethic of heroism, such an important component both for Serbianizing unitarist thought as well as Yugoslav multicultural ideology, is preserved intact here.

In the early Communist period Njegoš's work does not seem to have been a source of friction. *The Mountain Wreath* was a featured part of all school curricula throughout the country, and discussions of it were limited to scholarly commentary. The same could not be said of his resting place, however. Already in 1950, in preparation for the 100th anniversary of Njegoš's death, the idea of erecting a monument to the poet in Cetinje had been broached. In 1952, the republic government of Montenegro, through Yugoslavia's embassy in Washington, asked Ivan Meštrović (who was then teaching at Syracuse University) to design the monument. Meštrović responded with a plan for a mausoleum to replace the one on the summit of Lovćen.[26] This was actually the second proposal he made for the site, for he had produced some drawings in 1925 at the request of King Aleksandar (see photograph on p. 138).[27] The design that he proposed in the 1950s (and that stands on Lovćen today) differs considerably, although it retains the same overall Secessionist feel characteristic of most of the sculptor's monumental projects from the Kosovo Temple to the Tomb of the Unknown Soldier at Avala (see photograph).

It is unclear what drove Montenegrin officials to agree to replace the mausoleum that Njegoš himself had designed and that had been restored in

The present-day Njegoš mausoleum, built to designs by Ivan Meštrović and opened in 1971

1925. Most likely, it was a desire to de-Serbianize Njegoš, to make his resting place less Byzantine and thereby to bring his body into line with the interpretive paradigms that had already been developed for his work. Whatever the reasons, the project generated controversy, with Montenegrin and Yugoslav government officials mostly in favor and at least a portion of Serbian and Montenegrin cultural figures opposed. The final decision was not made until the late 1960s, after Meštrović's death. The destruction of the old mausoleum was ultimately a minor cause celebre, albeit one that was kept out of most public organs.[28]

As Yugoslavia began to collapse, Njegoš's position as Yugoslav national poet became shaky. The opening salvo appears to have been fired by a school teacher named Mubera Mujagić in 1984, at a public meeting sponsored by the Writers' Organization of Sarajevo to discuss proposed revisions in the nationwide required school curriculum.[29] Her suggestion, that *The Mountain Wreath* as well as Ivan Mažuranić's *The Death of Smail-Aga Čengić* be removed from the nationwide curriculum because they might "evoke national intolerance," led to a series of responses and counter-responses in the Belgrade biweekly *Intervju*.[30] While not disputing Njegoš's position as a great writer and thinker, Mujagić, who publicly identified herself as a Yugoslav, asked: "What kind of spirit can these works offer us? Can they evoke catharsis in the reader, a feeling of unity, Yugoslavism, accord, solidarity, toleration, and cosmopolitanism, or do they create bile, poison, and hatred towards anyone who belongs to another belief or nation." Mujagić's critics responded to her allegations in a couple of ways, either defending Njegoš as a great thinker and writer whose thought soars above all petty local differences and forms an indelible part of the national legacy that should not be removed just because it might offend someone in the present (Egerić), or by insisting that the characters and times described in Njegoš's work had nothing to do with the nations of contemporary Yugoslavia (Vučelić). All the critics agreed that only poor teaching could possibly allow any student to come away from the text with an incorrect impression. No one responded directly to the claims made by Mujagić, and backed up by a teacher named Jakov Ivaštović who reported having the same experience, that students did indeed interpret *The Mountain Wreath* in a nationalist vein. The most amazing aspect of the discussion, however, was not the specifics, but rather the fact that it took place at all. Despite the fact that this was, at least from an outsider's perspective, an obvious question to be raised about Njegoš's masterpiece, within Yugoslavia the subject was such a taboo that apparently no one in the previous 65 years had ever asked it before, at least not in public.

Perhaps as a result of these questions, by the late 1980s Njegoš's Yugoslav-oriented partisans clearly felt it necessary to defend the Yugoslav national writer against charges of chauvinism. Thus Jovan Deretić, in 1989 in the preface to the last "Yugoslav" edition meant for school use, felt constrained to prove that what had previously been considered the central action of the work was actually of secondary importance (see Document 4 for more of Deretić's strategy). "The annihilation of the converts to Islam, the fateful question of Montenegro appears first and foremost as an object of dread, hope and desire. It is presented in dreams, in poetic indications, and rumors. ... But Njegoš is least of all concerned with the course of events. He does not even show the annihilation of the converts on stage but rather presents it in mediated fashion, in the announcement of a herald ... and so one gets the impression that the poet wished to deemphasize the bloody clash as much as he could, to make it invisible."[31]

Once the collapse of Yugoslavia was final, the need to defend Njegoš's position as Yugoslavia's national writer disappeared. By 2002, two main schools of thought had emerged regarding Njegoš. One can identify, first, "Njegoš-bashers," whose goal has been at a minimum to remove Njegoš from his traditional position as national icon and at a maximum to blame his work for Serbian ethnic cleansing in the 1990s. This position is countered by a pro-Njegoš party that is itself split between Serbs and Montenegrins who are not in favor of Montenegrin independence, and pro-independence Montenegrins who would use Njegoš as a national symbol.

The theory that Njegoš provides a kind of blueprint for ethnic cleansing is widespread not only among Bosnian Moslems, but also among Serbian liberals. It appears as well in books by other authors intended for a more scholarly and Western audience. Thus, the Croatian researcher Branimir Anzulović puts it straightforwardly in his *Heavenly Serbia: From Myth to Genocide*, a book specifically designed to expose the dangers of Serbian myth-making in the wake of the wars of Yugoslav succession: "The rejoicing over the massacres and their description as a baptism in blood that leads to the nation's rebirth make the poem [*The Mountain Wreath*] a hymn to genocide."[32] The self-identified "Yugoslav" author Bora Ćosić is only slightly more circumspect in his assessment. Asked whether *The Mountain Wreath* can be seen as a kind of breeding-ground for atrocities, Ćosić replied: "Difficult to say. I do know that a criminal like Željko Ražnjatović (Arkan) ... is an admirer of Njegoš. And it turns out that he's not the only one whose heart begins to stir with black emotions at the reading of Njegoš's description of ethnic cleansing as a bloody baptism leading to the rebirth of Serbia as the most powerful nation in the region."[33] A similar understanding of Njegoš and his work prompted Carlos Westendorp, then the international community's High Representative in Bosnia and Herzegovina, to ban Njegoš from school textbooks in 1998.[34]

Recently, the question of how and whether Njegoš's work should be read has become less important. Rather, the issue is how he and his legacy can be used in the ongoing debate about whether there is or should be such a thing as a Montenegrin national identity separate from a Serbian identity. The opening salvos in this debate were fired as early as 1986 in a scholarly commentary by Slobodan Tomović. In the context of a careful, but controversial reading of *The Mountain Wreath*, Tomović claims that the terms Montenegrin and Serbian were not synonyms for Njegoš: "It is evident that Njegoš uses the terms "Montenegrins" and "Montenegrin" in all cases when his literary heroes address gatherings or their contemporaries directly, in distinction to "Serbian" which the author uses nostalgically to evoke pictures of the distant past."[35] This claim, even in a work that still presented Njegoš as a Yugoslav author (15–16), opened the possibility that Njegoš could be used not as a unifying symbol for Serbs and Montenegrins but rather as a wedge to demonstrate their essential difference.[36]

A companion piece to Tomović's commentary is a book published by the Montenegrin Academy of Sciences (CANU) in 1994 under a title that translates to *Anthropomorphological Characteristics of Petar II Petrović Njegoš*. Based on an analysis of the writer's bones carried out when his remains were transferred to the Meštrović-designed mausoleum in 1974, this book represents a bizarre combination of nineteenth-century racial theory, medieval respect for the bones of a saint, and modern national consciousness. The author, Božina Ivanović, carefully avoids any use of the word "Serbian" in his text, focusing exclusively on a meticulous, practically grotesque, analysis of Njegoš's skeletal remains in order to confirm the claims of Njegoš's contemporaries who, in his paraphrase, saw him as "an Adonis from the Montenegrin mountains … the Montenegrin Achilles and Orpheus, the Saul and the Samuel of his people, as handsome as Apollo, someone an artist would have chosen as a model for Hercules and a philosopher as a model for his life."[37] Along the way, Ivanović proves to the reader that Njegoš most likely stood between 191 and 193 centimeters tall, and that his brain mass was exceeded only by that of Turgenev (see photograph).

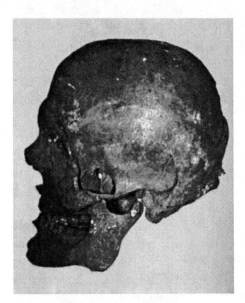

The skull of P.P. Njegoš, published in Božina Ivanović, "Antropomorfološke osobine Petra II Petrovića Njegoša"

Advocates of the view that Montenegrins are in fact Serbs have been quite vocal in attacking this position and in deploying Njegoš to buttress their own claims. As a rule, claims for Njegoš's Serbianism are accompanied by complaints about the destruction of Njegoš's mausoleum in 1971, an action that is interpreted, probably correctly, as the work of an alliance of Communists wishing to weaken potential symbols of Serbian identity and Montenegrins interested in building an independent non-Serb identity. Some Serbs, more inclined to full-blown conspiracy theories, blame the Vatican, the freemasons, and others for what is referred to on a website not accidentally registered as Njegos.org as "the pagan building known as the Njegoš mausoleum ... deed of a Croat nationalist Ivan Meštrović." Such a final resting place is clearly unacceptable to those who think like Zora Latinović: "Njegoš is a Serbian writer and this emerges logically from his work. Those who insist on a Montenegrin identity don't even try very hard to claim him" (*NIN* #2625, 19 April 2001).

In one thing at least, Latinović is correct. Those Montenegrins who are striving to create an independent state and an independent Montenegrin identity are not quite sure what they want to do with Njegoš. As opposed to the Montenegrin Academy of Sciences (CANU), which follows the Serbian line of its filial Serbian Academy of Sciences (SANU), and whose members insist at every turn on Njegoš's Serbian identity, members of the rival, Dukljanska akademija (DANU) seem rather conflicted. Thus, they were recently accused by the priest Velibor Džomić of believing that "the time has come to discard all the old canons, including Njegoš, and replace them with new ones" (as reported in *Vijesti*, 9 May 2001, and republished on the web at www.medijaklub.cg.yu/kultura/arhiva/maj2001/09.htm).

While this vituperative attack was clearly meant to shame partisans of Montenegrin independence (including the present governing political elite), it appears that some of them would in fact embrace the sentiments expressed. For them, it would appear that Njegoš and his cult is something of an embarrassment. He is archaic, violent, monocultural, and requires too much interpretation to remain acceptable. Thus, for the young writer Andrej Nikolaidis (born 1974), there is also no doubt that *The Mountain Wreath* played an important role in setting the stage for recent events.[38] Rather than banning Njegoš, however, this young writer recommends that he simply be put on the sidelines. "Today, I would say that there are several writers, and I number myself among them, who are close in age and who ignore Njegoš's legacy, although again, after us, there is pretty much no one. In particular, those who are younger than us again are returning to that retrograde tradition because they think that in this way they can affirm the idea of Montenegrin sovereignty and the need for independence."

Nikolaidis's position represents a truly new phase in the use of Njegoš.

For the first time, a group that could be expected to try to make use of him and his work in the process of identity creation is refusing to do so. Could this be an indication of a more general loss of prestige for literature in post-Communist Eastern Europe? Could it be an indication that Montenegrins are looking for new methods of creating national identity, based less on ethno-religious and cultural ties and more on contemporary European notions of citizenship? Probably not. Nikolaidis's own obsessive need to emphasize Njegoš's irrelevance is an indication that his cult simply cannot be ignored in Montenegro, even by those who most wish to do so.[39] It is thus almost certain that as their quest to create an independent national identity (with or without a state) continues, Montenegrins will have no other choice but to find a way to reincorporate Njegoš, peeling away from him and his cult the accretions of Serbian and Yugoslav nation builders and defending him from those who would see his work as nothing more than propaganda by literary means.

Sources

Document 1:

"Let there be then, all that there cannot be."

Nowhere in world poetry nor in the fate of any people can I find a more horrifying credo. But without that suicidal absurdity, without that positive nihilism (to make an oxymoron), without that stubborn negation of obvious reality neither the activity nor the very thought of action against evil would have been possible. And in this sense Njegoš is the fullest expression of our basic and deepest collective sense because it was under this motto, consciously or unconsciously, that our struggles for freedom were fought, from Karadjordje to the most recent days.

As in battle scenes painted by the old masters, in which you see two heavenly armies fighting with each other high above the battle of two human armies, so Njegoš's most important struggle plays itself out on two planes, the physical and the spiritual, the earthly and the heavenly. For the fateful battle with the Ottoman Empire would be both the subject of Njegoš's greatest poetic work as well as his biggest political and military problem. Njegoš frequently said: "I am also a martyr on these walls, like Prometheus in the Caucasus." And in comparing himself to Prometheus he would immediately add that the Turkish Empire was the hawk that gnawed at his insides.

It was not simply a struggle between two beliefs, two nations, and two races, it was a clash of two elements, the East and the West, and our fate willed that this battle be played out on our territories for the most part and that it divide and separate our whole nation with a bloody wall. We were all thrown and dragged into this elemental battle, and no matter which side we ended up on, we fought with equal intelligence, with equal bravery, and with equal belief in the justice of our cause.

The tragedy of this struggle was sharpened and deepened by the unavoidable fratricidal battles that our difficult history has frequently provided. The tragedy was all the greater for Njegoš in that from his high point of view, like all the great and light-bearing souls of our history, he could capture at a glance the totality of our nation, without differentiating between belief or tribe. (15–16)

Source: Ivo Andrić, "Njegoš, the Tragic Hero of Kosovo Thought" (1935); reprinted in Ivo Andrić, *Sabrana djela* (Sarajevo, 1984), 13: 9–32.

Document 2:
Led on by the great idea of the liberation of his nation and its amalgamation into a single great, free, and enlightened motherland, Njegoš felt equally close to Belgrade, Zagreb, Travnik, Dubrovnik, Skadar and Mostar. He had the same brotherly feelings toward the rebellious Bosnian Vizir Gradaščević, to Ali-Pasha Rizvanbegović and to Osman-Pasha Skopljak as he did toward Aleksandr Karadjordjević or Ban Jelačić. It was all the same to him whether one or another of them was baptized or not or what their names were; the important thing for him was that they were all sons of the same mother, of a single people, that they were brothers. (3)

Lonely Njegoš burned out quickly in his great love and pain. Like a meteor, he shined in the dark Yugoslav sky, leaving behind him a flaming path, by which resurrection could be achieved, a herald of the great future days of liberation. He has remained the highest exemplar of our race, as a priest, a ruler, and a patriot. His broad conceptions of Yugoslavism and of Slavdom, of freedom, fraternity, humanity and enlightenment raise him up high and place him among those individuals who have created an entire national program for years to come. They make him a national Messiah, the creator of a single bright and national religion of heroism, freedom, fraternity, love, and human dignity; they place him among the group of individuals who work for the ages for many generations and they make him truly immortal. (8)

Source: Dr. Nikola Skerović, "Njegoš and Yugoslavism," *Nova Evropa* [Zagreb] XI, 1 (1 January 1925), 1–8.

Document 3:

> *The Mountain Wreath* has played a gigantic role in the patriotic and
> martial upbringing of our younger generations over the past 100
> years. This role is no smaller today. Quite the reverse. The War for
> National Liberation, the most difficult and the most glorious period
> in the history of our peoples, brought it closer to us than it had ever
> been. Tito's generation embodies, in new conditions and in broader
> fashion, those very qualities of our people which were the key factor
> in all their triumphs, those qualities that are sung, with unheard of
> poetic strength, in *The Mountain Wreath*: self-sacrifice, heroism, the
> refusal to give in, and the noble hatred of enemies of and traitors to
> the fatherland, the highest conscience and answerability to the people
> and history. That is why, during the course of the War of National
> Liberation, the verses of *The Mountain Wreath* sounded like a pass-
> word on the lips of our fighters, and they could achieve their heroic
> feats, which enabled the realization of the ideals of national freedom
> and a better life. That is why when we read *The Mountain Wreath*
> today we see in its heroes the same qualities we see in the heroes of
> our War of National Liberation. Those same people who perfectly
> developed and completed the struggle for national liberation, ful-
> filled the ideals and dreams of the great Njegoš and the heroes of *The
> Mountain Wreath*. That is why *The Mountain Wreath* is today a true
> textbook of patriotism for today's and future generations. That is
> why we celebrate its hundredth anniversary not only as the most
> important cultural event of the new Yugoslavia, not only as a confir-
> mation of a new attitude toward great people and events from our
> past, but as a true national holiday.

Source: Niko Pavić, *Pobeda*, 7 June 1947, 1.

Document 4:

> In fact, in *The Mountain Wreath* … there is place for three worlds,
> three civilizations that have come into contact and become inter-
> twined on our territory: our heroic-patriarchal civilization whose
> exemplary expression was classical Montenegro; Turkish oriental-
> Islamic civilization; and Western European civilization introduced by
> the Venetians. To that openness to other peoples and cultures, which
> is present despite the fact that these nations were age-old enemies of
> Montenegro, must be added another openness of the poem, an open-
> ness to nature and the cosmos." (22)
>
> The annihilation of the converts to Islam, the fateful question of
> Montenegro appears first and foremost as an object of dread, hope

and desire. It is presented in dreams, in poetic indications, and rumors. The eye that can see into the future is able to see a vision of the land "liberated from internal evil." ... But Njegoš is least of all concerned with the course of events. He doesn't even show the annihilation of the converts on stage but rather presents it in mediated fashion, in the announcement of a herald ... and so one gets the impression that the poet wished to deemphasize the bloody clash as much as he could, to make it invisible. (26–7)

Source: Petar Petrović Njegoš, *Gorski vijenac,* preface by Jovan Deretić (Belgrade: Prosveta [Skolska lektira], 1989).

Notes

1 Quoted in Ljubomir Durković-Jakšić, *Njegoš i Lovćen* (Belgrade, 1971), 260.

2 "Njegoš je Crna Gora," *Stvaranje,* vol. 36, #11, 1981, 1311.

3 *NIN* #2625, 19 April 2001.

4 This was true even in Russia, a country that had obviously achieved political independence long before the appearance of Pushkin. Nevertheless, the forced Europeanization of Russian culture in the eighteenth century led to a national cultural inferiority complex, and Pushkin was seen to have marked the beginning of Russia's reappearance as a cultural nation.

5 James Frusetta's previous chapter in this volume discusses an analogous case in the history of the other major South Slavic peoples—the Bulgarians and Macedonians—albeit the subjects of dispute are revolutionaries rather than poets.

6 Actually, there is general agreement among contemporary historians that the massacre described in *The Mountain Wreath* never occurred. Njegoš, however, apparently accepted this legend as historical fact.

7 P. P. Njegoš, *The Mountain Wreath,* ed. Vasa D. Mihailovich (Irvine, Ca.: Charles Schlacks Publisher, 1986), 7. Further references to this work are made in the text by page number of this edition.

8 "*The Mountain Wreath*: Poetry or a Blueprint for the Final Solution?" *Spaces of Identity* 1/4 (www.univie.ac.at/spacesofidentity/vol_4/_html/pavlovic.html, 2.

9 Rešetar describes these editions in the introduction to the 1905 edition (Zadar, Izdanje hrvatske knjižarnice). Rešetar's commentary itself proved to be long-lasting, having been republished in various forms ten times between 1890 and 1940. See the commentary to the jubilee edition of the work (Belgrade, 1967) by Vido Latković, 224–25.

10 See Andrew Baruch Wachtel, *Making a Nation, Breaking a Nation: Literature and Cultural Politics in Yugoslavia* (Stanford: Stanford UP, 1998), 52–53.

11 *Primeri nove književnosti,* ed. Jeremija Zivanović (Belgrade, 1921), 139.

12 For a full account of Njegoš's design for the church, his burial there in 1855, exhumation in 1916 and reburial there in 1925, see Durković-Jakšić. For an excellent discussion of the general phenomenon of politically motivated reburial, see Katherine Verdery, *The Political Lives of Dead Bodies: Reburial and Postsocialist Change* (New York: Columbia UP, 1999).

13 See Durković-Jakšić, 127–268 for a full discussion of these debates.

14 Even the daily newspaper *Jutro*, in far-off Slovenia, gave the event quite a bit of space. On 22 September, it carried a long article on Njegoš and his significance, noting that he was "a great Illyrian, a great Yugoslav, and prophet of today's freedom." (5)

15 Quoted in Durković-Jakšić, 260.

16 Not everyone was willing to make of Njegoš and *The Mountain Wreath* exemplars of Yugoslav culture. As one critic complained at the time, "National ideologues have created a prophet out of him, a precursor to Yugoslav thought, and they have placed him as a link in the chain with which they avidly connect Gundulić and Kašić, and then through Strossmayer and Prince Michael to our days." Milan Bogdanović, "Vratimo Njegoša literaturi," *Srpski književni glasnik*, second series (16, #7), 1925, 577.

17 Jaša M. Prodanović, "Gorski vijenac kao vaspitno delo," *Srpski književni glasnik*, second series, (16, # 7), 1925, 562.

18 Ivo Andrić, "Njegoš, the Tragic Hero of Kosovo Thought," 16; reprinted in Ivo Andrić, *Sabrana djela* (Sarajevo, 1984), 13: 9–32.

19 P.P. Njegoš, *Izabrana pisma*, 152.

20 "Njegoš and Yugoslavism," *Nova Evropa* [Zagreb] XI, 1 (1 January 1925), 3.

21 It is, for example, the only passage provided in *Istorija jugoslovenske književnosti sa teorijom i primerima za III i IV razred gradjanskih škola*, ed. Franjo Poljanec and Blagoje Marčić, 2nd ed. (Belgrade, 1934). It is the featured passage in *Primeri nove književnosti*. The other, shorter, excerpts presented there are similarly "harmless." One finds the same tendency in post-Second World War readers. Vojvoda Draško is, for example, the only extended passage present in *Čitanka za VIII razred osnovne škole*, ed. Bojin Dramušić and Radojka Radulović, 8th ed. (Sarajevo, 1960, with approval of the Ministry of Ed. BiH). The same is true for *Naš put u jezik i književnost (Priručnik za drugi stupanj osnovnog obrazovanja odraslih)*, ed. Stojadin Stojanović, et al. (Belgrade, 1970).

22 It is interesting in this regard to contrast the treatment of the 100th anniversary of *The Mountain Wreath* with the almost complete silence that greeted the 100th anniversary of Ivan Mažuranić's *The Death of Smail-Aga Čengić* a year earlier.

23 After his fall from grace with his colleagues, Djilas would write a highly romantic biography of Njegoš—*Njegoš: Poet, Prince, Bishop*, trans. Michael B. Petrovich (New York: Harcourt, Brace & World, 1966).

24 The fact that Njegoš had been a religious in addition to a political leader was, of course, somewhat inconvenient. But Communist-era commentators were careful to play this down, noting the fact that he was not doctrinaire and that he usually wore civilian clothes.

25 *Pobeda* (Montenegro), 7 June 1947, 4.

26 The correspondence between Meštrović and the Yugoslav authorities relating to his mausoleum can be found in the publication *Sumrak Lovćena* (Belgrade, 1989), 36–47. This book is in fact a reprint of a double issue of the journal *Umetnost* that was banned by the Yugoslav government authorities in 1971 at the height of the controversy surrounding the erection of Meštrović's mausoleum.

27 For a discussion of Meštrović's 1925 plan, see *Nova Evropa* 1, 1, 1925. The illustrations are reproduced in *Sumrak Lovćena*, 221.

28 The book by Durković-Jakšić, which goes to great lengths to show that Njegoš's desire was to lie precisely in the building he designed and no other, is clearly an implicit polemic against the Meštrović mausoleum. More open criticism of the plan was suppressed, however, including the double issue of *Umetnost* discussed above.

29 These discussions were contentious all over the former Yugoslavia. For a discussion of their impact in Slovenia, see Wachtel, op. cit. 188–89.

30 The series of articles began with an attack on Mujagić by Miroslav Egerić, a professor of Philosophy at Novi Sad on 23 November 1984 (5) and continued with a long and sometimes rambling response by Mujagić on 4 January 1985 (16–18). It was followed a week later by another attack on Mujagić by Milorad Vučelić (36), and concluded with a group of four letters to the editor on 18 January (4). The quotations here are from Mujagić's response of 4 Januar, 18. My thanks to Dejan Jović for bringing this material to my attention.

31 Petar Petrović Njegoš, *Gorski vijenac,* preface by Jovan Deretić (Belgrade: Prosveta [Skolska lektira], 1989), 26–7.

32 Branimir Anzulović, *Heavenly Serbia: From Myth to Genocide* (New York: New York University Press, 1999), 54.

33 "The Hypnosis of an Unresisting Nation." Interview with Bora Ćosic by Tom Crijnen. First published in the Dutch newspaper *Trouw* (28 April 1999). Translated by Laura Martz and published on the archive of nettime.

34 As reported on the website www.truthinmedia.org/Bulletins/tim98-7-1.html.

35 *Komentar Gorskog vijenca* (Nikšić, 1984), 394.

36 A further elaboration of this theory can be found in a recent book on Montenegrin national identity by Milorad Popović. In his *Crnogorsko pitanje* (Cetinje/Ulcinj: Plima/Dignitas, 1999), Popović claims that Njegoš's "Montenegrin Serbianism" was a purely political position, developed in response to the contemporary situation. However, in Popović's view, Njegoš thought of himself as a Montenegrin not a Serb, and his *Mountain Wreath* is seen as being a purely Montenegrin work of literature, more or less incomprehensible to Serbs.

37 Božina Ivanović, *Antropomorfološke osobine Petra II Petrovića Njegoša* (Podgorica, 1994), 135.

38 See the interview with him in *Feral Tribune,* 3 June 2000, #768, 46–47.

39 I have found two other texts published by Nikolaidis in the period 1999–2002 in which he claims to see Montenegrins escaping the yoke of Njegoš.

CHAPTER 6

Ildiko Erdei

"THE HAPPY CHILD" AS AN ICON OF SOCIALIST TRANSFORMATION:
Yugoslavia's Pioneer Organization

"We are carrying youth, enthusiasm and strength through this once lifeless neighborhood ... echoes the loud refrain from the 'lower school' (Serbian part) in Starčevo, a small village in Vojvodina. They are following Tito's Torch of Youth and hurrying to meet the Pioneers of the 'upper school,' in a Croatian part of the village, to join their warm greetings and sincere wishes for a long life for our beloved Comrade Tito. Men and women merrily greet them on their way, leaning out of their windows and in front of their houses, cheering them on with a smile."[1] Although this was a local event in a village in Vojvodina, in the northern part of Serbia, in June 1953, the ritual embodied key images of the time—youth in action, the ideology of brotherhood and unity, the cult of the leader, enthusiasm and undivided support from the people.[2] It could have happened (and it did) in any other place in Yugoslavia. Demonstrating devotion to the ideals of revolution and socialism, and to the icon of the revolution—the (at that time) marshal and later lifetime president Josip Broz Tito—made up the entire content of a number of socialist rituals over the following years.[3] The main protagonists of the scene above were members of the children's mass organization, the Yugoslav Pioneer Organization—Pioneers for short. Mass Pioneer organizations came into being after 1945 in Yugoslavia as well as in the rest of the Communist world—in the Balkans (Romania, Bulgaria, Albania), in Central Europe (Hungary, Czechoslovakia, Poland) and outside Europe (China, North Korea, Cuba). Pioneer organizations were created on the Soviet model. Their objective was to build up patriotic emotions and develop a sense of belonging to the ideological collective from the earliest age. Organizations like "Kisdobos" (Young Drummers) in Hungary, and "Soimii patriei" (Falcons of the Homeland) and "Organizatia pionerilor" (Pioneers' Organization) in Romania, enrolled school children aged 6 to 14.[4] In Bulgaria, after the Second World War, three children's organizations were merged into one—the Dimitrov Pioneer Organization "Septemvriiche" ("Little children of September"), founded in 1944 under the guidance of the Bulgarian Communist Party; the "Stamboliiche," affiliated to the Peasant Youth Union and named after Aleksandar Stamboliiski, head of the Agrarian Party and prime minister from 1919 to 1923; and the "Red Swallow," affiliated with the Union of Socialist Youth . The new organisation was dominated by the Bulgarian Communist Party and its leader Georgi Dimitrov, whose name was incorporated, after his death, into the official name of the organization. The Pioneer organization in Bulgaria was closely linked to schools, and for the pupils in first and second school grade, "Chavdarche" groups ("cheti"), named after the legendary outlaw Chavdar and the partisan brigade "Chavdar," were formed for each school class.[5]

In every country where the Pioneer organization existed, its members were considered pioneering builders of the future, who would move the society forward, finding new paths to socialist goals. Their whole upbringing and education, both in and after school, was created with reference to the Communist Party, under the supervision of ideologically and class conscious teachers and Pioneer leaders, who monitored and controlled the "correct" way of growing up. At an early school age (or even before that, as in Romania and Hungary) children were converted from the status of "ideologically undecided" to "ideologically decided" members of the community through a political ritual of reception into this organization. The organization and its members were generally encouraged to appreciate the personality of Communist Party leaders, which could escalate into actual cults of adulation. The "difference between the former (child) and future (pupil/Pioneer) status was dramatically emphasized through the ritual of the reception into the Pioneer organization, as Miroslava Malešević has illustrated in the Yugoslav example[6]. The child was also reaching the first stage of social maturity, where he or she was expected to start fulfilling obligations of society. In that way, the state in socialist Yugoslavia took an active part in molding childhood, separately from the family's natural responsibility for early socialization. In short, admission to the Pioneer organization was the first initiation among many that would transform the person into a fully acculturated member of the socialist community. Unlike in traditional society, the socialization process was entrusted almost completely to various official organizations, all of which were organized and controlled by the Communist Party.[7]

The emphasis on children's upbringing and their role in the development of socialism was brought about through systematic monitoring of their growing up in a manner and to a degree incomparable with any other previous historical period. There are two interconnected reasons for this. First, the regime's future-driven utopian vision of a world changed by the personalities of its citizens made its interest in childhood inevitable. Investment in its own future was an on-going task of all the socialist regimes, and the "ideologically decided" children were the seeds of the promised future.[8] Another reason was the harsh social circumstances under which many if not most children in prewar Yugoslavia were growing up. In his study of the first postwar years of Communist rule in Yugoslavia and the cultural policy of "agitprop," Ljubodrag Dimić cites prewar statistics that reveal all too little schooling of any kind. According to his data, immediately before the Second World War, the population of Serbia (and the same could be said for Yugoslavia) was predominantly rural. Almost three-quarters of the population were living in villages, and there was a very high percentage of illiteracy. Just 30 percent of children had attended school. Since the majority of them were living in villages, they were obliged to help their parents in seasonal agricultural work; it was not uncommon for them to attend school only from time to time, in line with the agricultural season. Traditional customs may also have contributed to the very low percentage of children who continued their primary education. Members of some ethnic groups, for example Romanians, tended to marry early and usually dropped out of school at the age of 13 or 14. The new Communist regime used these failings to criticize the former government from the interwar era.

The new regime sought to develop a cultural and educational policy that would involve as many children as possible, in an effort to influence their lives and their thinking. In order to meet the needs of the population for basic literacy, the state initiated under Agitprop (the party body in charge of supervising and organizing cultural and educational programs, 1945–52) a mass campaign of "national enlightenment" *(narodno prosvećivanje)*, aimed primarily at increasing literacy. But, as Dimić notes, "the aim of the project of national enlightenment was not only to teach the people to read and write, *but to make them be able to use that knowledge in order to change their lives and the life of the whole community*" (my italics).[9]

Until now, there has been little ethnological, anthropological or historical research on mass organizations and upbringing in socialist Yugoslavia. Studies have chiefly concentrated on the party's ideological motivation in controlling all aspects of life, emphasizing the importance of the ritual of admission to the Pioneer organizations,[10] the appropriation of traditional holidays and the invention of new ones to celebrate the postwar transformation of society,[11] and "ideological indoctrination" through ABC books.[12] In this chapter, however, we consider the Pioneer organization as an institutional framework for producing childhood in Yugoslav socialist society.[13]

This chapter accepts the assumption of modern sociology that childhood is a "social construction," in other words that it represents not only a biological but also, and primarily, a social and cultural category. As Chris Jenks has put it: "Childhood is to be understood as a social construct, it makes reference to a social status delineated by boundaries that vary through time and from society to society ... Childhood then always relates to a particular cultural setting."[14] Studying children and childhood, according to this author, is actually a process of exploring various social contexts and sociological structures that set the limits in which a variety of childhoods are "created" and the normative system of expectation is generated. Jenks turns our attention to another important problem: the question of collective practices binding a child after he or she has become an independent social subject. He believes that "the way that we control our children reflects, perhaps as a continuous microcosm, the strategies through which we exercise power and constraint in the wider society."[15] The transformation of the Pioneer organization into a "true children's organization" began in the same year (1950) as "self-management" was established in Yugoslav companies. Along with the change in the content and method of work, the transformation also brought a change in the manner of social control of children. In the years that followed, a particular combination of "merry," "childish" forms with serious, ideological content was made. It created a way to control youth in a more indirect, informal and seductive, yet more innocent way—and one that was equally effective.

This reform of the Pioneer organization was of great consequence in the process of "childhood production" in socialist Yugoslavia. The early 1950s were important as a time of change both for Yugoslavia generally and for the Pioneer organization as well. Prior to 1948, the Yugoslav Pioneer Organization had given unequivocal support to the "first country of Communism," the USSR. Soviet influences were visible in every aspect of life, and particularly in a cultural and educational policy that in the immediate postwar period was under strong influence from the Soviet model. After the political departure of the Soviets, a period of political decentralization and a slow political and cultural liberation began. Part of that process was a transformation of mass organizations and of the Pioneer organization as well. This change was announced in a party document of 1950, which prescribed a change in the approach to children. But before we consider this important change, let us briefly summarize the history of the Pioneer organization in Yugoslavia.

ЖИВЕО ПРВИ МАЈ ДАН РАДНИКА И
СЕЉАКА
ЖИВЕО ВЕЛИКИ СТАЉИН ТИТО

*Remaking the impact of the Soviet influence—Pioneers celebrating 1 May 1946.
The inscription on the banner reads "Long live Great Stalin," but post festum the
word "Stalin" has been crossed out and Tito's name added*

"Short-Sleeved Heroes"

The Yugoslav Pioneer Organization was born during the Second World War
and died in 1991, during the first months of warfare between yesterday's
neighbors sworn to the Partisan motto of "brotherhood and unity" *(bratstvo
i jedinstvo)* and bonded by common Pioneer membership. The last generation of Pioneers tied red scarves around their necks on 29 November 1989,
when the country to which they swore their loyalty was living its last peaceful days. During the Second World War, many monographs on this organization claim, the Pioneers organized spontaneously or under the leadership
of the KPJ (Communist Party of Yugoslavia) and the SKOJ (Communist Youth
League of Yugoslavia). They joined Partisan units on front lines across the
whole of divided Yugoslavia. The first organized body was the Montenegrin
Children's National Liberation Movement, founded in November 1941. It
recruited boys and girls aged 10 to 15, on condition that they "do not drink,
do not smoke, and do not carry a sling-shot."[16] Youngsters throughout

Yugoslavia followed the example of the Montenegrin children. The Pioneer organization was officially constituted on 27 December 1942, at the First Antifascist Congress of Yugoslav Youth, when the main aims of the Youth organization regarding the new Pioneers were set down. According to *Children to the Sun of Freedom*[17] and *The Yugoslav Pioneers Organization 1942–1945*,[18] Pioneer organizations grew like mushrooms after the rain, on the front lines and on liberated territories. Such statements were intended to give the impression of a mutually reinforcing and constantly growing number of Pioneer groups.[19] As already noted, the concept, the basic organizational principles and the ethos of the Yugoslav Pioneer Organization came from the USSR. They drew on the Soviet experience of the "V. I. Lenin Pioneer Organization," established in 1922 and built "on the principles of collectivism and self-initiative, on the wide stimulation of children's initiative."[20] Articles from the first Pioneer newspaper, *The Pioneer,* first published in 1942 in different parts of the country, help to trace the influence of the Soviet model. Many articles focused on the attention Soviet authorities were paying to the upbringing and education of children. They stressed the benefits already achieved by growing up under socialism—the collective spirit, creative education, a stimulating atmosphere for learning and improving existing skills, and the development of a sense of discipline. The article "From the Country Where Happy Children Live" shows everyday life in a Soviet school collective, describing it as a "beautiful building, with marble columns, luminous rooms and big mirrors that reflect the happy faces of the Soviet children."[21] Much space was also given to promoting a belief in science and its capacity to liberate the minds of the people, particularly the young.

Young Pioneers were involved in a great number of activities, some being "civil" tasks (gathering food and clothes for soldiers and wounded), and some military duties (snatching weapons from German soldiers and giving them to Partisans, courier missions, guarding villages, enacting small diversions, and so on). Children left without families would join Partisan units and enthusiastically took part in battles.[22] Some, like Boško Buha, Sava Jovanović Sirogojno, Milka Mika Bosnić, Fana Kočovska and several others, became celebrities of the NOB (People's Liberation War) as child-heroes ("pioneer-national heroes").[23] They then became role models for the postwar generation. The basis for Pioneer activities was worked out during the war, when it was proclaimed that Pioneers should be recruited in villages and introduced to the basic features of Partisan organization and discipline, so that "the existing love of Pioneers for Partisans should grow deeper and more intense."[24] During the war in Bosnia, Herzegovina, Croatia, Slovenia and Montenegro, 356 community and 1,267 village Pioneers' councils, 7,120 labor squads and 13,000 Pioneer units were formed.[25] In May 1945, 40,000

Childhood in World War Two—Pioneers with wooden guns salute the commander

of the 800,000 Partisan total were under the age of 15.[26] They were organized as true military formations, with ranks, missions and real weapons actually used in combat. These children's lives were strongly affected by the war. The youngsters were not only the objects of wartime destruction and deprivation; they were also actors in the war. Thus the borderline between the world of adults and children was blurred, because a whole generation had prematurely to take on the duties and responsibilities of adults. The Communist leaders of Yugoslavia would often return to the role that these youngest fighters performed in war. This they used partly to underline the necessity of the liberation war, since "mere children" saw its importance and risked their lives for the cause. In addition, leading party officials, including Tito himself, used every opportunity to refer not just to the war years but to the prewar period as well as a time of "childhood deprivation" or "no childhood at all." On his birthday, Tito delivered the following message to the Pioneers that traditionally paid him a visit: "My childhood, like the childhood of my friends and of the great majority of children, was full of suffering and pain, filled with disappointments, because we couldn't achieve what we wanted to... Because of that, all of us who have had such a childhood now have a duty to care for the youngest—to create a pleasant childhood for you, since we did not have one."[27] Another example of this "child-centered ideology" came from the speech that Moša Pijade, one of the party leaders, gave in 1949 to a group of young researchers. He said that he regretted not being 50 or 55 years younger, and added: "I wish I could be young again to be able to have a childhood as you have. For our childhood was empty and meaningless, insubstantial, compared with all that our people's state offers you today, in order to make your childhood useful and pleasant, and colorful, interesting, bright and joyful."[28] Thus everything that had happened before the Communists took power was described mostly as lost time. More precisely, it was called a period of "stolen childhood," so the state and the party, as protectors of children, felt obligated to bring back this lost childhood.[29]

"Tempo, Tempo, Pioneers!"

The fundamental program aims, organization forms and symbols of membership to the Pioneers' organization had been created in wartime. In numerous Pioneers' groups, "Tito" caps with red stars were worn, and some elements of the admission ritual to the organization were recorded now and then (a formal song, the oath). The war's end brought new challenges for the organization. Tasks were to be more organized, internal organization and mutual communication among numerous Pioneer groups improved. The

Iconography of a Pioneer gathering in the first postwar years: party and state flags, portraits of the leaders and heroes frame the stage and watch over the performance

first task was to reformulate the main duties: military missions were to be exchanged for labor competitions contributing to rebuilding the home, the front and the victory of socialism. The new slogan for the whole society, including Pioneers, became: "All for the front, all for victory" (see Document 1). The new program of the Young Pioneers' Organization, from 1945, defines it as a "voluntary organization of children aged 6 to 14, regardless of sex," whose aim is to "develop self-discipline in work and learning on a daily basis and cultivate all aspects of cultural life, playtime and especially physical education among the youngest in a free country."[30]

There were already warnings that work with Pioneers, which was still the duty of the Senior Youth in the years that followed the end of the war, should not be reduced only to "marching and blind obedience of the adult's orders."[31] In the postwar setting, party leaders recommended that the social base of the Pioneer organization leaders be enlarged, accepting not just youth activists but also teachers and other professionals. In 1946, the organization changed its name to the Yugoslav Pioneer Organization and adopted formal regulations. According to that year's Statute of Organization, the symbols of the organization became the red Pioneer scarf and a blue cap with a badge; the Pioneers' flag, trumpet and drum were required for rituals. A Pioneer anthem was also established, and the slogan "For the country with Tito—to the future!" adopted.[32] A Pioneer oath to be sworn on admission to the organization was also created. The oath was slightly changed over the years, but its original message, emphasizing the Pioneer's undivided loyalty to the state and society, remained the same. (See Document 3.) The new program spelled out a range of Pioneer's duties that exceeded the narrow limits of responsibilities to the organization. Pioneers were "obliged to study well, respect their teachers and attend school regularly, to love and cherish their work, to respect their parents and help their families, to take care of younger siblings, to cherish love towards freedom fighters and Yugoslav army commanders, to help invalids, to be of assistance to the families of soldiers killed in action, to do favors to the old, needy and sick, to conduct themselves in a polite manner, not to drink or smoke, to be honorable, sincere and modest, to be true friends and to help each other, to be disciplined, to fully and correctly fulfill the tasks and duties given to them by the Pioneer organization."[33]

It is clear from this quotation that the program of the organization regulated the whole range of relationships of a child/Pioneer towards other persons, relationships previously taught in the family or in church (towards parents, among children in the family, attitudes towards the old and weak, basic moral standards). The primary social environment of the child was no longer his or her family but the socialist institutions and the mass organization that was to care for children. Documents that describe the organization

Discreet encounter of the "old" and "new" traditions: the decoration on which the young Pioneer stands is a traditional folk textile

of different newly invented socialist festivals subtly reveal the changing relations and prescribed attitudes of the Pioneer towards his or her family. It is expected from the Pioneer that the sense of belonging to the organization should outweigh all other possible identities, particularly that of belonging to the family. Thus, when the Pioneer had to perform certain tasks, he or she was instructed, as in one case, to "agitate their mothers to persuade them to bake cakes and prepare presents for Children's Day (the celebration of New Year in place of Christmas)."[34] The organizer of the celebration in the village of Crepaja judged the "agitation" as successful, for "almost all the children have brought the cakes at the time it was ordered."[35]

Beside the tendency to socialize children's upbringing and take over family responsibilities, the state tried to watch over children day and night and to become a regulator of children's behavior in every possible context. The instructions to Pioneer leaders directly in charge of carrying out government directives stated that Pioneers should always be aware of their role and the conduct that it required. The red scarf stood as a token of belonging

*Pioneer uniform (without the cap)—blue skirt,
white shirt, and red scarf (replicating the colors of
the national flag)*

to the organization and a reminder of moral obligations which were to be
fulfilled at all times. An instruction to Pioneer leaders in 1945 (see Document 2) explained why Pioneers should always wear their scarves. Apart
from representing a "symbol of Pioneer dignity" and "uplifting the spirit,"
the scarf is an "obstruction and reminder." As a sign of "ideological determination," it gives other Pioneers and adults the right to watch over the
wearer's behavior and warn him or her if needed. Thus the scarf "forces a
Pioneer to be well-behaved"[36] and becomes a powerful method of control
and self-control. This shows how the state used different methods, both
explicit and implicit, to convey desired messages and to shape the *habitus*
of children by regulating their body-space relations and prescribing proper
behavior in every possible situation.[37] The power of the red scarf did not
come just from its being the ultimate metonymical sign that could substitute

for the full Pioneer uniform. Nor was it just that it represented a powerful symbol of initiation into the organization. The red scarf was no ordinary piece of cloth. It was believed to have transformative power that could change the personality and affect the behavior of those who wore it. In this context we can talk about a belief in a transformative capacity for cloth, and textiles in general, that is well known in folk poetry and traditional rituals.[38]

All these efforts to organize and supervise the behavior of Pioneers proved to be inadequate for creating a socialist man[39]—the goal proclaimed in party and government top levels as the major measure of accomplishment for Yugoslav socialism. According to Milovan Djilas, then still a leading party official, if the goal was the creation of a "socialist man who loves his country and respects other nations ... a man of a rich inner life, physically and morally fit, strong and joyful,"[40] it was essential to start from the beginning, from the education of the youngest members—to start from the school and Pioneer organizations. This signed instruction from the Central Committee of the KPJ found its way to all Pioneer organizations by the summer of 1950. What needed to be changed, in the opinion of the party, was the way of recognizing the value of Pioneers in themselves and the methodology of working with them. The organization must become a "true children's organization."[41] The instructions went on to say that the Pioneer organization should be an educational-entertainment organization which will "satisfy the needs of children for play, entertainment and gymnastics, which will develop all characteristics and inclinations that contribute to proper and universal human development through organized cultural work, various excursions, expeditions, camping, etc."[42]

The former mandate of the organization was criticized for being too adult-directed and openly political, in content and overly militarized for children: "The weaknesses we have been faced with can be found particularly in rigid patterns of work with children, in too slowly finding out and developing different ways of work with them, in introducing certain obtrusive political matter (lectures and political information for children), in introducing an exaggerated military spirit and discipline which was inappropriate for children and their interests, with the result that the Pioneer organization was still not popular enough among children." Djilas concluded that one of the reasons for such a deficiency was that the organization did not offer to children "enough play, entertainment and everyday children's fun."[43]

This concern of the socialist community for its youth was not motivated, as one might at first assume, exclusively by the desire for ideological control over young members, as suggested by Miroslava Malešević.[44] The attention towards children and the young, as Petr Roubal argued for Czechoslovakia, rests at the very core of the socialist regime, and insistence on "childishness" can be considered one of its main characteristics. Roubal cites a semiotic analysis which shows children to be the only "true new people" because they are unburdened with a past, i.e., a bourgeois inheritance, and represent the future inhabitants of heaven.[45] Children are seen as a blank sheet of paper waiting to be filled with various qualities and overall ideologically correct contents. That is why, during the political process of reforming Pioneers' organizations, there also occurred a reconceptualization of the world of grown-ups and children, and the borderline between the two categories, that had been obscured and unbalanced during the war and shortly after. The authority of the older generation was again introduced.

The older generation alone was set up as responsible and authoritative in relation to others (children in this case). The only task to be performed by children was now to study. This indicates great confidence in the power of knowledge to change people and the community. Lisa A. Kirschenbaum has shown the strength of the revolutionary concept of knowledge in the Soviet model of preschool education. She talks about the Soviet vision of the "revolutionary generation in progress," which is expected to change not only its old-fashioned teachers, but also its parents.[46] This belief in the power of education to change life was shared by most prominent Yugoslav party and state leaders. They instructed children: "Your task is to study, that is your job ..." as a part of a general "people's enlightenment" campaign, organized and conducted under the strong guidance of the party. The belief in the power of knowledge to transform people and to make them able to change others too, with the final goal to create a new socialist man, was thereby spelled out. What was needed was a fresh start. Pioneer units were linked to schools and thus launched on the mission of producing a socialist childhood.

"More Fun, Please"—Creating One "Happy and Bright" Childhood

In order to get the reform going, a variety of activities for "correct creative development" and "encompassing personality" was to be set up with the necessary "material support." Newly planned children's activities would take place in specially created centers, and necessary symbols of the organization, plus now toys, books and magazines, would be supplied as soon as possible. Beyond the Pioneer corners and Pioneer residences, "Pioneer cities" were built near Belgrade and Zagreb, and a Pioneer valley near Sarajevo. Playgrounds were also supplied with equipment required for proper physical training. The world of children/Pioneers was gradually institutionalized in activities and content. Special Pioneer summer houses were built, Pioneer holidays set up, Pioneer magazines and radio stations founded, a "Pioneer railway" was created, and a later renowned child-orientated event called the Yugoslav Pioneer Games was organized for the first time. Artistic creation for children was stimulated (children's literature, children's movies), and children by themselves were encouraged to engage in different art forms.[47] During the first year of the reform, the accent was put on limiting the newly created Pioneer "children's world" to providing "children's joy," which was made the measure of a successful reform.[48] Determining and restricting "Pioneer areas," in which their activities could be planned out and supervised, was later followed by the planned organization of children's time in detail. So much time was scheduled that this left little space for the personal interests and the needs of their families.

Most of a Pioneer's time was to be planned and filled with "socially useful" work. Apart from attending school, they had to complete a number of "working classes," during which they would do chores to maintain the school area and the surroundings. Thus Pioneers would gain insight into the meaning of work, and be prepared to become creative personalities.[49] Projects for gathering litter and medicinal plants were organized on a regular basis. Not only was the time filled with "correct" subjects, but in the process Pioneers were given to believe that they were benefiting the national economy. Document 4 below recommends that all the activities organized by the Pioneer organization should connect joy with responsibility, health and morality, practice and creativity: "To build the characteristics of a socialist man within a child, the organization should help both school and family in the general education of children ... In the company of young naturalists children are eager to explore, for example, the life of certain animals ... The technical circle awakens an interest in technology, builds curiosity, creates a thirst for knowledge, and connects theory with practice ... In the physical education circle, attractive forms of sporting activities should be used to organize healthy free time filled with joy ... It is also vital that all Pioneers take part in socially useful work that is planned and systematic in helping the population—gathering scrap iron or medicinal herbs, cleaning and repairing rooms, taking part in village work and other tasks. Socially orientated Pioneer's work is of obvious importance. Children's work makes pupils self-disciplined ... more critical and strict with themselves and their friends."

Social improvement in general was one of the main aims of Pioneer organizations, and in the first postwar years particular emphasis was placed on technical and hygienic education. Reports sent "from the field," from villages and towns to regional and republic Pioneer organizations, comment daily on "hygiene measures" and issues of health. Concern with hygiene was an obvious example of how care for the bodies of the Pioneers came to be part of the creation of the "new socialist man."[50] In other areas, a whole week called Technical Week was devoted to getting acquainted with technology. It was considered that "polytechnic education and physical activities should be the key-work of the Pioneer organization in the development of socialist society."

Schedules were not organized purely on a daily or seasonal basis, nor were they left to be filled randomly with a mass of ideologically correct events. The flow of time was to be ordered on a longer-term basis and given meaning in order to serve educational and pedagogical purposes and systematically convey political and social messages. This was done by inventing a completely new calendar of festivals, by introducing new, "truly Pioneer" and "truly socialist" holidays, instead of the old, mainly family-centered traditions. Major Pioneer holidays and manifestations that mobilized the attention and energy of the young were the New Year ("a true Pioneer holiday"), A Salutation to Spring, Technical Week, Beginning of the School Year, Pioneer's Day (the end of a school year), and Republic Day (day of the admission to the Pioneer organization).

Although the "novelty" of the ritual calendar was emphasized in order to distance the new society from the past and its remnants, the efficacy of the new ritual system owed a lot to existing traditional ritual structures, cultural logic and systems of meaning. Lydia Sklevicky has shown in her analysis of the "New Year" celebration in the immediate postwar period how the resemantisation of "old" into a "newly created" socialist holiday, with children at the center, was accomplished. Christmas was switched to the New Year. Sklevicky argues that this was done in Croatia in the period 1945–50 and relatively "painlessly" because the basic ritual structure, its semantic and cognitive features remained stable and unchanged.[51] Data from the Kovačica area in the Vojvodina also show the interplay of the old, religious and family-based rituals with the new ones. Their frame of reference was indeed changed but their structural place in the calendar and sometimes their functions remained stable. An example taken from the teacher's notebook, an unofficial document for internal use only, suggests that, at least on the level of habitual use of language, it was very hard to separate "the old" and "the new." "For 'Vrbica' take them out to play; in case of bad weather, give them movies if there are cinemas, and onstage programs in other towns … Salutation to Spring will be held from 20 to 25 April … Mention to the squad councils that the program should be serious and ideological."[52] The terminology used to point out the time when the Salutation to Spring should be organized "around Vrbica" (Vrbica being an Orthodox Christian festival before Easter), reveals both the power of the old calendar and traditional rituals in times after the revolution and the continuing attachment of people to the old traditions and customs. Pioneer's Day was celebrated at the end of the school year, when the program of "inspection of work results" was prepared. According to the inscription released by the central committee of the NOJ, manifestations should last for two to three days and have three parts: a formal part, a cultural part and a public physical exercise part. This structure of the manifestation was based on three main "contents": political content in the form of a ritual, keeping the "tradition of revolution" through artistic forms, and manifesting the discipline of the "body of the unit."[53]

Preparation for the holidays and their celebration took a large portion of Pioneers' time after school. Apart from compulsory activities, Pioneers were organized into sections that had to relate a child's talents to the ideas and ideals of socialism, as outlined in Document 4. Even vacations, when children were free from school duties, were not left free for children's disposal. During the winter break, pioneer leaders were instructed to organize activities in the snow.[54] During summer, apart from the usual season projects for medicinal plant gathering, picnics were organized to stimulate "children's joy." Data from the Kovačica area show that while organizing picnics and arranging other children's festivals and activities, other local and mass organizations were involved (the Women's Antifascist Front, the People's Front, People's Youth, Yugoslav Army, work collectives, sport clubs, and so on). Sklevicky notes that these mass activities were initiated not only with enthusiasm, but also with subtle forms of repression, such as work release only to support the celebrations. In a report on the organization of a picnic which was supposed to make "joy" for children, we also find pressures to secure a massive outing of children, waiting eagerly for their free time: "Around 1000 of Kovačica's Pioneers saluted the spring on 27 April. Early in the morning, members of the administration took a truck and drove with music and trumpets and drums to wake up Pioneers, and collected those already awake and waiting in the schoolyard, which was the gathering place. Those Pioneers who liked to sleep longer were called out on the microphone ..."[55] Obviously, one was not even to decide about how much time to spend sleeping. The party preferred "dreaming with eyes open," instead of less controlled and proscribed dreaming in private.

During collective summer vacations, the children's day was also fully planned, and the organization of time and activities still resembled the military structure and organization of the army. Thus each day began with the salute to the flag and ended with the daily report to the leader (commander) of the group. Summer camps would generally end by the campfire with a program that would "bring the revolutionary tradition to life." In short, the party tried to arrange the entire life of Pioneers and fill it with content that "relates to the child's needs," as it determined those needs. Responding to needs it alone had created, the party produced the symbols of its own success—happy faces of young Pioneers. This policy of (presenting) happy

childhoods, identical to Soviet practice in the 1930s, was tied as much to
the desire of the state for discipline and recruiting dedicated Communists as
it was to the interests of the children themselves.[56]

Supervision of Pioneer's everyday life was also attempted, their time
arranged, activity areas outlined and controlled. In time, such activity did
become more engaging. Psychologists, pedagogues, writers, and poets entered
the organization, inventing and creating more appropriate and more attractive ways to spread the message of belonging to the socialist collective. We
may conclude that the aim of the reform of the Pioneer organization was
realized. A new basis for the ideological socialization of children was established, one that was not "overtly political" and "obtrusive," as was the case
during the first postwar years. Instead of complicated ideological litanies,
which were completely inappropriate for the children, the upbringing and
education of the young Pioneers in the years that followed the 1950 reform
were marked by the "ideology of the happy child." This ideology was not
original. As with many other aspects of Communist ideology, such as belief
in science and technology and permanent progress toward the utopian future
community of equals, and confidence in the transformative capacities of the
young generation, came from the USSR.

It is paradoxical that the "ideology of the happy child" that originally
came from Soviet influence on other socialist countries, was in the Yugoslav case used to exactly the opposite end. The reform of the Pioneer organization that initially represented the institutional setting for the production
of Yugoslav socialist childhood appeared shortly after Yugoslav Communist
leaders had broken with the USSR in 1948. Thus the "ideology of the happy
child" and the policy of creating a socialist childhood became the means to
differentiate Yugoslavia from yesterday's close friends and role models. The
latter were now accused of being corrupt and alienated from the original
ideas of Marxism–Leninism. As an article in a regular column called "IB
reality" in the local weekly *Pančevac* in 1953 noted, in every surrounding
country that belonged to the "Eastern Bloc" almost everything had gone
wrong. The column emphasized the dangers of bureaucracy that threatened
the Pioneer organization in neighboring Hungary. The professionalization
of the latter was criticized in order to support the new direction of the Yugoslav Pioneer Organization. The YPO was to promote individual initiative,
creative activities and rounded development of the personalities of the children. In addition, the "happiness" that was to be produced could be seen as
a safeguard against the rising bureaucratization that was seen as potentially
threatening to Yugoslav society as well. The investment in children with its
enormous symbolical potential supported the anthropological optimism of
the Yugoslav socialist project. Thus, the "ideology of the happy child" res-
onated both with Communist ideology's forward-looking orientation, along

with the more concrete social and political circumstances of the moment within which it was first created and then changed.

Yugoslavia's Communist leaders felt that investment in the proper upbringing of children was an investment in the future of the society as well. They carefully planned how the Pioneers would become the "bearers of the future," transformed through education and creativity, and therefore able to transform their parents, teachers, and the whole society. Through the ideological socialization of children in various contexts, party leaders and educators tried to connect the times past, the "founding myth" of the revolution, with a projected imagined future. Both past experiences and future perspectives were invested in the upbringing of children, making them the embodiment of the Yugoslav socialist project. It might seem self-evident that the "ideology of the happy child," with its ideological aims and content, did not leave any room for the genuine happiness of children. However, as childhood memories of different generations of Yugoslav Pioneers demonstrate, such a conclusion would be only part of the truth.

It would in fact be difficult to call an institution of such long standing as the Pioneer organization simply a success or a failure. It might well seem a total failure to those who witnessed the "real future" of the country and the organization in comparison with the "utopian vision" that was imagined in the 1950s. Many of those who grew up being guided by the "ideology of the happy childhood" took part in the most unhappy warfare of the 1990s. Belgrade's Pioneer City, built during the early 1950s as a place to celebrate children's creativity, is today a home for war refugees. It stands as a sad metaphor for different stages of a once confident ideology.

Nevertheless, it would be incorrect to conclude this chapter by picturing childhood in socialist Yugoslavia only in such dark tones. True, there were a lot of children not so pleased, if not unhappy, at not being able to celebrate publicly church or other religious holidays, or having different views of past and present events. Still, as Lydia Sklevicky also argues for the social transformation of the 1950s in Croatia, newly introduced holidays must have been a source of real pleasure for children. Indeed, brand-new clothing, exciting festive events, visits to the seaside or just a handful of candies, always with cautious reference to the state and party as the noble donors, must have brought joy. As Sklevicky put it, such experiences certainly offered, at least temporarily, "separation from the difficulties of everyday life, relief from the shortages on the harsh road to the bright future."[57]

Sources
Document 1:

Today a great part of our country is free. We must have that in mind in order to strengthen our work and to standardize it. There are two main tasks in front of our country;

1. To drive out the enemy and liberate the whole of the country

2. To build up the liberated parts of the country and to prepare for the grand effort of building new, free, federal democratic Yugoslavia.

Two tasks: our people must deal with the war and work. Pioneers must help them and must prepare for new efforts.

1. The major war task is: "Everything for the front, everything for victory." That slogan should be written and exposed in a visible place in every room where Pioneers meet. Every gathering, every meeting should have as its first point for discussion the motto: "Everything for the front, everything for victory." Pioneers should talk and decide what they can do to make a contribution to victory (to collect garbage, to visit the wounded Partisans, etc.). Those comrades who are exceptional in their work should be praised, and those whose results do not satisfy should be warned ... Both successes and failures should be mentioned and referred to in the school paper. ...

2. In order to grow up as true renovators of our country, we should be decent Pioneers at first. Therefore, every Pioneer must know very well the aims of the Pioneer's Organization and be a good pupil. We shall start to standardize the work of the Pioneer's organization in the whole country soon: You will get regulations concerning uniforms, internal organization, etc... An organization standardized in such a manner should be looked forward to with joy and you should be proud to be its members. Until then, it would be useful to talk over certain questions. In the following ten days organize about two meetings with all the members. At each of these meetings the first discussion point is going to be: "Everything for the front, everything for victory." The second issue at the first meeting should be: "Why do we need to be good pupils?" At the second meeting have proper discussion on the following question: "Which are the most important tasks of Tito's Pioneers?"

The Pioneer's leaders should be well prepared to chair and facilitate these meetings. Take notes about the course of the meeting. These scripts should be sent to us.

Source: "Our new tasks," in *Pioniri*, Belgrade, 5. III, 1945, 8.

Document 2:

Demand that Pioneers always be attired properly, making sure that they wear the Pioneer's scarf. The scarf is a sign of the Pioneer's dignity and honor. The scarf helps to lift the spirit. But the scarf is also an obstruction, a reminder as well. If a Pioneer is wearing his scarf it would be shameful for him to hang on a tram, to climb a tree, to shoot at birds. Besides [if he is wearing the scarf—I.E.] the other pioneers and the adults will remind him to behave properly. The scarf forces the Pioneer to be good.

Source: Instructions to the Pioneers' leaders, published in the brochure "Pionirski rukovodilac," May 1945, cited in Dragoslav Ognjanović and Rada Prelić, *Pionirska organizacija Jugoslavije, Dečje novine, Gornji Milanovac,* 1982, 217–18.

Document 3:

Pioneer's Oath

Today when I'm becoming a Pioneer
I give my honorable Pioneer word
That I will diligently learn and work
Respect parents and teachers
And be a faithful and honest friend
Who keeps his word of honor;
That I will follow the path of the best Pioneers,
Appreciate the glorious deeds of Partisans
And all progressive people of the world
Who stand for liberty and peace;
That I will love my Homeland
Self-managing socialist Yugoslavia
And its brotherly nations and nationalities,
And that I will build a new life,
Full of happiness and joy.

Document 4:

The Pioneer organization complements school in the universal education and upbringing of pupils, and together with family culture, gives a unique educational and upbringing system to children in the FNRJ (Federal People's Republic of Yugoslavia).

The Pioneer organization should be an educational organization gathering children aged 6 to 14, which will provide the pleasure of play, and physical education with its joyful features, and through organized work with children, create artistic initiative, a sense of living in a collective, friendship, love of work and study, and love of our motherland. Building the characteristics of a socialist man within a child, the organization is supposed to help school and family in the general education of children ... In the company of young nature-lovers, children are eager to explore, for example, the life of certain animals ... The technical circle awakens interest in technology, builds curiosity, creates a thirst for knowledge, and teaches to connect theory with practice ... In this [physical education] circle, beautiful forms of physical activities should be used in organizing healthy free time filled with joy ... It is also vital that all Pioneers take part in socially useful work that is planned and systematic in helping the population —the gathering of old iron and medicinal herbs, cleaning and repairing rooms, taking part in village work and other things. Socially orientated Pioneer's work is of evident importance. The use of child activity in work makes pupils self-disciplined, and makes them more critical and strict with themselves and with their friends.

Source: Report from the annual council of the vicinity council of the Pioneer Organization of Kovačica, 18 February 1951.

Notes

1 "Škola—nosilac kulturnog života," *Pančevac*, 6 June 1953, p. 4.

2 The main sources used in this paper are published and unpublished archives on Pioneer organization's activities in the Kovačica district of Vojvodina, between 1950–1955, from the Historical Archive of Pančevo, the Vojvodina Archive, and various publications about the history of the Pioneer's Union. Also used are articles taken from the specialized Pioneer magazines, Pioneers' letters to Tito, directions for creative work for the Pioneer instructors, songs and poems about Pioneers and their duties, Pioneer oaths, all published in special issues for the Pioneers themselves and those working with them. In addition, during my research I organized a workshop entitled "A Childhood in Socialism" in Belgrade in February 2002, where anthropology students from Ljubljana, Zagreb, Belgrade and Skopje took part in sharing their experiences of growing up under socialism as the last generation of "Tito's Pioneers". Their oral testimonies were of use in interpreting "the old material" and locating it in a longer time frame. Although this chapter is a case study, its assumptions relate not only to other parts of Yugoslavia but to other countries too, due to the nature and organization of Communist governments.

3 In 1948, a resolution was made that a Pioneer Union would celebrate the following holidays in a formal way: Republic Day (29 November), A Salutation to Spring, Pioneer's Day (27 November), New Year (31 December) and the beginning of the school year, together with other ordinary public holidays. Some of these holidays died out over time, while others arrived on the scene. The most important Pioneer and youth-related holidays remained Republic Day, when new members of were admitted to the organization,

New Year's Day—which was declared "a true Pioneers' holiday"—and, from 1957, the Day of Youth, when young people organized and involved in the birthday celebrations of the president of the Republic, Josip Broz Tito, by carrying the Torch of Youth and taking part in a mass patriotic gymnastics show. The central event was performed on 25 May, on Tito's birthday, in the JNA (Yugoslav People's Army) stadium, and it was called a *slet*. Apart from this central manifestation, numerous local *slets* were organized in each community which the Torch of Youth passed through.

4 Milan Ristović, Dubravka Stojanović, eds., *Childhood in the Past, 19th and 20th Century (Additional Teaching Materials)* (Belgrade: Association for Social History, 2001), 64–66.

5 *Kratka Bulgarska Entsiklopediia* (BAN: Sofia, 1964), 2: 177–78; I wish to thank Rossitza Guentcheva for providing me with information about the way the Pioneer organization was constituted and the way it worked in socialist Bulgaria.

6 Miroslava Malešević, "Prijem u Pionirsku organizaciju," *Etnološke sveske V* (1984), 80.

7 The whole of one's personal life could be seen as an obligatory and constant succession of initiations into one after another mass organization—first one became a Pioneer, than a member of the youth organization, afterwards a member of the party. All adults were obliged to be members of the People's Front, and women had an organization of their own called the AFŽ. One could also be organized according to personal interests and skills. The reason is that the state wanted to organize, observe and control every possible activity of its citizens. An excellent picture of the way the Communist Party organized political and cultural life in the late 1940s and early 1950s is given in Ljubodrag Dimić, *Agitprop kultura* (Belgrade: Rad, 1988).

8 About the Communist vision of the future and the role of the party in representing it, see chapter 11 in this volume.

9 Ljubodrag Dimić, *Agitprop kultura* (Belgrade: Rad, 1988), 128.

10 Miroslava Malešević, ibid.

11 Lydia Sklevicky, "Nova godina: Od 'mladog ljeta' do 'političkog rituala,'" in *Konji, zene, ratovi* (Zagreb: Druga, 1996), 175–85.

12 Radina Vučetić, "ABC Textbooks and Ideological Indoctrination of Children: 'Socialism Tailor-Made for Man' or 'Child Tailor-Made for Socialism'?" in Slobodan Naumović and Miroslav Jovanović, ed., *Childhood in South East-Europe: Historical Perspectives on Growing Up in the 19th and 20th Century* (Belgrade and Graz: Zur Kunde Sudosteuropas—Band II 28, Udruženje za društvenu istoriju—Ideje 2, 2001), 249–65.

13 In this paper I rely on two important concepts in studying childhood, which both suppose the socio-historical condition of childhood as a social experience. One of them is a historical concept introduced by Filip Aries in his work *Centuries of Childhood,* which presumes that childhood is a historical phenomenon of more modern times. According to Aries, only from the eigtheen century onwards can we talk of childhood in the modern sense, because from then on we can follow the separation and division of the children's world from the adult's and the establishment of specific ideas, modes and cultural codes concerning children; this Aries and his disciples named "the discovery of childhood." The other concept is related to modern approaches in the sociology of childhood, which

identifies childhood as a "social consequence," in other words which, believe that there are different socio-cultural modes of nurture and child upbringing in different times and space, which are also "sociologically subtle, or rather socially distinguished" (S. Mihajlović-Tomanović, "Childhood in History, between Ideas and Practice," *Sociology*, vol. XXXVIII, nr. 3 (1996), 440). And the last but not the least of the research tradition is the anthropological approach to growing up, established and developed in the school of "culture and personality," most particularly in Margaret Mead's works. More about these approaches is to be found in F. Aries, *Vekovi detinjstva* (Belgrade: Zavod za Udzbenike I nastavna sredstva, 1989); S. Mihajlović-Tomanović, ibid. 429–43; S. Mihajlović-Tomanović, "Perspectives and Problems in the Sociological Study of Childhood," *Sociology*, vol. XXXVIII, nr. 2 (1996), 327–31; Chris Jenks, *Childhood* (London: Routledge, 1996). These sources provide the operational definition of childhood. In this chapter, the term childhood will consider not only the age of life itself but also certain forms of social practice (principles, institutions, activities) determining this age and making it differ from other intervals of life producing a specific social experience.

14 Chris Jenks, *Childhood*, 7.

15 Ibid., 69.

16 The Youth Movement magazine wrote about this first Pioneers organization on 2 February 1942: "The youngest Montenegrin people's liberation organization has a board of five persons: three boys and two girls. It organizes conferences each Saturday in which literary essays are read. One of the essays had the topic: How do I imagine/see Hitler? ... The Pioneer organization gathers donations for the NOF. Our youngest comrades—while older ones are on the front line—watch carefully over the village; Partisan couriers and Partisan explorers are greeted with "Death to Fascism," and they conduct themselves as friendly hosts in their villages." Petar Kačavenda, *SKOJ* (Communist Youth League of Yugoslavia) *i omladina u ratu i revoluciji* (Belgrade: NIRO "Eksport pres," 1979), 76.

17 Momčilo Stefanović, *Deca suncu slobode* (Beograd: NIRO "Cetvrti juli," 1979).

18 Dragoslav Ognjanović and Rada Prelić, *Jugoslovenska Pionirska organizacija 1942–1945* (Gornji Milanovac: Dečje novine, 1982).

19 Data on the organization of Pioneers' groups, their squads and divisions, were not reported systematically, but announcements of a huge overall total nonetheless appeared regularly in publications on Partisans, Pioneers and the Liberation War in general. The unreliability of these totals was all the greater because Pioneer organizations were "fluid" and unstable during the war, being formed and disbanded depending on military demands and the size and stability of liberated territories.

20 *Kratka Bulgarska Entsiklopediia* (Sofia: BAN, 1964), 2: 177; translation by Rossitza Guentcheva.

21 "Kako žive deca u Sovjetskom Savezu," *Pionir, list najmlađih u Sremu*, 1942, 16.

22 There are indications that the child-Pioneers' participation in Partisan units was used as a strategy for the mobilization of adults; tales about the voluntary involvement of Pioneers in Partisan units and details of their extraordinary bravery put grown-ups to shame and forced them into joining the Partisans (Ognjanovic, Prelić, 186). Staša Zajović witnessed a similar strategy in the warfare of the 1990s, when women war volunteers in Montenegro were used to induce men to join the fighting in larger numbers

and to mobilize public support (S. Zajović, "Women and Militarism in Serbia," *Women Against the War*, 3–4 (1995): 36–43.

23 In NOB literature Pioneer-soldiers and Pioneer-national heroes were all claimed to be children under 15 at the end of April 1941. New research shows that some of those Pioneer-heroes were over 15 at that time, and that they belonged in the Youth category instead.

24 Mihajlo Ogrizović, *Hrvatski pioniri u narodnoj revoluciji* (Zagreb: Savez društava "Naša djeca" republike Hrvatske, 1977), 17–20; in D. Ognjanović and R. Prelić, 80.

25 Kačavenda, 77.

26 Ognjanović and Prelić, 202. Since most of the data are based on the memories of participants of the National Liberation War, and because there is no official recorded evidence, the data on the total number of organized Pioneers must be treated with reservation.

27 Momčilo Stefanović, XV.

28 Ognjanović and Prelić, 232.

29 A childhood in socialism is more likely a "produced" than "invented" social phenomenon (according to Aries' theory). It is certain that Yugoslav Communists did not "invent" childhood, although they consciously exploited the metaphors of children and childhood in political communication. As for the practice of childhood, the sets of specific activities, images, and principles that constitute and culturally define an age group, it was now to be democratized, to be made accessible to all social levels.

30 "Program Organizacije mladih pionira Demokratske federativne Jugoslavije," in D. Ognjanović and R. Prelić, 216–17.

31 Ognjanović and Prelić, 217.

32 There are indications that in different republics of Yugoslavia over time the colors of the scarves or the caps changed. Thus there is information that in Bosnia in certain periods the color of the cap was white, while in Slovenia there are examples of yellow scarves. I have no idea when this differentiation started or with what intention.

33 Ognjanović and Prelić, 220.

34 History Archive Pančevo, Fund of the Pioneer Vicinity Council in Kovačica 1950–1952.

35 Ibid.

36 "Pionirski rukovodilac" (May 1945), in Ognjanović and Prelić, 218.

37 This happens to be true not just for the 1950s but also for the period after Tito's death, although there were some changes in what was meant by the wearing of the red scarf. During the 1980s, on every 4 May (the day Tito died), different ways of commemoration were organized. These included memorial hours at the beginning of every school day, dedicated to the memory of "beloved Comrade Tito" and "revolutionary traditions." According to one student, the Pioneers in her school (in Belgrade) were obliged to wear their complete Pioneer uniform on that occasion, which was already unusual at that time. If, during the 1950s, the red scarf was understood as an effective means to control the behavior of the Pioneers, its function was expanded during the 1980s to help preserve and refresh memories of the "revolutionary past" and to remember "the founding father" of Yugoslav socialism.

38 This can be clearly seen in the famous oral poetry cycle dedicated to the Battle of Kosovo. Everything that either the heroes wear, or that was put on their horses, has an evident meaning whose purpose was to support the strength, faith, morality and other important characteristics of the heroes and to further strengthen their abilities; belief in the transformative capacity of cloth can be found in some of the traditional rituals, where it is believed that, for example, "the shirt made for a day" *(košulja jednodanka)* has the magical power of being bulletproof in times of war. Magical and transformative capacities are particularly ascribed to the cap, which is believed to be synonymous with the person who wears it. Therefore, in some parts of Serbia a widow is obliged to wear her late husband's cap for a year after his death, which is intended to ensure his presence around her and control her behavior for a prolonged period. See Tihomir Đorđević, *Zle oči u verovanju Južnih Slovena* (Beograd: Prosveta, 1985); Veselin Čajkanović, *Mit i religija u Srba* (Beograd: SKZ, 1973).

39 At the Third Plenary Session of the CK KPJ (Central Committee of the Communist Party of Yugoslavia) in 1949, we find a resolution concerning educational measures, which Milovan Djilas took part in formulating. The necessity of reforming the educational system was emphasized, with the intention of making it more comprehensive and efficient in creating a "new, liberated and brave socialist man, whose perspectives are broad and versatile, and to whom foreign bureaucracy and narrow-mindedness are unknown" ("Resolution from the Third Plenary Session of the CK KPJ," *Savremena škola 8–10* [Belgrade, 1949], 1). On 29 September of the same year, during Children's Week, Marshal Tito, speaking to Pioneers, said: "What is most important for our country today, what is most precious? People are! And people will be what we make of them in their education. That is why we have to pay attention that children, who will become the responsive citizens of this country, are given conditions for a fine and proper upbringing, that they are healthy and well brought up citizens of socialistic Yugoslavia … Whom do we build factories and other structures for; whom do we build this country for? We are building it for our future inhabitants …"; *Tito među nama* (Ljubljana: Dopisna delavska univerza, 1972), 43.

40 Milovan Djilas, "Problemi obrazovanja u borbi naše zemlje za socijalizam," *Savremena škola* 8–10 (Belgrade, 1949), 13.

41 Realizing the sensitivity of the social context, the proposed reform of the Yugoslav Pioneer Organization could be understood as a realization of a then popular slogan: "Factories to the workers, land to the peasants," in the context of the children's world. It was under this slogan, on 27 June 1950, that an *Act on ruling private companies and larger economy associations by working collectives*—Act on Self-management, for short—which "outlined" the Yugoslav "way to socialism," was passed.

42 History Archive Pančevo, Fund of the Pioneer Vicinity Council in Kovačica 1950–1952.

43 Ibid.

44 Miroslava Malešević, 81.

45 Petr Roubal, *Display and Disguise: the Place of the Czechoslovak Spartakiads in Socialist Regime and Society*, MA Thesis (Budapest: Central European University, 2000), 21.

46 Lisa A. Kirschenbaum, *Small Comrades—Revolutionizing Childhood in Soviet Russia, 1917–1932* (London: Routledge, 2001), 131.

47 Srđan Karanović, one of the famous Yugoslav movie directors, made his first film

as a Pioneer. His was also the very first Pioneer film in Yugoslavia. The film was shown at the Pioneer Film Festival in Zagreb in 1961.

48 Since the reform of the Pioneer organization started during the first five-year plan, its rhetoric fits into that of the "plan." Those who were to carry out party's orders to create a "true children's organization" had the task of "producing" as much children's joy as possible. This devotion to producing joy, élan, creativity, naturally related to children, happened at the same time that Communist leaders, including Tito, publicly declared "bureaucracy" a chief danger, a "contagious disease" for society. This production of children's joy, or the socially organized enhancing of children's true élan, and creating the symbolic value of enthusiasm, could be seen as an antidote to bureaucratic infection.

49 This practice was based on another Leninist revolutionary concept: the transformative capacity of creative work that would appear after abuse and control were removed. This idea was the foundation for the concept of workers' self-management and workers' control, proclaimed in Yugoslavia in 1950.

50 Insistence on the importance of hygiene was certainly one of the longest lasting features in socialist upbringing. An anthropology student from Croatia recited the following Pioneer verse that she remembered from childhood as an important message. This rhyme remains, ten years after the disappearance of the Pioneer organization, still a part of the educational program in Serbian kindergartens. It goes: "Little soap, little soap, make bubbles on my head; clean face, clean hands, cheeks of red; we shall ask the mirror who is looking clear, little mirror shall reply: A clean Pioneer."

51 Sklevicky, 184–85.

52 History Archive Pančevo, Fund of the Pioneer Vicinity Council in Kovačica 1950–1952.

53 Ibid.

54 A report of the Republic Council of Pioneers to the Vicinity Council in Kovačica, No. 110, History Archive Pančevo, Fund of the Pioneer Vicinity Council in Kovačica 1950–1952. The report consists of an instruction for celebrating New Year and organizing free time during the winter break; "winter work" consists of details for the organization of games in the snow, a description of the games, and how to arrange the play according to the *"Pioneers in the Snow"* and *"To the Snow, Pioneers"* manuals.

55 History Archive Pančevo, Fund of the Pioneer Vicinity Council in Kovačica 1950–1952.

56 Compare Kirschenbaum, 134. In the Yugoslav case, instructions for organizing Pioneer manifestations reflects the intentions of the organizer. For example: " ... if in the course of arranging the celebration we get every Pioneer's attention, those Pioneers will look forward to the celebration and attend happily; thus the success of the program would be greater" "... to avoid the big crowd that could spoil the children's mood, Pioneers are to be divided into small groups ..." " ... leaders of the groups gather their Pioneers for physical games and fun, but it is to be done in a clever way so that children alone ask to go to play" "... then the whole group can spare some time gathering edible plants or killing some pests. All the work should be carried out according to the preference and interest of the Pioneers, so that children see play in all the work". Scenery of the *"Salutation to the Spring"* celebration, March 1951, Fund of the Pioneer Vicinity Council in Kovačica 1950–1952.

57 Sklevicky, 186.

CHAPTER 7

Maja Brkljačić

POPULAR CULTURE AND COMMUNIST IDEOLOGY:
Folk Epics in Tito's Yugoslavia

When he started translating the story of Tito's life and work into a series of
epic poems, Milorad P. Mandić, a thirty-nine-year-old Montenegrin and
tractor driver by profession, already had considerable experience in the
field. He had published three books on various episodes from the Second
World War. In two more describing new achievements in science and technology, he was especially fascinated with and dwelled long on the Soviet
"space heroes" Yuri Gagarin and German Titov. These two men with the red
star on their foreheads were like "heroes on the battlefield" who conquered
the Universe.[1] The decision to tackle the life of Tito came, in his own words,
as a result of an "unrelenting desire" to have his verses "talk about dear
Comrade Tito."[2] Unrelenting desire or not, his decision to record a rather
long biography of Tito in verse (composed in twenty-seven songs over forty-
three pages, starting with Tito's birth and ending with the year 1965, when
the book was published) brought Mandić into the ranks of epic folk poets.
The tradition of oral epic folk poetry, commonly but wrongly identified with
the *guslar* tradition only,[3] has a long and important history in the Balkans.
In general, the verbal art of East and South Slavs has been predominantly
epic in character.[4] But by the time Mandić was composing his songs, much
had changed in the culture that nurtured epic poetry. Keep this in mind as
we read the introductory verses of Mandić's rhymed biography of Tito:

This is the book to be read
> About the path of life of Comrade Tito.
> Even if I had the knowledge of Njegoš,
> It would hardly help to sing this song.

It would not satisfy me
Had I the artistry of Gorky
Or of Tolstoy from the country of Russia,
It would not meet my desires.
Had I the talent of Pushkin,
I would not have the desired song.
Or the talent of Balzac or of famous Socrates,
It could not please me.
(...)
If I knew the meaning of all words,
It would not fulfill my wishes.
(...)
It is not easy to sing about a genius,
Whose past shines like the sun,
And it will shine as long as the world lasts
For our future generations.[5]

Although he finished only four grades of primary school before the war broke out and a short course for tractor drivers after the war in Tito's Yugoslavia, Mandić was socialized in a predominantly literate culture, in which he had access to the works of Tolstoy, Pushkin and Balzac. And yet this did not mean that oral culture, which was the originating ground for epic, had disappeared entirely from the scene. As this chapter hopes to demonstrate, many traces of the traditional culture and traditional social structures could be encountered in the modernized Communist society of Yugoslavia. There they underwent a certain transformation but did not lose their essential features, nor did their performance lose popular appeal. Even to the present day, oral epic performers enjoy fame in the eyes of the general public. Hence they were readily employed by politicians of quite different political leanings—Franjo Tuđman in Croatia and Slobodan Milošević in Serbia, to give the two most obvious examples.

Remembering in Songs and Verses

One of the most important functions of oral epic poetry is, as I will argue later in more detail, recording and preserving the memory bank of a given group. Epic singers are custodians of memory and tradition, and thus of the identity of the group. The spread of literacy does not mean that they lose their position in society; it only means that they are no longer the only ones in charge of safeguarding the content of memory. The epic poem is thus a competing medium for upholding the group memory. It is precisely through the epic's content that I want to explore the perception of the Second World War and the Communist revolution in Yugoslavia. The purpose of this article is to investigate the way in which the war and the rise of a new era were interpreted by the folk poet, who was, as I argue below, decisively influenced in his performance by the group of which he was a member. The attitude of the Communist Party, as the newly emerging historical arbiter, towards folklore is crucial for the proper understanding of the role folk singers played. As is shown below, this attitude is best described as ambivalent: at the early stage of the war the party was opposed to folklore, because it was considered as "irreconcilable with the party style." Yet the party had ultimately to give in if it wanted to win the support of the broader population. With power firmly in its hands, the party again thought itself strong enough to banish folk performances. This, however, was only a short-lived experiment, especially because the party did not want to abandon the heroic tradition of the folk epics, from which it learned to derive a significant part of the explanation of its "historical mission." Already in the early sixties, the League of Yugoslav Communists saw before its eyes the revival of folklore performances, much to the discomfort of some older members. All the same, folklore, and together with it the oral epic poem, ultimately became an integral and incontestable part of everyday life in Yugoslavia.

In order to understand the persisting appeal and attraction of this specific poetic genre, we must turn our attention to the more distant past. The first epic poems were created as far back as the twelfth century.[6] Leading scholars hold that epic poems, "like medieval chronicles, safeguarded popular ... consciousness," and that "[ordinary] people claim they could not have had any other history but [the one sung on the] *gusle*."[7] To comprehend it properly, it is necessary to clear this picture of its romantic overtones and break it down into its component parts. According to Jan Assmann, an awareness of unity, uniqueness and belonging to a group is created and reproduced through what he calls cultural memory. It is concretized through linguistic objectifications, symbolizations, rituals and sacred (canonical) texts. Rituals and texts fulfill two functions: normative (prescribing orientation points for acting) and formative (defining the group identity).[8] In order for cultural memory to be effective, it has to be objectivized, stored, reactivated and circulated in the group. This can be achieved in one of two ways: through the repetition of a ritual in an illiterate society or through the interpretation of a text in a literate society.[9] The former creates what is called ritual coherence, while the latter results in textual coherence within a given group.[10] When there is no possibility to preserve the content of cultural memory in writing, human memory (and material culture) is the only place where the knowledge necessary to secure the identity of a group can be stored. In that case, the content of the memory will be most commonly saved in poetic form, for the purpose of easier remembrance. Reactivation follows through ritualistic enactment, usually in a multi-media fashion: through singing, playing and dancing, when the content of memory is actively re-lived. The reactivation of memory requires collective participation: a story-teller and an audience.[11] Through the ritualistic repetition and reliving of the content of memory, the coherence of the group is created and recreated through time and across space.[12]

This short summary of Assmann's admittedly complicated theory identifies the function of oral epic poetry. Matija Murko defined the epic poem as "a chronicle in verses, the purpose of which is [the promulgation of] truth, entertainment, education and the instruction of successors."[13] In a predominantly illiterate society, the population at large has no means to record the content of tradition when it wants to communicate it outside of the so-called synchronic space of communication comprised of three generations (this being the temporal frame of communicative memory). In order to transmit any subject matter vertically, along the generational axis, something seemingly anchored in the distant past is needed that will at the same time enable group members to communicate and exchange news both about the past and the present. This "something" is, for the society we deal with here, the oral epic poem. While it is undoubtedly also a source of aesthetic pleasure to the listener, the main function of the epic poem is the mediation and transmittance of recent news and the exchange of the relevant collective experiences.[14] In 1963, a folk poet from Herzegovina, who most probably never in his life left his small town, sang about his role while taking for himself the old folk name *Radovan*:

> Radovan is old history,
> He breathes through wind and talks through darkness.
> I will tell you truthfully, my dear brothers,
> I remember all kinds of devils.
> I remember [the Roman emperor] Diocletian
> And the Mongolian leader Batu-khan,
> And Attila, dragon of fire,
> I remember each and every tyrant.[15]

A precondition for the existence of oral tradition is the existence of a group that accepts and sanctions the products of this tradition. Jakobson and Bogatirjev have called this "preventive censorship by the group."[16] What it means is that if we regard oral folk poems as a process of communication, then the sender (folk singer) and the receiver of the message (the group) are to be found in the same field in interaction. The receiver inspires and thus to some extent controls the sender.[17] Only if the singer offers the tones and

text that please the group can her/his song live. It is the group that grants
the singer the authorization to translate into verse the group's way of per-
ceiving and interpreting social developments. This means that by using the
singer's stories we can reconstruct the popular understanding of different
events the group lived through and thought important to "put into verse."
But we should also be aware that the narratives sung by the folk poet do not
represent some kind of unspoiled, true version of history, liberated from
interventions or pressures by those in power. They are neither true nor false
versions of the past. They represent a repository of names, dates and events
that were meaningful to the group at the moment the songs were created,
and the stories they convey from times of war or peace are stories the group
exploited to make sense of its present reality.

The *Gusle* in the Holy Space

The oldest references to folk epic poems on the territory of former Yugoslavia are found in 1557 in the writings of a Croatian poet from the island
of Hvar, Petar Hektorović. Probably the most influential and widespread
printed collections of the poems are the anthologies compiled by Vuk Stefanović Karadžić and printed in their first editions in the periods 1823–1833
and 1841–1862. In the first half of the twentieth century Matija Murko
observed that still the most popular book among the Croats was *Razgovor
ugodni naroda slovinskog* [A pleasant talk of the Slavonic people] by Andrija Kačić Miošić, first published in 1756. Even though it was written by one
man, and an educated one on top of that, the book owes its enormous appeal
to its form, which faithfully follows the pattern of the oral epic poem.[18]
Kačić composed his collection of poems with the intention of making it
accessible to "the poor peasants and shepherds of the Slavic people."[19] Its
style is deliberately close, indeed almost identical, to the style, metrics and
themes of oral epic poetry. As a consequence, many researchers later mistakenly believed numerous poems in the collection to be of folk origin. Kačić
has been a constant inspiration to folk singers. In 1987, the *guslar* Mile
Krajina proclaimed: "When I learned to read and write in the primary school,
I started reading the old heroic poems by Father Andrija Kačić Miošić."[20]
The population at large used Kačić's book to learn the alphabet, and through
it, history.[21] It should not come as a surprise that in 1952 in certain areas of
the counties of Šibenik and Drnić in Croatia, Kačić's collection was a universal synonym for the book: whatever they had read and irrespective of
when they read it, people believed they had read it in his collection.[22]

   The fate of Kačić's collection eloquently demonstrates that the introduction of writing does not displace oral expression: it merely opens another

channel of communication.[23] Oral, that is, natural or direct communication, is taken by the older generation of scholars to be the fundamental feature of folkloric text. They hold that the circumstances of oral communication conditioned a so-called secondary feature of folkloric creations: the stability of the basic structure of the text or the formulaic style. *Formula* is defined as a word or a group of words that is often used in the given metric conditions for the purpose of expressing an important idea;[24] when grouped, *formulae* make up a system of expression, and these systems create different narrative patterns.[25] Champions of this approach to the study of oral epic poetry are Albert Bates Lord and Millman Parry. They have related the formulaic style of oral communication to the uninterrupted variability of the content of the folkloric text, but always within constant systems of expressions. Matija Murko noted many years ago that "our printed epic poems have only once been sung or dictated [in the form printed] and never again,"[26] because the folk singer changes and moulds the song with every new interpretation (s)he makes. As a consequence, it would appear that when written down (or recorded on tape), the text ceases to be a part of folklore, because it can no longer be reshaped and modified by a performer.

The more recent approach to the study of folklore has repudiated this view and focused instead on the "[e]xamination of the performance of folklore in concrete situations of use."[27] Detailed empirical research in the 1930s into oral texts has demonstrated that an orally performed folkloric text is directed foremost to the problems related to the existing conduct of social life.[28] It is not concerned with some distant or exotic past; rather, it tackles issues that bear relevance in the moment of its creation. This means that the folkloric text cannot be seen as a natural object that somehow survives from the past into the present: if we want to believe it to be a part of tradition, then we must also take into account that tradition does not exist by itself as an unspoiled link with some imagined past. Rather, tradition is "a selective, interpretive construction, the social and symbolic creation of a connection between aspects of the present and an interpretation of the past."[29] It is thus wrong to assume that we can distinguish between "real" and "false" or "authentic" and "fake" folklore, because folklore itself is a symbolic construct.[30] If modern epic folk songs appear to bear little resemblance to the folk songs told by epic singers two hundred years ago, this does not mean that they are any less part of folklore. What it means is that social life in the modern culture has changed, but that in spite of that, folk songs do not cease to have "an important role in the personal, familial and social life of the widest population strata," and that through them symbolical communication between members of different communities takes place.[31]

With the dawn of the twentieth century, oral epic folk songs and folk singers did not lose their appeal and power. Existing literature leaves no doubt that up until the outbreak of the Second World War, folk singers were not only present but were very popular and widely distributed throughout the territory of interwar Yugoslavia.[32] They were admired by the broader public, while each house and region took special pride in its own singer(s).[33] In the area of Dubrovnik, when a folk singer with a *gusle* appeared, the entire village gathered. In Nova Varoš, the singer occupied a place next to the icon: a holy space. In Dalmatia at the time, people reportedly listened to the singer more closely and faithfully than to the priest in church.[34] Epic song was considered by the broad masses as the main entertainment and "the main type of sport."[35] The practice of epic singing was most strongly present in the *zadruga* (extended household) where several families and generations lived together. It should also be noted that prior to the formation of the first Yugoslavia in 1918, a *gusle* used to hang over the bed of each candidate for the priesthood in the Catholic catechism school in Mostar.[36] While it is generally believed that epic poems are inspired primarily by war, we know that after 1918, in addition to the songs about the First World War, there was an entire cycle of folkloristic texts about the murder of the Croatian Peasant Party leader, Stjepan Radić, in the Yugoslav Parliament in Belgrade in 1928. I have also tracked down epic songs that were performed in the course of the pre-election campaigns and agitation in Croatia in 1935, 1936 and 1939.[37]

> O, peasants, martyrs,
> You poor people, sufferers,
> The election day has arrived
> The twenty-eighth is here.
> Be careful, my brother, where you go,
> As one has to give a vote.
> Be smart, make no mistake,
> And relieve yourself of the evil destiny.
> (...)
> We should vote for no more pasha,
> He is not for our kind,
> We need someone who is cautious with money
> And who is the real peasant brother.
> Our Vasa Mihajlović,
> He is the real peasant and our kind.
> He will make the people proud,
> He will be the real president.[38]

If we consider that the majority of the population of interwar Yugoslavia was illiterate, none of this comes as a surprise. All social strata were represented in the ranks of the singers of epic: peasants, factory workers, sailors, fishermen, county clerks, military officers, notaries, professors, school principals, engineers, artisans.[39] Murko identified among female singers women who were widows of lawyers, mothers of drama writers, daughters of shipowners, and "ladies with Italian family names."[40] There were quite a number of county prefects who were epic singers, and often the reason behind their election was precisely the prestige they enjoyed for the ability to recite folk tales, with or without the *gusle*. The age structure ranged from the youngest reported singer who was only 3 years old, to the oldest one who was allegedly 120.[41] Despite the arrival of the Communist regime and vigorous educational efforts targeting the illiterate populace, all of these singers did not simply disappear from the scene. Additionally, we know that in the 1980s the commercial market for the distribution of epic folk songs, most notably those accompanied by the *gusle*, was highly developed. It was not exceptional for a *guslar* to sell more than 50,000 copies of a recording. One joint-edition of four *guslars* sold out its 100,000 copies in a short period. An engineer in Podgorica, Boško Vujačić, was able to sell half a million records and tapes by 1980, while in 1990 a tape by Milomir Miljanić, "The Wings of Kosovo," was selling at the amazing rate of three hundred copies per day.[42] And it was around this same time that the Serbian singer voiced his concerns:

> O, Slobodan, our sharp sword,
> Will the battle at Kosovo take place soon?
> Will we call upon Strahinjić,
> Stari Jug, nine Jugovićes,
> Or Boško to carry our flag
> And to wield his sword at Kosovo.
> (…)
> If needs be, just let us know,
> We will fly like gun bullets.[43]

On the Croatian side, the same atmosphere was echoed, but the names were different:

> O, I create a new song
> To be sung in my Čista Provo.
> Our Tuđman, prince and knight,
> Has been shot upon.
> (…)
> I made a new *gusle*,
> To revive the Croatian princes—
> Rise, lion Tomislav,
> Who touches each Croatian heart!
> (…)

> Earth is warmed by the rays of the warm sun,
> And Croatia by the Croatian heroes.
> Let Zrinski-Frankopan arise
> And return me *banus* Jelačić.[44]

Like many others of the same kind, these poems were composed by a (more often than not) anonymous author. Alois Riegel held that in folkloric art, there is no difference between the producer and the consumer; in other words, products of folklore are not intended for the open market but rather for the producer's own consumption.[45] This allows us to claim that in the late 1980s people in Yugoslavia still felt it appropriate and desirable to express their emotions using the form and style of an oral epic folk song. What is important here is not only the fact that in both cases the singer resurrected old folk heroes, knights and princes, to help the great leaders, Milošević and Tuđman respectively, in fighting some very modern battles which were considerably different from those in which the epic heroes originally took part. It seems more significant that these are only two examples of the kind of communication that was intimately familiar to many persons in former Yugoslavia during the years when their country was breaking apart.

To Make Communist Epics?

Prior to the Second World War, the population of Yugoslavia was predominantly rural: it is estimated that roughly 80 percent of Yugoslavs inhabited rural areas and lived from agricultural pursuits. Like many other Communist countries, Tito's Yugoslavia embarked on an ambitious program of industrialization and urbanization. As a result, in 1971 less than 50 percent of the population lived off agriculture. In the period 1948–1971, 6.5 million people migrated from rural to urban areas. This was a sudden, almost brutal migration, which did not result in turning peasants into workers but in creating a unique combined stratum of peasant workers. Its outcome was not a city with an urban population, but what Dunja Rihtman-Auguštin aptly called "a village in the city."[46] Among the features of the pre-industrial life in the *zadruga* (community), we count things such as a very strong pressure toward conformity within the community, group solidarity, and radical egalitarianism in division of goods.[47] The latter is connected to the "theory of limited goods": due to a peasant's inability to enlarge the quantity of goods possessed by the *zadruga* this quantity is permanently unchangeable and cannot be influenced. If one member of the community receives more bread, this will mean that another member will inevitably receive less. This custom not only strengthens group solidarity, but it also means that much attention will be paid to each division of goods. Such social structures proved to be very resilient, even in a historically new, supposedly modernized situation. According to research related to the strikes caused by firings of workers (carried out in 1969), group solidarity was still of great importance to the new working class: 89 percent of all interviewed workers said that they advocated putting an end to the firings, even though they were aware that their factories would in that case perform less efficiently and that their living standards would correspondingly drop.[48] In 1966, the Economic Institute in Zagreb conducted research into the effects of the economic reforms of 1965 in the companies and factories in the area of Zagreb. A number of them did not want to raise the salaries of their workers, even though they had the means to do so, because "they did not want to differentiate too much in earnings from others."[49] Finally, if the workers believed that the distribution of earnings was not "egalitarian" enough, they took matters in their own hands. There were cases of building and construction companies where, each month after they received their salaries, workers would meet in their quarters and there bring together on the table all the money they had received, in order to distribute it among themselves in exactly equal portions.[50] Similar patterns were observed in other professions, too. As one fisherman explained: "When salaries of different amounts arrive ..., we first put all of it together, then divide it with the number of people [who went to sea that month to fish], and only then does each person take his share. We believe this to be best, and that is how we work."[51]

The new working class, the migrants, also brought their folklore with them. It was not a rare sight immediately after 1945 to see in the cities original folklore groups performing on the streets and city squares, while the spectators either voiced their approval or joined the performance. For the party this was a large problem to deal with, but something they had encountered already before. In the course of the Second World War, the Communist leadership of the Partisan movement faced a major obstacle in its efforts to secure the support of the broader population for their cause. Educated in somewhat stiff party discourse, they were unable to explain "the party line" to the people. Their words simply did not resonate with the peasant majority in particular. As it was quickly noticed, village school teachers, who were very well versed in folk poetry, knew much better how to rally popular support—either to encourage people to join the fighting on the Partisan side or to persuade the peasants to give food freely to Partisan units.[52] The reason for this was quite simple: they were able to recite long lines of the older heroic epic poems, mingling their motifs with events from the current war.

Epic vocabulary, which was as different from party discourse as can be, was considered suspicious by party commissars and unwelcome, but with the need to enlarge the Partisan units they had little choice.[53] The section of the propaganda department of ZAVNOH (the Antifascist Council of the National Liberation of Croatia), which had charge of culture and the arts, published in the course of the war two editions of *Our songs*, a collection of folk songs with motifs from the liberation struggle. Moreover, from 1943 the same propaganda department had one person whose only job was to record and collect Partisan folk songs.[54] When we read them today, it is not difficult to understand what it was that so bothered Communist commissars in those songs: the repeated invocation of the name of God, fairies taking part in people's destinies, voices from the graves commanding the acts of the living—a world of spiritual forces and actors with which the Communist Party could not do much. While waiting for better times to come when it would become possible to dispense with folklore, the party took an active part during the war in supporting and promoting folk performances and production. Milovan Djilas, for example, embellished his war-time speeches to the Montenegrin peasants by quoting repeatedly from anti-Turkish folk songs or lines from Njegoš's *Mountain Wreath*.[55]

Once power was seized, the Communist Party changed its positive attitude towards folklore. Much in agreement with the interwar policy of the USSR that the products of folklore were "a worthless remnant of patriarchal society,"[56] the party in Yugoslavia also labeled folklore "primitivism of the worst kind" and banned it by decree from social life.[57] With their full efforts directed towards industralization and urbanization, scenes of groups of people singing folk songs and dancing *kolo*, a traditional folk dance, in the center of Zagreb or Belgrade were hardly a welcome sight for the party; they suggested that the revolutionary transformation was not succeeding as originally envisaged. As an example reflecting their negative feelings on the matter, the choir "Joža Vlahović" was not allowed to perform on the final evening of the Festival of Yugoslav Youth in Belgrade in 1948. The folk song they prepared for performance, which had as its main motif the conversation between a grieving mother and her dead son speaking from his grave, was considered mystical and was thus forbidden.[58] But the relation of the party towards folklore was in no sense unequivocal and clear. While perhaps disinclined to listen to "mystical" songs, the party happily seized upon the popularity and prestige enjoyed by heroes of the older epic poetry in order to create its own symbolic imagery. The published editions of Partisan songs were usually carefully arranged. The collection, whose subtitle reads "Folk songs about the war and the revolution," opens with several old folk songs which include motifs from the peasant uprisings, the anti-Turkish wars and the resistance the ordinary peasant offered against his feudal master. The first song to follow after these is "To the Communist Party, leader of the popular uprising."[59] The line of continuity is clearly and consciously emphasized, and historical legitimacy thereby imparted.

While the Partisan folk songs were accepted in this sense as valuable, the same did not hold true for songs with themes from contemporary life. This negative attitude provoked protests among folklorists and ethnologists. Partly in defense of the integrity of their own profession, they complained about the "habitual practice" of consigning folkloric production prematurely to oblivion.[60] When people were hired by institutions researching folklore to record in various communities the songs that were commonly recited, they rarely returned with poems about contemporary themes such as the rebuilding of the country or life in the new peasant collectives;[61] only old songs were considered good, the new ones were deemed not worth recording. When they heard songs with new themes, the researchers simply switched off the recorder.[62]

In spite of the disapproving attitude of the party towards folkloric performances, the folk songs lived on. In the new peasant collectives, Bosnian writer Mak Dizdar heard people singing them both during work and in late evening popular gatherings.[63] Some ethnologists noted a song or two with motifs from contemporary everyday life. There were workers' unions in Belgrade which organized *guslar* sections, and their members performed in factories and sometimes even in schools.[64] After existing for some time unofficially, the folk poets were ultimately allowed onto the public scene in the early sixties. In 1961 the first *guslar* society was founded in postwar Yugoslavia. From then on, epic poets were regularly invited to perform on local radio stations, and they toured the country singing before enthusiastic audiences. Sometimes it was possible to discuss through the medium of the epic poems subjects that were otherwise considered a strict taboo in society, such as the Partisan reprisals after the Second World War. On one occasion a folk poet, who described in his poem the bad economic situation in his company, was accused of "disturbing the citizens and spreading false information."[65] *Guslars*, who initially accepted the claim that their performances were obsolete and primitive, were back.[66] And they were there to stay.

Singing the Songs of War

We know that the Second World War was a very painful time for the general population in Yugoslavia. It does not then surprise us that the folk singer found that there was a special quality to this war.

> When furious winds start blowing on Earth
> When an animal without law becomes judge
> That was the year 1941;
> The black earth hit by the plague.

The sun over Kordun goes into eclipse
And everything falls into nightly darkness.
Mad wolves scream everywhere,
And the devil holds rifles in his hand.[67]

Animals in control of human life, wind and plague, darkness: this is the familiar set of popular *topoi* used to describe the end of the world.[68] For the epic singer, one from the area of Kordun especially, the apocalypse seemed to capture perfectly the reality they had to face from one day to another during the war. This was no time for humans; it was an era of animal rule. Document 1 bears eloquent testimony to what was enacted in the darkness: heinous crimes, the magnitude of which was unprecedented. The poem refers to an event that took place on 18 April 1942, in the village of Furjan, when a squad of Croatian Ustaša soldiers attacked the Serb village, set it on fire, tortured and killed the young and the old, and raped and then killed local women. Interestingly though, according to the folk singer, the evil times did not begin with the arrival of fascism but much earlier with the arrival of the Serbian "tyrant Pero Živković,"[69] King Aleksandar's closest military advisor, whom the king appointed as prime minister at the start of his royal dictatorship in 1929. Complete darkness then descended with the appearance of the "three-headed dragon"—Adolf Hitler.[70] The folk song tells us through the mouth of Ante Pavelić that Hitler's forces created the Independent State of Croatia and that the Ustaše were aware of the weak support they enjoyed among the people,

Which rejected them a long time ago
And followed Radić Stjepan instead.[71]

Even though the epic poems describing the Ustaša massacres provide an exact chronology with full names for those affected, and often with their birth places as well, they very rarely identify a single person on the Croatian side who inspired the crimes.[72] To be sure, the Ustaša soldiers and their leaders are called "bastards," "Hitler's servants," "dogs," and "beasts," but the origins of the idea for the massive slaughter of Jews and Serbs are found in Hitler's Berlin. However, the clouds and darkness he brought could not last forever.

In Montenegro, the appearance of clouds signified a new temporal plane: "Thunder reverberated / Across the hills and valleys of former Nemanja's Zeta / The lightning struck near Vir Pazar / And cut the cloud over Zeta in pieces."[73] Zeta was the medieval Serbian kingdom, and Stefan Nemanja is considered to be its founder. For the folk poet, the rather large time lapse did not cause a problem. On the contrary, the popular uprising, aiming "to free the people from slavery" and "expel executioners from the country," was seen by the folk poet as a "rebellion like before." The original word used in the poem for "rebellion" is *buna*, and we know from older songs that this is the word used to refer to the Serbian uprising against the Turkish rule (*buna na dahije* or, in English, "rebellion against *dahijas*").[74] The beginning of the National Liberation Struggle (NOB—*Narodnooslobodi-lačka borba*) or the Partisan war is never referred to in official Communist discourse as a *buna* (rebellion) but as an *ustanak* (uprising). The resistance did not come by itself, it was initiated literally by someone "from above":

> O, people, what a miracle—
> A great lake has been created
> And within it, a three-headed dragon
> That wants to swallow the people.
> With unhappiness, comes luck, too:
> There was a hard nest in the world,
> In which white swans were hatched,
> Among them, a grey bird falcon,
> That spreads his wings all over the country—
> Underneath the wings, he scatters his feathers,
> From which white swans will arise,
> And with them grey falcons,
> All together to smash the dragon with force.[75]

The lake is the Third Reich, the dragon, as we have seen, is Hitler. The nest in which fighters are born is the homeland (Yugoslavia), and there we find Communists (white swans) and the grey falcon, Tito, who flies over the country and sheds feathers, that is, calls for uprising, which stimulate more people to join the struggle. "The cradle of the young Partisans" is the mountain Romanija in Bosnia and Herzegovina,[76] probably the strongest demonic *chronotopos* in Yugoslav epic poetry; the place where time and space meet and open a new dimension, in which supernatural and demonic forces reign. This is the holy space, which, as Ivo Žanić has noted, must be crossed by each person wanting to become a true hero: it is a stage set for the rite of passage, and only the individual who, in the poem, sets foot there can claim his heroism.[77] Tito was no exception in this regard.

Set against grey falcons and white swans, there was a wide range of enemies. What becomes readily obvious when reading the poems is that they pay considerably more attention to the "traitors to the homeland" than to non-Yugoslav foes. With the exception of Hitler, foreign adversaries of the Partisan army are dubbed simply "enemies" or are given their national designations (Italians, Germans). Mount Romanija, on the other hand, remembers vividly "black days and black dungeons" that were opened with the treason allegedly committed by the Serbian noble Vuk Branković who did not appear (or appeared too late) at Kosovo in 1389 and thus, according to the folk poem, caused the greatest of all defeats. For the folk poet singing about the Second World War, the black days of treason extend from humiliation and shame provoked by Vuk Branković's betrayal, all the way: "To executioner Ante Pavelić / Notorious Milan Nedić / Dense Captain Ljotić / Kvaternik, General Draža / And Rupnik, old traitor / King Peter, Paul and Stepinac / The worst of the Balkans' sons."[78] The folk poet saw no difference between various Chetnik leaders, the Ustaša *Führer*, young Yugoslav King Petar in exile in London or Archbishop Stepinac; these were details that did not matter. What mattered was the heroism of the freedom fighters. They had a range of predecessors, as the source of strength and inspiration. Partisan youth could exclaim in a poem, "We are the children of Obilić,"[79] referring to the greatest Serbian hero who was killed in the Kosovo battle. In similar terms, Ratko Pavlović from Toplice, the legendary organizer of the popular uprising in southern Serbia, was seen "As equal to Prince Marko / And Miloš Obilić. / He was an excellent orator / As if he were taught by Njegoš! / If Njegoš were to rise from his grave / Ratko from Toplice would be in his company."[80] When such a hero dies in the battle, he falls silently: "Without cries or shouts,/The young boy sleeps in the grass."[81] Interestingly enough, bodies of the fallen heroes do not emanate any kind of special power that would prevent wild animals from eating them.

> When heroes touch the grass,
> Crows and ravens fly to them,
> And drink from their hot blood,
> Eat their heroic flesh.
> At night, a wolf comes from the woods
> And scatters corpses all over the forest.[82]

The destiny of a young Bulgarian fascist was not much different:

> The raven ate of the flesh,
> And searches now a place where to rest.
> His legs are bloody to the knees,
> Bill and head almost to the shoulders!
> In the bill he holds the eyes of the hero,
> Among them there is no star
> But a cockade washed in blood,
> Punched by a bullet through the middle.[83]

A few seconds later, when the bird finds a branch on which to sleep, it swallows the eyes of the Bulgarian soldier. The only way in which we can then differentiate the dead Partisan hero from the dead fascist, the poems seem to suggest, is through the record of history: it will have the last word, and its judgement will be final. On top of that, there comes the scream of the mother. Each fallen hero leaves behind him, again in accordance with the existing folk tradition, a weeping mother, sometimes also a sister. Unlike the archetypical mother in the folk tradition, the mother of the nine young Jugović's, who died of grief caused by the deaths of her husband and all nine sons at Kosovo, the mother of the Partisan hero lives on and finds the cure for her sorrow in the hope of revenge: "I will not curse my destiny / But everyone who won't avenge my son."[84]

Even though the folk singer makes a conscious effort to explain that "[t]he [liberation] battle was fought not by Communists only,"[85] he never questions the party leadership of the Partisan troops. And this is how he explains who these Communists were: "These people who incite rebellion,/ Who despise masters and the crown, / Who want the same law for everyone, / These people are called Communists. ... They want to build the house anew / To bring peace among brothers and peoples / And fight against the masters."[86] And yet, in spite of all their strength, there were moments when Communists and Partisans just could not move ahead. These instances did not come as a consequence of their weakness, for in direct conflict with the enemy they were always victorious. They had to bow their heads, as the singer shows, when Mother Nature stood in their way.

Probably one of the most beautiful epic poems about the Second World War describes the battle on the river Neretva. This was one of the bloodiest but also the most renowned episodes in the war. The German army, together with the Ustaša and Chetnik forces, surrounded Partisan troops in March 1943. Partisans were additionally slowed down in their advance by the 4,000 wounded they carried with them. Had they chosen to leave the wounded behind, they could have easily fled from the enemy; but the Partisan headquarters, together with Tito, decided that the wounded had to be saved. Even though they suffered great losses, they managed to create confusion in the enemy's ranks by blowing up the only existing bridge on the river Neretva that could have saved them. Immediately upon doing so, they built a provisional bridge for Partisan forces (which consisted only of infantry) that could not support German tanks. Ultimately, the Partisan army successfully escaped from the encircled area.

The folk song about this event relies heavily on the existing folk tradition, but it also introduces several new elements into the poetics of the genre. The narrative revolves around the inability of Tito's army to build the second bridge: whatever material they bring, they manage only to get halfway across the river, when the wild water demolishes it: "What Tito's soldiers build, / Until they reach half of the river, / Wild Neretva takes all away."[87] Anyone familiar with Yugoslav folk poetry will recognize this motif from another, much older source—the poem about building of the city of Skadar on Bojana: "What constructors build during the day / A fairy destroys during the night."[88] In order to find the solution, Tito sends 900 couriers to bring him "the old books of wisdom." There he reads that the bridge will be built only after a young couple in love is sacrificed to the river—an unkissed girl and an unmarried boy. In the old poem, the fairy reveals to the king that in order to erect the city, he needs to find two children, a brother and a sister, with similar names, and build them into the foundations of the city. In both cases, this is the old Greek concept of φάρμακου: the need to make a sacrifice of innocent humans which will please the gods (or Nature, which amounts to the same), ease their rage and allow human actors to continue with their plans. And while in the old poem the king was unsuccessful in finding two children and instead built his sister-in-law into the foundations of the city, Tito did locate his young couple in love, the young courier Ivan and Janja, his proletarian sweetheart. They understand the situation and willingly submit their bodies to the river. The Neretva is tamed, and the story has a happy ending. On the other side of the river, Ivan and Janja are buried, "Their crosses decorated with [red] stars."

The last line, describing the crosses with red stars on the grave markers, proves Maja Bošković-Stulli right when she notes that two completely different eras meet in this poem.[89] While old folk songs often began with the line "Dear god, what a miracle!" this one opens with "Dear comrade, what a miracle!" Untamed Nature that can be domesticated only by a human sacrifice is also from an older world: in the new one, machines will take care of that. The actors on Neretva are, however, fresh. This is not just any innocent couple, it is a Partisan courier and a proletarian girl. And they do not meet their death blindly and unknowingly (as happens regularly in the old songs), but with eyes open and fully aware of their actions. Mythical ambience may still be present, but people are no longer entirely helpless when facing their destiny.

The wide range of heroic sacrifice and human loss among Partisans and civilians made dealing with prisoners of war more complicated. As noted above, the call for revenge was loud and could not be simply disregarded. In official Communist accounts, historiography especially, mention of Partisan reprisals was an absolute taboo. Questions about retaliation were suppressed to the extent that even today it is difficult to estimate the number of victims. However, as Document 2 testifies, the folk poet and thus his community were very well aware of the massacres and their extent, and their talk about these painful issues was tolerated, as we see, despite the tasteless tone employed by the poet (the large quantity of decomposed enemy bodies fertilized what had hitherto been barren land). That this was acceptable behavior should not surprise us, because in the traditional heroic codex of honor, vengeance is something desirable.

When the Communists, people who fought during the war "For Freedom and for ideals / So everyone would equally have bread,"[90] seized power, many things had to change. Numerous songs describe the process of rebuilding the country, celebrating what was indeed an incredible work ethic on the part of the mostly youthful brigades. A folk poet observed: "Each person works on reconstruction / There is no more hunger."[91] When compared to the war years of starvation and the prewar experience of the Great Depression of the 1930s, the latter claim must have made a particularly strong impression. Advancing industrialization and electrification prompted the folk singer to state: "America has been created now in our country."[92] In spite of the change of the ideological paradigm, America stayed in the folk imagination as a synonym for a prosperous country offering limitless possibilities. The USSR, the proper ideological mate, never came to occupy that place. Moreover, the conflict with Stalin that soon followed in 1948 left no space for anything like that. It is interesting that folk poets in relation to the split spoke much more about attacks coming from other Communist countries than from the USSR. Quite appropriately, the whole campaign was perceived by the poet as directed against Tito, and he chose thus to defend the country and the party by defending the Yugoslav marshal. Tito's superiority over other Communist leaders was easily established on the basis of his war record as in this reference to the Hungarian Communist leader, Mátyás Rákosi.

> O, Rakosi, where were you
> When Tito spilled his blood?
> You rested in the coolness of Moscow,
> Whilst Tito fought the war!
> You, the coward of this war,
> Pretend now to be a democrat!
> If a battle develops again,
> The old story will repeat:
> Our Tito will be the leader,
> And you will hide again.[93]

A similar strategy was employed when the poet had to stand for "our people." As shown in Document 3, Yugoslavia's postwar history is differentiated from the history of other Communist countries by the argument that Yugoslavs fought hard for their freedom, whereas others received it as a gift. The unstated conclusion was that because they did not invest much in their freedom, these countries were ready to submit to someone else's (i.e. Stalin's) rule. Even though the initial prospect was, as we know, very daunting, the folk singer never lost his optimism: "The truth has to win."[94] But it was quickly noted that as the consequence of "the politics of the blocs" things were not developing smoothly. In Document 4 we notice a concern for world peace. The song opens in a way similar to the poems about the beginning of the Second World War. The threat to peace is epitomized again in the dark cloud, "the Big Two" (i.e. leaders of the US and the USSR), much like Hitler in 1941, concoct their infernal plans, while the hungry do not even have bread. The real novelty in this poem is its mention of grieving widows. In the old traditional folk poems, women could grieve for sons, fathers and brothers, but mourning for husbands was considered a taboo. Murko claims that even if such poems existed, they were not recorded by the collectors because of shame.[95] The new era, among other changes, evidently brought a revolution in this respect, too.

∗∗∗

It is often asserted that the Communist Party of Yugoslavia had a rather easy path to power in 1945, because, unlike its counterparts in the rest of Eastern Europe, it enjoyed popular support and legitimacy on the basis of the recently won war. My reading of Yugoslav oral epic poetry suggests that this is only part of the answer. That the victory in the war was an important asset for the party is clear. But perhaps equally important was the way in which this victory was perceived by the broader public. The Second World War was for the folk singer not just any war in which just any two sides fought each other. The poems analyzed here suggest that because bloody reality was encountered on a daily basis, the war was experienced as an ultimate clash between good and evil, the white swan and the black devil. In the Serb-populated parts of Croatia, the beginning of the war introduced all too often scenes such as this: "Many a sister seeks her brother now / A little child calls for his daddy. / Above the cave, crows scream / For the caves are badly covered / And the crows have found piles of flesh. / Crows scream, the skies cry. / In the cavity a small creek originates / Bloody creek that runs into the river; / The river is no longer blue / But runs on filthy and bloody."[96] As the end of the poem puts it, only the Party is able to end this darkness and in the only way it knew—by turning on the light of the red star.

Since the Yugoslav Communists came to power in a country with a predominantly rural population, they had to create *ex post facto* the working class in whose name they seized power. But despite that problem, the Communists were not faceless or abstract people to the folk poet and, with him, the wider community. We have seen that they inherited in the popular imagination a place in the line of heroes reaching as far back in history as the fourteenth century. We know that every new power-holder asserts the legitimacy of his rule by building a line of continuity with some distant past. Great origins, as Pierre Nora noted, magnify the greatness of the present generation.[97] Past heroes are a reservoir of bones on which the present rulers can feed and from which they draw their strength. Due to the fact that, as Funkenstein explains, collective memory is entirely topocentric and is insensitive to the passage of time (i.e., it is basically ahistorical),[98] it was very easy for the Yugoslav folk poet to tell his story of the war, in which Communists led "our" army, by inserting the names of the brave Partisans in the long line of popular heroes. Miloš Obilić from the fourteenth century, Njegoš from the nineteenth century, and Tito from the twentieth century rub shoulders in the folk poem; consequently, the glory and brilliance of one hero were easily appended to another one. Tito's Communists were thus given a chance to avenge all "our" tragic heroes who died in their various struggles, and this chance they did not want to miss. When the Ustaše slaughtered more than five hundred Serbs in the small town of Veljun in Croatia, the folk poet reasoned: "[The Ustaša executioner] made Kosovo out of Veljun."[99] When Tito's Partisans were killing the Ustaša soldiers, this too was vengeance for the dead bodies that remained at Kosovo. If looked at from this perspective, the arrival of Communists, often portrayed as discontinuity in historical development, was for the folk poet a natural sequel in the story of a glorious and heroic past. The conflict with Stalin served only to enhance this point.

The desired continuity was obvious in at least one more respect. Yugoslavia's historians of the Communist period who dealt with the Second World War are often reproached for their simplistic stories about "the good Partisans" and "the evil foreign occupiers and domestic traitors." Such stories left a lot of empty and unexplained space for competing versions of the past that would ultimately return to haunt the country and its inhabitants, still today unable to cope with the more complex picture. While I do not disagree, it seems important to state two qualifications. First, the analysis of the folk poems shows that they were in their very origin a narrative about "the good us" and "bad them." Folk poems have long since cultivated the story about the Good, the Bad and the Ugly. The Good is the young hero who defends his land. The Bad is the foreign aggressor who launches an assault on his land. And the Ugly is the hero's brother who commits treason and sells his loyalty to the aggressor for a handful of golden coins. Yugoslav historiography merely filled these roles with concrete names. Tito and his Partisans were the Good, Germans and Italians the Bad, while the role of the Ugly was taken over by the Ustaše, Chetniks and other "domestic traitors." The golden coins for which, e.g., the Ustaše sold themselves to Hitler, was, obviously an independent Croatian state—no matter of what kind. And secondly, one has to wonder whether it was possible at all for Yugoslav historians to change this naive narrative and insert more tones of grey in it. If, as stated before, the legitimacy of the Communist Party depended upon its fulfilment of the tasks posed by predecessors from the distant past, any shifting in the ruling narrative would have undermined the party's position in the hierarchy of power.

Benefiting from the distant heroic past, the Communists presented themselves, as the folk poet tells us, as people "who want the same law for everyone."[100] They came bringing with them the principle of ending class exploitation. This theme was familiar to the peasant mind, which recalled through poems the burden imposed by the feudal master. In the course of the war, the party offered to the peasant a possibility for change. The call for an uprising asked the peasant: "For whom do you work the land, for whom sow, / For whom do you spill your blood? / There has been enough of pains and suffering, / enough of robberies and the *kuluk*! / Wake up, take off the dark veil, / break your heavy chains!"[101] According to Momčilo Zlatanović, this was one of the favorite peasant songs of the uprising.[102] True, it sounded much like the call for peasant uprisings from earlier centuries, but this only enhanced its appeal and strength. Seen by the folk poet as liberators from the foreign oppression, walking in the footsteps of glorious ancestors and with the promise to bring bread to everyone, Communists must have appeared to be the winning combination. And this is precisely what they were.

Sources

Document 1:

> "Bloody song"
> (...)
> As they spoke those words,
> The first houses burst in flame,
> From houses people emerge
> Naked, bare-foot, hardly awake,
> In disarray they don't know what to do.
> The mother grabs her four children,
> One on her back, another dragging by the hand;
> The old man grabs three grandchildren,
> Drags children, himself stumbling
> For his old body is aged,

Misery is pushing him forward,
It does not let him die in peace.
The little brother, not even eight years old,
Carries his one-year-old sister;
The young daughter-in-law, last year married,
Carries the old woman,
Under her belt an unborn child;
(…)
From the bush then jump slayers,
Jump, take out their knives;
Those heroes from Cetingrad,
That bunch of filthy bastards
They start slaughtering women and the old,
Stab children with blades,
Smash heads with guns;
Creeks of blood flow.
(…)
When the slaughter ended,
They start their dirty work;
Collect chained girls
Take them out of blood,
Tear down their clothes,
Push them to the black ground,
Place knives near their heads
To show what awaits them,
What awaits them, if they resist,
What awaits them, they know well,
No matter submissive or not;
They grab them with their bloody hands,
Grab their white bodies;
Again you hear screams and cries,
As if people were slaughtered by wolves;
(…)
Dear brothers, what else is there to say,
Fifty of them did the same,
Then butchered them with knives
And left them naked in blood.

Source: "Krvava pjesma," in Stanko Opačić-Čanica, ed., *Narodne pjesme Korduna* (Zagreb: Prosvjeta, 1971), 16.

Document 2:

In 1945, beginning of April,
Our army penetrated the front of Srijem,
Tito's great offensive
Surrounded then its opponent
In Croatia and Slovenia
It cut off the road to Austria
So the enemy could not slip away
But so it would pay for what it did yesterday,
So did Tito tell to the comrades
That they do not allow the fascists to run away
Tito's belligerent army
Fulfilled his plan,
On 15 May 1945
It defeated the Germans completely,
When the last battles were fought
The army killed many of the German soldiers
The number of the dead
Was almost one hundred thousand,
And the large number of the prisoners
Over two hundred thousand soldiers,
While the military equipment then acquired
Was also very great,
The so-far barren land
Was fertilized by the bodies of the Germans
Sponges, great eaters of the world,
They stink all through our hills and valleys
Their bones have been spread around
From Africa all to famous Moscow
There, they soaked the soil with blood—
And they thought to conquer the Kremlin,
Millions of German heads
Await to be cultivated
In the broad fields of the *kolkhoz*
By the strong Soviet tractors,
Their land became fruitful then
The Germans from the West fertilized it
The whole people was then happy
With the defeat of the aggressor of the world.

Source: Milorad P. Mandić, *Pjesme o životnom putu druga Tita: U čast sedamdese-togodišnjice* (Bački Petrovac: Novinsko-izdavačko štamparsko preduzeće "Glas ljudi", 1965), 38–41.

Document 3:

Tito led us in the battle
He spilled his own blood,
He did not lie in a soft bed,
But he fought on the real battlefield.
It has not been achieved as a joke
That Tito is called the Marshal,
But it has been gained through the battle
That Tito is called the hero.
Where were those from different countries
When our people were dying?
They were all over the place,
But not there where one had to defend the people.
They were not there, where the battlefield was.
Or else they would know to value freedom more.
Donated freedom is easy
And servility must be such, too.
Our pure blood has been spilled,
So the freedom gained would be more valued.

...

Our people knows also
That Comrade Tito before the war
Had raised the Communist cadre
For the uprising against the fascists.
Lies are coming from some countries
That our party is no good,
That in the countryside there is anarchy
That we are heading toward capitalism.
They lie even much more
But their lies cannot be proven
Because the party headed by Tito
Stays on the correct path.
Let the speculating contemptible hear and see
What goes on in our midst
Let them see and be ashamed,
Let them see how the *zadrugas* work.
Everyone will say to the one who asks
That we love the party and Tito.

...

Let them come and see
What our heart is made of,
They will see it is made of granite,
That it dies and lives for Tito.

Source: Savremene narodne pjesme (Sarajevo: 1957), 275–81.

Document 4:

"Peace, Freedom and Equality of All People"
A dark cloud is menacing the Earth,
Such a dark one nobody has ever seen before.
People would like to live in freedom,
Peace is wavering like a boat in the water.
Major powers keep threatening us with rockets,
At any time they can be hurled to the sky.
The Big Two govern insolently the world,
Determined to realize their infernal plans.
Eight hundred billion bucks, my dear,
For armament has been spent in a year!

The twentieth century is coming to its end,
But the oppression of men has not stopped yet.
There are still tyrants in the government,
They don't obey human laws and will.
Millions of people are dying from hunger now,
And the neutron-bomb is being constructed.
The atomic arsenal is big enough
To destroy the whole globe, the land and sea.
Poisonous gas and bombs of all kinds,
Together with life-dangerous laser beams
Can burn down the Earth in a minute.
All mankind could die in no time.
Europe would be all in a flame,
Not a stone would remain upon stone.
Those lucky ones who remained in a shelter
Would die from the radiation afterwards.
What man has built in hundreds of years,
The bomb can destroy at once.

So I ask all the rulers of the world:
Spare and save this planet of ours, please!
If you don't want to give us our daily bread

Don't kill our children and our friends.
For us all there's enough killing and war,
Enough blood, evil and heavy pain.
Our mothers still black shawls wear,
Pulling out their hair for their dead sons.

Every mother weeps deeply for her boy killed,
Like a bird with a broken wing.
Poor wives still mourn for their husbands
With tears in their eyes, sobbing is still heard.
Grieving widows forever they will be—
Raising and taking care of their children.
Woe! This damn foolish tragedy war!
Why must man kill man?
How much humiliation we've been through!
How many murders and bestial tortures!
Why don't people come to an agreement,
Knowing that nobody can really win?

Let the army serve the people,
All the people in the United Nations!
Pass the laws all together,
Thwarting all plans of despotism.
These laws should be fully obeyed,
Tyrannical regime mustn't exist.
Let every man live in freedom
Using natural resources as he pleases,
Let him elect democratically the best.

If people don't come to an agreement,
It will be too late when they find the truth.
The birth-rate can be controlled and decreased
Without killing innocent unborn children.
Make the deserts yield crops,
They will be the granary for all people.
There is sunshine enough, make rain,
Everybody will have plenty of bread.
All powers should be directed to peace,
All energy should be in the service of man.
Instead of bombs, make tractors,
Let's use all the land and sea.

No country will lack food,
And starving children won't die any more!
(trans. by Antun Šimunić)

Source: Mile Krajina, *Guslarske pjesme i pjesnički zapisi* (Osijek: 1987), 41–42.

Notes

1 Milorad P. Mandić, "Predgovor," in Milorad P. Mandić, *Pjesme o životnom putu druga Tita: U čast sedamdesetogodišnjice* (Bački Petrovac: Novinsko-izdavačko štamparsko preduzeće "Glas ljudi," 1965), 1. He takes special pride in the fact that his poems were mentioned in a radio show broadcast by Radio Moscow.

2 Mandić, "Predgovor," 2.

3 A *guslar* is a player on the *gusle*, a one-string folk instrument used for musical accompaniment of the recitation of an epic poem.

4 Svatava Pirkova-Jakobson, "Introduction," in Vladimir Propp, *Morphology of the Folktale*, 2nd edition (Austin: University of Texas Press, 1968), xix.

5 Mandić, "Uvodna pjesma o Maršalu Titu," in *Pjesme o životnom putu druga Tita*, 5–6.

6 Matija Murko, *Tragom srpsko-hrvatske narodne epike, Putovanja u godinama 1930–1932* (Zagreb: JAZU, 1951), 453.

7 Murko, 375.

8 Jan Assmann, *Religion und kulturelles Gedächtnis* (Munich: Verlag C.H. Beck, 2000), 53.

9 Chapter 5 in this volume by Andrew Wachtel tackles one such case.

10 Assmann, 54. However, in spite of the introduction of the sacred canonized text, the crucial components for the achievement of cultural coherency of a given society remain customs, festivals, and rituals. Evidence of their importance for Yugoslavia's Pioneers is provided in Chapter 6 by Ildiko Erdei.

11 Assmann, 54.

12 Assmann, 55.

13 Murko, 421.

14 Ivo Žanić, *Prevarena povijest* (Zagreb: Durieux, 1998), 37–38.

15 The song was performed by Jozo Karamatić from Posušje, and written down by Zlatko Tomčić, *Hrvatske narodne epske pjesme iz Hercegovine i Dalmacije*, 1963, Archive of the Institute for Ethnology and Folklore, Zagreb, manuscript 3.

16 Jakobson and Bogatirjev, as quoted in Zdenko Škreb, *Studij književnosti* (Zagreb: Školska knjiga, 1976), 93.

17 Jovan Janjić, "Narodno stvaralaštvo o ustanku i revoluciji u nastavnim planovima i programima," *XXVIII Kongres Saveza udruženja folklorista Jugoslavije* (Sutomore: 1981), 79.

18 Up to the official beginning of the Croatian national re-awakening in 1830, Kačić's work was published in seven editions, in 1756, 1759, 1780, 1801, 1811, 1816, 1826.

19 Andrija Kačić Miošić, as quoted in Josip Vončina, ed., *Andrija Kačić Miošić, Razgovor ugodni naroda slovinskog i Matija Antun Reljković, Satir iliti divji čovik* (Zagreb: Liber, 1988), 10.

20 Mile Krajina, *Guslarske pjesme i pjesnički zapisi*, 2nd edition (Osijek, 1987), 136.

21 Murko, 64. Some people learned to read just so they would be able to read Kačić's and other collections of epic poems.

22 Maja Bošković-Stulli, *Narodne pjesme, pripovijetke i običaji iz okolice Šibenika i Drnića*, 1952, Archive of the Institute for Ethnology and Folklore, Zagreb, manuscript no. 102, 3. Murko encountered Kačić's songs recited as far apart as in Kruševac and Macedonia (Murko, 252).

23 Jack Goody, "Oral Culture," in Richard Bauman, ed., *Folklore, Cultural Performances, and Popular Entertainments: A Communications-Centered Handbook* (New York, Oxford: Oxford University Press, 1992), 12. And further: "The notion of an oral tradition is very loose. In a nonliterate society the oral tradition consists of everything handed down (and *ipso facto* created) through the oral channel—in other words, virtually the whole of culture itself. In a society with writing, both the literate and oral traditions are necessarily partial. Moreover, elements of the oral tradition, like folktales, inevitably get written down, whereas elements of the written tradition are often communicated orally, like the Indian Vedas." (13)

24 In the case of oral poetry, some of the formal classificatory features are: prosodic elements (metrical patterings, alliteration, assonance, end assonance), parallelism (a type of repetition with variation in meaning or structure), distinctiveness of the language of oral poetry from everyday speech. Ruth Finnegan, "Oral Poetry," in *Folklore, Cultural Performances, and Popular Entertainments*, 122–23.

25 Vladimir Biti, *Pojmovnik suvremene književne teorije* (Zagreb: Matica hrvatska, 1997), 401.

26 Murko, 12.

27 Richard Bauman, "Folklore," in *Folklore, Cultural Performances, and Popular Entertainments*, 33.

28 Ivan Čolović, *Divlja književnost*. Etnolingvističko proučavanje paraliterature, 2nd edition (Belgrade: XX vek, 2000), 319.

29 Bauman, 32.

30 Bauman, 32.

31 Čolović, *Divlja književnost*, 319.

32 The literature is weakest in the case of Slovenia. I therefore cannot equally strongly claim that what follows applies in the same degree for Slovenes.

33 Murko, 367.

34 Murko, 368.

35 Murko, 376.

36 Murko, 43.

37 See *Narodne pjesme Korduna*, ed. Stanko Opačić-Čanica (Zagreb: Prosvjeta, 1971), 190–98.

38 Opačić-Čanica, 197–98.

39 Murko, 61.

40 Murko, 191.

41 Murko, 62.

42 Žanić, 67.

43 As quoted in Ivan Čolović, *Bordel ratnika*, 3rd edition (Belgrade: XXth vek, 2000), 35. All names, except of course Slobodan Milošević, are of legendary Serbian heroes who died during the Battle of Kosovo in 1389.

44 As quoted ibid., 36–37. Čista Provo is a small town in Croatia. Tomislav is believed to have been the first Croatian king, crowned allegedly in 925. Petar Zrinski and Fran Krsto Frankopan are two Croatian nobles executed on the orders of the Habsburg emperor Leopold in 1671. Josip Jelačić was a governor of Civil Croatia and Slavonia in the middle of the nineteenth century.

45 As quoted in Arnold Hauser, *Filozofija povijesti umjetnosti* (Zagreb: Matica hrvatska, 1963), 204.

46 Dunja Rihtman-Auguštin, "Tradicionalna kultura i suvremene vrijednosti," *Kulturni radnik* 3 (1970): 34.

47 Ibid., 30–31.

48 Ibid., 39.

49 Ibid., 36.

50 Ibid., 36.

51 Branko Đurica, "Kako su Cvitkovići shvatili Marksa," *Politika*, 20 July 1967, as quoted ibid., 36.

52 Žanić, 313.

53 Gojko Nikoliš, *Korijen, stablo, pavetina* (Zagreb: Liber, 1980).

54 Maja Bošković-Stulli, *Pjesme, priče, fantastika* (Zagreb: NZMH, 1991), 199 and 215.

55 For the content and importance of this work, see the article by Andrew B. Wachtel in this volume.

56 Frank J. Miller, *Folklore for Stalin: Russian Folklore and Pseudofolklore of the Stalin Era* (Armonk, New York—London, England: Studies of the Harriman Institute, M. E. Sharpe, 1990), 6.

57 Rihtman-Auguštin, "Tradicionalna kultura i suvremene vrijednosti," 33.

58 Bošković-Stulli, *Pjesme, priče, fantastika*, 201.

59 The collection referred to is *Plameni cvjetovi: Narodne pjesme o borbi i revoluciji*, ed. Tvrtko Čubelić, Svetozar Petrović and Grigor Vitez (Zagreb: Mladost, 1961).

60 Maja Bošković-Stulli, "Narodna poezija naše oslobodilačke borbe kao problem savremenog folklornog stvaralaštva," *Srpska akademija nauka, Zbornik radova*, vol. LXVIII, Etnografski institut, vol. 3, ed. Dušan Nedeljković (Belgrade: 1960), 421.

61 Mak Dizdar, *Narodne pjesme iz borbe i izgradnje*, ed. Mak Dizdar, Narodna knjižnica, sveska I (Sarajevo: Seljačka knjiga, 1951), 141.

62 Renata Jambrešić-Kirin, Institute for Ethnology and Folklore in Zagreb, personal conversation.

63 Dizdar, 141.

64 Žanić, 65.

65 B. Marjanović, "Crnom vrhu se crno piše," *Politika*, 4 April 1970, as quoted by Dunja Rihtman-Auguštin, "Četiri varijacije na temu kultura poduzeća," *Kulturni radnik* 3 (1972): 149.

66 Krajina, 137–38.

67 Kordun is a part of Croatia where a great number of the Croatian Serbs lived. The area experienced some of the worst Ustaša pogroms in the Second World War. The quotation is from the song "Crni Đurđevdan," in *Narodne pjesme Korduna*, 268.

68 *Topos* (from the Greek word *tópos* for "a place") denotes in literary theory a conventional formula.

69 "Crni Đurđevdan," in *Narodne pjesme Korduna*, 269.

70 "Čvrsto gnijezdo—naša domovina," in Sait Orahovac, ed., *Narodne pjesme bunta i otpora: Motivi iz revolucije, borbe i obnove* (Sarajevo: Svjetlost, 1971), 99.

71 "Crni Đurđevdan," in *Narodne pjesme Korduna*, 269–70. Radić is in general a positive hero in the poems, while the same cannot be said about his successor, Vladko Maček.

72 This pertains especially for the poems from the Serb-populated areas of Croatia that were composed by the Serbian folk singer.

73 "Ustanak Crne Gore trinaestog jula 1941. godine," in Šefćet Plana, "Ustanak 1941. u albanskoj i crnogorskoj narodnoj epici," *XXVIII Kongres Saveza udruženja folklorista Jugoslavije* (Sutomore: 1981), 58.

74 Tvrtko Čubelić, ed., *Epske narodne pjesme* (Zagreb: n.p., 1970), 287–303.

75 "Čvrsto gnijezdo—naša domovina," in Orahovac, *Narodne pjesme bunta i otpora*, 99–100.

76 "Ustanak na Romaniji," in Orahovac, 21.

77 Žanić, 204–25.

78 "Ustanak na Romaniji," in Orahovac, 21.

79 "Pjesma partizanske omladine," in Orahovac, 188.

80 "Ratko Pavlović-Ćićko," in Tatomir P. Vukanović, *Srpske narodne partizanske pesme* (Vranje: Narodni muzej, 1966), 82–83. For the position of Njegoš in the national pantheon, see chapter 5 by Andrew B. Wachtel in this volume.

81 "Čolića majka," in Vukanović, *Srpske narodne partizanske pesme*, 114.

82 Ibid., 114.

83 "Bukilića majka," ibid., 110.

84 "Zašto narod tol'ke suze lije," ibid., 88.

85 "Ustanak Crne Gore trinaestog jula 1941. godine," in Šefćet Plana, "Ustanak 1941. u albanskoj i crnogorskoj narodnoj epici," 58.

86 "Ustanak na Romaniji," in Orahovac, *Narodne pjesme bunta i otpora*, 22.

87 Bošković-Stulli, "Narodna poezija naše oslobodilačke borbe," 413–14. The entire poem is given on those pages.

88 "Zidanje Skadra," here quoted from Čubelić, *Epske narodne pjesme*, 17–23.

89 Bošković-Stulli, "Narodna poezija naše oslobodilačke borbe," 414.

90 "Zašto narod tol'ke suze lije," in Vukanović, *Srpske narodne partizanske pesme*, 88.

91 "Na Titov govor preko radija 31.12.1946," in Orahovac, *Narodne pjesme bunta i otpora*, 266.

92 Milivoj Rodić, ed., *Sunce iza gore: Revolucionarne narodne pjesme sa tla Bosne i Hercegovine* (Banjaluka: "Glas," 1983), 166–67.

93 "Oj, Rakosi," in Orahovac, *Narodne pjesme bunta i otpora*, 284.

94 Ibid., 283.

95 Murko, 267.

96 "Krvavi pokolj kod Krnjaka," in Opačić-Ćanica, *Narodne pjesme Korduna*, 281.

97 Pierre Nora, "Between Memory and History: *Les Lieux de Mémoire*," *Representations* 26, (Spring 1989) 16.

98 Amos Funkenstein, "Collective Memory and Historical Consciousness," *History and Memory* 1 (1989): 5–26.

99 "Đurđevdan," in Opačić-Ćanica, *Narodne pjesme Korduna*, 275.

100 "Ustanak na Romaniji," in Orahovac, *Narodne pjesme bunta i otpora*, 22.

101 Nikola P. Ilić and Momčilo Zlatanović, ed., *Narodne pesme južne Srbije o oslobodilačkom ratu i revoluciji* (Leskovac: Književni klub "Glubočica," 1985), 19.

102 Momčilo Zlatanović, "Uvodne napomene," in Ilić and Zlatanović, 6.

CHAPTER 8

Rossitza Guentcheva

SOUNDS AND NOISE IN SOCIALIST BULGARIA

"I would have died if, for a man concentrated on work, silence had indeed been so indispensable as it seems at first glance. I live quite near the baths and at this very moment I am surrounded by a multitude of sounds. Imagine, there are all types of sounds able to make anyone start hating the very organ of hearing. There is the noise of those who do physical exercises, and the noise of the swirling of the plumb-heavy ball, and the panting of those working, or better said pretending to work; I can hear how they breathe heavily, hold their breath, and then emit hoarse and rough exhalations. I can hear the slapping of a greasy hand on the shoulder of a body being massaged with oil; from the type of the sound I can even infer how the oil is being applied, with a stretched or with a curled palm ... 'Oh, you will exclaim, you are either made of iron or are deaf, if your mind is not affected by so diverse and inharmonious shouts, when the stoic Chrysippus was brought to death by some endless cheers alone.' ... I swear, this noise does not bother me more than the murmur of running water, although it is known that one people changed the site of their city just because they could not stand the noise produced by the river Nile ... I force my mind to remain concentrated and unaffected by any external phenomenon ... Calmness is not reached but by the mind."

Seneca to Lucilius, Letter LVI, *"On unpleasant sounds"*

This chapter is about the perception of sounds in socialist Bulgaria. Either wanted or unwanted, sounds are an intrinsic part of the everyday life of people, and, for the present case, of Bulgarians in the socialist society of the period 1944–1989. I explore the fragile threshold between sounds and noise and attempt to explain why certain sounds qualified as appropriate for the ears of the socialist citizen. The inquiry will also address the fate of undesirable sounds disgraced as noise, and the Bulgarian Communist Party's (BCP) ideological rationale for sanctioning the soundscape.[1] Inasmuch as sounds belong to the domain of the everyday, the chapter will throw light on an aspect of people's everyday existence which has remained as yet largely unexplored by historians. Equally, this research on human senses and their social control will reveal the reverse effects of categorization and regulation on broader everyday experiences. My intention is to capture the specific meaning attributed to sounds and noise during the four socialist decades in Bulgaria through the concepts elaborated by Communist Party leaders and intellectuals.

At the end of the 1940s and through the 1950s, Bulgarian citizens were left almost entirely unassisted in judging the desirability of different sounds that surrounded them. The problem of noise, and especially of its control, regulation, and reduction, practically did not exist at that time. Far from the explicit endeavor to combat noise that developed in the late 1960s and the anti-noise euphoria which took shape in the 1970s, few sounds qualified as noise in the two preceding decades. At a time when massive industrialization was under way and building up heavy industry was the daily duty of citizens and authorities alike, the noise of machines in the factories was welcomed and celebrated. Workers, poets, and officials delighted in the roar of engines, recognizing in their squeaking and rattling the first sounds of modern industrial Bulgaria, successfully leaving behind its now outdated rural image. "Instead of birds singing—winches are grating" were the words by which one of the key figures of Bulgarian socialist realism, the poet Penio Penev, summarized this atmosphere. Like the whole generation of the 1950s, he was enchanted by the oily smell of motors, the seductive scent of lime, and the coarse voices of turbines and cement mixers.[2]

In the late 1940s and throughout the 1950s, fighting rural backwardness and modernizing the country through rapid industrialization were the paramount tasks of the Communist regime. In 1956, Bulgaria was still an agrarian country, where the rural economy still outweighed the industrial sector, and the village population was twice as large as the urban.[3] Even the capital city of Sofia still exhibited traces of a small town, where some residents raised domestic animals and planted vegetables in their private courtyards and gardens. A 1957 edict of the Executive Council in one of the Sofia districts designated the specific locations in the district where domestic animals and poultry could be bred.[4] For more than a decade after the socialist revolution, district authorities in Sofia were still working to assure large agricultural crops and the productivity of domestic animals. The sounds of Sofia at that time were closer to the sounds of the countryside than to those of a burgeoning urban agglomeration. The average Bulgarian citizen in the 1950s was most likely to be disturbed by the mooing of cows, the quacking of ducks or the grunting of pigs.

At the same time, because one of the paramount goals of the Communist Party was to transform backward rural locations into modern and shining socialist sites, sounds associated with rural life acquired a pejorative connotation. They were identified with useless romanticism and harmful nostalgic longing for a peaceful way of life. A quiet existence was incompatible with the proletarian zeal needed to build a new socialist Bulgaria, to erect new cities and factories, and with the revolutionary drive forward to an ideal Communist society. A feuilleton, published in the daily *Otechestven Front* on 22 September 1955 and entitled "Noise in harmony," ridiculed the sentimental yearning for the "tender ringing of guitars" and the singing of telegraphic wires and restless blackbirds. The author derided the idyllic verses to Nature written by three Bulgarian poets, and implicitly promoted rough proletarian enthusiasm and the raw beauty of pouring concrete.[5] Silence was also associated with the capitalist enemy, "who now acts secretively and furtively, and tries not to make noise on the squares," ruining socialist institutions covertly from within.[6]

This notwithstanding, rural sounds were not the only blight to the soundscape of the early socialist decades. A host of musical sounds turned out to be unwanted and marginalized, for varying reasons. The operetta "Deliana" was labeled a "harmful work" immediately upon its first performance at the season's opening at the State Musical Theatre in Sofia.[7] It was considered an "attack against our new cooperative village, a thoughtless, trite caricature of the new relations in that village," which "nurtures petit-bourgeois vestiges in people's consciousness." In this instance, the libretto rather than the music itself was conceived as tasteless and pernicious. Depicting the protagonist in his romantic relationship with a woman ("and not in his relations to the cooperative villagers"), a village girl as "intriguer" and one villager as "drunkard" ("there are no such personages in our socialist village"), the authors were blamed for "having followed the canons of the tasteless and decadent Western operetta" and "espoused the reactionary bourgeois dream of a rural idyll." Although the music itself was found worthy and accessible for a mass audience, it was turned into noise by a deviant text that did not conform to the rules of socialist realism.

Yet music itself could easily acquire dangerous connotations and thereby become noise. Such was the fate, for example, of modern atonal music inspired by Schönberg, Hindemitt, Debussy and others. Bulgarian composers Konstantin Iliev and Lazar Nikolov, who wrote such music in the 1950s, were severely criticized as "militant formalists" and "imitators of decadent bourgeois music." Here is how an article of 1956, proclaiming itself as "defending real music," described their artistic experiments:

> Their works represent pandemonium, a senseless accumulation of dissonance, a sort of musical equilibristics. They have supplanted the piano's melody with a clapping drum-drum. The charming cantilena of violins, the tender expression of wooden instruments, and the masculine beauty of brass are sacrificed to shrieks, twangs, and screams unbearable for normal human hearing ... For such debased music, the words of Maxim Gorky in his article "Music for the fat" are the most appropriate: "Suddenly, in the deep silence, a stupid hammer starts clanking dryly—one, two, three, ten, twenty clanks, then, as a ball of mud splashing in the purest of water, savage

shouts, screeching, thunder, clamor, crashes and creaks come
in. Inhuman voices are invading, which remind one of a horse
whinny; the grunt of a brass pig is heard, the braying of don-
keys, a slimy croak of a frog."[8]

Strictly following the official Stalinist line of suppressing atonal music
in the USSR, even the works of Soviet modernist composers like Shostako-
vich, Stravinsky, and Prokofiev were criticized as "noisy decadent propaganda."[9] Jazz also figured prominently on the list of offensive sounds, being
judged tasteless, erotic, vulgar, unserious, and American (see Document 1).
Yet such noise was easier to control, as ideologically incorrect musical
pieces were simply banned or deleted from public performances. Censorship—
together with self-censorship—was sufficient to assure that the degrading
sound of degenerate bourgeois music did not reach the ears of socialist
Bulgarians.[10]

New Sounds and New Problems

By the late 1960s, the official policy of forced industrialization and urbanization had brought significant changes to the urban as well as rural landscape of Bulgaria. By 1969, the number of urban dwellers for the first time
surpassed that of rural inhabitants, following a rapid concentration of population in the cities.[11] It was precisely the speed of this urbanization and its
attendant abruptness which had crucial importance for the transformation of
the everyday life of Bulgarian citizens. The policy of accelerated urbanization, going hand in hand with an ideological concern for town planning,
also led to the concentration of population in multi-story buildings. Under-
taking public works in widely spread villages and towns was considered
time-consuming and expensive, and thus inefficient. In order to develop
exemplary socialist cities and villages quickly, authorities adopted a policy
of "shrinking the regulated inhabited territories" and "maximizing the concentration of building activities."[12] Compact multi-story buildings would
allow faster and more efficient urban development that was measured in
kilometers of asphalt roads constructed, linear meters of sidewalks and
water-pipes laid, and numbers of trees planted.[13]

While the increasing number of factories, cars, buses or trams diversi-
fied street and city sounds, the concentration of residents in multi-story
buildings further multiplied neighborhood sounds. These "inner district"
sounds came from public parks and playgrounds but most of all from private apartments: they were generated simply through too close co-existence
in the crowded socialist-style buildings. Not only was the number of floors

per building increasingly high, the number of apartments per floor also rose. Initially, the projection for the general town plan of Sofia envisaged just 7 square meters of occupied space per person, yet until advice from foreign architects helped to change this to 15 square meters.[14] The small size of apartments followed from the urgent need to house a rapidly growing urban population and the authorities' desire to fulfill and even surpass targets in the five-year plans for economic development. Since they were set at numbers of apartments constructed, the smaller their size the more the plan target was met. Since people were fitted to flats rather than the other way round, the average size of a Bulgarian flat was set by the Council of Ministers at 75 square meters.[15]

Data from one of the first sociological surveys of living conditions in a central Sofia district revealed that in 1967 more than 97 percent of those interviewed shared a room with another person. (Yet only 29 percent declared that their flats were uncomfortable, meaning "flats where more than two people share a room or where two families are accommodated in one apartment.") Not only were Bulgarians densely packed in residential buildings, but by the mid-1960s they also acquired enough modern appliances to produce, or expose others to, new types of sounds. Of those interviewed 54 percent said that they had washing machines, 46 percent possessed vacuum cleaners, and 25 percent had refrigerators. The survey showed that 89 percent of the respondents owned a radio, 33 percent had a TV set, 14 percent owned record players, and 7 percent tape machines.[16]

In this way, a new category of sounds emerged throughout the 1960s. They were specifically urban, that is, not related to socialist industry and the construction of the socialist homeland. They necessitated a new classification. Unlike rural sounds, they were not expected to die out gradually; unlike industrial sounds, they were not ideologically correct. Nor could they be easily suppressed through censorship, as was the case with undesirable music. These sounds demanded categorization which would change the existing perception of sounds. New classificatory work, however, started with the industrial sounds. A few more years had to pass before the multitude of urban sounds were officially interpreted as noise, account taken of them in the rules of socialist cohabitation, and measures prescribed for their avoidance on the path to the attainment of perfect socialist coexistence.

From Sounds to Noise

Instrumental in the process of changing perceptions and sensibilities whereby sounds were degraded to the status of simple noise was the Bulgarian Communist Party's policy of *intensified* industrialization, which was adopted in the mid-1960s.[17] Industrialization in the preceding decades had been extensive, and involved the building of new factories and enterprises. Intensive industrialization meant that the already constructed industrial plants and machines had to be made more efficient.[18] This was thought possible to achieve by raising the productivity of the labor force. Yet in the mid-1960s, contemporary scholarship, armed with new techniques, instruments, and sophisticated methodology, discovered that loud sounds negatively affected workers' health, concentration, and productivity. The first sound to fall under direct regulation as harmful and inadmissible was the roar of machinery, now dethroned from its place as a palpable symbol of socialist Bulgaria in the late 1940s and 1950s. To be sure, *machines* continued to function as such a symbol until the very end of the Communist regime; it was only their *roar* which was now found offensive and damaging. From being a welcome sound it became unwanted noise, dissociated from the representation of machines as pillars of socialist development.

Attention focused first on conditions at the workplace and on production noise, for it was in factories and plants that diminished concentration, lower productivity and illness-generated absences were judged to be most detrimental. From 1965 onward, a host of Bulgarian specialists, most of them medical doctors and acoustic engineers, published books on the great social harm of noise. Calling noise a "public enemy of contemporary life," "a dangerous enemy," and even "enemy number one," they campaigned for a rationalization of the workplace and workforce.[19] Summarizing these concerns and calculating the multiple damage noise did to productivity, Liliana Todorova wrote:

> With the country's industrialization, with the growth of productive capacity, and the automatization and mechanization of work processes, conditions have appeared that lead to an increase in workplace noise too. A huge percentage of workers in different branches of industry and agriculture are exposed to noise which lowers their productivity and increases traumatization... It has been established that productivity at noisy workplaces is 20 to 60 percent lower than at quiet ones, the volume of waste production is considerably higher, while the number of mistakes during calculations rises by 50 percent... All this lowers work capacity and the precision of routine movements, while raising production errors by 20–25 percent in comparison to a noise-free environment.[20]

Todorova also noted that in noisy environments the ability to understand speech decreased. This could endanger communication among members of a working collective and the ability to hear orders, whereas in professions requiring good hearing, the very ability to execute one's professional duties could be reduced.[21] She concluded: "Experience demonstrates that lowering the intensity of production noise is an important though as yet unused resource. It is established that reducing noise by 1dB raises productivity by 0.3–1 percent. Hence every defeated decibel would bring our socialist economy millions of leva."[22]

Other sounds quickly suffered the fate of industrial noise as Bulgarian researchers realized that noise outside the workplace might equally imperil productivity. It was the Marxist notion of *reproduction* (i.e., restoration) of the capacity for work which formed the bridge to interpreting a growing number of sounds as noise. Reproduction of the labor force, which took place outside of working time, was crucial for the maintenance of the processes of work and production. Noise jeopardized the restoration of the ability to work by not letting people rest and relax, by harming their sleep and by destroying their leisure time. Since sleep and leisure had little meaning in the Marxist doctrine outside of their being a reservoir for renewed work capacity, damaging the socialist citizen's sleep and leisure represented an unsuccessful renewal of the ability to work hard. Leisure was conceived of as a "sphere which continues human self-accomplishment in work," hence contributing to the self-accomplishment of the socialist personality and its harmonious development.[23] Leisure was not an alternative to work, it was its extension; if its effectiveness was impeded by noise, this would undermine the central tenet of socialist society, productive work itself.

The logic of protecting productivity required that noise be regulated; it also determined its regulation along a public-private axis. Three types of noise were distinguished. To the production noise of industrial enterprises and machines, which was to be prevented from undermining workers' productivity, two other types were added—public noise of private origin (the noise of cars, motorcycles, lifts, pipes), and private noise, incorporated in the notion of the socialist way of life, or *bit* (the noise of neighbors, family arguments, the loud playing of radios, television or musical instruments). Both of them negatively affected workers' reproduction outside of the workplace.

Some specialists singled out public noise of private origin as the worst offender, although they were divided over which was more harmful, the noise of vehicles or that produced by shops, restaurants, bars, and manufacturing facilities located on the first floors of occupied buildings.[24] Others thought private noise was the worst, with the human voice being the chief culprit and silence the optimal sound.[25] Still others appealed for a "conscientious and civilized use of modern appliances, especially of radio and television sets, record and tape players, etc., which means reducing their volume so that some people's entertainment and pleasure do not interfere with the tranquillity of their neighbors."[26] Music could also become pure noise. "The radio station at the factory, which thunders louder than the machines, tires the worker and increases waste, is also a source of noise, although, formally speaking, it broadcasts (entertaining) music," said Iasen Moskov. And he went on:

> Noise is all around us—both at the workplace and in the street. It penetrates already into our homes which are supposed to be hearths of tranquillity. How many people are awakened in the morning by the ringing of the alarm clock or by the thunder of motorcycles and vans, then work in noisy conditions, and upon returning home when they need to rest, are again exposed to shouts, tapping, the piano of the neighbor, or to the street loudspeakers, in some small provincial towns still used at any hour.[27]

Public or private, noise was any unwanted, harmful, confusing or embarrassing sound. But being contingent on perception, it was relative, and because of that, elusive and extremely hard to combat. Sharp sounds might be inoffensive for some but disturbing for others. Still, noise was aggressive.[28] It invaded and strained people's ears against their wish, leaving them passive, defeated and incapable of reacting. Noise attacked human flesh by raising blood pressure, causing ulcers and cancer as well as an array of nervous, psychological, cardiac and gastric diseases.[29] It was an enemy, but an invisible and hidden one, which no person could either touch or see.[30] Noise was permeable, defying obstacles, and able to assault a disproportionately high number of city dwellers. When doctors found out that noise could injure the human body even during sleep,[31] it was clear that a holy war would have to be waged against it. "A vital imperative of our society is to initiate a decisive fight against noise," wrote a physician, adding "'More quietly! Silence!'—these are vital imperatives which should be embodied in our everyday life, because they promote enthusiasm, health, and long life."[32]

In the Vanguard of Combating Noise

Once the point had been reached where the paramount assets of a socialist society—work, productivity and their reproduction—were believed to be at stake, it was time for official authority to step in. From the early 1970s, a massive campaign against plant noise as well as city, street, neighborhood, and private noise was initiated by the highest Bulgarian ruling bodies. The problem of noise moved onto the agenda of the Politburo of the Central

Committee of the BCP and started being discussed at the meetings of the Council of Ministers. In the absence of private enterprise and an independent business sector, it was the central institutions of the socialist state which were obliged to control, regulate, and ensure the health of the labor force. Inevitably politicizing noise, these institutions would be the most effective not only in putting forward but also in enforcing prescriptions on what noise was and how to overcome it.

Before the 1970s, the control of unpleasant sounds—chiefly public noise—had been entrusted to the trade unions and the organs of the Fatherland Front, a BCP-sponsored mass organization which dealt with the public sphere and the socialist way of life. At that time, noise was not perceived to pose a particular danger to the whole socialist citizenry and economy; it affected relatively few people (predominantly industrial workers) and was not regarded as a major social and public evil. "The history of the campaign against noise in our country is relatively short," commented a Bulgarian scholar in 1976, referring to the fact that it was at the beginning of the 1970s that the initiative was taken "by the state, which started organizing, leading and implementing a complex of measures for combating noise."[33] Noise, according to a high-ranking official who addressed a session on environmental protection at the National Assembly in 1973, was a new problem which socialist Bulgaria had to address extremely seriously by adopting appropriate legislation.[34]

The BCP's engagement against noise coincided with the design and inception of the *Program for raising the standard of living of the Bulgarian people*, announced by state and party leader Todor Zhivkov in 1971.[35] The concept of "standard of living" (*zhizneno ravnishte*) combined concern for environmental protection, citizens' health and the socialist way of life, as well as the need to lengthen their leisure time, where the anti-noise drive would smoothly fit in. Raising the standard of living was to be achieved through 12 separate programs, from accelerated housing construction, the manufacture of scarce commodities (meat, fish, vegetables, fruits and things for children), and the building of kindergartens, sport facilities and youth clubs, to improving public dining, transportation networks, and the organization of working time, and training specialists through secondary and higher education.[36] A polluted environment damaged the health of Bulgaria's citizens, thus endangering their performance as socialist workers. Safeguarding the worker's body would guarantee the increasing pace of socialist production. Bodies could be strengthened and made competitive through sports and improved diet. Since the Marxist notion of reproduction of the labor force depended extensively on material conditions outside of the workplace, the Communist Party found a rationale for participating in the management of these as well.

Although the new socialist way of life was conceptualized as being outside of the sphere of production and politics, it had a strong reciprocal connection with them.[37] One's productive and public work depended on the way
one was eating, dressing, satisfying one's needs, and renewing and improving one's strength, knowledge and creative capacities.[38] The problem of the
new socialist way of life and the manner in which socialist citizens "satisfied their everyday material and spiritual needs" became more important in
the early 1970s when the state set out to reduce working hours and adopt a
five-day work week. A central pillar of the increased socialist standard of
living, the two-day weekend, extended the amount of leisure time, hence
accenting time dedicated to reproduction of the workforce.

At the same time, the question of how workers spent their leisure hours
became even more important. Since the official premise was that every person organized their personal and familial *bit*, "using leisure time as they
want and like,"[39] from the 1970s onward socialist citizens had more time at
their own disposal. Marxist research on time-budgets warned, however, that
leisure time should have nothing to do with passive rest, loitering, or empty
entertainment, nor even with spending time "alone" or "on one's own."
Only activities oriented to physical, intellectual, professional, spiritual and
social development of the personality should count for leisure time.[40] The
two-day weekend was a "direct investment in raising the education and professional qualifications of working people and in this sense the sixth working day which became a holiday will not be an empty day."[41] It would be a
working day par excellence, spent on reproduction and improvement of
one's capacities for work.

Thus from the early 1970s, the standard of living was conceived of as
the "other pole of economy"; it depended on the state of the natural environment, the socialist citizen's health and a meaningful way of life. Noise
could put all three of these at risk. Todor Zhivkov summarized its negative
effect on the environment in his report to the 10th Congress of the BCP in
1971: "The flourishing industrialization of the country has had some negative consequences too. I mean above all the pollution of air and water, the
increase of noise, vibrations and infrasounds, etc... These phenomena should
not be underestimated or treated lightly. They must be stopped through
strict legislation and the active involvement of society."[42] The minister of
construction and architecture, Grigor Stoichkov, also spelled out the detrimental influence of noise on human health, productivity, and way of life:

> Construction acoustics treat the problems of sound isolation in
> private and public houses, of limiting and reducing the noise
> and vibrations in the production areas of industrial buildings
> and human settlements. These are problems relating to acoustic

comfort in the way of life of the socialist citizen, industrial productivity, and the population's health in general. Solving these problems now is of utmost social, economic and political importance and is linked to making the work environment healthier and to stabilizing the workforce in industrial enterprises.[43] (See also Document 2.)

The Bulgarian authorities were convinced that it was socialist societies, especially the USSR, which could best preserve the environment, because their relationship to nature was not contaminated by predatory exploitation. Quoting Soviet Supreme Court decisions of 1972 on environmental protection, as well as Leonid Brezhnev's words on nature preservation in his report to the 24th Congress of the Soviet Communist Party, they initiated a massive, complex, and large-scale attack on noise. It started at workplaces on the outskirts of cities, proceeded to streets, shops, and public gardens, then after going on to specify the location, size and shape of buildings and private apartments, it entered into apartment kitchens and sitting rooms and finally ended in the bed of the socialist citizen. Its ultimate goal was not to intrude into citizens' private lives—as already noted, personal and familial *bit* was supposed to remain their own business—but to protect and improve their healthy relaxation and ensure useful reading and self-education in an atmosphere of calmness and tranquillity.

Directive No. 67 of the Council of Ministers of 6 April 1973 listed numerous initiatives for reducing noise and vibrations in industrial, public and residential buildings, and in all inhabited places.[44] Identifying noise as "one of the cardinal problems of the living environment," it required that all noisy activities in industrial enterprises be grouped together and isolated behind doors and special glass. All machines produced in Bulgaria or imported from abroad had to have their noise and vibration characteristics clearly defined, while all regional people's councils were ordered to take all noisy productive activities out of residential districts. The directive authorized the Ministry of Interior to withdraw from circulation noisy motor vehicles and barred the use of cars with two-cycle engines between 10 pm and 6 am. It decreed that night deliveries to shops and supermarkets be reorganized so as to ensure silence in all inhabited places.[45]

A variety of institutions turned to enforcing the new restrictions. By 1976, when the directive's implementation was first monitored, regional district authorities had started putting asphalt on central streets (concrete pavement increased noise by 10–12 dB) and designing protective green screens against noise. The regional people's councils in 11 cities elaborated programs for moving noisy industrial enterprises outside of residential neighborhoods. The Bulgarian refrigerators Mraz 160 and Mraz 200 were already being advertised with reduced noise as a feature. So were a host of other electrical products (ventilators, electric trucks, washing machines, air conditioners, etc.). The Ministry of Interior carried out more than 2.3 million checks and suspended from circulation about 30, 000 motor vehicles because of loud engines. In order to alleviate inner-city traffic noise, ring roads encircling the towns were built in Sevlievo, Pazardzhik, Sliven, Lovech, etc. In the major train stations, steam engines were completely replaced by diesels. The Ministry of Transport prescribed a list of measures for reducing noise in the area of train and bus stations, encouraging the use of light signals, radio-telephones and other noiseless means of transmitting information.

From the cities' industrial hinterland through their streets and stations, anti-noise concerns moved to the buildings where the socialist citizen lived, mobilizing town-planning and architecture to join in the struggle. Since greenery helped reduce noise, trees and bushes were to be planted around the main city transport arteries, with special attention to their seasonal growth. The parks of Sofia, which in the 1961 general town-development bill were located at the outskirts of the capital, were moved inside the city, closer to the population. Residential buildings were to be set apart from main city roads by two rows of public buildings—first shops and restaurants fronting the streets and behind them two- or three-story public garages to act as barriers to noise. This asymmetric zonal arrangement was intended to break up the boring sequence of identical blocks of flats and enhance the pleasure from contemplating beautiful architectural ensembles, since "the perception of architectural aesthetics was also contingent on the experience of noise." The optimal height of residential buildings was set at 10–12 floors; their optimal position was parallel to the road.[46]

Anti-noise activities penetrated within the buildings, too, and affected the size and architecture of the apartments themselves. Size related to the flat's orientation to north, east, south or west.[47] Floors and ceilings of apartments were to be laid down with special anti-noise insulation (containing penopolystirol, rubber, cork, etc.).[48] Balconies and loggias—those long-honored sites of public communication within private property—were found to reflect street noise and blamed for letting it inside the flat; therefore their construction was not recommended. On the contrary, interior furnishings such as carpets, thick table-cloths and heavy curtains were especially endorsed.[49] In order to best protect the socialist worker, state hygienic and epidemiological inspectors together with acoustic engineers were granted the right to examine citizens' apartments, measure the level of sounds emitted by their refrigerators and washing machines, as well as the noise penetrating in their rooms from the outside.[50] The new categorization of sounds did prove to be a powerful social agent, transforming the everyday environment of citizens and dictating the shape and size of their homes.

Citizens' Response to the Anti-noise Crusade

There was one last type of noise where regulation and control were the hardest to enforce, namely the noise produced by human beings in the course of their daily existence and communication. Sound-proof walls, ceilings and floors could indeed help enforce the duty of sleep and rest, protecting citizens from noisy neighbors, loud music, shouting in the street and lively conversation in the nearby district garden. Yet as Document 3 indicates, this was not always the case. People were often left with the dubious privilege of listening unwillingly to others' conversations or with the temptation of eavesdropping, spying on and even participating in their neighbors' private day-to-day activities. The Council of Ministers attempted to regulate that kind of noise too by approving a lengthy and extremely detailed *Model Guide on Internal Order in Residential Buildings*, produced by the Ministry of Justice (Document 4). Prescribing minutely when, where and what kind of sounds were permissible, it had to be posted in all buildings throughout the country with the goal of preventing conflicts among neighbors and assuring peaceful socialist cohabitation.

The struggle against human noise was carried on by more subtle means as well. Noise was progressively associated with uncivilized behavior, with savage manners and primitive conduct. Uncultured style and habits, betrayed by untamed voices and careless night-long parties, were to be confronted by the Fatherland Front, which struggled to uproot and replace them with considerate human relations devoid of aggression, rage and discontent. Eradication was practiced in gentle and mild forms, such as organizing children's detachments for spending time meaningfully and courtyard squads for protecting order in residential buildings.[51] Despite the military terminology, the techniques the Fatherland Front preferred were friendly persuasion, benevolent instruction and patient inculcation of the principles of polite behavior. There were other instruments of re-education, such as the fine of four leva codified in the *Model Guide on Internal Order in Residential Buildings*,[52] or the district "comradely courts" which were empowered by a law of 1961 to enforce the rules of socialist coexistence in buildings and private flats.

Respect for the right—and duty—to calmness, peace and tranquillity in interpersonal relations was also promoted through associating noise with remnants of bourgeois manners and sensibility. Describing noisy capitalist environments allowed clear anti-Western rhetoric to be deployed. Such depictions also associated Western noise with an outdated, unhealthy way of life. This is how Geno Tsonkov described the atmosphere in a typical Western bar:

> It is certainly a happy phenomenon that the *bit* of the Bulgarian
> in the past was not contaminated by the habit of spending a
> great part of his leisure time in pubs, coffee houses and bars,
> which is a habitual and extremely widespread practice for cer-
> tain Western people. Facts are showing convincingly that time
> spent in pubs, coffee houses and bars is not meaningful. Air
> inside them is filthy, impregnated with the smoke of tobacco,
> alcoholic fumes, carbon dioxide and noise. Hence it is self-evi-
> dent that no sensible rest is possible in these places. In addi-
> tion, too much time is lost unnoticeably there, most of all in
> empty talk.[53]

Middlebrow fiction also encouraged the association of noisiness with
old ideological villains.[54] Vividly portraying loud-voiced and noise-addict-
ed characters as the conservative petit-bourgeois or the modern trickster,
Iulian Vuchkov hoped to expose these sins as inadmissible in a socialist
society (Document 5). Unlike in the early 1950s, the enemy was not silent
and secretive anymore but stood out in the open, and his sharp voice made
him ridiculous and unpleasant. He was not particularly dangerous any longer,
but just a sad relic of the past which, with the readers' effort, could be
stricken from the face of the socialist society. Calm conversations, tranquillity and peacefulness were markers of the exemplary socialist way of life.

Bulgarian citizens were quick to lend credibility by their now authorized
complaints. That noise bothered and tormented them was evident from
scores of letters of complaint sent to the highest institutions in the country,
the Council of Ministers, the State Council, and quite often to the top state
and party leader, Todor Zhivkov himself.[55] These personal pleas abounded
with descriptions of pain and agony inflicted by noisy neighbors, restaurants and light industry situated near or inside residential buildings. They
were taken seriously by the authorities and always duly investigated,
although some of them included grossly exaggerated and even entirely
implausible assertions.[56] When light industry plants came under attack, they
were rarely closed down, as citizens wanted, but the noisy machines were
taken out, fines were often levied, while precise measurements of noise
were invariably made.[57]

These sources indicate that the majority of the protesting citizens had
skillfully endorsed the motives behind the state's concern with noise, namely
that noise ruined their calmness, harming their productivity and the ability
to replenish their energies for work. "Dear comrades," began a letter of several Sofia residents on Struma Street, "with the feeling of people who seek
assistance and protection from the highest state institution in our country,
we write to you asking for help," and then went on complaining about the

noisy ventilator of a nearby snack bar. To back their appeal, the inhabitants of Struma Street nicely adopted the official standpoint: they claimed that the sleep and tranquillity at night of hundreds of people had been broken, that they could not sleep at all, and *"on the next day we feel ill."*[58] A much longer letter of residents on Alabin Street in Sofia, complaining of loud restaurant music, displayed a more poignant argumentation:

> This noise is unimaginable and unbearable, accompanied by a terrible roar and unexpected echoes. Peaceful life in any of the surrounding buildings is unthinkable. But most of their inhabitants—we—are working people, workers and clerks, who seek their basic indispensable rest in order to gather forces for the next working shift ... The repertoire of the orchestra lasts for a long time every day, and consumes the hours meant and destined for our relaxation. We ask you to interfere most energetically and order that the harmful consequences of the unwarranted impact of this extreme and obnoxious noise be liquidated.

Having attached to their complaint excerpts from anti-noise regulations and instructions, published in the *State Gazette* and the daily press, the inhabitants of Alabin Street summoned a supreme authority whose pronouncements were given due emphasis with the help of capital letters:

> We refer to the thought of comrade Todor Zhivkov, expressed by him on multiple occasions, namely that MAN IS THE MOST VALUABLE GOOD in our socialist country. Everything is done and should be done IN THE NAME OF MAN AND FOR THE GOOD OF MAN ONLY. Especially now, in the months preceding the Party Conference of March 1984, for which we should demonstrate maximum achievements. Yet they presuppose and necessitate at least a MINIMAL TRUE REST—FOR RELAXATION FOR THE NEXT WORKING DAY![59]

It would be inaccurate, however, to assume that official rhetoric had in all cases been deeply or honestly internalized and that citizens sincerely believed that noise had to be evaded because it hurt their productivity at the workplace. It is difficult to discern the internal motives of ordinary people simply by reading their letters to the government. At least in one case, the anti-noise correspondence between ordinary people and official power discloses that noise was used as an instrument for settling inter-personal disputes between neighbors. In 1981, Nedko Nakov from the village of Bukovets sent a complaint to the Presidium of the National Assembly against the village doctor. In an almost unreadable text full of grammatical and orthographic mistakes, he accused the doctor of being a hooligan and of gathering at his home large groups of people who shouted all night long. Since Nedko Nakov requested the doctor's replacement on the ground of his not being able to rest calmly, an investigation was launched. It discovered that the doctor had not done anything of which he was accused, but had publicly exposed Nakov's son who had stolen money and fishing tools from his house.[60] Noise had been called in to settle a score between neighbors; the official policy of combating noise was used to serve individual ends, albeit unsuccessfully. What was more remarkable, though, was the deploying of this rhetoric by an almost illiterate villager.

****

The exploration of the perception of sounds in socialist Bulgaria reveals a significant cultural transformation that took place in the late 1960s and early 1970s. Sensual experiences, which are most often thought of as homogeneous and immutable over longer spans of time, underwent a remarkable change whereby calmness and tranquillity were restored as values for socialist Bulgarians. This shift was predicated on concern for raising the productivity of labor and assuring the successful reproduction of citizens' capacity for work. Throughout the four socialist decades, particular sounds were ascribed different meanings that were contingent on the pace of industrialization and the phases of building a Communist society. The revolutionary roar of machines and the thundering song of marching workers were admissible only in the first two decades of socialist construction. In that period, revolution was indeed noise, a literal raising of the voices of the masses. By the early 1970s, however, the socialist infrastructure was already in place while socialism entered its second, developed stage. The revolution was over, and the voices of the masses could be allowed to subside. As a consequence, several sounds were reconceptualized as harmful and damaging to the productivity of workers. Quietness and peacefulness were reintroduced into the life of the Bulgarian citizen as barriers to noise, and new sensibilities were promoted.

In addition to discerning a trajectory of sensory alterations, we were able to observe how the conceptual tools designed by Communist Party theoreticians affected the everyday life of Bulgarian citizens. The official assumption that noise damaged productivity resulted in notable transformations in plant safety, inner-city transportation, the provision of services, and even in architecture and interior design. Moreover, it was related to an ambitious project of social engineering, namely, to produce the new socialist personality which would be an amalgam of decency, propriety, and impeccable civility. These exemplary qualities were cherished as a viable channel for pushing calmness and tranquillity into citizens' domestic space, where they depended entirely on individual expediency.

Therefore by blocking unpleasant sounds, policies for limiting noise were designed to envelop the socialist worker in silence and grant him the chance for efficient reproduction and rest. A particular space was thus formed around the socialist worker, a space where offensive sounds and noise were not admitted. This space was not a private space: it sprang neither from interest in the individual, nor did it leave personal conduct to the discretion of the citizen. Yet it was meant to accompany the workers throughout, from the workplace to bed, shielding their repose in both public and domestic spaces. Although it was by no means free from state interference, it was created in order to protect the body, health, and meaningfully spent leisure time of the worker. This notwithstanding, it is interesting to consider how the authorities were able to discuss questions of leisure, lifestyle, and even eating and dressing, without touching on the problem of the private sphere. Even more interesting is how ordinary people, in accepting the rhetoric of calmness and tranquillity, came closer to the classic bourgeois notion of privacy as well, though still without conceptualizing it. Their reliance on the state to protect them from noise and their genuine belief in its power to do so places them very far, however, from the stoic individual endeavor of Seneca to defeat noise in his own head.

Finally, to return to the quotation, we cannot forebear to add that Seneca succumbed to noise and lost the fight. Concluding his letter to Lucilius, he confessed: "Calmness is not reached but by the mind ... Yet from all this it does not follow that it would not be easier to escape from noise. That is why I will leave this place. I wanted only to test myself. There is no need of further tormenting my ears, when Odysseus, protecting his fellow-travelers, invented a wonderful and simple means, even against the Sirens."

Sources

Document 1:

> We arrive [in the city of Vidin] by steamer exactly on 9 September this year. In the Danube capital there reigns a festive, happy mood. The restaurant-garden in the city park is full of young people. Jazz is being played! We listen and cannot believe our ears. Amidst the sound of 'Boogie-woogie' and 'Rumba', stooped silhouettes of long-haired swingers are twisting. Among them healthy and robust young people from the masses attempt to imitate them. In the orchestra, a dozen musicians are smiling self-contentedly. We look more carefully

and recognize one after another the leading Vidin symphonists. The 'symphonist' Slavkov, instead of a trombone, on which he plays not badly, has taken two hollow pumpkins and in 'artistic trance' tries to capture the foreign American rhythm of the rumba. The rest of the 'symphonists' chime in. Amidst the sounds of this cacophony, the city cultural leaders drink their wine with dignity. Nobody even thinks to protest against this musical barbarity ...

Source: Muzkor, "Vidinski neblagopoluchiia," *Bulgarska muzika* 9 (1953): 44.

Document 2:

The technical and scientific revolution resulted in significant positive transformations in the life of the people, but at the same time it brought about some negative consequences for people's living environment. I refer to the pollution of water, air, land, to erosion and the intense increase of noise and vibrations, to the accumulation of solid waste, as well as to the over-use of natural resources, etc., all of which are of crucial importance ... Increasingly, growing noise represents a paramount threat for a big part of the population. In some cases it reaches 80–100 decibels, which is 1.5–2 times higher than the approved standards. Long-term experimental research demonstrates that the constant pressure on the hearing organs changes the conditional reflex activity of the main brain, decreases attention and working ability, rases blood pressure, has a negative impact on the stomach-intestinal tract, and speeds up the decrease of hearing. Psychic damage and nervous diseases caused by noise have become everyday cases in the hospitals. Unfortunately, no other harmful agent is so difficult to overcome and eliminate as noise ...

Source: TsDA, f. 136, o. 56, a.e. 520—Decision No. 56 from 10 October 1973 of the Council of Ministers, adopting the report of Mako Dakov [deputy-president of the Council of Ministers] on the protection of the natural environment, 1–44.

Document 3:

Behind the corners of new buildings, still unthreatened by rigid requirements for green-planting, neighbors continue to gather from time to time, possessed by a hereditary passion for making compotes and jars of vegetables on inter-building fires. But those are the last Mohicans, for tomorrow the straightforward alleys, the grass and the trees will take over from them the compote-jar good-neighbor relationship. Would these relations be able to flower on the common concrete plane of floors in the building and the common corridors in basements and attics, fenced by thick concrete cages, well-closed windows with blinds and curtains, and doors barred by intricate locks? It is true that with the present type of construction one can hear everything through the walls, windows, and doors, thus neighbors can communicate in a strange modern fashion. But this is only temporary (let us hope!).

Source: Ivan Stoianovich, *Susedut—moi priiatel?* (Sofia: Izdatelstvo na OF, 1983), 6.

Document 4:

Art. 1. This guide regulates the internal order in the residential building located in................/town/, on ..../street/, .../No/, ... /PO Box/.............

... Art. 7. /1/ The dusting of carpets, clothes and other objects must be executed only at the places reserved for that end in the building's courtyard. During weekdays, this can be done between 7 and 10 am in the morning and 4–7 pm in the afternoon, and on holidays, from 8 to 11 am.

/2/ When no place is reserved for it, dusting cannot be done from the balconies and windows on the building's facade.

Art. 8. Washed clothes can be left to dry only in the courtyard or on the balconies, verandas and terraces which are not situated on the building's front.

Art. 9. It is forbidden to put boxes, cartons, and other objects on the balconies, verandas, and terraces on the side of streets, squares, and public gardens.

Art. 10. Garbage containers must stay on the places specially reserved for them.

Art. 11. The glass of windows cannot be replaced by newspapers, wooden or plastic pieces, etc.

Art. 12. It is forbidden to keep domestic animals and birds on balconies, verandas, terraces, and in attics and basements.

Art. 13. Wood can be cut only at the places specially reserved for this in the courtyard and the basements. This can happen daily between 7 and 12 am and 4 and 8 pm.

Art. 14. Playing on instruments, singing, making noise, turning on the radio loudly and other similar things are forbidden between 10 pm and 7 am and 2 and 4 pm. Exceptions are allowed in special cases only for families which have received permission from the building's warden or the president of the managing council.

Art. 15. Parents are obliged to not allow their children to make

noise during the above-specified hours, as well as to write on walls
and damage the building.

(...)

Art. 18. Inhabitants must clean the places of public use and the
areas around the building. It is forbidden to pour water out of balconies and windows, as well as to throw out paper or other rubbish.
This can be done only at the places reserved for this.

Source: TsDA, f. 136, o. 66, a.e. 40—Decree No. 44 from 8 September 1978 of the
Council of Ministers, about the changing and supplementing of the *Guide on
Management, Order, and Surveillance in Buildings,* and the adopting of a *Model
Guide on Internal Order in Residential Buildings,* 8–21:

Document 5:

[T]he petit-bourgeois moves around like a dark cloud, filled with a
sense of territorial supremacy. Where his intelligence fails, his tongue
comes in, and the rude man walks with an open mouth. When you win
the battle with him, he loses his temper. And he sinks to the "enchanting"
sound of a yell. And in a gradual release of the content of his vocal
cords. Then he gesticulates and points at you as at a thief in a bare
field. Then the voice of the boor resonates and winds about as a whip.
It reverberates freely and powerfully. And you faint before you can
hear the end of his phrase. Because the boor within the conservative
petit-bourgeois likes to explain things and strip them of their sense,
until we start hating them before we understood them. When he
argues, he breathes heavily and does not allow you to move even
if you are about to lose consciousness ... Understanding between you
and him is like a postponed quarrel. Your calm conversations are
something like a digging in a desert ...

The modern trickster conceives of conservative petit-bourgeois as
incomplete, raw persons. They like the noisy chaos of the rooms,
attics, basements, and villas or the walk in the neighborhood. He seeks
the urban noise of boulevards, cars, and restaurants where he feels like
a son of his century ... What happens with leisure and pleasure from
the beauty of nature, when one is chased by the habits and 'services'
of urban noise?

Source: Iulian Vuchkov, *Choveshki nravi* (Sofia: Narodna Mladezh, 1975), 204–17.

Notes

1 Jo Tacchi, "Radio texture: between self and others," in Daniel Miller, ed., *Material Cultures: Why Some Things Matter* (Chicago: University of Chicago Press, 1998), 25–45.

2 Penio Penev, *Kogato se nalivakha osnovite* (Sofia: Narodna mladezh, 1965), 43–44.

3 In 1946, the number of urban dwellers in Bulgaria was 1,735,000, compared to 5,294,000 in the rural population. In 1956, the numbers were, respectively, 2,556,000 against 5,058,000. See *Demografiia na Bulgariia* (Sofia: Nauka i izkustvo, 1974), 438.

4 Sofiiski Gradski i Obshtinski Durzhaven Arkhiv, f. 65, o. 1, a.e. 613, II-4.

5 Georgi Bitsin, "Shum v kharmoniiata," in Ivan Radev, ed., *Literaturnite pogromi: Poruchkovi "ubiistva" v novata ni literatura* (V. Turnovo: Slovo, 2001), 59–62.

6 Consider, for example, the portrait of the enemy in the first Bulgarian socialist operetta "Deliana," written by Parashkev Khadzhiev in 1952. The librettist was criticized for erroneously describing the village kulak as "noisy, open, and straightforward" while "now the enemy acts secretively in the village," etc. See "Vredno proizvedenie," *Bulgarska muzika* (1952): 5.

7 "Vredno proizvedenie," 4–8. I thank István Rév for having brought my attention to instances where music becomes noise and to the content of noise, not only its level.

8 Blazho Stoianov, "Protiv formalizma—v zashtita na istinskata muzika," *Bulgarska muzika* 3 (1956): 51.

9 "Postanovlenieto na TsK na VKP(b) za op. 'Velikata druzhba' ot Muradeli i bulgarskata muzika," *Muzika* 1–2 (1951): 3–11.

10 For a variety of sounds in 1953 Warsaw see B. Brzostek, "Dźwięki i ikonosfera Stalinowskiej Warszawy anno domini 1953," *Studia i Materialy* 5 (2001): 11–27.

11 In 1969, the number of urban dwellers was 4,374,000 while the number of rural inhabitants was 4,090,000. During the first 25 years of the socialist regime, the share of the urban population in the total rose from 24.7 percent (in 1946) to 54.7 percent (in 1971). See *Demografiia na Bulgariia*, 437–38.

12 Tsentralen Durzhaven Arkhiv (TsDA), f. 136, o. 32, a.e. 162, ll. 1, 7, 41.

13 Even settlements of less than 4,000 inhabitants—as, for example, Gara Kaspichan, with its 3,960 inhabitants—had seven blocks of flats by 1961. The project for its center envisaged the construction of several three-story buildings. See TsDA, f. 136, o. 32, a.e. 162, l. 25. In order to limit the territory of the capital, the 1961 bill for the general town plan of Sofia restricted the number of low-rise buildings to around 5 percent of all new housing construction. This notwithstanding, in 1970 the Council of Ministers of Bulgaria expressed concern that "Sofia had spread over too large a territory, which has resulted in complications in the development of communication and transport links, public utilities, housing construction, industry, the supplying of provisions and services, etc." It was not until 1978 that the Council of Ministers contemplated limiting the number of stories per building, ordering 60 percent of all new dwellings constructed throughout the country to be at a maximum five stories. See TsDA, f. 136, o. 32, a.e. 198, ll. 2, 4; o. 50, a.e. 460, l. 7; o. 66, a.e. 187, ll. 4–5.

14 Compare Svetlana Boym's comment on the mathematical and bureaucratic division of home space during socialism, "as if it were not a 'living' space ... but some topological abstraction." Note also her personal memories of living in a Soviet communal apartment, her attempts to "muffle the communal noises" and her experience of the "fluttering sound of a curious neighbor's slippers." Svetlana Boym, "Everyday Culture," in Dmitri Shalin, ed., *Russian Culture at the Crossroads: Paradoxes of Postcommunist Consciousness* (Boulder, Co., and Oxford: Westview Press, 1996), 157–83.

15 This average socialist apartment had also a fixed average price—6,800 leva (7,200 for Sofia). Those Bulgarian regional authorities which allowed the average size of a flat in their areas to reach "80–90 and even more square meters" were severely criticized by the center because these deviations reduced the pace of planned progress in house construction. See TsDA, f. 136, o. 55, a.e. 790, l. 15.

16 Geno Tsonkov, "Korenni kachestveni izmeneniia i tendentsii v obshtestveniia, semeiniia i lichniia bit na naselenieto ot Blagoevski raion na Sofia," *Nauchni trudove na Visshata partiina shkola "Stanke Dimitrov" pri TsK na BKP* 32 (1967): 58–60.

17 For a similar approach explaining social reality through the conceptual tools elaborated by Communist Party theoreticians, see Dejan Jović's chapter in this volume.

18 See Todor Zhivkov's speech to the 9th Congress of the BCP (14 November 1966) in Todor Zhivkov, *Intenzivno razvitie na sotsialisticheskata ikonomika* (Sofia: Izdatelstvo na BKP, 1967), 7–11.

19 For the rationalization of productivity, see Ulf Brunnbauer, "'The League of Time' (Liga Vremia): Problems of Making a Soviet Working Class in the 1920s," *Russian History/Histoire Russe* 4 (2000): 461–95.

20 Liliana Todorova, *Shumut—vrag No 1* (Sofia: Meditsina i fizkultura, 1978), 15–16.

21 For a similar concern see Nikola Zarkov and Maia Konstantinova, *Akustichna kharakteristika na Sofia* (Sofia: BAN, 1988), 7.

22 Ibid., 17–19.

23 Vesela Tabakova, "Svobodnoto vreme i mladezhta v burzhoaznoto obshtestvo," *Novo vreme* 2 (1987): 115. Contrary to socialist reality, Tabakova claimed, leisure time in bourgeois societies did become an alternative to unhappy, cheerless work, offering an illusory possibility for self-accomplishment and a refuge for the devastated personality.

24 Eduard Gazdov, *Shumut—vrag na suvremennia zhivot* (Iambol: HEI, 1967), 15.

25 Mitko Enchev, *Tishina i zdrave* (Sofia: Meditsina i fizkultura, 1973), 18, 14.

26 Emil Efremov, *Nashata otgovornost* (Sofia: Meditsina i fizkultura, 1969), 23.

27 Iasen Moskov, *Shum i zdrave* (Sofia: Meditsina i fizkultura, 1970), 6, 3. Such a small provincial town was, for example, Smolian; the use of street loud-speakers there was even codified in the town-development plan approved by the Council of Ministers in 1973. See TsDA, f. 136, o. 56, a.e. 264. Street loud-speakers were more often used for propaganda purposes in the towns and villages of the compact Turkish minority in Bulgaria, allegedly because of its more pronounced backwardness and higher level of illiteracy.

28 *Shumut kato faktor na zhiznenata sreda* (Plovdiv: H. G. Danov, 1976), 6.

29 M. Angelova, "Khigienno znachenie na shumoviia faktor v proizvodstvoto i bita" in *Izsledvaniia i borba s shuma v stolitsata* (Sofia, 1970), 5.

30 TsDA, f. 136, o. 72, a.e. 143, l. 65.

31 "Children who sleep in a noisy environment become nervous and troubled, and their appetite reduces; if they are of school age, their grades in school drop" (Moskov, 10–11).

32 Gazdov, 14–15.

33 *Shumut kato faktor*, 155–56.

34 *Za opazvane i podobriavane na prirodnata sreda v N.R.Bulgariia. Dokladi i izkazvaniia na Osmata sesiia na Shestoto NS 1973 god.* (Sofia: Izdatelstvo na OF, 1974), 61.

35 I thank Ivan Elenkov for having brought this point to my attention.

36 Todor Zhivkov, *Za posledovatelno izpulnenie resheniiata na X-ia kongres na BKP za povishavane zhiznenoto ravnishte na naroda* (Sofia: Partizdat, 1972).

37 For an excellent discussion of shifting concepts of *bit* reform in the USSR see Victor Buchli, *An Archaeology of Socialism* (Oxford and New York: Berg, 1999).

38 Izidor Levi, *Shiroko dvizhenie za nov sotsialisticheski bit* (Sofia: NS na OF, 1969), 3.

39 Tsonkov, 49.

40 Zakhari Staikov, *Izsledvaniia na biudzheta na vremeto* (Sofia: BAN, 1989), 6–7.

41 Kolio Kolev, Atanas Dimitrov, *Vsichko za choveka* (Sofia: Izdatelstvo na BKP, 1969), 87.

42 Todor Zhivkov, *Otcheten doklad na TsK na BKP pred X-ia kongres na partiiata* (Sofia: Partizdat, 1971).

43 TsDA, f. 136, o. 65, a.e. 37, ll. 23–24.

44 TsDA, f. 136, o. 56, a.e. 173, ll. 10–17, 30.

45 Ibid., l. 15. This measure was taken against Trabant and Wartburg cars. Yet after a protest from the Union of Bulgarian Automobilists it was revoked with Directive No. 278 of 30 December 1973. Expressing ultimate support for the protection of the "reproductive relaxation of working citizens," the Union nonetheless reminded that these cars were produced by a sister socialist state, the German Democratic Republic. See TsDA, f. 136, o. 56, a.e. 353.

46 N. Kamenov, N. Zarkov, "Shumozashtita na zhilishtnite teritorii," in *Mikroklimat i shum v zhilishtnata sreda* (Sofia: BAN, 1972), 91–98. See also Nikola Zarkov, "Otsenka i zashtita na akustichnata sreda v zhilishtni teritorii," *Tekhnicheska misul* 6 (1980): 87–90.

47 Kamenov, Zarkov, 100. See also *Shumut kato faktor*, 154.

48 TsDA, f. 136, o. 56, a.e. 173, ll. 58–65.

49 Kamenov, Zarkov, 85, 108.

50 Ibid., 63–70. On 2 July 1967, for example, noise measurements were executed on the southern balconies on two floors of building No. 13 on Vladimir Zaimov Boulevard in Sofia, between 8 and 9.45 am. Measurements continued on the balcony and in the liv-

ing room on the fourth floor, between 9.50 and 11.30 pm. The door of the living room was left ajar, "as it stays usually during that season of the year." The observation team arrived at the alarming conclusion that the level of noise in Sofia at night was significantly higher than permitted.

51 TsDA, f. 136, o. 35, a.e. 616, l. 31.

52 Which, during discussion of the draft guide, the Fatherland Front found too small to be effective and proposed the fine be raised to 10 leva. See TsDA, f. 136, o. 66, a.e. 40, l. 111.

53 Tsonkov's survey demonstrated that only 10 percent of those interviewed stated they visited pubs, coffee houses or bars, while 42 percent said they did not visit them. Slightly embarrassed by the high number of non-respondents, the author nonetheless concluded that the percentage of people who did not attend bars was not small and that this was a great advantage of the socialist *bit*. See Tsonkov, 66.

54 I rely here on the notion of middlebrow fiction which Vera Dunham uses as a source to capture the relationship between the Soviet regime and the Soviet middle-class citizen in the years between the end of the Second World War and Stalin's death. Echoing official views, this literature is compliant, didactic, unimaginative, gray, routine, pedestrian and uninspired. Because of its prescriptive purpose and its linking the social with the political realm, it lends characters from the immediate present an intense verisimilitude. See Vera Dunham, *In Stalin's Time: Middleclass Values in Soviet Fiction* (Durham and London: Duke University Press, 1990), xxv, 28–9, 31, 22.

55 For letters of complaint see Sheila Fitzpatrick, *Everyday Stalinism. Ordinary Life in Extraordinary Times: Soviet Russia in the 1930s* (Oxford: Oxford University Press: 1999), 175–8.

56 Such was, for example, the complaint of Kostadinka Ilieva from Sofia, addressed directly and personally to Todor Zhivkov. She insisted that noise from a neighboring light industry enterprise caused dilapidation and destruction of her apartment as well as the severe illness and subsequent death of her husband. See TsDA, f. 136, o. 72, a.e. 143, ll. 116–117.

57 For several examples see TsDA, f. 136, o. 72, a.e. 142 and TsDA, f. 136, o. 72, a.e. 143.

58 TsDA, f. 136, o. 72, a.e. 139, l. 20 (emphasis mine).

59 TsDA, f. 136, o. 72, a.e. 143, ll. 61–61a.

60 TsDA, f. 136, o. 72, a.e. 140, ll. 89–91.

CHAPTER 9

Robert C. Austin

GREATER ALBANIA:
The Albanian State and the Question of Kosovo, 1912–2001

The goal of this chapter is to examine Albania's official relationship with Kosovo in the twentieth century. Its intention is not to address "grass roots" attitudes towards Kosovo before the 1990s but simply state policy. We should remember that for the overwhelming majority of the period in question, Albania's population had virtually no stake in the political process. In the interwar period an illiterate and impoverished peasantry were subject to the authoritarian regime of King Zog. In the Communist period Albanians confronted the most oppressive form of Stalinism. Nevertheless, despite the earlier inability to affect official policy, popular attitudes may now reflect Tirana's policy. Even with the end of one-party rule in 1991, there was no noticeable clamor to re-evaluate long-established policy towards Kosovo. Why has official Albanian policy been based on Realpolitik vis-à-vis Kosovo rather than openly pursuing a policy of Greater or Ethnic Albania?[1] This question is interesting for several reasons. Albanians, unlike some of their neighbors in the region, have not been tempted by claims based on medieval statehood. This is an anomaly especially when one considers that Albanian borders, agreed upon in 1913 and reconfirmed after the First World War, left just as many Albanians outside the state as inside it.[2]

Moreover, despite having all the conditions present for revisionist and irredentist thinking, the twentieth century did not offer up a single serious political leader of the state who could be called pan-Albanian, and there are hardly any political forces that have called (or call) for the creation of a Greater Albania. This is not to say that there have been no revisionist or extreme nationalist parties in Albania, only that they have never been able to gain substantial popular support. In fact, the very forces that have called for a more openly revisionist policy were more often than not undermined by the policy of the Albanian state itself. Just why this is the case is an important question, especially since Albania's neighbors have consistently portrayed Albania and Albanians as bent on revising their borders at the expense of Serbia, Montenegro, Macedonia and Greece.

There are several reasons why Kosovo was marginalized in Tirana's policy prescriptions. It is impossible to speak of a single Albanian nationalism. Rather, Albanians need to be viewed as still in the process of building a unified nationalism that would bind all the Albanian communities that were separated by Great Power diplomacy. In fact, at this juncture, one may well speak of at least two Albanian nationalisms with distinct centers and agendas, namely Prishtina and Tirana. Separated in 1913, when nation building was still in an embryonic stage, the Albanians have never been able to begin sustained work for a unified identity, and the governments in Tirana have done little towards the creation of a truly national program. As well, the Albanian state has been consistently weak since its inception in 1913 and, especially in the interwar period, more concerned about defense against hostile neighbors and maintaining existing frontiers than with the quest for national unification. In the Communist period in particular, the isolationism of Enver Hoxha's government contrasted sharply with the relative prosperity and openness of Yugoslavia. Moreover, cut off from the world, Communist Albania's policy towards Kosovo appears as rhetorical, half-hearted and almost theatrical. Finally, the Albanian elite in Kosovo has not always looked to Tirana for leadership. That is especially true in the post-Communist period when Albania's transition has been so fraught with catastrophes and setbacks that it can hardly be called "the motherland."

To explore these themes, we will look at Albania's relationship with Kosovo at four critical junctures. It is only at these points in the twentieth century that one can even seriously speak of an official Albanian policy toward Kosovo. Kosovo was only significant for Tirana in the aftermath of the First World War, during and after the Second World War and after the collapse of Albanian Communism. The years between these episodes were marked by disinterest in the fate of Kosovo. Readers will note that the documents correspond roughly with these watersheds. Document 1 outlines the difficulties faced by the Albanians in the aftermath of the First World War in defending their existing geo-political frontiers. Documents 2, 3 and 4 look at the Communist public and private musings on the Kosovo question, and Document 5 speaks to the issue of transition Albania's relationship with Kosovo.

The Legacy of Albanian Nationalism

Not surprisingly, the foundation of the relationship between Albania and Kosovo is rooted in the Albanian national awakening. Albanian nationalism emerged only in 1878 and was the direct result of a fear of partition in the wake of the Russo-Turkish War. Albanians were not unified, and the elite, who were largely the large landowning class of Islamic beys that dominated political life in the Ottoman period, played on this disunity. The main obstacles to national unity, which in many respects still remain, fall under four broad headings: religious, regional, linguistic, and socio-economic. Five hundred years of Ottoman rule had exacerbated disunity within Albanian society. Roughly 65 percent of the population had converted to Islam.[3] Some 10 percent were Catholics, living primarily in and around the northern city of Shkodër [Scutari]. A compact community of Orthodox Albanians, roughly 20 percent, lived in the south, coexisting alongside a community of both Greeks and Slav Macedonians in the provinces of Gjirokastër [Argyrokastron] and Korçë.[4] Ottoman policy toward the Albanians had added its own obstacles to national consolidation. The Ottoman Empire had traditionally tried to preserve adherence to Islam and pursued a divide and rule policy, openly encouraging divisions between Moslems, Catholics and Orthodox Christians. While Moslem Albanians often rose to the heights of the Ottoman administration, Catholic and Orthodox Albanians were marginalized and enjoyed few benefits. The Turks, realizing that language was the key unifying component of the Albanians, also made a conscious effort to undermine Albanian culture by severely restricting the teaching of the Albanian language and forcing Albanians to learn Turkish or Arabic. Orthodox Albanians largely fell under the influence of the patriarchate of Constantinople and were thus subjected to Greek influence in terms of language, religion and culture.

Albania's national awakening was thus delayed when compared with other Balkan nationalities. In June 1878, Albanian leaders had met in Prizren and established the Albanian League for the Defense of the Rights of the Albanian Nation, often called the League of Prizren. This was the first time that Albanians spoke with one political voice. The League's fundamental goal was to prevent the partition of Albanian lands by the Treaty of San Stefano (1878) between Russia and the Ottoman Empire. It also sought to set up the framework for a form of administrative autonomy within the Ottoman state for the four vilayets (provinces) with a sizeable Albanian population, Janina, Shkodër, Kosovo, and Monastir [Bitola]. It is worth noting that at the outset, Albanians were not secessionists. However, owing to regional and religious differences, the League of Prizren was dominated by Moslem conservatives and never established a single center of direction or

concerted action.[5] As such the League was hardly a truly national organization. Some patriots suggested that the League should be an Islamic organization, others pushed the Albanian aspect and viewed the League as a force
for Albanian autonomy within the Ottoman Empire.[6] While the League was
later crushed by the Ottoman authorities in 1881 and its leadership exiled, it
did make nationalist leaders "aware of the wide gap that existed between
their immediate political aspirations and the deep-seated social, economic
and cultural backwardness of the overwhelming majority of people whose
rights they defended."[7] Realizing that much remained to be done if Albanians were to survive as an independent people, patriots turned their attention to a cultural awakening and focused on the one component that unified
the Albanians: language.

Denied a long period of cultural preparation, Albanians set out again on
the path of nation-state building in 1920 only to find that many of the obstacles to national unity that had become apparent after 1878 were still there.
The country was overwhelmingly illiterate and there were gross deficien-
cies in political, cultural, and economic development. There were, moreover,
two distinct Albanian-speaking communities within Albania, the main division being north-south. Gegs, essentially northern Albanians, inhabit the
primarily mountainous regions north of the Shkumbin River including Kosovo, while Tosks dwell in the low-lying regions south of that river. Southern
Albania, with its proximity to Greece and its less rugged terrain, was far
more accessible and possessed better communications to the outside world.
The Tosks were by and large better educated than their brethren in the
north. Village life was more developed and the clan-style existence that still
prevailed in the north had largely been eroded by the end of the nineteenth
century. The standard of living was higher, literacy was more widespread,
and "the populace more sensitive to material deprivation."[8] Equally important was the fact that Orthodox Albanians, who lived in the south, because
of their disadvantaged position within the framework of the Ottoman Empire,
were more inclined to emigrate. It was these émigrés preeminently the cler-
ic Fan Noli who emerged in the interwar period as the spokespeople of
Westernized Albania that was free from the legacy of Ottoman rule.

The south had traditionally been more open to foreign stimuli, more prone
to politically sophisticated ideas, and in many ways better suited to truly
national, as opposed to regional, thinking. Tosks also possessed a sense of
superiority owing to what they identified as the south's more advanced cultural and economic position. Because of the inaccessibility of the north,
emigration there was marginal and the region maintained a form of quasi-
autonomy under Ottoman rule. Tribal life, embodied in the centuries-old
Canon of Lek, a fifteenth-century tribal customs text, was still dominant.[9]
Even in the post-independence period, this region continued to distrust any

form of central government and the hereditary clan chiefs worked to thwart attempts to bring them under the control of Tirana.

Gegs and Tosks spoke different dialects, and within them numerous sub-dialects existed as well. Albanian patriots attached great significance to the creation of a unified Albanian language as integral to the country's national awakening. Until the beginning of this century, Albanian nationalists had yet to choose even an alphabet for their language. Prior to the 1908 Congress of Monastir, which adopted the Latin script, several alphabets were in use throughout the country.[10] The adoption of Latin script, "although innocent in appearance, not only was a powerful factor in unification, but also signified a breaking away from Turkish-Islamic culture and an orientation toward the West."[11] In 1916, at a meeting in Shkodër, a first attempt was made to create a common literary Albanian. The participants chose the Geg idiom from the town of Elbasan as the basis for the gradual convergence of the Geg and Tosk dialects. However, no further progress was made and nothing else was undertaken in the interwar period to unify the principal dialects. It was not until 1972 that a Unified Literary Albanian was adopted. It represented a fusion of both Geg and Tosk, although drawn primarily from the latter which, as some observers noted, was because of Tosk predominance in Albania's Communist leadership.[12]

Albania after the First World War

The Albanian national awakening was thus hardly complete when statehood was achieved. If one were to apply Miroslav Hroch's model on national awakenings, the Albanians were in the beginning of Phase "A" in that patriots were developing national culture, language and ethnography.[13] Illiteracy was widespread, as even by 1939 some 80 percent of the population could not read.[14] One could not speak of an attempt at patriotic agitation among the population, or the development of mass nationalism. In fact, these later stages were largely completed, in a deeply politicized way, by Albania's Communist rulers who undertook a sustained nation-building campaign. It aimed at eliminating all divisions and hence any challenge to their authority that could come from religion and regionalism. Patriots like Ismail Qemal, the founder of the Albanian state in 1912, were not unmindful of the fact that the independence declaration was premature.[15] However, the alternative was partition among its Balkan neighbors.

Albania's 1913 borders were largely an expression of geo-political bargaining. The First World War subsequently destroyed Albania's brief independence and it was only in its aftermath that Albanian leaders could begin seriously the process of state and nation building. The paramount agenda for the majority of Albanian political leaders was to ensure Albania's survival as an independent state and to find a place within the Southeastern Europe shaped by the Paris peace settlements. This was no easy task. Albania found itself weak, without allies (either big or small), and its territory was coveted by far more powerful neighbors. This is not to say that Albania's leaders did not seek much larger borders in Paris. It would have been absurd not to put forward maximum demands especially when Italy, Greece and Yugoslavia were making claims that would have left Albanians with little more than a triangle linking Tirana, Durres and Vlora. That said, since the Albanians lacked a Great Power benefactor, the main task for the Albanians in Paris was not the creation of a greater Albania, but rather to ensure that they were left with what they achieved in 1913. Given the limited borders it did receive, Albania might well have fallen into the revisionist camp of East Central and Southeast European states, like Bulgaria and Hungary. Yet it pursued a policy during the interwar period that was largely based on preserving the territorial status quo.

The internal situation also forced acquiescence to the peace settlement. Albania's political culture was rudimentary, and few of the political parties, personalities or groups that emerged were capable of taking their appeal beyond religion, region or even more narrow, often careerist, interests. There was no general agreement as to where the state was heading: to the East, retaining the authoritarian legacy of 500 years of Ottoman rule, toward a West European parliamentary government, or somewhere in between. Albania remained essentially unintegrated, dominated by a class of politicians that had a vested interest in the maintenance of a socio-economic status quo, established under the Ottoman Empire, which was essentially feudal. The vast majority of the populace were landless peasants who had no stake in the political process.[16] For our purposes, what is most important is that the Balkan and First World Wars delayed the opportunity to create a single Albanian national consciousness, and borders separated the Albanians on all levels.[17] In short, separated long before any serious work was done in creating a single identity, Albanians in Albania and Kosovo largely went their separate ways.

As Document 1 indicates, Albania's interwar political leadership was focused on the much more pressing task of survival, as between 1920 and 1925 Albania's neighbors did their utmost to promote instability and call into question the very existence of an Albanian state. The country's leaders were thus forced to dedicate scarce resources to defending the postwar status quo, not to fighting the "injustice" of the frontiers. Albania's two principal interwar politicians, Fan S. Noli[18] and Ahmed Zogu,[19] both opted for policies that would preserve the existence of Albania within existing borders. Any adventurous pursuit of incorporating Kosovo could only invite disaster for Albania. It was only Noli, who was briefly prime minister between June and December 1924, who attempted to make Kosovo an international issue. He did this not as a revisionist but because he owed his power partially to support from Kosovars, the Albanian majority in Serbian-controlled Kosovo, and he actually believed that the League of Nations promised a new order and that minority rights treaties were there to be upheld.

The years between 1920 and 1924 were a chaotic time for Albania but also the only democratic period in Albanian history prior to the end of one-party rule in 1991. There were indeed domestic forces that called for a more aggressive policy towards Kosovo and they were very much a part of the intense political debate inside Albania. For many Albanians, especially those in the northeast, who had found their prewar trade, family and other links with Kosovo severed, there was a strong desire for ethnic unification. Also, Belgrade's policy aimed at Serbianization after five centuries of Ottoman rule, manifesting itself in multiple abuses including forced migration. In a 1921 petition to the League of Nations, the Albanian community in Serbia alleged that since 1918, some 12,371 people had been killed and 22,000 imprisoned.[20] The Kosovo Committee, fundamentally a clandestine resistance movement, which drew its membership from both sides of the border, was formed in 1918 to promote a more aggressive Albanian policy on Kosovo. It sought the national unification of all Albanians. Its minimum goals were Yugoslavia's adherence to the rights of its Albanian minorities as stipulated by the postwar minority treaties, while its long-term ambition was the annexation to Albania of the territories primarily inhabited by Albanians.[21] Its leadership, especially Bajram Curri, Hasan Prishtina, Zia Dibra and Hoxha Kadriu, were men who had little use for diplomacy and preferred armed action. (They had come together in order to confront Ottoman authorities in Kosovo in 1912. By 1933, with the assassination of Prishtina by an agent of Zog, all of them had died violent deaths at the hands of their opponents.) The Committee had fundamentally two enemies: the government in Belgrade, which they maintained was waging a war on the Albanian community, and politicians in Tirana, who preferred a hands-off policy in Kosovo. Interestingly, for Ahmed Zogu, the main challenge to his leadership in the early 1920s largely came from disgruntled Kosovars who expected more concern from Tirana, and judged Zogu as pro-Yugoslav. The Kosovo Committee reached its zenith in 1924 when they helped Noli seize power in a coup d'état of sorts that briefly unified the political forces opposed to Zogu.

Noli, eager to avoid offending international opinion and also seeking to appease his Balkan neighbors, did not include members of the Kosovo Committee in his government but he did accompany them to the League in the fall of 1924 to help plead their case. Noli's decision to re-open the Kosovo question after four years of relative neglect was not merely because the circumstances of his June victory dictated it. As an idealist and committed to the vision of new world order offered by U.S. president Woodrow Wilson, he believed that the Kosovars were not accorded full rights in accordance with the postwar minority guarantees and he hoped that through the League of Nations he could improve his brethren's plight. He felt strongly that while Albania was meeting its obligations to its much smaller minorities (Greeks and Serbs), Belgrade and Athens were violating the new League of Nations standards. Nevertheless, Noli's support for the Kosovo Committee was judged by Belgrade as hostile. Ahmed Zogu, who chose Belgrade for his brief exile just prior to Noli's seizure of power, ousted Noli in December 1924 with vital aid from the Yugoslav army. This ended not only Albania's brief experiment with democracy but also Tirana's activism in the affairs of Kosovo. Zogu, a master of realpolitik and political survival, had no stomach for the Kosovo cause. In exchange for Yugoslavia's support, he made some modest border changes but more importantly he agreed to eliminate the Kosovo Committee.[22] In due course, its leadership was exiled or killed by Zogu's agents.[23]

The Second World War

National division and isolation following the First World War was not much altered by Zogu in the interwar period. Albania's population was left largely as Zogu found them—poor and illiterate. As to Kosovo, it would not be an exaggeration to say that Zogu's only acknowledgement of the Albanians in Kosovo was his decision in 1928 to call himself "King of the Albanians" as opposed to the "King of Albania." The interwar experience for the Albanians in Kosovo was worse than their brethren in Albania—they were not only poor and illiterate but they also faced consistently hostile policies from the Belgrade government.[24] That said, neither Albanians in Albania nor Albanians in Kosovo were taking concrete steps to establish a unified national identity and the Second World War did little to erode the cleavages within the Albanian communities. Significantly, the wartime division between Communists and nationalists was largely a reflection of the old Geg-Tosk split as the Albanian Communist movement was very much a southern phenomenon. Not just First Secretary Enver Hoxha[25] but also the rest of the early Communist leadership was, and essentially remained, Tosk in origin. This led one observer to note that "Communism came to Albania as a revolt of the more advanced Tosks against the political domination of the more backward Gegs."[26]

During the war, the question of Kosovo became a major bone of contention between Albania's potential liberators. The nationalist Balli Kombetar

(National Front) formed in November 1942 by Midhat Frasheri,[27] called for the creation of a greater Albania while the Communist-dominated National Liberation Movement, which later became the National Liberation Front, owed much of its existence to crucial assistance from Yugoslavia's Communists. It unsurprisingly opted for a policy that left Kosovo in Yugoslavia. Only briefly did the two groups agree on a common front that included a commitment to a "Greater Albania" in the ill-fated Mukje accord of August 1943. The accord briefly papered over differences between Communists and nationalists but, under Yugoslav pressure to reject the deal, Communist leaders did so. According to an official history of the Albanian Communist Party, the Balli Kombetar accepted the "ethnical Albania hoax, a weapon of the fascists and reactionaries to beguile the Albanian people into forgetting who their main enemy was at that time and to stir up antagonisms against the neighboring peoples."[28] As Document 2 indicates, Hoxha was eager to ensure that territorial expansion did not undermine the solidarity between Yugoslav and Albanian Communists as Yugoslav support took precedence over other concerns. On an official level at least, the solution to Kosovo lay in victory by Albanian and Yugoslav Communists.

Even the development of a "Greater Albania" under fascist auspices during the war cannot be taken as a serious manifestation of Albanian official policy. As Bernd Fischer noted, it was largely an Italian enterprise designed to win over mass support.[29] The plan eventually backfired as there was not enough enthusiasm outside of Kosovo to "win any lasting support for the Italians."[30]

After the war, Enver Hoxha focussed attention on eliminating the social and political power that Gegs and their cultural elite enjoyed in the north. He also assisted the Yugoslav state in repressing Albanian nationalists in Kosovo.[31] As early as 1944, at the request of Tito, the Albanian Communists sent troops to disarm the population of Kosovo and "to prepare the way for the resumption of Yugoslav control."[32] Finally, when looking at the Albanian state in the Communist period it is important to keep in mind that it was, with few exceptions, a Tosk government.[33] As Documents 2, 3 and 4 indicate, not surprisingly, Albania's Communist leaders had one policy meant for public consumption and another that was the "real" policy. Documents 2 and 3 were published in Albania and elsewhere and they can hardly be taken as serious policy statements or a reflection of the wartime reality. Document 4 was released in 1994 after the collapse of Albanian Communism and was part of an effort to discredit the Albanian Socialist Party (former Communists). Albania's Communist leaders consistently sought to portray themselves as nationalists pushing for unification but were deterred by Tito's reluctance. As we now know, Hoxha did not push for unification at all. He did offer it as something that might happen in the long run but without ever considering its pursuit as a serious policy. Like Zog before him, the question of political survival was his biggest concern and the relationship between Yugoslav and Albanian Communists precluded any attempt to push for a different policy for Kosovo. After leaving Kosovo to its fate, and surviving a personally near-catastrophic break with Yugoslavia in 1948, Hoxha was free to turn up the heat on the question of Kosovo. Given Albania's limited role and influence in world affairs, Hoxha was able to say what he wanted without fear of repercussions.

Transition Albania

The collapse of Albania's Communist regime between 1990 and 1992 offered a real opportunity to reassess official policy on Kosovo and it certainly gave the country's democratic forces added strength in the electoral battles of 1991 and 1992.[34] Moreover, any Albanian claim to Kosovo would not have been unreasonable given the harsh policies of the Milošević regime there after 1989. However, despite fertile ground for revisionism, interest in Kosovo only briefly rose to the foreground of Albanian policy. Early statements from the Democratic Party (DP), formed in 1990 as Albania's first post-Communist opposition party, suggested that Albania finally had pan-Albanian leaders. Party co-founder Gramoz Pashko criticized Communist rulers for "supporting the Kosovars with polemical propaganda rather than action during periods of unrest and Serbian oppression in Kosovo."[35]

In 1991, DP leader Sali Berisha noted that his party "could not accept the division of the Albania nation as eternal."[36] Berisha also enjoyed very close relations with Ibrahim Rugova, leader of the Democratic League of Kosovo, the dominant political force there. Rugova and his party strongly supported Berisha in Albania's elections of 1991 and 1992. It appeared that change was in the air in Tirana and that the long-suppressed issue of unification was on the table. When elected with a resounding majority in the March 1992 elections, Berisha enjoyed great respect in Albania and Kosovo which he could have used to articulate a long-term vision for a pan-Albanian national state.

In concrete terms, however, Berisha did little to advance this cause. There are three reasons for this. Firstly, he was no doubt warned by Albania's patrons in Washington and Europe to avoid advocating border changes. Secondly, he realized that pan-Albanian nationalism was not something that unified Albanian voters, and it was especially useless among a population fed up with slogans and cut off from the outside world for so many years. Finally, Berisha sacrificed almost all his programs in favor of a devastating battle with the opposition Socialist Party that poisoned Albanian political life. As a result, Berisha softened his line on Kosovo once he was in power.

In 1993, he suggested that believers in a Greater Albania were naïve and added that "Albania has not sought, does not seek and will not seek any change in existing borders."[37] Berisha also noted that Albania could not speak for Kosovo.[38] This provoked a lengthy battle with Kosovar academician Rexhep Qosja. Although his constituency in Kosovo was increasingly small, Qosja called for steps to be taken, primarily on an academic level, which would move forward the process of national unification by calling for the creation of a pan-Albanian council. Qosja made it clear that Berisha was wrong when he said that Albania "will not seek" border changes as he was not entitled to speak for future generations. He also criticized him for downgrading the issue of Kosovo to a question of human, i.e. individual, rights.[39]

Until 1992, Albania's official policy toward Kosovo derived from a legacy of state weakness, political survival and an incomplete national awakening. After democratic changes swept the region in 1989, many leaders in Kosovo were not prepared to follow a line from Tirana, especially since democratization came to Kosovo before Albania. In 1996, important differences between Tirana and Prishtina became more apparent. In the wake of pro-democracy demonstrations in Serbia in late 1996, the government in Tirana urged Kosovo's Albanians "to stage their own peaceful demonstrations."[40] Rugova, who was reluctant to provoke any crackdown by Belgrade, rejected the advice and was no doubt disturbed that Tirana was trying to tell him what to do. In 1997, as the Albanian state collapsed in the wake of failed pyramid schemes, it was Prishtina calling on Tirana to exercise restraint and hold fresh elections.

More recently, the Albanian Socialists, the successors to Berisha's DP government in an internationally sponsored election in 1997, made it clear that Greater Albania was not on their agenda. In April 2001, the Socialists, whose support came largely from the south, stated that they did not support the creation of a Greater Albania.[41] Then Albanian prime minister Ilir Meta said that the "Albanian communities should be integrated into the different countries where they are based. These liberal and democratic countries will join the European Union, which will allow in the future the Balkans of today to become an open region. ..."[42] The flurry of activity and rush of public statements from Tirana in 2001 was the result of statements to the contrary by a cabinet member of the then governing coalition. Arben Imami, secretary general of the Democratic Alliance and the minister of justice, stated that his party declared as "one of its future political commitments to devote itself to inspiring and accelerating the unavoidable peaceful unification of Albania with Kosovo."[43] Imami, later explaining the remark to journalists, noted that "as for the idea of viewing my statement as feeding the desire of Albanians for a Greater Albania, I am of the opinion that we are speaking about a contemporary trend for a divided nation to unite: there are not two Vietnams or two Germanys any more, and there will not be two Koreas in the future."[44] Imami's statement was immediately denounced by all mainstream political forces in the country.

As far as official Tirana is now concerned, Greater Albania is not a realistic policy. Document 5, from former Albanian foreign minister Paskal Milo, made it clear that official Albanian policy is about integration into Euro-Atlantic structures and not about unification. Milo's statements, which might well be considered judgmental and insulting to Kosovars, were a response to the regional and international clamor about the growing threat of Albanian nationalism after the NATO-led war in Kosovo. The insurgency of Albanians in Macedonia led many to believe that the next big threat to the region came from Albanian unificationists. In conversations with analyst Tim Judah, Milo made it clear that Tirana does not seek border changes but would like to see borders become irrelevant.[45] Even during the armed conflict between Macedonians and Albanians in Macedonia in 2001, official Tirana's statements were "indistinguishable from those issued by the international community."[46] Even the Albanian press avoided a descent into nationalism and jingoism. Cynics will simply argue that Milo (and the rest of Albania's political elite) is simply telling Western leaders and journalists what they want to hear. But as the preceding pages have made clear, Sali Berisha, Paskal Milo and the post-Communist governments are merely following Albania's traditional hands-off policy. Although they now couch it in the "Euro-speak" of not wanting to change borders but to eliminate them, the Albanian leadership retains their predecessors' reluctance to offer anything that looks like a pan-Albanian program—even on a philosophical, intellectual or psychological level.

There are political forces within Albania that do call for the creation of a Greater Albania, yet they have remained insignificant and exist on the margins of Albania's political scene. The successors to the wartime parties Balli Kombetar and the monarchist Legaliteti have, it must be admitted, both called for territorial revision. The Balli Kombetar (BK), which is primarily a party of émigrés, has consistently maintained that the Communist abandonment of Kosovo after the war was criminal. While the more right-wing Democratic Party was in power (1992–1997), the BK pressured the government to take a harder line on the Kosovo issue.[47] Legaliteti, which advocates a return of the monarchy, also supports revised borders. As noted earlier, the BK's commitment to Kosovo is real and very much based on its wartime struggle. Legaliteti, on the other hand, is revising history when they claim that Zogu fought for a unification of Albanian-inhabited territories. Regardless, these two parties and others have yet to influence the political discourse in Albania and rarely secure more than 5 percent of the popular vote.

Conclusion

Throughout the twentieth century, official policy in Tirana has continually rejected nationalist pursuits. When Albania achieved its fragile independence in 1912 and again after the First World War, to sacrifice claims to Kosovo was a simple matter of survival. This is especially true in the interwar period when Albania's neighbors sought to ensure that Albania remained weak and divided. Lacking Great Power support, revisionism would have invited a catastrophe. Only Fan Noli, for a brief six months in 1924, tried to put the Kosovo issue on the international table. He did this not as a revisionist, but merely as a naïve believer in the League of Nations minority rights treaties. This cost him dearly, as his inability to maintain "good neighborly relations" resulted in his ouster. Noli's political survival meant he needed to find a modus vivendi with Albania's neighbors and that meant he needed a policy based on state weakness. Ahmed Zogu, as president (1925– 1928) and king (1928–1939), worked against a claim to Kosovo for the sake of staying in power. Enver Hoxha could not have "won" Kosovo from his Yugoslav allies in 1944, but he did not fight for it either, despite his "official" pronouncements. He did not even turn it into a serious human rights issue as Albania's peculiar foreign policy, especially after the break with China in the late 1970s, stripped Albania of its limited means to lobby for the Kosovars.

Albania's post-Communist leaders found that the past really was a prologue; it seemed like 1920 all over again. For the sake of security and Western aid, they dropped any claim to Kosovo but did their best to pursue the problem from a human rights perspective. This consistent hands-off policy towards Kosovo may be the result of the simple fact that the "Albanian political elite preserves a traditional belief in great power patronage."[48] Just as important, with the exception of the Communist regime's brief foray into a peculiar form of self-reliance after their alliance with China collapsed in the late 1970s, external forces have in fact played a key role in shaping Albania's destiny. Still, much has been made of the threat or promise of a Greater Albania especially since the events in Kosovo in 1999 and Macedonia in 2001. One observer noted that the war in Kosovo radically transformed relations between Tirana and Prishtina and that all Albanians recognize that while the road to Albanian national unification is likely to be complex and protracted, "the ultimate goal remains a unitary state of all Albanians."[49] When war came to Kosovo in 1999 and an estimated 500,000 Kosovar refugees arrived in Albania, a chance for national "oneness" was briefly on the table. However, while certain barriers were knocked down, many still remain. The war did little to change the cool official relations between Tirana and Prishtina. In addition, it is not certain that it did anything to bring ordinary Albanians from Kosovo and Albania closer together. A great

number of refugees, in Albania for the first time, were no doubt surprised
by the state of the economy. Tim Judah noted that many Kosovar Albanians
"were shocked by the poverty and corruption of Albania and, as many were
also robbed there, they were more than happy after the war to leave."[50] In
any case for Albania, even more so than in the past, Tirana is largely unable
to influence events outside the country.

Sources

Document 1:

The Albanian nation has suffered cruelly from the unjustifiable dismemberment of which the country was a victim in 1913. The vast
districts of Kosovo and the districts of Dibra, Hotti, Gruda, Plava and
Gussinje, with a population of more than a million Albanians, have
been annexed to Serbia and Montenegro as a result of political manoeu-
vres; the same fate has befallen the Albanian region of Chameria, which
has been annexed to Greece. Albania cannot endure to be further
manipulated. The surrender of even the smallest part of her territory
would, to her, be equivalent to the renunciation of her very existence.

Source: Fan S. Noli speaking to the League of Nations in Geneva in June 1921.
Noli was fighting further reductions in Albanian territory. Quoted in *Publications of
the Permanent Court of International Justice at The Hague.* Series C, No. 5–II,
Fifth Ordinary Session—Documents Related to the Advisory Opinion No. 9. 4
September 1924. *Question of the Monastery of Saint Naoum.*

Document 2:

Meanwhile [during the Second World War], the Communist Party of
Albania took a consistent internationalist stand and did not allow
itself even the slightest manifestation of chauvinism. ... As to the
problem of Kosova and other regions of Yugoslavia inhabited by
Albanians, the CPA had never accepted the fascist slogan of "Greater
Albania." It saw the correct solution of this problem in the victory of
the people's revolution in both Albania and Yugoslavia. The CPA had
declared publicly that, through the victory of the revolution in both
countries, the Kosova people would win the right to decide their own
fate. Otherwise, they would fight against any Yugoslavia that would
try to oppress and enslave them."

Source: History of the Party of Labor of Albania, (Tirana: Institute of Marxist–
Leninist Studies at the Central Committee of the Party of Labor of Albania, 1982).

Document 3:

After we [Enver Hoxha and Tito] talked about the development of education and culture in our country and I put forward some requests in this direction, too, especially about sending a number of Albanian students to the University of Belgrade, Tito asked what I thought about the solution to the problem of Kosova and the other Albanian regions of Yugoslavia. After a moment's silence to sum up our views on this important problem so that I could present them in the most complete and concise way, I said:

"You know about the historical injustices which the various imperialist and Great-Serb reaction have done to Albania. You also know the principled stands of our Party during the National Liberation War and the desire of our people for friendship with the peoples of Yugoslavia."

I went on to express to Tito the opinion of the Albanian side that Kosova and the other regions in Yugoslavia, inhabited by Albanians, belonged to Albania and should be returned to it.

"The Albanians fought," I told him, "in order to have a free and sovereign Albania with which the Albanian regions in Yugoslavia should now be united. The time has come for this problem to be solved justly by our parties."

President Tito replied:

"I am in agreement with your view, but for the time being we cannot do this, because the Serbs would not understand us."

Source: Enver Hoxha's account of his meeting with Tito in June 1946, as quoted in Hoxha, *The Titoites*.

Document 4:

Affiliated with this is another issue. Some members of the party want to philosophise, saying that we should not ask what Kosovo is doing. In case that one member of the party understood clearly the line of the party, he understands the issue of Kosovo. Democratic Yugoslavia is more advanced and more progressive than we are. Our interest is that Yugoslavia is strong, because with a strong Yugoslavia we will have a democratic Balkans. Is it in our interest to seek Kosovo? This is not progressive. Therefore, in this situation, we should do everything we can so that Kosovars are brothers with the Yugoslavs. When we arrive at socialism, there [Yugoslavia] and here, when the remnants of capitalism are beaten, in this situation, Kosovo will be together with the Socialist Republic of Albania. This is the line, this is what Marxism teaches. We will explain this. For those who do not understand this, we are obliged to fight them.

Source: Enver Hoxha's speech to an Extraordinary Plenum of the Central Committee of the Communist Party of Albania, 18–20 December 1946. Quoted in *Marredheniet-Shqiptaro-jugosllave, 1945–1948* (Tirana, General Director of the State Archives, 1996).

Document 5:

The platform of a "Greater Albania" is not popular in Albania. This does not mean that the Albanians of Albania are less nationalistic than others or that they do not want close relations with their compatriots in other countries. There is no connection between the two. A number of reasons explain this attitude to the platform. Political culture and education in Albania are at higher levels than in Kosova and Macedonia concerning the public at large. They understand better the anti-Albanian core and substance of the slogan. Living in the mother-country, they have conceptualised their future in the development of Albania and its orientation towards Euro-Atlantic structures. Human contacts during the last decade between Albanians on both sides of the borders have shown differences not only in mentality, psychology, and cultural background, but also in economic development. This gap cannot be filled in a short time.

In the official policy of the Government of Albania there is not, nor has there been, any reference to or any aim at the creation of a "Greater Albania." On the contrary, there have been clear and unequivocal statements that such an idea is counterproductive and contrary to the objectives of Albania to be integrated into a United Europe.

Source: Paskal Milo, *Greater Albania—Between Fiction and Reality.* Published by the Albanian Ministry of Foreign Affairs, 2001. At the time of writing, Milo was Albania's foreign minister.

Notes

1 Throughout this chapter I will employ the term Kosovo, as it is the accepted international designation, instead of Kosova as it is spelled in Albanian. I will also use the term Greater Albania as opposed to Ethnic Albania. Both mean essentially the same thing.

2 On the number of Albanians in Yugoslavia, Ivo Banac writes that "the official census probably halved their number (reducing it from probably 800,000–1 million to 441,740 in the preliminary report on the 1921 census and to 439,657 in the final report).

See Ivo Banac, *The National Question in Yugoslavia* (Ithaca, 1984), 298. According to Magocsi, the figure for 1931 was 505,000. See Paul Robert Magocsi, *Historical Atlas of East Central Europe* (Toronto, 1993), 141.

3 Albanians are primarily Sunni Moslems, although there is a smaller number belonging to the Bektashi sect.

4 In 1922 Albania's religious breakdown was as follows: out of a total population of roughly 900,000, 563,729 were Moslem, 181,051 Orthodox and 88,739 Catholics. T. Selenices, *Shqipria ne 1923* (Tirana, 1923).

5 Stavro Skendi, *The Albanian National Awakening, 1878–1912* (Princeton, 1967), 464.

6 S. Pollo and A. Puto, *The History of Albania—From its Origins to the Present Day* (London, 1981), 119.

7 Anton Logoreci, *The Albanians—Europe's Forgotten Survivors* (London, 1977), 41–42.

8 R. V. Burks, *The Dynamics of Communism in Eastern Europe* (Princeton, 1961), 145.

9 Leke Dukagjini was a fifteenth-century feudal lord. For more details on northern tribal life see Margaret M. Hasluck, *The Unwritten Law in Albania* (Westport, 1981).

10 Skendi, 139–42, 370–76.

11 Ibid., 468.

12 For an interesting polemic on linguistic developments in Albania see Arshi Pipa, *The Politics of Language in Socialist Albania* (Boulder, 1989).

13 Miroslav Hroch, *Social Preconditions of National Revival in Europe* (New York, 2000), 22–23. Phase B is marked by the attempt or growth of patriotic agitation or growth of patriotic agitation among the population. The final phase, C, is defined by the growth of a mass movement.

14 In 1944, 80 percent of the population is estimated to have been illiterate and the ratio of pupils to total population was 58 per thousand." Toussaint Hocevar, "The Albanian Economy 1912–1944: A Survey," in *Journal of European Economic History* (Italy) 1987, 16 (3): 565.

15 Ismail Qemal (1844–1919) declared independence in November 1912 from the Albanian coastal town of Vlora [Valona]. Qemal was a prominent official in the Ottoman Empire and a member of the Young Turk Parliament. He later rejected the centralizing trends of the Young Turks and began lobbying, especially in Vienna, for support for the creation of an independent Albania. For details on Qemal's career see Raymond Hutchings, *Historical Dictionary of Albania* (London, 1996), 187–88.

16 Eighty-five percent of Albania's population was rural even though only 9 percent of land was arable and there was no industrial development prior to 1925. Orjan Sjoberg, *Rural Change and Development in Albania* (Boulder, 1991), 29.

17 Isa Blumi, "The Commodification of Otherness and the Ethnic Unit in the Balkans: How to Think About Albanians," *East European Politics and Societies*, V, 12, No. 3, (Fall 1998): 561.

18 Bishop Fan Noli (1882–1965) was an Orthodox Christian who spent his early

years in the U.S., attending Harvard University and proclaiming his Albanian church as autocephalous in 1912 (without recognition from the patriarchate in Istanbul). He represented Albania at the Paris Peace Conference in 1919–20 before his brief period as president in 1924, which began and ended in conflict with Zogu. He was obliged to leave the country and never returned.

19 Ahmed Zogu (1895–1961) was born of Moslem Gez parents in the Mati area and acquired military experience during the First World War as commander of the new Albanian army formed in 1916 by occupying Austrian forces. He played a leading role in the departure of all foreign forces in 1921 and consolidated his power as interior minister until 1924. On expelling Fan Noli's brief regime, he became president and proclaimed himself king in 1928, ruling until himself expelled by the Italian invasion of 1939.

20 Swire, 291.

21 *Records of the Department of State Relating to the Internal Affairs of Albania, 1910–1944*, Record Group 59, National Archives Microfilm Publication M1211, National Archives, Washington, D.C. (hereafter Department of State), U. Grant-Smith to the secretary of state, no. 354, 19 November 1924. 875.01/256. Grant-Smith, U.S. minister in Albania, had a brief conversation with Curri on 18 November.

22 See Paskal Milo, *Shqiperia dhe Jugosllavia* (Tirana, 1992), 300–03.

23 According to Communist historiography, Zogu ordered the assassinations of both Bajram Curri and Hasan Prishtina. See Aleks Buda et al., *Fjalori Enciklopedik* (Tirana, 1985), 145 and 867–68.

24 For details on the interwar experience of the Albanians in Kosovo, see Noel Malcolm, *Kosovo—A Short History* (New York, 1998), chapter 14.

25 Enver Hoxha (1908–1985) was the son of a Moslem Tosk merchant who was drawn into Communist activities during his studies in France, 1930–33. Returning to Albania as a school teacher in Körce in 1936, he was dismissed after the Italian invasion of 1939 and joined in forming the small Albanian Communist Party (Party of Labor) in 1941. By 1944 he was first secretary as the Nazi retreat left the party's partisan forces in a commanding position.

26 Burks, 147.

27 Midhat Frasheri (1880–1949) had opposed Zog's regime earlier in the 1930s but headed a government for him from 1935 to 1937. The NLF's Communists rejected postwar accommodation with him or the National Front.

28 Institute of Marxist–Leninist Studies at the Central Committee of the Party of Labor of Albania, *History of the Party of Labor of Albania*, 2nd ed. (Tirana, 1982), 126.

29 Bernd J. Fischer, *Albania at War, 1939–1945* (West Lafayette, Indiana, 1999), 71.

30 Ibid., 88.

31 Blumi, 564.

32 Nicholas Pano, *The People's Socialist Republic of Albania* (Baltimore, 1968), 18.

33 Pipa, 223–24.

34 For details on the Albanian elections of 1991 and 1992 see Robert Austin, "What Albania Adds to the Balkan Stew," *Orbis* V, 37, No. 2, Spring 1993: 259–79.

35 Louis Zanga, "The Albanian Democratic Party," *RFE/RL Research Report*, 1 March 1991: 3

36 Quoted in Elez Biberaj, "Albania at the Crossroads," *Problems of Communism*, September–October, 1991: 3.

37 *Rilindja Demokratike*, 3 February 1993.

38 Elez Biberaj, *Albania in Transition* (Boulder, 1998), 251.

39 Shkelzen Maliqi, "Kosovo: What Next?", *Aimpress* (www.aimpress.org,) 7 February 1995.

40 Biberaj, *Albania in Transition*, 255.

41 *RFE/RL Newsline*, 13 April 2001.

42 AFP, 4 April 2001.

43 International Crisis Group ICE Report, *Albania: The State of the Nation 2001*, Tirana/Brussels, 25 May 2001: 3.

44 Ibid., 4

45 Tim Judah, "Greater Albania?" *New York Review of Books* V, XLVIII, No. 8, 17 May 2001: 37.

46 ICG Report, "Albania: State of the Nation," 22.

47 James Pettifer and Miranda Vickers, *Albania: From Anarchy to Balkan Identity* (New York, 2000), 155.

48 Ibid., 22.

49 Elez Biberaj, "The Albanian National Question," in Michael Mandlebaum, *The New European Diasporas—National Minorities and Conflict in Eastern Europe* (New York, 2000), 279.

50 Judah, ibid. My own work in the field during the war confirms Judah's analysis.

CHAPTER 10

Marko Bulatović

STRUGGLING WITH YUGOSLAVISM:
Dilemmas of Interwar Serb Political Thought

"The Serb people have no more sacred object than that of the state, before the war—Serbia, today—Yugoslavia. That which you cannot obtain from them by invoking ideas of Serbdom, Orthodoxy, or freedom, you can always get by calling upon the interests of the state."

Dragoljub Jovanović, 1941

In December 1918, following the four-year tragedy of the First World War, crown-prince and regent of Serbia Aleksandar Karadjordjević solemnly proclaimed the Kingdom of Serbs, Croats, and Slovenes.[1] The new kingdom—usually referred to as Yugoslavia from its very inception—would join a long array of newly founded states. At the same time, the profoundly restructured political map of Europe no longer had a place for four great empires—the Ottoman, Russian, German, and Austrian-Hungarian. Alongside the great quartet, however, were some lesser absentees. The small Kingdom of Serbia, which had credentials as first an autonomous and then a sovereign state for almost a century, also vanished. The Kingdom, a winner in the Great War, willingly transferred its sovereignty to the new Yugoslav state. The terms of this transfer would however prove to be controversial, not only among Croats, Slovenes and other non-Serbs, as is well known, but also among the Serbs themselves.

This chapter assesses the meaning and importance of Yugoslavism as a national identity and state ideology among the Serb elites from 1914 to 1941. Arguably, no other national elite in Yugoslavia embraced both of these concepts with more enthusiasm than the Serb elite. The chosen period is a compact one in the history of Serb political thought—the year 1914 gave birth to the official Yugoslav program, while 1941 would bring about a collapse of both the Yugoslav state and the idea of Yugoslavism as a single national identity. Neither Yugoslavia nor Yugoslavism would ever again be resurrected on similar terms.

If there had been any single thread within political thought in Serbia before 1914, it would have been the unification of all Serbs into a larger

Serbian state. Likewise, many prominent Serb politicians and intellectuals living outside the Serbian state had long cherished the political ideal of joining an expanded Serbia, their perceived fatherland. That desired state, however, had never been seriously conceptualized. And yet, in 1918 the Serbs found themselves in a single state, albeit one where they were at most a plurality, far from a majority. Given this turn of events, any "ideology of unification" lost its meaning while, at the same time, the challenges of the new political framework did not allow for an ideological vacuum. Coming to grips with the reality of the newborn state required the Serb elite to search for another national ideology. Yugoslavism was the obvious candidate.

Yugoslavism, in its original nineteenth-century form, was a romantic idea cherished by a few. It was a notion of a common South Slav culture and society, sometimes combined with wishful thinking about a future common state in which that society would grow free and prosperous. By the turn of the century, this idea had gained, and lost, more definite contours in Croatian politics. Once the state of the South Slavs was formed in 1918, Yugoslavism, in its various shades, would be transformed from its socio-cultural setting into an ideology which seems to have been the dominant political concept among Serbs in the interwar years. This is not to say that Serb political thought would become less heterogeneous once the Yugoslav state was established. It only means that—as in the case of the prewar drive towards unification—Yugoslavism, in its versions, was the only common denominator in Serb political discourse.[2]

Towards a "Centuries-long Dream"

In the days following the establishment of the Yugoslav kingdom, Prince-Regent Aleksandar issued a manifesto addressed to "his people" stating that a "vow, repeatedly affirmed through centuries by generations of our predecessors, has been fulfilled."[3] Throughout the interwar period—and especially during the early euphoria of liberation and unification—the idea of a long-sought-after common state of the South Slavs was repeatedly stressed. However, the Yugoslav idea in Serb political thought seems to have been of much more recent origin. While the nineteenth-century Serb intelligentsia undoubtedly recognized the need for cooperation among all South Slavs, their notions of a common South Slav nationality were hardly well defined. The "age of nationalism" had slowly but surely ushered in a set of rules for defining national allegiances and in it the Serb identity would become fairly well established. However, this is not to say that the limits of that identity were clearly set. Whereas the development of Serb national consciousness had begun before the "age of nationalism," the idea of Serb "linguistic nation-

hood" would gain prominence by the 1840s. Furthermore, in the course of
the nineteenth century, this linguistic nationalism would merge with the
concept of Serb "political nationhood" as a consequence of Serbia's autonomy (from 1830) and independence (from 1878).[4]

Thus, the emergence and subsequent strengthening of the Serbian state
immensely furthered the development of Serb national identity among
Serbians (Serbs from Serbia) as well as Serbs living outside of Serbia. As a
self-governing state with budding political institutions, an active foreign
policy, and an increasingly homogeneous ethnic composition, Serbia became
a core state with which most Serbs could easily identify. By the early twentieth century, it became attractive as a political model to the other peoples in
the region which strove for national states of their own.[5] However, the real
power of the Serbian state should not be overestimated. Its dominant ideology of liberation and unification of all Serbs was very vaguely defined and
never written down as a complete political program.[6] On the other hand, the
increasingly defensive Ottoman Empire and the still assertive Habsburg
Monarchy were incomparably more powerful neighbors which stood in the
way of Serbia's desired expansion. Thus, Serbia's drive towards cooperation
with other South Slavs was conditioned by the need to preserve its vulnerable independence as much as the prevalent ideology of Serb unification.

An elaborated concept of multi-ethnic pan–South Slav unification, coupled with the notion of a common South Slav nationality that transcended
the separate Serb identity, was nowhere to be found in nineteenth-century
Serbia. Serbian leaders had, up to the start of the First World War, never
really reached beyond the prospect of underpinning and expanding their
Serbian nation-state. Although programs for creating a Yugoslav or Balkan
union had occasionally been advanced in the region, Serbian statesmen
never considered them as anything but a wider framework which would
enable Serb unification. Likewise, their co-nationals living in the surrounding empires were increasingly drawn to identification with their perceived
national center. Despite some attempts by the Habsburg Serbs at acquiring
civic rather than ethnic nationhood, the Balkan Wars of 1912–13 provided a
final push to identify with the ethnic core in Serbia.

The First World War brought about a dramatic shift in approaches to the
Yugoslav question. For the first time, amidst the wartime chaos, the idea of
creating a new state encompassing most of the South Slavs began to take
shape. Serb politicians and intellectuals took part in the two principal advocates of unification which would arise from the Habsburg framework—the
Yugoslav Committee operating out of London from 1915 and the National
Council convened in October 1918 in Zagreb. More importantly, the Serbian
state would, early in the war, declare its war aims as the "struggle for liberation and unification of all our fettered brethrens, Serbs, Croats, and Slovenes."

True, this statement, advanced by the Serbian National Assembly in the temporary capital of Niš in December 1914, was just a vague formulation intended to win Entente support against Austria–Hungary. Yet, the so-called Niš Declaration was the first official document in the Serbian shift from the policy of exclusive Serb unification towards the creation of a single South Slavic state.[7]

From December 1914 on, Serbian war propaganda would push for South Slavic unification and advance the concept of a "trinomial people." This concept implied that a single people with three names were legitimately striving for their national state. However, sometimes within the same document, we find the "trinomial people" to be interchangeable with the "Serb people." In Document 1, there is ample evidence of this confusion. Stanoje Stanojević,[8] who was, together with many other distinguished scholars, charged with articulating Serbia's war aims for the international public, wrote of a single people of Serbs, Croats, and Slovenes, but he also identified the unification of "our people" with the unification of Serbdom. Consistently, throughout the war, Serb elites dedicated their energy to explaining and justifying the program for the creation of a new, Yugoslav state, but they offered no precise formulation on the sensitive questions of its internal structure. Although Serbia's war effort undoubtedly drained all of its energies—and a detailed elaboration of a future state framework was hardly an option—these questions were so important that the unclear notions and delayed considerations forecast serious trouble for the would-be Yugoslavia.[9]

Stubborn adherence to traditional political principles and deep mistrust of "outsiders"—and this included the Serbian opposition—distinguished the wartime premiership of Nikola Pašić[10] in general and in respect to the Yugoslav idea in particular. Nevertheless, even among opposition circles, consideration of the crucial questions about the future state would be deferred until the postwar period. Therefore, the following comment from Prime Minister Pašić from 1917 provides a good illustration of the general Serb attitude towards the arrangement of the projected state: "A Serb, wherever he is, wants to unite with Serbia without questioning her state structure or her constitution. Instead, he says: I want to live with my brothers in a free and independent state; if its internal structure is not good, we shall fix it together."[11]

The Formative Years—Adapting to "Yugoslavdom"

After 1918, Serbia would completely fold into the new framework. Aside from the Serb name listed in the new state's title, all elements of its statehood perished within Yugoslavia. In the first years of the new kingdom,

alongside the central government there were also several provincial governments, but Serbia did not have one. And as the former Serbian constitution
was suspended, so the Serbian Parliament was dissolved in December 1918.
The main pillar supporting such a transformation was the perception of the
Yugoslav kingdom as a natural and painless continuation of Serbian state
tradition: there was a Serbian monarch on the throne, Serb political domination in political life, and a Serb plurality.[12]

With the principles of state formation so fluid, it is no wonder that the
Kingdom of Serbs, Croats, and Slovenes began its life with a major problem in structuring itself. The formative years proved how incongruous was
the initial watchword—"national oneness and state unity"—as it soon
became evident that "tribal" designations dominated the political stage.[13]
The constitutional question would exhaust almost all the energies of political participants, ending in a solution that hardly satisfied anyone but the
two leading Serb-dominated parties—the Radicals and the Democrats.
Despite substantial differences between them, both parties insisted on the
unitary nature of the new state and they managed to impose their will on the
rest of the country.[14]

Given the persistence of unification as a desired end throughout the
modern history of Serbs, the creation of Yugoslavia could have been perceived as a great, or even final, accomplishment of their national goals.
When Yugoslavia emerged, the outlook among South Slav elites could have
hardly been free from ethnic nationalism. Thus, the Serb elites were unlikely to view their new and deliberately chosen state framework as anything
but the continuation of their old and jealously guarded Serbian statehood.
The uneasy adaptation to the state's multi-ethnic composition, and the fact
that Serbian statehood was invested in the new state, would steer the Serbs
toward Yugoslavism as the most promising substitute for their "lost" ideology. The newly embraced ideology was basically a two-part response to the
new circumstances: one part preserved the state framework within which
"all Serbs are united"; the other attempted to broaden their sense of national
identity and thus make their adaptation to the previously unknown environment easier. Interwar developments reveal that while the former aspect proved
to be long lasting, the latter did not take a firm hold over Serb politics.

Already during the war, as mentioned above, the notion of merging Serbia
into the Yugoslav framework irrevocably tied the prospects of the Serb national question to the new state. Pašić was convinced—from at least 1917—that
another Serb homogeneous state could not be made out of the new framework without sacrificing the already accomplished pan-Serb unification.
Any speculation about a federation and, subsequently, a separation ("amputation") of the "non-Serb" areas made leading Serbs very apprehensive.[15]

The foundations of prewar Serb political thought inevitably changed during the 1920s. Yugoslavism undoubtedly was a widely accepted ideological response, but it also introduced much confusion among Serb elites as soon as the first crises arose. Although "national oneness" was the operative word in public discourse, it was often questioned as an ideal hardly achieved as yet. We can see in Document 2 that Ljuba Stojanović[16] realized the complexities of this favorite slogan and considered national oneness only as a process in the making, whose ultimate success was far from guaranteed. A common nationality might be achievable sometime in the future, but the essence of Yugoslav orientation was, as he saw it, the need of all the constituent nations for a common state.

It became obvious, at least to some leading Serb intellectuals, how complicated the building of their new state would be. Živan Spasojević, a professor of law from Belgrade, was one among many who expressed caution in dealing with the question of national oneness since, in his words, "our road is not to assume that we are already one, but only with time is there going to be a true merger of all the elements." He added that "... there is one dangerous error—the wish to implement mechanically that which used to be valuable, albeit outmoded, for one homogeneous part of the people, to all and different parts of the people in the new age."[17]

The heated atmosphere of the first decade was hardly conducive to further elaboration of Yugoslavism as national ideology. Prospects for a normal political life had been gloomy even before the first constitutional feuds began. It was obvious that, in the absence of a firmly established state structure and order, the king would assume an exceptionally large role. Most Serbs would embrace the crown as the strongest remaining symbol of former Serbian statehood. There was a widespread belief that the crown, as the only real guarantor of both Serbdom and Serbian statehood, would provide for the continuing, albeit virtual, existence of the Serbian state and the Serbian national body within the new multinational setting. On the other hand, by vesting the crown with too much power, the Serb elite would render the entire Yugoslav establishment vulnerable to its abuse.

One gets the impression that almost none of the prominent Serbs questioned the need for the Yugoslav state during the first postwar decade. However, Serb politics in the 1920s was marked by divisive partisanship and growing disillusionment. Even the aforementioned Ljuba Stojanović, one of the most informed contributors to a number of interwar journals and newspapers, would bitterly conclude that "... writing rarely bears fruit anyway; people are either illiterate or do not have time for reading anything aside from the partisan pieces written by party agents who lack the ability of independent and critical thought."[18]

The Royal Coup—Dictatorship for "Integral" Yugoslavism

In 1928, in the midst of a heated discussion in the Yugoslav parliament, a Radical deputy from Montenegro killed two Croat deputies and mortally wounded the leader of the Croat Peasant Party, Stjepan Radić. This event was a tragic yet symptomatic act in the long-lasting national and political crisis. In response, the single strongest supporter of the Yugoslav state made a radical move—King Aleksandar Karadjordjević decided to strengthen the state and establish national unity by means of royal dictatorship. He proclaimed, on 6 January 1929, that there was only one constitutive nation in the state—a Yugoslav one—in place of what he called "tribal" exclusiveness. Later that year, the country's name was changed to the Kingdom of Yugoslavia, while the laws replacing the 1921 constitution inaugurated a major effort for state and national integration. Moreover, the king proclaimed the process of formation of the Yugoslav nation as being already completed. "The hour has come," said Aleksandar, "when there cannot and must not be any intermediaries between the People and the King. Preserving national and state unity is the highest goal of my reign and it must be the highest law for me and everyone else ..."[19]

Therefore, the crown, which had been the bearer of Serbia's merger into Yugoslavia, now assumed leadership in the process of national transformation. This undoubtedly provided a huge impetus for the Serb political body to participate in the new project—to affirm a new national identity, one that, if carried through on the French pattern, would exclude all others. Whereas most Serbs never needed any incentives to accept the state component of Yugoslavism, they did need them for its national component. It quickly became apparent that the experiment with so-called integral Yugoslavism would be a task even more daunting than it was for interwar Romania.[20]

Lazar Marković, leader of one of the many factions in the suppressed Radical Party, justified the king's decision to foreign representatives: "The reason for the abrogation of the people's will by the act of 6 January, lies in the fact that, at a certain moment, the people proved to be incapable of expressing a common will, one which would have enough strength and authority to emerge as the true people's will. This weakness forced the king to undertake extraordinary measures in order to protect the highest interests of our whole people—Serbs, Croats, and Slovenes. The coup was sudden and strong, but its makers expect a beneficial outcome for the people."[21]

The king's coup would lead, among other things, to a total collapse of Serb political life. The dictatorship shut down parliamentary life and the activities of the established political parties. Furthermore, more and more publicly active interwar intellectuals withdrew from politics. Although the ebb of independent thought was felt throughout the entire country, Serbia in particular withdrew into total silence. At the same time, an array of "nonentities" appointed to higher public office kept parroting the official proclamations about state and national unity and about a single Yugoslav nationality. The stage was also set for those who had not been able, during the preceding decade, to convince their fellow intellectuals that Yugoslavism meant more than the idea of the state itself. Velibor Jonić, whom contemporaries perceived as one of those "rightists impressed by the sheer power of the state," wrote passionately about the special mission imposed on the Yugoslavs by their destiny, which strongly resembled the rhetoric spreading across the European right: " … The first question we must ask is: are we, as Yugoslavs, today a historical people or not? Do we have a universal purpose? … Centuries of suffering, victimization and humiliation, which we Croats, Serbs and Slovenes have endured, have not been in vain. All of this was part of the long, difficult and fundamental preparation. However, all this has ended with the day of unification. … Therefore, our destiny is in our own hands. It will be such as we make it. The opportunities before us, however, are great. … Yugoslavism and its fulfillment have to be our ideal. That ideal is here, it is set. He who embraces it, he will live in bliss."[22]

Likewise, some Serb historians offered their "good offices" to explain for the governing clique the spontaneous nature of Yugoslav national integration. The well-regarded Vladimir Ćorović paid tribute to the official ideology in his monumental *History of Yugoslavia*. "Yugoslavia, as a state-political term, is quite a new phenomenon … However, the Yugoslav ideology which led to the Yugoslav state is not of recent origin. When the history of the South Slavs is approached broadly, when you observe the history of peoples instead of the history of states, it is evident that in our national life political boundaries did not mean real divides between the tribes." Ćorović continues, "There have been so many close relationships and common actions which tell us that among the people there has always been a certain consciousness of a community; or, it tells us that farsighted minds have always relied on it."[23]

When the dictatorship entered its third year, however, it became clear that the concept had been far from successful. First of all, it could not improve the economic viability of the state. The timing could not have been worse given the world economic crisis which hit Yugoslavia with full force in 1931. Furthermore, the lack of popular support and obvious reluctance of even Serb intellectuals forced the king to reduce somewhat the rigors of his dictatorship. In 1931, the regime claimed to pull away from its autocratic framework and return to constitutionalism. The new constitution was "given to the people" by the king, but the return to parliamentary life proved to be only nominal. The new parliament and the newly established senate consisted of appointed rather than elected deputies. One of them claimed that with the advent of dictatorship, "… instead of the former romanticism, a wholly new period began, a period of realism in our country which was opened and carried out by our king."[24] And yet, nothing was further from the truth. Document 3, in which Jovan Dučić[25] poetically celebrates the new name of the state and supposedly long-awaited national integration, reveals how utopian indeed was the concept of integral Yugoslavism.[26]

At the same time—supranational exhortations and economic troubles aside—Aleksandar's regime did enough to keep state sovereignty intact during the restless 1930s. Therefore, even those Serbs who raised their voices against the regime did not attack its principles, but only its authoritarian practices. The fact that state unity was indeed preserved, albeit by dictatorial methods, rendered the Serb opposition incapable of making an unconditional alliance with various national-based resistance movements in the country. Thus, while angry Croat leaders were writing memoranda to influential foreign statesmen, asking for protection from the "terror of the Serb king," even their greatest Serb ally, then émigré Svetozar Pribićević, would object to Croat initiatives that bordered on separatism and the resolution of the so-called Croat question outside the framework of Yugoslavia.[27]

Ultimately, the dictatorship fulfilled almost none of its stated goals, but shifted the political spectrum onto somewhat different lines from the first interwar decade. The dictatorship radicalized Croat nationalism. More broadly, it became apparent that Yugoslavism—both as a state and national ideology—was losing support outside the Serb political body. Also, the public presentation of integral Yugoslavism accelerated its demise. Numerous state-invented organizations with "Yugoslav" designations—which were overly intolerant toward non-state-sponsored groupings, particularly the "tribal" ones—represented the stronghold of Aleksandar's policy and contributed to the overall radicalization of Yugoslav society.[28]

While the Croat opposition grew more cohesive and stronger,[29] Serb parties grew weaker and more disorganized. In essence, the dictatorship reopened the Serb question as well. Yet the fact that the former Serbian, now Yugoslav crown undertook the project of national and state integration furthered the very tenuous identification of Serb national ideology with this new integral Yugoslavism. Although the "non-Serbs" often perceived the king's rule as Serb absolutism and terror, his dictatorship was not intentionally undertaken with a Serb agenda—his was to be an authentically pan-Yugoslav program. It attempted to dissolve all separate "tribal" national bodies, including the Serb body, and to melt them, as quickly as possible, in a new supranational pot. Undoubtedly, the dictatorship made Yugoslavism—if not Yugoslavia itself—into a virtual reality. Although dissenting voices were suppressed, restlessness was already detectable during the early 1930s. After 1934, the mounting discontent would soon boil over.

The King is Dead—Shift Towards National Exclusiveness

In October 1934, King Aleksandar, arguably the foremost Yugoslav of the interwar era, was assassinated by a joint action of Croat and Macedonian terrorists on the streets of Marseilles. His death would be followed by a period of royal regency which would last until the end of the first Yugoslavia in 1941. During this period, the tenets of Aleksandar's Yugoslavism were only nominally kept intact. Under the 1935–1939 regime of Premier Milan Stojadinović,[30] it became clear that the relationship between Yugoslavia and Yugoslavism changed significantly.

Stojadinović often referred to his time in office as the era of "real Yugoslavism." As shown in Document 4, the program of his newly founded and state-sponsored Yugoslav Radical Union acknowledged the existence of the worrisome national question. It clearly recognized the division within the country and promises a "high degree of self-rule," although retaining, at least formally, the concept of state and national unity. But, in the same document, as well as in the prevalent political discourse of the time, the late king's program of integral Yugoslavism was criticized for leaving "the unresolved Croat question" as its legacy. The Croatian Peasant Party pressures for autonomous rights would make the appearance of exclusively Serb pressures, as a belated reaction, only a matter of time.

R. W. Seton-Watson characterized this period as a "dictatorship without a dictator." The announced "political ideal" of regional self-rule was not followed by the necessary legislative and constitutional changes. However, Stojadinović would bring into political life an element which had previously been painfully absent—economic reform. His was the most ambitious program for industrial modernization of the interwar era. Dragomir Minović, a banker from Serbia, emphasized the importance of economy to further state and national integration. He identified the rationale behind Stojadinović's pan-Yugoslav program: "The ethnic element does not suffice to preserve the union—neither we, Yugoslavs in the narrow sense, even less all the South Slavs. It has to be combined with another important factor—the economy—which can hold us together. ... Once the rule of law is established and strengthened, and once the awareness of the common economic interests regains and strengthens national oneness, the feeling for the state, i.e. the feeling of the need for union, will come by itself and develop according to the fulfillment of people's expectations. Only then will Yugoslavia become what it should be for all of us: our common house."[31]

This "real Yugoslavism" of Stojadinović provided just a temporary respite in the decline of the Yugoslav national concept. The very first declaration of his government acknowledged national divisions and prompted a group of "integral Yugoslavs" to leave Stojadinović's party. It was obvious that their concept of Yugoslavism had lost its primacy. Members of the former state party (Yugoslav National Party), which was now in serious disarray, attacked the Yugoslav Radical Union for betraying integral Yugoslavism. They perceived Stojadinović's alliance with political parties which predominated in the 1920s as a return to the "tribal politics" which had brought so much trouble to the country before 1929.[32]

The Serb question was also looming on the horizon. Miloš Crnjanski, one of the most provocative Serb writers, launched a new journal in the mid-1930s which flirted with then fashionable European right-wing ideologies. Despite advocating unconditional adherence to the late king's political principles, Crnjanski would in time turn toward Serb exclusiveness. In one of his articles, he bitterly stated that "… everything that was Serbian has been briskly erased, while the respected other side operates with things such as autonomy, separatism, and demands," and concluded that the Serbs "…should make the same demands! … While on one side every problem is advanced through the prism of Slovenism and Croatism, on the other side it is forbidden to view the same thing through the Serbian position. That is not fair. … I may be the only one today, but I am convinced that there will soon be a million of us who will say that everything is nice and pretty, and good for them, but—let us be rid of this nonsense. Let's see how things look as purely Serbian interests."[33]

The Desperate End—the Collapse of Pan-Yugoslav Nationalism

Integral Yugoslavism had already proven bankrupt as a national identity by the mid-1930s; and the looser pan-Yugoslav multinational ideology of Stojadinović would suffer a total collapse in the final years of the Kingdom. The internal divisions became deeper than ever, and only the adherence to the Yugoslav state framework would keep the Serb political body together.

Although anti-government forces had assumed the leading role in seeking an accord between Serbs and Croats throughout the 1930s, formal agreement would eventually be reached between the Belgrade government and Croatian representatives in 1939. Once this agreement afforded an enlarged Croatian *banovina* (province) some attributes of separate statehood within Yugoslavia, a substantial part of the Serb elite began to panic. Their established adherence to the Yugoslav state was now joined by an ardent Serb nationalism. This uneasy combination represented the last refuge of their interwar Yugoslavism.

Within the Serb political scene, the formation of the Croatian *banovina* was widely perceived as the single most harmful act in the short history of Yugoslavia. The 1939 agreement, concluded after the ousting of Stojadinović, made Yugoslavia into something between a federation and confederation. At that time, there were few who had not realized that the unitary conception was no longer possible. Yet the new restructuring sought to secure the survival of the Yugoslav multinational framework only by the resolution of the Croat national question. Whereas that question had been politically prominent since 1918, the final two interwar years witnessed the heated discussions of the newly reopened Serb question.

The uncertain new structure of the state, looming external danger, and still more demands from the Croatian side, greatly alarmed the Serb elite. Even on the eve of the approaching collapse, however, the dominant stream in Serb political thought would turn to yet another idea of Yugoslavism— this time as a pure state concept. As discussions on how to save the state from dissolution continued, the very principle of the preservation of Yugoslavia remained indisputable.

The only attempt at creating a wider and better organized Serb movement was the founding of the Serb Cultural Club, which would briefly progress from a cultural to a purely political institution. The Club assembled a number of members of the Serb political, intellectual, and financial elite and attempted an all-encompassing Serb national program.[34] Such a program seemed imperative after the creation of the Croatian *banovina*. For the first time on a large scale, many prominent figures, mainly from Belgrade, spoke of the need for Serb national mobilization and the formation of a Serb unit within newly restructured Yugoslavia.[35] Nevertheless, most of these elite members would remain loyal to the Yugoslav framework. Document 5 provides a full exposition of this late Serb Yugoslavism from Slobodan Jovanović,[36] who headed the Club and was widely perceived as the "hidden hand" behind Serbian political and intellectual thought. Jovanović's "unsentimental approach to politics"[37] tied the Serb national question closely to the Yugoslav state, but also to the Croat question.

The article by Jovanović was one of many that appeared in the Club's journal *Srpski glas* (Serb Voice) seeking to address the thorny Serb question. The aforementioned Vladimir Ćorović, who only a few years before had acted almost as an official state historian, now wrote that "... from 1918 until today, the centralistic regime, with its immature—and often unconscientious and arbitrary—bureaucracy, has compromised the idea of national oneness ..." He further claimed that the Croats, who had once been the champions of Yugoslav ideology, began to work against national oneness and Yugoslavism "... when it became clear that Belgrade, instead of Zagreb, would become the center of the Yugoslav action. They began identifying Yugoslavism with Great Serbianism and developed an integral Croat nationalism. They exaggerated the danger of the idea of national oneness and imposed their own doctrine on many Serbs." Appalled by the 1939 agreement, Čorović concludes: "To us, the state structure is not as important as the spirit which governs that state."[38]

Some articles from *Srpski glas* proceeded to the still greater anxiety that while Yugoslavs had not been created and would likely not be ever created, the Serbs' own national identity had begun to dissolve. This sentiment grew stronger when it became obvious that part of the Serb community—in the exaggerated form then perceived—began to question their Serb identity. This could have been a sign of the struggle for regional power and domination which could not but leave an imprint. It could also have been a consequence of the loosening of the Yugoslav concept which, as a result, left many alternative avenues open. "When we enter a debate over Serbdom throughout Yugoslavia," wrote Slobodan Drašković, then a young university professor, "we are quick to doubt ourselves, to renounce everything, to discuss everything humbly. We even permit the discussion of whether the Vojvodina Serbs are the same as Serbs from Serbia, or whether Bosnians, Herzegovians, or Montenegrins are Serbs! If this continues, soon we will agree to discussions on whether Serbs exist at all, so that in the end we will manage to renounce even ourselves!"[39]

Among the Serbs, the last interwar years would bring about further reassessment of their position in the Yugoslav context. Part of the Serb community reckoned that Serb national identity had consistently been overshadowed by Yugoslavism and suffered for it in the process. Slogans like "Serbs, rally together!" were mushrooming up by the end of the 1930s. Higher Serb officials from Bosnia warned of the grave dangers awaiting the Serbs if they failed to close ranks as soon as possible.[40] Still, this idea of an exclusively Serb mobilization also had numerous opponents in Serb public opinion. Some staunch supporters of Yugoslavia as it existed claimed that a strong state concept could not be built without relying on a strong national concept involving solidarity among all the peoples of Yugoslavia. Belgrade journalist Miloš Milošević severely criticized those from the Serb Cultural Club who advocated an end to cooperation with the Croats since that was the only proper way of providing for Yugoslavia's survival. While holding Jovanović responsible for not acting resolutely many years before against the royal dictatorship, he was harder on the other rhetoric coming from the *Srpski glas*. "One might think", wrote Milošević, that "... instead of sowing, reaping, working, or even breathing, the Serbs have always and only been guarding the state," and proposed including most of the *Srpski glas* articles in a "pocket encyclopedia of idiocy."[41]

Sharp criticism of this "closing of Serb ranks" also came from Dimitrije Ljotić, the leader of perhaps the only proto-fascist movement in Serbia. Ljotić acknowledged the absence of a common Serb front, but objected to these calls for Serb separatism. He wrote: "Where can you find a greater

Serb unit than within Yugoslavia, which generations prior had made for the Serbs, just as much as for the Croats and Slovenes? We were never against such an association, but there has to be something else, for not only Serbs, but also for Croats and Slovenes, to which Yugoslavia means just as much as to the Serbs, must. ...."[42]

Likewise, the wave of Serb exclusiveness ran into opposition among the old "Yugoslav" guard. The long-time "Yugoslav" from Zagreb and editor-in-chief of *Nova Evropa*, Milan Čurčin, whose journal was rapidly losing influence just because it had preserved its traditional multi-ethnic Yugoslav orientation, reacted to this new separatism with despair. Lamentation over the apparent death of Yugoslav nationalism and disgust with "tribal" nationalisms dominate his last prewar articles. "It is hard to believe that ever, in the history of our people, was there more wrongful and sinful a watchword than this ["Serbs, rally together!"], which Belgrade attempts to spread amongst Serbs," wrote Ćurčin. "This is perhaps the most humiliating testimony of the political lunacy of the current Serb intelligentsia and the incompetence and powerlessness of Serbian politicians. ... In theory, who can determine the difference between Serbs and Croats; ... who will separate them one from the other, and where should the borders be erected?" asked Ćurčin.[43]

Thus, by the early 1940s, intra-Serb disputes about their "national space" were almost bigger than those between Serbs and Croats. Whereas Yugoslavism undoubtedly solidified the Croat national movement as a reaction against it, it confused and deadlocked any separate Serb mobilization. No wonder therefore that the Second World War would find the Serb elite in disarray, incapable of implementing any serious national program, including the most important one in their perception—preserving the Yugoslav state at a time when stronger and more integrated states would be falling like dominoes.

Epilogue—Interwar Serb Elites and Yugoslavism

The preceding inquiry shows that, in the last years of the Kingdom, the adherence of the Serb elite to the Yugoslav state framework seems to have been the only remaining basis of their Yugoslavism. In fact, most of them had already realized during the 1920s that national oneness had not been achieved, but they continued to perceive Yugoslavism as a viable, or at a minimum, a necessary state concept. It seems, however, that the ideological vacuum was not sufficiently filled. The pre-1918 unification ideology had the luxury of being loosely defined. It spoke of future prospects in general terms, of a "dream" perceived as the final step and main goal of Serb nation-

alism. However, interwar Yugoslavism represented adaptation by the heterogeneous Serb political body to real-life circumstances; it had to react to
the existing context of the Yugoslav state. Their incessant ideological wavering reveals that the interwar Serb elites could not come up with an appropriate way to transfer their former primary principle of unification into a stable
and viable political doctrine.

On the one hand, there was the problem of national identity. The Yugoslav component sometimes led leading Serbs to believe that a genuine
transformation of their nationhood was under way. However, the identification of Serbdom with Yugoslavdom ran into serious obstacles. Not only did
they themselves constantly challenge the national aspect of Yugoslavism;
there was also Serb discontent with the evident lack of adherence to Yugoslavism among non-Serbs. The previously recognized peoples of Yugoslavia—Serbs, Croats, and Slovenes—had long fostered their separate identities, albeit not always with clear-cut notions. Even if we assume that a new
multi-ethnic Yugoslav identity was as achievable as any other, that process
would have required a longer, much better organized and more systematic
process of "imagination" and "invention."

On the other hand, there was the traditional allegiance of Serbs to their
national state. What actually replaced the former drive towards pan-Serb
unification was the idea of a large metaphorical hat under which all Serbs
were covered. The "hat" was the Yugoslav Kingdom which, it seemed to
Serb elites, would offer better prospects for preserving the Serb nation than
any other likely framework. Thus Yugoslavism, although admittedly suspect
as an ethnic national concept, would remain consistent as a state concept in
Serb political thought. It also advanced, more often than not, the need for a
large and strong state, which deemed it attractive for a part of the non-Serb
population as well.[44] However, as the previous ideology of Serb unification
was never thoroughly conceptualized, the concept of the state as an end in
itself was also ill-defined.

Although deeply divided by the end of the interwar period, Serb leaders
remained agreed only on the need to work out their own national identity
within a state that was still called Yugoslavia. As seen in Document 5,
Slobodan Jovanović made the best case for this last recourse of interwar
Serb Yugoslavism by stating that "... neither Serb nor Croat nationalisms
can show us the right way if they are not tied to the Yugoslav state idea. Nor
does the Yugoslav state idea have any vitality if separated from Croat and
Serb nationalisms." While Serbdom and Yugoslavdom definitely parted
ways, Serbia and Yugoslavia became inseparable.

Sources

Document 1:

... The Serbs, Croats, and Slovenes are one and the same people by origin and by language. The Serbs and Croats are totally identical, while the differences between them and the Slovenes are quite insignificant. Although historical development, from the twelfth century on, has separated the Serbs from the Croats, forcing them to go their separate ways under different influences, and although they were, especially in the recent times, artificially alienated, the Serb and Croat peoples have nevertheless been conscious of the fact that they constitute a single people, have the same interests, and depend on each other. All the clashes, quarrels, and battles between the Serbs and Croats have always ended with the belief in national oneness and with the idea that the Serbs and Croats need to be one whole.

... We want all the Serb, Croat, and Slovene peoples, who have the same origin, language, and mentality, to be united in a single state, for that is the only way we can contribute—as members of the larger international community and in accordance with our capabilities—to the strengthening of the universal human, intellectual, and material culture. The unification of our people in a single state is not our goal. The unification of Serbdom is only a means which would enable the Serb people to work—faster, easier, and better—on the fulfilling of the great ideals of all humanity: all people and all peoples should be free, healthy, enlightened, financially secure, and—if possible at all—happy and pleased.

Source: Stanoje Stanojević, *Šta hoće Srbija?* [What Does Serbia Want?] (Niš, 1915), 21–27.

Document 2:

Following the centuries-long battle and slavery, due to a fortunate conjuncture of events in world affairs as well as the huge efforts and sacrifices of our people—especially the Serbs from Serbia—the Serbs, Croats, and Slovenes have cast off the shackles of slavery and become *free*. Now, it's up to us to build the structure of our free and independent state ... Do the Serbs, Croats, and Slovenes want to live in a *single* state union, in a single *simple* state? I trust that every reasonable Serb, Croat, or Slovene would reply in the affirmative. Everyone with common sense must seek the construction of a *single* state since, if for no other reason, it comes out of our natural instinct for self-preservation.

If we were united, we would be stronger and able to keep our freedom ...

However, from the time they moved to these areas, the Serbs,
Croats, and Slovenes have never been together in a single state. Nor
have the Serbs themselves been united in a single state ... During
many centuries, they have lived either in independence or slavery and
developed—under the influence of various cultures and faiths—different mentalities, different worldviews, and, to some extent, different
national ideals ... No doubt that our living together in a state of our
own will bring us closer to each other ... Will that lead to a total and
pure national oneness? Let time decide that. For our part, we must
look to that which connects us and not to that which sets us apart.

But we should bear in mind one thing—when part of a certain people develops a consciousness about its individuality, when it develops
its own culture, intelligentsia, and literature, this is not likely to be forgotten or abandoned. Thus, we should take this into account especially
now when we are laying the basis of our governmental structure. Our
state will be strong and stable only if it is based on reality. If we build
it on wrong premises, either consciously or unconsciously, then we
shall live in constant friction with each other. That will arrest our economic and cultural development which is so crucial for us since we
lag behind other nations.

Source: Ljuba Stojanović, *Nekolike misli o našem novom državnom uredjenju* [Some
Thoughts on Our New State Structure] (Belgrade, 1919), 11–14.

Document 3:

We have turned over a new leaf and found ourselves on a new page of
history ... One blood and one country! One destiny and one life formula! One fatherland and one patriotism! One future and one duty!
One language and one national culture! One tradition and one history!
Or, in a short and splendid definition: *One history and one state!* That's
the new and powerful energy which has been given the name Yugoslavia ... This could not have happened ten years ago when we had a
country with internal borders which caused doubts and ambiguities,
borders which were *unscientific, illogical,* and not created by our people *but by the circumstances and by our historical enemies.* The old
name of the country emphasized the *differences between the three tribes
and not the sameness of the people's blood and* ideals ... Serbia, as
always, had the courage to start with herself. Never have her sacrifices
been bigger or higher. By doing so, she has abandoned neither her past
nor her glory; she has only changed her state name into a name which

is better suited for the development of her history and ideals. Today, the powerful name of Yugoslavia is a synthesis of all those innumerable evidences which point to the one and only direction of our national energies. This time, the idea of nation and state has risen above people's instincts and passions. If Serbia ceased to be one big province within the state, one that used to be shaped only by circumstances, that's because *the nation has now become wider than her borders!*

Source: Jovan Dučić, "Reč Jugoslavija" [The Word Yugoslavia], *Politika*, 30 October, 1929; in J. Dučić, *Sabrana dela*, vol. IV (Belgrade–Sarajevo, 1989), 609–12.

Document 4:

    ... The Serbs, Croats, and Slovenes need to build the internal structure of their own house together and in good faith. In that regard many errors have been made on all sides. Until now, we have suffered the most from the "integral" patriots, who proclaimed themselves the sole guardians of Yugoslavia and the sole fighters for state and national unity ... From 1932 until eleven months ago, the people from the Yugoslav National Party governed this state ... What did those gentlemen leave us as their legacy? Among many other failures, they have bequeathed us the unresolved Croat question.

    ... Our program stresses the principle of a high degree of self-rule. That is our political ideal ... We are for the respect of the three names of our people: Serbs, Croats, and Slovenes. We are for the respect of their equality and their traditions. We want to arrange the structure of government with respect to the people's wishes and needs. At the same time, we leave it to the individual regions to arrange their own administrative, economic, financial, and social needs, granted that those arrangements are not contrary to the state's, that is, contrary to the state goals and needs.

Source: Milan Stojadinović, "Program Jugoslovenske Radikalne Zajednice" [Program of the Yugoslav Radical Union], *Novosti*, 2 July 1936; cited from F. Čulinović, ed., *Dokumenti o Jugoslaviji: Historijat od osnutka zajedničke države do danas* (Zagreb, 1968), 331–32.

Document 5:

    ...Yugoslavism was a product of a national calamity; there was much more political realism in it than people usually think today. Let us remember the circumstances on the eve of the world war in which the Croats and Serbs respectively found themselves. The Croats were afraid that their hard-fought autonomy could not be protected from the systematic attacks by the Hungarian government ... The Serbs under King Peter I realized that they could not extend their borders in any direction ... As the Croats were facing a life-and-death struggle against the Hungarians, in the same way the Serbs were facing a life-and-death struggle with the Habsburg Monarchy; and as the Croats deemed help from the Serb brethren precious, so the Serbs badly needed help from the Croats. Yugoslav thought was nothing but an awareness of the need for political cooperation between the Serbs and Croats.

...Were the circumstances after the war changed in such a way as to allow the Serbs and Croats to part ways? Are they now sure they can make it on their own, one without the other? ... Serbia would lose the bigger and more important part of the Adriatic coast ... She would, more or less, become something she used to be before the world war—the only landlocked state in the Balkans ... Nor would the position of the Croats be less difficult. An independent Croatia, even if it encompasses all of today's Croatian *banovina*, would belong to the rank of smaller states. We live in a time which is un-favorable even to middle-sized states, let alone smaller states ... Therefore, it is clear that the same reasons which propelled the Serbs and Croats to strive towards unification before the world war, are still valid today. If the circumstances have changed at all, they have not changed for better but for worse ...

The question is not whether the Serbs and Croats want to stick together, but whether they have to stick together ... Yugoslavism as a national idea ran into obstacles and was opposed by Serb as well as Croat nationalisms. However, this does not mean that Yugoslavism as a state idea has to run into trouble ... Neither Serb nor Croat nation-alisms can show us the right way if they are not tied to the Yugoslav state idea. Nor does the Yugoslav state idea have any vitality if sepa-rated from Croat and Serb nationalisms."

Source: Slobodan Jovanović, "Jugoslovenska misao u prošlosti i budućnosti" [Yugo-slav Thought in the Past and Future] (lecture given at the Serb Cultural Club on 4 December 1939); cited from S. Jovanović, *Sabrana dela*, vol. 11 (Belgrade, 1991), 567–75.

Notes

1 1) Except for some widely accepted Anglicized forms, names in this article have been rendered in their original spelling; 2) "Serbian" (noun and adjective) refers to Serbia proper, that is, pre-1912 Serbia (its territory and inhabitants) as well as the language of Serbs, while "Serb" refers to all Serbs, regardless of territory; 3) all translations in this article are made by Robert Momich and the author (italics in translations are used only if found in the original texts).

2 The cultural component of Yugoslavism, which was most prominent during the pre-Yugoslav era in the form of so-called cultural Yugoslavism, would lose its separate standing after 1918. While interwar intellectuals almost never stopped contemplating a unified Yugoslav culture, their visions became ever more inseparable from the dynamics of national and state structuring of Yugoslavia. Thus, all the endeavors intended as strictly cultural expressions of Yugoslavism were hardly ever free from its other two, national and state, components. On cultural Yugoslavism see Andrew Baruch Wachtel, *Making a Nation, Breaking a Nation: Literature and Cultural Politics in Yugoslavia* (Stanford, CA: Stanford University Press, 1998).

3 In F. Čulinović, ed., *Dokumenti o Jugoslaviji: Historijat od osnutka zajedničke države do danas* (Zagreb, 1968), 298.

4 See Ivo Lederer, "Nationalism and the Yugoslavs", in Peter Sugar and Ivo Lederer, eds., *Nationalism in Eastern Europe* (Seattle: University of Washington Press, 1969), 403–8; also Stevan K. Pavlowitch, *Serbia: The History behind the Name* (London: C. Hurst & Co, 2002), 26–64.

5 See John Lampe, *Yugoslavia as History: Twice There was a Country* (Cambridge: Cambridge University Press, 1996), 81–87; also Gale Stokes, *Politics as Development: The Emergence of Political Parties in Nineteenth-century Serbia* (Durham: Duke University Press, 1990).

6 Much has been written in this respect on Ilija Garašanin's "Načertanije" of 1844; however, it would be too much to view this document as a "Yugoslav" program; see D. Bataković, "Ilija Garašanin's Načertanije: A Reassessment," *Balcanica*, vol. XV–1 (Belgrade, 1994): 157–83.

7 See D. Janković, *Srbija i jugoslovensko pitanje 1914–1915. godine* (Belgrade, 1973).

8 Stanoje Stanojević (1874–1937) was a prominent historian, professor at the Belgrade University and member of the Serbian Royal Academy. He was the editor-in-chief of the *Serbo-Croato-Slovene People's Encyclopedia* (1924–1929) and founded the *Yugoslav Historical Journal* (1935). His works include *A History of the Serb People* (1908). He participated in the work of the Yugoslav delegation at the Paris Peace Conference.

9 Certainly, the prospects of interwar Yugoslav political dynamics were not dependent solely on the outlook of the Serb elites, but their inconsistent attitude towards the structure of the would-be state contributed a lot to later difficulties.

10 Nikola Pašić (1844–1926) was a primary founder of the Serbian Radical Party and prime minister of Serbia 1908–1918 and of the postwar Kingdom of Serbs, Croats and Slovenes from 1921 to 1926.

11 In Dj. Stanković, *Nikola Pašić i Hrvati (1918–1923)* (Belgrade, 1995), 407–08.

12 See Lj. Dimić, *Istorija srpske državnosti: Srbija u Jugoslaviji* (Novi Sad, 2001).

13 Certainly, "national oneness" was not an exclusively Serb formula. Aside from being accepted as a true belief among many, the formula was also quite convenient for Yugoslav foreign policy and, as such, readily welcomed by the Serbs and non-Serbs alike. Having a common national front *vis-à-vis* the neighboring states proved to be a very important pillar of the new state not only during the postwar border delineation, but throughout the interwar period when, as Slobodan Jovanović put it, "nationalism was liberalism in foreign affairs."

14 On state structuring during the first years of Yugoslavia see Ivo Banac, *The National Question in Yugoslavia: Origins, History, Politics* (Ithaca: Cornell University Press, 1992).

15 The "amputation" of "non-Serb lands" gained some prominence as a possibility in the early 1920s; the issue would be raised again in 1928 by King Aleksandar himself but it would be too much to view this move as anything but an additional method of putting pressure onto the quarrelling political parties.

16 Ljubomir Stojanović (1860–1930) was a well-known historian and linguist. Like Stanojević, Stojanović was a university professor and Serbian Royal Academy member who industriously collected and published sources for Serbian history. In the Kingdom of Serbia he was a member of the Radical Party and, later on, the Independent Radical Party, and served as a prime minister, minister of education, and minister of interior. After the First World War, he was a founder of the Yugoslav Republican Party.

17 Ž. Spasojević, "Savremeno pravo i država," in *Jugoslovenska demokratska liga*, (Geneva, 1919), VI.

18 Lj. Stojanović, "Još o 'Srpskom pitanju,'" *Nova Evropa* 12, no. 14 (1925): 413.

19 Cited in F. Čulinović, ed., *Dokumenti*, 291–92.

20 See Constantin Iordachi's chapter in this volume.

21 Cited in L. Marković, *Jugoslovenska država i hrvatsko pitanje* (Belgrade, 1935), 347.

22 V. Jonić, "Jugoslovensko misionarstvo," in V. Novak, ed., *Antologija jugoslovenske misli i narodnog jedinstva, 1390–1930* (Belgrade, 1930), 882–83; in 1941, Jonić would become a commissar in the German-imposed wartime government in Serbia.

23 V. Ćorović, *Istorija Jugoslavije* (Belgrade, 1933), 1.

24 M. Dimitrijević, *Tri govora u Narodnoj skupštini* (Belgrade, 1932), 13–16.

25 Jovan Dučić (1871–1943) is one of the most distinguished Serb poets. Born in Herzegovina, by the end of the nineteenth century he was a member of a prominent Serb literary circle. In 1907 he entered the ministry of foreign affairs of the Kingdom of Serbia. From 1910 on, he would occupy various posts in both the Serbian and Yugoslav diplomatic service. He served as Yugoslav ambassador to Budapest, Rome, and Madrid.

26 Dučić, who was already viewed by some as an ardent Serb nationalist at the time of writing this "hymn to Yugoslavia," would, in 1941, turn to Serb exclusivism; reacting bitterly to the crimes committed against his co-nationals in the Independent State of Croatia, Dučić would write that the Serb people in 1918 had no idea that they would

take such a huge obligation while getting nothing in return from the others: "Yugoslavism was a journey on a road with no end, it was madness and suicide." Cited in J. Dučić, *Verujem u Boga i u Srpstvo* (Belgrade and Prishtina, 1996), 51.

27 B. Petranović and M. Zečević, eds., *Jugoslovenski federalizam—ideje i stvarnost: Tematska zbirka dokumenata, vol. 1 (1914–1943)* (Belgrade, 1987), 317–21.

28 On the radicalization of the youth movements see Sandra Prlenda's chapter in this volume; also, N. Žutić, *Sokoli: Ideologija u fizičkoj kulturi Kraljevine Jugoslavije 1929–1941* (Belgrade, 1991).

29 True, the Croat political front would remain divided, but the Croatian Peasant Party became so dominant that most of the Croat population gathered around this party. On these developments, see Mark Biondich's chapter in this volume.

30 Milan Stojadinović (1888–1963) was one of the leading political figures of interwar Yugoslavia. In the 1920s, as a member of the Radical Party, he served as a minister of finance under several governments. In the 1930s he was a founder and president of the Yugoslav Radical Union. From 1935–1939 he was the prime minister and minister of foreign affairs and strengthened Yugoslavia's economic and political dependence on Germany. In 1941 he was transferred to the British authorities who interned him on the island of Mauritius. After the Second World War he moved to Buenos Aires where he served as a financial advisor to the Argentinean government.

31 D. Minović, "Pravni poredak, i narodno jedinstvo," *Nova Evropa* 28, no. 9 (1935): 301–302.

32 *Interpelacija na gospodina Pretsednika Ministarskog saveta*, Archive of Yugoslavia, holding fund 74, box 13, unit 24; the Yugoslav Radical Union was a coalition of the Slovene People's Party, the Yugoslav Muslim Organization, and a part of the Radical Party.

33 Cited in M. Crnjanski, *Politički spisi* (Belgrade, 1989), 63–66.

34 See Lj. Dimić, *Kulturna politika u Kraljevini Jugoslaviji 1918–1941* (Belgrade, 1996), 506–61.

35 As a reaction to the creation of the Croatian *banovina*, for the first time calls for the creation of a separate "Serb land" could be heard. There was one such project conceptualized by some prominent Serb jurists in 1940, which had for its aim the creation of one unified Serb unit centered in Skopje. Despite being presented for public debate there were no formal policies to this effect (see Petranović and Zečević, *Federalizam*, 569–70).

36 Slobodan Jovanović (1869–1958) was an eminent jurist, historian, literary critic, and politician. He was one of the most respected intellectuals in modern Serbian history. His outstanding scholarly work includes a voluminous and still unsurpassed political history of nineteenth-century Serbia. Later on, he would become the prime minister of the Yugoslav government-in-exile (1942–1943).

37 See Aleksandar Pavković, *Slobodan Jovanović: An Unsentimental Approach to Politics* (New York, 1993).

38 V. Čorović, "Pitanje preuredjenja države," in *"Jako srpstvo—jaka Jugoslavija. Izbor članaka iz "Srpskog glasa", organa Srpskog kulturnog kluba, objavljenih 1939–1940* (Belgrade, 1991), 13–15.

39 S. Drašković, "Današnji položaj i zadaci Srba," in Ćorović, *Jako srpstvo,* 125–28.

40 B. Kaludjerčić, *Zašto smo protiv granice na Drini i protiv cepanja Bosne i Hercegovine,* AJ, holding fund 37, box 9, unit 48.

41 M. Milošević, *Otvoreno pismo gospodinu Slobodanu Jovanoviću: O njegovoj odgovornosti za defetizam "Srpskog glasa,"* (Belgrade, 1940).

42 Cited from *Dimitrije Ljotić u revoluciji i ratu* (Munich, 1961), 164–67.

43 Ć. [M. Ćurčin], "'Srbi na okup!'", *Nova Evropa* 33, no. 5 (1940): 129–35.

44 Interestingly enough, as Dejan Jović discusses in the next chapter, following the radical ideological transformation of society in Communist Yugoslavia, the "cult of the state" would be seriously challenged even among Serb Communists. That aside, the late 1980s witnessed yet another return to Yugoslavism as a state concept and the Serbs would once again become the only champions of it on the same old ideological basis—Yugoslavia was seen as the only possible framework to include "all Serbs."

CHAPTER 11

Dejan Jović

COMMUNIST YUGOSLAVIA AND ITS "OTHERS"

This chapter focuses on the construction of official identity in postwar Yugoslavia (1945–1991). More specifically, it analyses the construction by the Yugoslav political elite of a political frontier[1] between "Us" and "Others." In states led by Communist parties, the political elite has perceived itself primarily as an intellectual elite. After all, the Communist party was supposed to play the role of an enlightened vanguard,[2] which represented not reality as it is, but a vision of the future as it ought to be. In Yugoslavia, the party increasingly saw itself as a *scientific institute*, a vision-formulator—a *guiding* rather than *commanding* force in society.[3] At the same time, the party still had in reality the decisive role in the policy-making processes. The politics of Yugoslav socialism was based on an attempt not only to interpret reality but to change it. Formulating this vision in Yugoslavia's case was its main ideologue (and long the likely successor to Tito), Edvard Kardelj.[4] This chapter maps out the main elements of Kardelj's (and thus the official) view of what Yugoslavia was and what it ought to be, and likewise what it was not and ought not to be. His was an ideological answer to the question of national identity. This identity, however, was constructed more on negative considerations of who "We" are not and who "We" ought not to be than on positive identification with who "We" are and who "We" ought to be. Identifying the "Others" played a central role in constructing a single Yugoslav identity under socialism.

After 1989, the "Others" changed, and the Yugoslavs had to reformulate that identity-definition. It was no longer possible to define Yugoslavia simply as "different from the Soviet Union," or "different from the prewar, bourgeois statist Yugoslavia." These Others were no longer viable as antipodes against which Kardelj's vision of Communist Yugoslavia had been constructed. Lacking a positive ideological vision of the future and internal cohesion, Yugoslavia faced an identity crisis which soon led to its disintegration.

Constructing Identities in Communism

For all identities and in all societies, it has been argued, the Other has a defining importance.[5] The process of defining ourselves is one of creating a frontier between "Us" and "Others." We cannot define who "We" are without determining who "We" are not. This process has its analytical and normative dimension. By creating a frontier between "Us" and "Others," the identity-definers tell us not only who "We" are / are not, but who "We" ought / ought not to be (thus issuing a normative statement).

The normative dimension of identity-building is much stronger in vision-driven political systems, in which the enlightened vanguard legitimizes itself by its own vision of the future.[6] Socialism (as a period of transition to Communism) was a vision-driven project in which the elite did not primarily represent reality (i.e. what *is*, as in representative democracies) but the desired future. Even more, the vanguard (the Party elite) aimed at radically changing, not representing, reality. Socialism was by definition a denial of reality. Reality was not to be represented but to be changed. To every socialist ideocratic[7] system, the first Other was therefore reality. This is why elections were not considered a crucial element of the political system. Elections are instruments of mapping out reality as it is; those who are elected represent social reality. The goal of socialism, however, is to change this reality, not to represent it. Communist opposition to elections was not primarily motivated by hunger for complete power (although this element was certainly present too), but by their ideological belief that reality should be overcome. Unlike reality, the future is portrayed as "bright" and promising. While, for example, the elite in a socialist society might admit that in reality "there are many problems," they *knew* that the future would bring solutions to these problems. The party itself was the representative of this "bright future" in which the unfulfilled ideals of the Enlightenment—equality, freedom and solidarity—were to be achieved. Its members viewed the Communist party as a model for the future society, a miniature society-of-the-future. Principles such as egalitarianism in intra-party relationships, complete openness to criticism and self-criticism, activism and intellectualism would for the present be possible only within the party. The aim was to extend them to the whole of society.[8]

The past was another "Other" against which the Communist vision was formulated. The past was described as a period of darkness replete with inequality, lack of freedom and injustice. It was treated as a "previous life," a "pre-history" of mankind. The socialist revolution was the final break with the past. The official narrative of socialism divided people into "forces of the past" and "progressive forces." Revolution was the final and forceful victory of the latter over the former. This victory was historical ("an epochal change"), and thus the former stood no chance of restoring its power in society again. Counter-revolutions were of course possible—but to expect the return of capitalism once it was defeated by socialism would be the same as to expect the restoration of feudalism once it had been destroyed by the bourgeois revolutions.[9]

Socialism was a process in which the past and present was deconstructed in order to make space for the construction of the future. Constructed by the enlightened vanguard, this bright future is to be built in opposition to the present and the past. The forces of the past and present, "retrograde elements" and "conservative forces," are thus the main enemy of socialism. The stronger they are, the more brutal the violence against them must be. Violence is justified if it serves social progress, but should, of course, be minimized and then become unnecessary as the class consciousness of the population arises. But even in a later phase of the revolution (once its first, brutal phase is over) the vanguard needs to be aware of the existence of the forces of the old, because, as the saying goes, "the enemy never sleeps." The Revolutionary army and militia are instruments of this instrumentalist understanding of violence. They are essentially revolutionary institutions, whose purpose is not only to defend the country and prevent violence (as in liberal democracies) but to increase class consciousness and safeguard the revolution. The army and police in socialism do not defend the state as such, since the state is a conservative institution of the past and present. They defend the revolution, the vision of the future and its supreme visionaries. In a socialist society, these institutions are by definition ideological.[10]

It is just because of the presence of the forces of the past and present that the existence of the state is still justified, even in socialism. In principle, socialism is a process in which the state is to be replaced by a self-governing society, while the main state functions are to be *socialized*.[11] However, this is a gradual process (controlled and led by the vanguard), in which at no time should the forces of the past be permitted to think that they would be tolerated beyond a strictly minimal level, let alone invited back to power. In socialism, the state is not justified *per se*, but only because of the existence of the "Other," of the "enemies of socialism" which one had to deal with in an "administrative way." The existence of the state itself is thus conditioned upon the existence of the "Others," that is, of "anti-socialist forces."[12] Although the forces of the past are the most dangerous enemies of the socialist state, the forces of the present are enemies too. Stagnation, for example, is also an enemy, because the purpose of socialism is to radically *change* society, not to consolidate it. Although to many of their liberal critics, socialist societies were bastions of conservatism (i.e., that permitted no change at all), a more subtle analysis of their real politics would offer a different conclusion. Sudden and brutal changes of elite personnel, radical turnabouts in policies, a lack of written rules, exposure of virtually everybody to unpredictable actions by those in power—these are examples of socialism's policy of permanent revolution or (at least) "permanent reform."[13] All were supposed to eliminate either forces of the past or of the present.

All these elements defined official identity in Communist-Party led socialist states. The main identity-definers were the members of the elite, that is, of the party/vanguard. The state was a temporary instrument of the revolution. Its main task was to keep an eye on both "the forces of the past" and "the forces of the present." However, in the long term the state itself, as a remnant of the past, should wither away. It was to be "socialized," its main functions replaced by a self-regulated society of class-conscious working people. The new society would be a stateless association of free producers.

The vanguard had a monopoly in defining the vision and in leading society towards its realization. It was legitimized not by elections, but by its "far-sightedness" and by possessing knowledge of the "general laws of history." The future was to be radically (i.e. revolutionarily) different from the past and the present. It would be made—by the will and action of the "subjective forces of socialism"—as a mirror image of the past. Or, as the words of the "Internationale" puts it: "The Earth shall rise on new foundations, we have been naught, we shall be all!"

The Official Construction of Yugoslavia's Identity

Although the Yugoslav Communists did not follow the ideological and political line formulated mainly by Moscow for all other Communist countries since 1948, they remained Communists and Marxists. As Tito explicitly said in 1953, there was no attempt to invent "Titoism," but only an original, Yugoslav, interpretation of Marxism, which would then become a basis for a "Yugoslav way to socialism."[14] In fact, the Yugoslav Communists claimed that they understood Marxism better than the Soviets, and of course, better than the East European countries too.

Very much unlike "East European" countries, the Yugoslav interpretation of Marxism (and thus the official identity developed as a consequence of such an interpretation) was based not on following Soviet Marxism but

on criticizing it as "revisionism." Throughout its socialist period, the Yugoslavs introduced elements of "original Marxism" in order to replace and/or
counter Soviet "revisionism." This process of criticizing the Soviets, while
still remaining Marxists, occupied a central place in identity-construction
for the "New Yugoslavia." This identity was no longer based on ethnic similarity between the Yugoslav (South Slavic) nations, nor was it justified by
the very fact that there was a Yugoslav state, as was attempted for interwar
Yugoslavia (see the previous chapter by Marko Bulatović). Neither ethnic
similarity nor the existence of the state could have served as pillars of identity within a Marxist framework. As in all ideocratic systems, Yugoslavia
insisted on a "clear vision," without which, as Kardelj famously said in
1977,[15] there would be no possibility to construct Yugoslav unity, and thus
no possibility of preserving either socialism or the country's independence.
(See Documents 1 and 2.) For Yugoslav Communists the process of vision
formulating performed the same function as election-based institution building in liberal democracies. Not only "the unity of the nation," but its very
existence as a nation would be endangered without a "clear vision."[16]

In constructing their vision of the future, Yugoslav Communists had to
identify the "Others," both the "forces of the past" and the hostile forces of
the present against whom the process of socialism is directed. Without the
presence of these forces the state would not have been justified.

There were two main "Others" against which Yugoslav socialism tried
to construct itself, one related to the past and the other to the present. The
first was invented by the party before 1948, the other after 1948. Both of
them were then preserved as "Others" until the end of Yugoslav socialism,
in the late 1980s. These were (1) prewar Yugoslavism, based on the concept
of South Slavism, which in ideological terms was a form of liberal, i.e. representative democracy; and (2) Soviet-style socialism, with its strong state
and fairly centralized political structure—if not in theory and legal framework, then certainly in reality. These two Others were antipodes against
which the new Yugoslav identity (post-1948) was to be constructed as a
"mirror image." Yugoslavia ought to be radically different from both its
interwar incarnation and its brief but stormy Stalinist period (1945–1950).
To some extent, both of these hostile Others remained as threats into the
present. Internationally, the world of "capitalism" (controlled by the "forces
of the past") was still strong. At the same time, the other half of the world,
although socialist, was based on a revisionist concept of Marxism. "Soviet
socialism" (often called "state socialism" or simply "Stalinism") was the
socialism of "stagnation," not of social progress towards a stateless society
as an association of free producers. (See Document 3 for Tito's explicit
repudiation of "statism.") Thus, both alternatives to Yugoslav self-managing
socialism were potential threats. These two Others had their domestic repre-

sentatives too: on the one hand "liberals" and "techno-managerial forces" (representatives of the "forces of the past," i.e. of liberal democracy), and on the other "dogmatists," "unitarists," "bureaucrats" and "Stalinists" (representatives of "Soviet-type socialism")[17]. A spectrum of socialist Yugoslavia's political enemies was developed along the line of "right" and "left" deviations from the Yugoslav model. The next two sections reconstruct the mainstream representation of these two historical mega-Others in order to demonstrate how the enlightened vanguard used them in the process of identity-construction.

Interwar Yugoslavism

The Yugoslav Communist Party (CPY) had revolutionary aims and thus its hostility towards the interwar bourgeois Yugoslav state was unquestionable. Illegal since 1920, the CPY used all methods (including violence) to overthrow the royal Yugoslav regime. We are, however, concerned here primarily with those elements of Yugoslav identity before the Second World War which were central to the old state and which the Communist interpretation of the past had sought to eliminate in postwar (socialist) Yugoslavia. Interwar Yugoslavia was based on its ethnic, i.e. South Slavic character. It was a country of all the South Slavs (minus only the Bulgarians), in which three recognized "tribal" groups (Serbs, Croats and Slovenes) were supposed to become one Yugoslav nation. Yugoslavia was to creat a Yugoslav nation, primarily in a political, but also in an ethnic sense.

This nation-creating project was in fact based not only on ethnic similarities between Yugoslav groups, but also on the prevailing liberal concept of nationhood.[18] Yugoslavia followed the French political model of a unitary state (at least before the agreement of 1939, when Croatian specificity was recognized), using at the same time the unification of Germany (1870) and Italy (1871) as models for its own unification. The Serb-dominated political elite of interwar Yugoslavia decided to centralize the organization of the state, in part to bar separatism and Communism. The latter, a universalist doctrine, not only relativized the borders of the states, but also challenged some of them as products of bourgeois *imperialism* after the First World War. The main elements of Yugoslavia's domestic and foreign policy were in fact expressions of this political concept. Based on a democratic principle of counting individual votes (not ethnic groups or ethno-political territorial units), interwar Yugoslavia was more popular with Serbs, the largest Yugoslav ethnic group, than with the smaller ones, although the logic of coalition politics created exceptions to this rule. The most prominent were the Slovenes and the (not officially recognized) Bosnian Muslims. Like the other newly created states in Europe, the interwar Yugoslav state was grounded in principles of representative democracy. But these principles would remain essentially a vision which was to a large extent imported from abroad. While Yugoslavia as a state was not created by foreigners (and is thus not a "product" of Versailles), both its constitutive ideology (liberal democracy) and its model for state structure were imported from the West. Essentially, the first Yugoslav state was a vision-driven project, an experiment based on a nation-state-building ideology. Although liberal democracy was not entirely new to some of the population, its combination of liberalism with the nation-state was a new one. As with all other countries into which this combination was introduced after 1918, Yugoslavia, too, failed to become what was desired by its identity constructors.

The new, socialist Yugoslavia was from its beginning constructed as the opposite of all this. Firstly, it was a republic, not a monarchy; and it was a federation, not a unitary state. Secondly, it did not seek to construct a Yugoslav nation, nor did it aim at building up a Yugoslav nation-state. Finally, it was not a liberal democracy and it felt no need to "import" their "second-hand" institutions, such as political parties, parliaments and elections.[19] As explained above, the new Yugoslavia was to be based on a radically different concept of the state. While in the liberal concept a state might be "minimal" or even "ultra-minimal,"[20] it would never "wither away." According to all Marxists, the state is considered to be an institution of a class-divided society and an instrument of oppression of the exploited majority by the ruling minority. Once the majority takes over, the state is on its way to becoming redundant. For Yugoslav Communists too, it was to be weakened and ultimately replaced by the "association of free producers" and a "self-managing society."

Even less was the new Yugoslavia aiming to build up a nation-making state. The Yugoslav Communists" interpretation of the collapse of both the Austro-Hungarian Empire and interwar Yugoslavia attributed these state failures, albeit mistakenly, to attempts by the elites in these "states" to deny the existing nations and invent a new supra-nation created by the state itself. Being on the side of the weak, exploited and unrecognized nations in these multi-ethnic "states," Marxists fought against them both. Now, when they got an opportunity to direct the identity-defining process, they were determined not to commit the same "mistake." This is what they promised to the smaller (and weaker) Yugoslav nations, many of whom supported the party precisely because it offered an answer to both the national and social problems they experienced. It would have been a deception if the party failed to deliver on its promise.[21] The consequences of not delivering on that promise would be especially grave in Yugoslavia, which was composed of small and weak nations, and where even the largest nation (the Serbs) was not a majority of the total population (only 36.6 percent in 1981).[22] The Marxist concept of nationhood, Yugoslav Communists claimed, therefore suited all Yugoslav nations, including the Serbs. It was not only that all of them were (historically) victims of foreign exploitation, but they all could easily fall victims to foreign and domestic threats to their national identity and security.

The fundamental difference, then, was that postwar Yugoslavia did not attempt to create a Yugoslav nation, either in an ethnic or a political sense.[23] It viewed "unitarism" and "great-statist" tendencies as one of the main potential or real enemies of socialist Yugoslavia. Its policy of recognizing existing conditions instead of attempting to change them, was, however, a paradox from the Marxist point of view. In all other areas of social life, Yugoslav Communists repudiated previous reality and wanted to eliminate the past. But on the "national question" they were conservative, favoring preservation of the existing over change. This conservative view on the nationality issue was best expressed by Edvard Kardelj's notion of "completed nations." While the state was to wither away once socialism advanced, nations were not meant to disappear. This paradox was in fact at the core of the controversy which ultimately destroyed Yugoslavia both as an ideological concept and as a state.

Finally, the new Yugoslavia aimed at a radical decentralisation of the state. This was viewed as a step towards direct economic as well as political democracy. Decentralization of the state was not only, and perhaps not even primarily, a result of pressures by those who pointed to the continued existence of the "national question." It was also an inevitable task if socialism was to succeed in replacing the state with a "self-governing society." Because the only real democracy was based on the rights of those who produce to decide upon the fruits of their labor, decentralization and de-etatization was a *conditio sine qua non* for democracy. In the narrative developed by the Yugoslav Communists, democracy did not mean "liberal democracy" but direct, or semi-direct, economic and political democracy via a complex system of *delegates* and *delegations*. Its focus was not on political power but on the distribution of goods and services produced by the "working people." Political power in Yugoslav socialism was to be taken away from the state apparatus, and thus from *bureaucracy*,[24] and decentralized to the level of "a housewife," as Lenin famously said. This process of decentralization was to be at the same time a process of democratization.[25]

In its opposition to interwar Yugoslavia, the new socialist Yugoslav discourse identified the following "Others": (1) unitarism (a doctrine and action aimed at creating a state-nation by gradually challenging elements of the identities and/or rights of existing smaller constitutive nations); (2) centralism (an attempt to centralize state apparatus); (3) statism (a doctrine which considered that states are irreplaceable, and that the state, not society, should have the ultimate decision-making power; also expressed through the notion of "sovereignty," which is a remnant of the liberal theory of the state); (4) bureaucratism (often characterized as "petrification" of the existing structures, and thus an enemy of change). These four Others were all related to the state and its functions. The new socialist narrative was also hostile to liberal democracy *ipso facto*. As noted in the introduction to this volume, Marxism characterised liberal theories as "ideologies" that hid the reality of class exploitation both domestically and, in the form of imperialism, globally. The electoral system of a liberal democracy, for example, provided representation for an "abstract person" rather than for a person as he/she is by social class. Elections are thus a mere farce, in which "abstract citizens" have an occasional chance to choose between one or another capitalist. In reality, decisions are taken by "extra-parliamentary" powers. Real change, by which those who exploit the majority would be overthrown, is not possible within the institutional structure of liberal democracy but only through a socialist revolution. All these elements (hostility towards parliament, political parties, elections, capitalists and the bourgeoisie) were preserved and developed in the Yugoslav official narrative. (For the flavor of this argument, see Documents 4 and 5 by Edvard Kardelj.) They resulted in an institutional and political structure which indeed was radically different from that of interwar Yugoslavia.[26] The main task of the state in socialist Yugoslavia was to safeguard these "achievements of the revolution" (*tekovine revolucije*) and to prevent the intrusion of the elements of the old into the new structures. As Tito said already in 1945, there will be no return to the Old. The new Yugoslav identity was to be anti-capitalist and anti-centralist, anti-statist and anti-unitarist. It was a system of permanent, especially constitutional, reform by which both the Past and Present were to be replaced by the Future, as envisioned by the enlightened vanguard.

Soviet-style "State Socialism"

After 1948, Soviet-style "state socialism" became the second "Other" against which the new Yugoslav identity was to be constructed. The Yugoslav enlightened vanguard maintained that it was the Soviets, and not them, who misunderstood and misinterpreted Marx's vision of the future. They (the Soviets), and not Us, were the "revisionists."[27] The main disagreement concerned the Soviet assessment of the state in socialism.[28] Soviet Communists, much more than the Yugoslavs, believed that the state was still needed. Instead of weakening it, they strengthened it.[29] In addition, all four enemies of socialism ("unitarism," "centralism," "statism" and "bureaucratism") which the Yugoslav Communists feared from the Yugoslav past, were still strong in the USSR. For all these reasons, the Yugoslav Communists said, the Soviets betrayed the main aim of socialism: the reduction of state functions to the minimum.[30] Actually the Soviets, having lived for more than 30 years already under socialism, were in some ways more realistic and less ideological about the state-society relationship. Emancipation from Soviet influence, consequently, did not in fact introduce a less, but a more ideological and less realistic basis for identity construction in Yugoslavia. In the decades following the split with the USSR, Yugoslavia was becoming, as well as a more pleasant country in which to live, more and more ideological. Its identity was now based increasingly on a vision of the future, rather than on connective elements such as ethnic, historical or political similarities between its constituent nations.[31]

The self-management concept, invented in 1950, and the new orientation towards a "non-aligned" foreign policy were the Yugoslav responses to Soviet statism in domestic policy and "hegemonism" in foreign affairs. In its nationality policy, Yugoslavia not only recognised the existence of small nations and "nationalities," i.e., non-Slavic ethnic groups such as Albanians. It also decentralized the federation, turning it by the early 1970s into a "specific community of self-governed nations and nationalities" which could no longer be characterized as either a federation or a confederation in the conventional sense of the word. (See Document 5.) A new narrative was invented, based on the three pillars of the new Yugoslav official identity: (1) self-management, (2) non-alignment, and (3) confederalized federalism. They were all inspired by the desire to be different not only from interwar Yugoslavia but even more so from the USSR. Whereas the state was strong in the USSR, just as in interwar Yugoslavia, Yugoslav self-management was anti-statist, and thus a true socialist project. (For Kardelj's views on this see Document 5.) While the USSR was one of the two superpowers, and thus exercised hegemonic power over the socialist half of the globe, Yugoslavia fought against both Western ("capitalist") and Soviet ("hegemonic") imperialism. Its ideological concept of anti-imperialism and anti-hegemonism (i.e. opposition to both military-political blocs) was rooted in the Marxist rhetoric of global (internationalist) action against global injustice. Finally, just as Yugoslavia sided with the exploited in global terms, Kardelj justified the further decentralization of Yugoslavia itself with the same argument, namely the protection of the weakest against the strongest (and thus, potentially—the most dangerous). Serbia, and to a lesser extent Croatia, being the two largest populations, were treated as the potential "hegemonic powers" in Yugoslavia. Their power was to be controlled and scaled down, while the real political power of other, smaller nations (Bosnian Muslims, Montenegrins, Macedonians and Slovenes) and "nationalities" (Albanians, Italians, Hungarians) was to be protected and increased in real terms. This was not, as today many argue, inspired by Tito's and Kardelj's "anti-Serbian bias," although they indeed feared that a "return to the past" might mean a return to Serbian domination over the others in Yugoslavia.[32] The reform of the nationality policy in the 1960s and 1970s was primarily motivated by the ideological beliefs that weaker nations (domestically as well as internationally) deserve protection against potential exploiters.

The Yugoslav Communists were not forced to make concessions to the nationalists, as today many claim. Given apparently favorable circumstances both domestically and internationally in the 1960s and 1970s, they believed that the time had come to take a further step towards realizing their own vision of a decentralized political community. Smaller and larger ethnic nations would be equal, and none would be exploited by another. They also believed that only by defeating "unitarism," "centralism," "statism" and "bureaucratism" would they advance the socialist project and leave "capitalism" further behind. Not to continue would mean stagnation and the death of their revolution. As Kardelj concluded, they could simply not afford not to have changed further if they wanted to remain genuine revolutionaries. The reforms of the second half of the 1960s and the first half of the 1970s were not therefore a result of a crisis but of perceived success over the previous decade (the mid-1950s to mid-1960s). This confidence made Yugoslav Communists think that their political system indeed was the best alternative to both capitalism and state Communism.[33]

The same positive assessment of global conditions led Yugoslavs to declare Soviet-type statist socialism as *the main* threat, a more important "Other" than the liberal-democratic system. It was not only because of the real political pressure by the Soviet Union (especially in moments of crisis, such as in 1968 with the invasion of Czechoslovakia or in 1971 with the Croatian Spring)[34] or because in these years it indeed seemed that liberalism was in worldwide crisis while socialist democracy looked victorious even in West European countries.[35] Although Yugoslavia was by no means certain to receive American military or even political support in the unlikely case of Soviet aggression, it was clear that such a step would by this time be too risky for the USSR to take. (But see Document 6 for fears from the Yugoslav leadership that Tito's death in 1980 would yet tempt the Soviets to take such a risk.) The main reason why Soviet-type socialism had nonetheless been ranked as the main "Other" by Yugoslavia's elite was ideological. Yugoslav Communists shared the Marxist beliefs that it would be against the "general laws of history" to expect liberal democracy to return successfully in societies in which a socialist revolution was successful. This would be especially true in Yugoslav society, where revolution was domestic in the making and not imported. In Kardelj's words, the *old society* "had absolutely no chance of success."[36] If liberalism in any of its forms was unlikely to come back, then socialism indeed remained the only game in town. This meant that the real political choice was not between liberalism and socialism, but between various types of socialism. As Edvard Kardelj explicitly explained in 1973, "it may be claimed that today the ... choice [is] between socialist self-management ... and the system of bureaucratic-technocratic statism."[37]

This is why Soviet socialism was considered to be more dangerous than liberal democracy. But it also seemed that this ideological explanation corresponded well with reality. People were indeed more worried about the possibility of an attack from the East[38] than from the West. In addition, within Yugoslavia itself, there was potentially more support for Soviet-state socialism than for Western-type liberal democracy. Political and economic protests in 1968 (Belgrade and Priština) were in fact inspired by demands for "alternative forms" of socialism, not for liberal democracy. The main values advocated were egalitarianism and social justice.[39] Thus, the party elite had indeed reason to fear that not liberal democracy but an alternative form of socialism could endanger its position. Paradoxically, while the elite promoted less state and more society (self-management), many in the population demanded more order and more state intervention, especially when the downward spiral of the economy and of political disintegration was well advanced by the 1980s. To many, for example to Albanians in Kosovo, even Enver Hoxha's Albania was not totally unattractive, precisely because at least in the blurred perceptions about life "over there" it offered more equality.[40] But also elsewhere in Yugoslavia the elite still needed to convince people that Yugoslav socialism, in which the state was "withering away" faster than elsewhere, was indeed better than Soviet or any alternative socialist system.

The elite did so by portraying the Soviet Union and its socialism as (only a milder form of) "Stalinism"—using images not much different from those developed and promoted by the West, sometimes even by directly importing and/or translating books, films, plays, and academic books which portrayed the USSR in very unfavorable lights. The myth of Tito's "historical No!" (in 1948) received equal treatment as the myths on the Partisan struggle against occupiers and "domestic traitors."[41] The borders were now, since the early 1970s, wide open to the West, and thus the West itself was in a position to influence the image-creating process in Yugoslavia. The image of the West was now in sharp contrast with that of the East. Support for Tito was almost in linear correlation with the danger people felt from the Soviet Union.[42] The Yugoslav identity was now more than ever before based on a thin narrative of "self-managed socialism," one that is different from Soviet statism yet still remaining socialism. It was becoming more and more dependent on the existence of the Soviet Other. This would have dramatic consequences once the Soviet Other ceased to exist, in the second half of the 1980s.[43]

Domestically, this would have political consequences too. Ranking the Soviet danger above any other, the Yugoslav political elite declared "dogmatic" and "statist" Communists within the country to be their main enemy. It opposed them with much more vigilance than the liberal democrats and pro-Western groups. In the 1940s, pro-Soviet politicians such as Andrija Hebrang (a Croat wartime party leader) and Sreten Žujovic (a Serb) were arrested together with tens of thousands of pro-Soviet Communists who were jailed at Goli Otok. In the 1960s, potentially pro-Soviet members of the elite, such as the state's vice-president, Aleksandar Ranković, and the defence minister, General Ivan Gošnjak, were removed from office. In the 1970s, the founding congress of a new alternative Communist Party of Yugoslavia in Bar (1975) was prevented from meeting and the organizers were all arrested. The alternative socialist Praxis group was removed from Belgrade and Zagreb Universities in 1981; the Belgrade Six (a group of "Trotskyites") were arrested and tried in 1983–5; and so on. Finally, the conservative (pro-Kardeljist) forces within the LCY leadership were especially keen to point out that some Montenegrin supporters of Slobodan Milošević and his "antibureaucratic revolution" (1988) were in fact supporters of the "Russians," and that the whole project (led by Milošević) would lead the country closer towards the East.[44] Even the political assassinations of a number of prominent Croatian political émigrés may have been carried out because of their links, or at least the intention to establish them, with the USSR.[45] Finally, the elite insisted that the Kosovo unrest of 1981 was a "counter-revolution," organized and led by dogmatic Marxists–Leninists. To call it "nationalist" or "separatist" would, for them, actually diminish the importance of the problem. And indeed, as would be discovered a decade later, many of those who protested in Kosovo in 1981 (and later) were inspired by an alternative form of Marxism, whether they were "Hoxhists" or "Titoists."[46]

Their confidence in using Soviet ideology as the defining "Other" against which the Yugoslav "mirror image" ought to be created was based on the Yugoslav enlightened vanguard's firm belief that Yugoslavia simply could not collapse; thus separatism had no chance of succeeding.[47] Yugoslavia's ethnic nations—so the elite believed—had no reason to reject socialism, which offered them full recognition and an institutional framework that no other system had in the past. In fact, Yugoslav socialism offered them more than either a Soviet or Western sort of political system would, as some would discover a decade after the break-up of the state.[48] As believers in rationalism, the enlightened vanguard simply could not have imagined reasons why anyone in Yugoslavia would want to turn towards nationalism once they had achieved their strategic objectives in post-1974 Yugoslavia, of republics as their nation-states.[49] They were also, the Yugoslav Communists believed, sufficiently "conscious" to reject nationalism, as a doctrine of the dark and by many hated past. The trends towards globalization (as Kardelj dubbed it back in 1970)[50] would make nationalism and separatism a relic of the past. Barriers between states, including the Berlin Wall, would be torn down, and Yugoslavia would become an example of diverse cultures living side by side with one another in their own republics, with their own rights and in peace. Nationalism simply could not prevail over such a prospect. Thus, there was no real danger of it.

On the contrary, there was still a danger of "unitarism," "statism," "centralism" and "bureaucratism." They could link themselves with "hegemonic" forces both domestically—primarily, that is, with Serbia, but also with Croatia—or internationally—that is, with the Soviet Union. Yugoslav official rhetoric against "unitarism" now replaced (at least among non-Serbs) the campaign against "nationalism." A keynote speech by the Croatian long-standing party leader, Vladimir Bakarić, at the Tenth Session of the Central Committee of the LC Croatia (15 January 1970) expressed this well. Weighing the chances for nationalists or unitarists to establish a government, whether in Yugoslavia or in Croatia, Bakarić said that only the second group would have a chance:

"Would they [the "unitarists"] be able to realize their program? They would be able to find a program, to find allies in Yugoslavia, to find them outside of Yugoslavia. Their chance to realize this program has gone, it does not exist in Yugoslavia, but with pressure on Yugoslavia from abroad this would become possible. And I think that it is possible for them, if not exactly to form a government, then certainly to create a serious political movement supported by this pressure from abroad, and also by their own forces within the country. Of course, the main support for this program would be bureaucratic centralism and Cominformism."[51]

And if that was the case in Croatia a year before the eruption of Croatian nationalism, one may just imagine how significant was any threat of unitarism, in Bakarić's view, that would come from Serbia.

It is within this context that one may understand why the threat from liberalism—i.e., the West—and nationalism was rather overlooked, while that of "statism" and "unitarism" was overestimated. Ultimately, one may now better understand why the Yugoslav elite was totally unprepared and surprised when the Soviet system collapsed and liberalism, contrary to their expectations, entered the Yugoslav identity-making arena and emerged victorious. The fact is, it came hand in hand with nationalism.

Conclusion

The official identity of socialist Yugoslavia was towards its end almost exclusively based on a vision of the future, i.e. on ideology rather than on common ethnic, political and cultural characteristics shared by its constituent nations. Even more than earlier, the vision of a future was the key element, and for the party's own narrative the only element, that kept Yugoslavia together. Only if socialist was Yugoslavia worth preserving and fighting for. The other possible Yugoslavias, such as the interwar liberal-democratic regime or a statist/unitarist Yugoslavia similar to the USSR, were undesirable. But not only that: to Yugoslav Communists they were ultimately impossible.

Yugoslav Communists indeed had a vision of internal cohesion, which was based on Edvard Kardelj's interpretation of Marxism. But instruments that would in other types of social projects help strengthen internal cohesion, such as ethnic similarities, state centralism or nationalism in both the civic and ethnic sense, were treated as hostile Others. They were essential parts either of past domestic concepts (interwar Yugoslavism) or parallel but undesirable concepts of socialism (such as Soviet statism). They were therefore unacceptable to Yugoslav official identity formulators. Without these potential instruments of cohesion, Yugoslav Communists placed not only the identity but also the existence of Yugoslavia entirely on the back of their own ideology. Their commitment to Marxism prompted them to underestimate the chance for liberal democracy or nationalism to compete with socialism as a vision of the future society. By declaring alternative models of socialism, especially the Soviet model, as the only real threat (since socialism was "the only game in town"), they ended up exactly where they did not want to be, more dependent than ever on the existence of the Soviet Other. The collapse of their own ideology, and the collapse of that Soviet Other, left Yugoslavia without both pillars of identity: internal cohesion and an external difference. This joint collapse, and not ethnic hatred, nationalism or the economic crisis, was the main reason why it disintegrated.

Sources

Document 1:
> Ranković's whole line was conservative. In Serbia, we felt him to be a heavy burden. ... Tito exercised full control over foreign policy and the army, while Ranković controlled the Party and police. We wanted to put the lid on this. ... Everything that Kardelj initiated and promoted in our political system distinguished us from the East and

it was a guarantee that we would not return to the past. In general, he was a reformist and a Yugoslav.

Source: Petar Stambolić, as quoted in Slavoljub Djukić, *Kako se dogodio voda* (Belgrade: Samizdat B92, 1992), 212. Petar Stambolić was the leading Serbian politician in the forty years between 1944 and 1984.

Document 2:

For, as I have already stated, the alternative here is not whether Yugoslavia will survive or not but whether it will continue to develop as a socialist, self-managing and democratic community of equal peoples or whether it will fall into the hands of hegemonic forces in any political or ideological guise (Kardelj, 1969/1981: 228).

Source: Edvard Kardelj, "Yugoslavia—the Socialist Self-Managing Community of Equal Peoples" (speech given in 1969) in *The Nations and Socialism* (Belgrade: STP, 1981), 228.

Document 3:

The federal leadership is always being accused of statism. There have been in this criticism of statism overtones of national postures, i.e. complaints about the federal government being in Belgrade, about Serbia squeezing the most out of this situation, and so on, and about such statism being harmful to other nations and other republics. Well and good, we are now liquidating that statism and the federal government will have left to it very little of the kind of competence and very few of the kind of affairs which could be said to favor one or the other republic. But we must now see to it that this statism is not divided up among the republics. ... Statism should go right out of our lives and out of the relationships existing in this country.

Source: Josip Broz Tito, "No republic can be sufficient unto itself" (speech given in 1971), in *The National Question* (Belgrade: Komunist, 1983), 162.

Document 4:

Engels ... wrote: "It is pure nonsense to talk of a free people's state. So long as the proletariat uses the state, it does not use it in the interests of freedom but in order to hold down its adversaries, and as soon as it becomes possible to speak of freedom the state as such shall cease to exist." ... Every state represents authority, and as such is a form of dictatorship. Democracy itself as a political system is a form of authority, and therefore a form of dictatorship. Hence the long-range objective of socialism in Yugoslav conditions should be *not to create a state-sponsored democracy, but rather to socialize state functions* [Kardelj's emphases], and to promote self-management and self-managing democracy. Such efforts simultaneously create the conditions for the withering away of the state in general and, by the same token, for the withering away of the state characterized by the dictatorship of the proletariat in all its forms, including the present self-managing democratic form. Instead of democracy as a form of state system, there will be a democracy and freedom of the individual, who is no longer the subject of the state but governs himself and regulates social relationships as the relationships between man and things and not between man and man. In such circumstances, the state apparatus will turn into a specialized public service of the self-managing society. Therefore, there is no contradiction between the dictatorship of the proletariat and democracy, but there is a contradiction between the centralized power of the state and its apparatus, whatever form it may take, on the one hand, and the self-management aspirations of man and his interest unions on the other.

Source: Edvard Kardelj, *Democracy and Socialism* (London: The Summerfield Press, 1978), 92.

Document 5:

When we say that the political pluralism of bourgeois society cannot serve as the political system for socialist self-management, we must add that a one-party system as a variant of this system will not do either. ... From a socio-historical point of view, the one-party system is a permutation of the political system borrowed from the bourgeois state in the era of capitalism. It in fact performs the same role as the multiparty system of bourgeois pluralism, the only difference being that power is wielded by one party rather than by several parties in turn. Actually, there is very little difference there, because the political parties in bourgeois society—with the exception of the revolutionary parties of the working class—do not differ greatly in their attitude towards the existing social system. However, the one-party system, even more than political pluralism, is susceptible to serious deformations of various kinds. In the first place, there is a tendency for the party leadership to form a personal union with the state executive apparatus, and thus the executive becomes the tool of technocratic and bureaucratic forces in society. ... The one-party system may thus change gradually from being a class weapon to being an instrument of technocratic and bureaucratic rule over class and society. The Paris Commune and Marx were both aware of this danger, but it has never been more real than in contemporary socialist practice today. ...

Our society was bound to make this break [with the one-party system, D.J.] as soon as it opted for self-management, and the socialization of state property on the basis of self-management, instead of the perpetuation of state-owned forms of social production relations. The one-party system of the Stalinist type came about when the mechanism of bourgeois parliamentarism was simply grafted on to the system of socialist socio-economic relations. The one-party system took two features from the political system of bourgeois society which make it incompatible with the system of self-management. Firstly, like the bourgeois parliamentary system, it excluded the individual from having a direct hand in governing society. Secondly, by reducing the individual's role to that of a political citizen, it transformed him into a caster of votes for personalities and not for interests, so that at the polls the citizen surrendered his general warrant to administer society and his own personal interests in favour of political and state executive officials and bodies. ...

The primary concern of the [one-party] political system, therefore, is no longer to establish socio-economic and democratic conditions in which the real worker can freely and autonomously pursue his class interests and aspirations, but rather to secure the functioning of the centralized state machinery. This kind of dogmatic theory has fundamentally affected the development of the political systems in contemporary socialism. Of course, everyday life has modified it and continues to do so, but it has caused socialist practice—particularly the development of socialist democracy—considerable harm. ...

It is precisely the struggle for a more progressive democratic system of socialism to which we should be committed. Socialist practice has shown what pitfalls and hazards are involved in an exclusive orientation toward a one-party political system. The greatest danger presented by such a system for Yugoslavia would be that the League of Communists should become an integral part or even an appendage of a technocratic-bureaucratic monopoly. The mechanism of monopoly is conservative by nature, and therefore it imposes a conservative ideology on the workers" movement. Hence such a system does not suit our system of self-managing pluralism precisely because of its machinery. ...

It is clear, however, that as the political role of anti-socialist and anti-self-management forces weakens, which is historically inevitable, this special role of the League of Communists, and with it this single feature of the one-party system, will also weaken and wither away. The long-term creative role of the League of Communists consists primarily in its efforts and ability to make a theoretical and scientific assessment of the objective laws ruling the trends and development of socialist society, to correlate these trends on a day-to-day basis with the aspirations and interests of the self-managing subjects ... and to mobilize the broad working masses in a drive to achieve the goals which are set on the basis of these assessments. This means that the Yugoslav political system, far from being a one-party system, actually precludes any such system, just as it precludes the multiparty pluralism of bourgeois society. Self-management and self-managing democracy cannot tolerate political monopoly by any forces outside the democratically integrated system of social self-management. It is precisely from this self-managing democratic integration that the organization of the state and of its highest executive organs emanates. If a feature of the one-party system is still present in this state system, it is only as an instrument to defend the survival and further development of our self-managing and democratically integrated socialist society. The more stable the system of self-managing democracy becomes, the less prominent this attribute of the one-party system will become.

For all these reasons, our self-managing society would be taking an extremely reactionary step backwards if it were to embrace the political pluralism of bourgeois society or its one-party variant. What needs to be done above all is to democratize society even further on the principles of self-management by the working man and citizen. Only such a status of the working people in society can lead to the withering away and abolition of the class system of society in general, and thereby secure democracy and freedom for all.

Source: Edvard Kardelj, *Democracy and Socialism* (London: The Summerfield Press, 1978), 68–79.

Document 6:
The only real threat perceived by us [the state and party leadership of Yugoslavia in moments of President Tito's illness in 1980] was a sudden aggression by the Warsaw Pact countries with a radical objective. The aggressor would, according to estimates by the Yugoslav military leadership, with no special preparations, be able to move against our country about 15–20 divisions, of which four were air and parachute divisions with seven brigades. They would deploy strong air and tank units. ... At the meeting [of the National Defence

Council, on 13 March 1980] we all agreed that, according to all indicators, one must count on a long-term war in the case of aggression. ... The Soviet leadership had not given up on its pressure against Yugoslavia.

Source: Raif Dizdarević, *Od smrti Jugoslavije do smrti Tita* (Sarajevo: Oko, 1999), 49. Raif Dizdarević was the representative of Bosnia and Herzegovina in the Yugoslav State Presidency in 1986–1989, and from 1988–1989 its president.

Notes

1 For an explanation of the category of political frontier see Aletta Norval, *Deconstructing Apartheid Discourse* (London: Verso, 1996), 4; Ernesto Laclau and Chantal Mouffe, *Hegemony and Socialist Strategy: Towards a Radical Democratic Politics* (London: Verso, 1985).

2 The concept of the enlightened vanguard is explained by J. L. Talmon, *The Origins of Totalitarian Democracy* (London: Sphere, 1970). In Marx's version, the intellectual and political elites merge into one—since philosophers have only interpreted the world, but the point was, as he famously said in his 11th Thesis on Feuerbach, to change it. The role of the enlightened vanguard in socialism was to be both the ultimate interpreter of reality (and visionary of the future) and the force changing it in the direction of the vision. Communists, therefore, had a duty to study (and then to teach) Marxism. For the importance of studying Marxism for young Communists in the USSR, see Sheila Fitzpatrick, *Everyday Stalinism* (Oxford: Oxford University Press, 1999).

3 This vision was promoted by Croatian party leader Vladimir Bakarić, who had taken the Italian Communist Party as a role-model. It was then developed in Edvard Kardelj's last book *Pravci razvoja političkog sistema socijalističkog samoupravljanja* (Belgrade: Komunist, 1977), which was declared (by the LCY Presidency) the official preparatory document for the Eleventh LCY Congress (1978).

4 Edvard Kardelj (1910–1979) was for the whole postwar period the main ideologue of Yugoslavia's political system. He was both the supreme interpreter of Marxism and the chairman of the Constitution Commission for all postwar Yugoslav Constitutions. A Slovene school teacher before he joined the Yugoslav Communist Party in 1939, Kardelj was a member of Tito's inner circle of Partisan party leaders by the time that the Jajce meeting outlined the postwar Federation in November 1943. For Kardelj's role in this period see my "Yugoslavism in post-WWII Yugoslavia: from Tito to Kardelj," in D. Djokić, ed., *Yugoslavism: Histories of a Failed Idea* (London: Hurst, 2003), 157–81.

5 For a comprehensive statement of this argument, see Charles Taylor, *Sources of the self: the making of the modern identity* (Cambridge: Cambridge University Press, 1989).

6 This, however, does not mean that vision does not exist in "non-ideological," i.e. liberal-democratic societies. It is, however, widely felt that politics in these societies is more "pragmatic" and less vision-driven. It is more about what is than what ought to be;

its political elite is representative, i.e. elected. Politics in a liberal democracy is "about power" or "all about economics." However, this is not the case in vision-driven societies—they are legitimized by denial of reality and, if need be, by violence.

7 For the notion of ideocracy see Jaroslaw Piekalkiewicz and Alfred Wayne Penn, *Politics of Ideocracy* (Albany: Sunny Press, 1995).

8 Party members, for example, addressed one another (and even the party leader) with the informal "Ti" rather than formal "Vi" to emphasize the egalitarian character of Communism; meanwhile, all party members were requested to be moral and political role-models to others. For role-models in socialism see Sheila Fitzpatrick, *Everyday Stalinism* (Oxford: Oxford University Press, 1999).

9 In his *Notes on Social Criticism* (Belgrade: STP, 1965), 64, Kardelj explained this by saying that "a man who would today try to make gold following the recipes of medieval alchemists would be considered a charlatan or a ridiculous ignoramus." Once defeated, capitalism simply could not come back—this would be just like "medieval alchemists" returning back once modern chemistry and medicine have been established.

10 To understand the implementation of this general conclusion to the Yugoslav case, see Miroslav Hadžić, *Sudbina partijske vojske* (Belgrade: Samizdat B92, 2001). For the treatment of the ideological character of the army in socialism, see *Nova Revija* 57 (1987) and later issues, especially the articles by Spomenka Hribar.

11 In Serbo-Croat, the word was *podruštvljavanje države*. The word "society" was often used instead of "state." For example, "societal ownership" (not "state ownership"); "socio-political communities" (instead of state-territorial units), etc.

12 To be clear: in most liberal-democratic concepts, too, the existence of the state is justified by the threat of violence, which might occur because of the presence of the Hostile Other, either within society or from outside (that is, in the form of "internal" and "external" enemies). No state is neutral, and none rules out violence to preserve social order, as defined by its ruling class or elite. The difference is that liberal democracies do not consider the present as such an enemy that it should necessarily be excluded from political representation. On the contrary, they allow representation of the present via elections. On a higher level, within the extra-parliamentary sphere, they too are future-oriented, often driven by a vision (for example, by an "American dream"), and structured not as neutral instruments of all citizens but as tools of their own elites. In this chapter, however, we do not focus on other states but on Yugoslavia.

13 That socialism was a period of ongoing "revolutionary" reforms was evident especially in Yugoslavia, whose postwar political history is in fact a history of constitution-writing and endless economic and political "reforms." In socialist societies the difference between "reforms" and "revolution" is much less clear-cut than those who are coming from liberal-democratic tradition would assume. Gorbachev's and Marković's reforms in the late 1980s were therefore perceived by many in those societies as yet another of these "reforms," not as an announcement of the collapse of the regime. Thus they were tolerated for much longer than one would have expected even by the most conservative factions of the political elite.

14 For this see Vladimir Dedijer, *Tito* (New York: Simon and Schuster, 1953), 432. Dedijer says that Tito told him: "Titoism as a separate ideological line does not exist. ... To put it as an ideology would be stupid. ... It is simply that we have added nothing to

Marxist–Leninist doctrine. We have only applied that doctrine in consonance with our situation. Since there is nothing new, there is no new ideology. Should 'Titoism' become an ideological line, we would become revisionists; we would have renounced Marxism. We are Marxists, I am a Marxist and therefore I cannot be a 'Titoist.'"

15 As Kardelj expressed it, "the unity of the nation is not possible unless based on a clear platform, on a clear outlook for the future development of society." Edvard Kardelj, "Ways of Democracy in a Socialist Society," in *Self-management and the political system* (Belgrade: STP, 1980), 263.

16 This is why the Party occupied the central place in the army and the defence system in general. By formulating a "clear vision," the party was making a decisive contribution to defending the nation. In the Yugoslav case, the supreme position of the party in defence issues was guaranteed by legal provisions which made presidents of the party committees the "presidents of the Social Self-Defence Councils" in war or any situation of imminent threat of war.

17 The political leadership tagged its opponents with some of these labels to indicate that they were not only opponents of socialism in Yugoslavia, but of Yugoslav independence too—because there was no difference between Yugoslav self-managing identity and Yugoslav identity as such. To support any "foreign" ideology would mean to undermine Yugoslav identity, i.e. its independence. For example, Milovan Djilas was in 1954 declared an "anarcho-liberal" (pro-Western) and Aleksandar Ranković in 1966 a "bureaucrat" and "unitarist" (thus pro-Soviet); the Croatian leaders of 1971 were "nationalists" (pro-Western), the Serbian leaders in 1972 "liberals" (also pro-Western), etc. Even after Tito's death, the labeling continued. Slobodan Milošević was treated by the members of the elite most loyal to the Kardelj discourse as a "unitarist" and "dogmatist" (thus pro-USSR) when he appeared on the political scene in 1984.

18 When talking about the liberal concept of nationhood, one needs to be aware of the historical context in which all this happened. In the aftermath of the First World War the liberal doctrine seemed victorious (at least in Europe), and thus it expressed itself in its unrestricted, i.e. unreformed form. Only later were liberal concepts amended in order to respond to the issues of minorities, collective identities and group rights. In the period we analyze here, liberalism had no answer to these problems. Nor did it recognize the importance of the ethnic definition of a nation, reducing the term to the political, i.e. civic nation only. This is the main reason for its failure in Germany and throughout East and Southeast Europe, where the concept of "nationhood" was primarily ethnic, not political. Even when (after the Second World War) it moved to include the social dimension (as social-liberalism and/or left-libertarianism), liberal democracy offered to minorities less than socialism. This is why the introduction of (even such reformed) liberal concepts in post-Communist societies failed to convince so many (and especially ethnic minorities) that they would gain anything in terms of their social and political status, rather than lose everything.

19 See Edvard Kardelj, "Ways of Democracy in a Socialist Society," in Edvard Kardelj, *Self-management and the political system* (Belgrade: STP, 1977), 130.

20 For example, in Robert Nozick, *Anarchy, State and Utopia* (Oxford: Blackwell, 1974).

21 Famously, Tito himself acknowledged this in his 1942 article in the party gazette *Proleter*: "The words *national liberation struggle* would be nothing but words, and even

deception, if they did not have, together with their meaning in the overall Yugoslav context, a specifically national meaning for each people individually, if they did not mean, together with the liberation of Yugoslavia, the liberation at the same time, too, of Croats, Slovenes, Serbs, Macedonians, Arnauts [Albanians], Moslems and the rest; if the national liberation struggle did not contain the substance of effective freedom, equality and brotherhood for all the peoples of Yugoslavia. This is the real essence of the national liberation struggle." See Josip Broz Tito, "Nacionalno pitanje u Jugoslaviji u svjetlosti narodno-oslobodilačke borbe," *Proleter* 17 (1942): 3.

22 For the importance of such fears of becoming a minority, which was growing in all Yugoslav nations by the end of the socialist period, see my article "Fear of becoming a minority as a motivator of conflict in the former Yugoslavia," *Balkanologie* 1–2 (December 2001): 21 36. The socialist narrative did not know of either majorities or minorities. The concept of minority was excluded from this narrative—it was politically incorrect to name anyone as a "minority." With the introduction of liberal democracy (which was based on counting votes, and thus counting citizens too), both of these concepts were promoted. Since in Yugoslavia nobody was a majority, and nobody wanted to be "demoted" to the status of a minority, all ethnic groups felt unhappy with prospects of being forced to become a minority. Those fears then created aggression, especially among those segments of the ethnic groups which were left outside their new nation-states with the status of a minority: Serbs in Croatia and Bosnia–Herzegovina, Croats in Bosnia–Herzegovina, Albanians in the FR Yugoslavia, Serbs in Kosovo, Albanians in Macedonia, etc.

23 The Marxist concept did not recognize the *demos* because the very concept of *demos* is linked with elections and the state—none of which was central (or even desirable) in Marxist views on society. The reasons for not promoting a Yugoslav nation in an ethnic sense have been already explained above.

24 Hostility towards bureaucracy was not specific to Yugoslavia but a feature of all socialist narratives, which were ideologically anti-statist. Bureaucracy is a network of public servants, and thus of a state. Good examples of anti-bureaucratic rhetoric and action were the Chinese Cultural Revolution and, later, the anti-bureaucratic revolution of Milošević (1988).

25 From the discourse of liberal democracy, such an equation of decentralisation with democratization does not make much sense. On the contrary, the *demos* cannot be created through decentralization, but only through centralization, via, for example, the construction of a nationwide "electorate." Neither elections nor *demos* were, however, part of the Communist discourse on nation.

26 New terms were constructed to explain the "new forms" and institutions of social activism. These terms are almost impossible to translate into the vocabulary of liberal-democratic societies.

27 For this explanation, see Tito's speech in the Yugoslav People's Assembly on 17 June 1950, on the occasion of proposing the Law on Workers' Self-management. The speech is a theoretical discourse against the Soviet interpretation of Marxism. Similarly, Kardelj's speech at the Third Plenum of the CC LCY (March 1954) criticized the "theories of spontaneity" in Milovan Djilas's writings. At crucial moments in Yugoslav political history, the Central Committee meetings turned almost into philological seminars on the meanings of Marx's writings and of sentences/texts written/said by various "revi-

sionists." Being the enlightened vanguard, the party was, of course, always right, even when its interpretation clashed with the author's. For example, the Eighth Session of the CC LC Serbia in September 1987 denied Dragiša Pavlović the right to interpret the meaning of his own words (on "easily promised speed"); the party was there to interpret their "real meaning." For the importance of words and their interpretation in socialism, see Vaclav Havel, "A Word About Words" (1977), in *Open Letters* (London: Faber and Faber, 1991), 377–89.

28 An excellent account of the debates between Soviet and Yugoslav Marxists on the "withering away of the state" is given in Ivo Lapenna, *State and Law: Soviet and Yugoslav Theory* (New Haven: Yale University Press, 1964).

29 They differed also in the understanding of the role of the party. In Tito's words soon after the split with Stalin: "The role of the party is historically limited to a certain period. The party withers away gradually. That does not mean that a one-party system will be superseded by a multi-party system. It merely means that the one-party system, having superseded a multi-party system, will in turn vanish. ... Therein lies the very difference between our view and that of the Soviets." Vladimir Dedijer, *Tito* (New York: Simon and Schuster, 1953), 430–31.

30 Criticism of the USSR as such was more sophisticated, since Yugoslavia could not afford open conflict. However, criticism of "Stalinism" had no limits. Tito had more understanding for the Soviets than some other members of the political elite, for example, Edvard Kardelj, Koča Popović and Stane Dolanc. Some political conflicts between Tito and these three political leaders (with Kardelj in 1967, with Popović in 1972, and with Dolanc in 1978) were the result of different views on how far Yugoslav criticism of the USSR could go.

31 This is certainly one of the reasons that Yugoslavs found more difficult than others in restructuring their identity once ideology had collapsed. The violent break-up of Yugoslavia was the result of the weakness of the state, which was a direct consequence of the elite's commitment to the anti-statist concept of self-management.

32 In this conclusion Kardelj was supported by leading Serbian Communists as well. For the reasons why the Serbian elite accepted Kardelj's political narrative, see my "Zašto je Srbija prihvatila Ustav iz 1974?" *Ljetopis* (1998), 3: 63–104; see also the authorized minutes of the Fourteenth Session of the Central Committee of the League of Communists of Serbia, 29 and 30 May 1968 (Belgrade: Komunist, 1968).

33 Indeed, many others (both in the East and in the West) shared this enthusiasm for Yugoslav reforms and Yugoslavia's original "third" way.

34 For perceptions of the Soviet threat in 1968 and 1971, see the memoirs of members of the Yugoslav political elite of that time, e.g. Miko Tripalo, *Hrvatsko proljeće* (Zagreb: Globus, 1991); Dragoslav Draža Marković, *Život i politika* (Belgrade: Rad, 1987 and 1988); and Latinka Perović, *Zatvaranje kruga* (Sarajevo: Svjetlost, 1990). For this threat related to the 1979 Soviet invasion of Afghanistan, see Branko Mamula, *Slučaj Jugoslavija* (Podgorica, 2000); and Raif Dizdarević, *Od smrti Tita do smrti Jugoslavije* (Sarajevo: Oko, 1999).

35 As exemplified by the Paris protests, the anti-war campaign in the U.S., and the rise of the left throughout Western Europe in 1968–1972; also, Allende's victory in Chile in 1970.

36 Edvard Kardelj, "The National Question in Yugoslavia and Its Foreign Policy" (speech given in 1973), in Edvard Kardelj, *The Nations and Socialism* (Belgrade: STP, 1980), 236.

37 Ibid., 286.

38 A journalistic account of this was given in Duško Doder, *The Yugoslavs* (London: George Allen and Unwin, 1978). For opinion polls conducted in Slovenia (among other issues, on perceptions of threat) see Niko Toš, ed., *Slovensko Javno Mnenje 1987: pregled in primerjava rezultatov raziskav SJM 69–SJM 87* (Ljubljana: Delavska Enotnost, 1987).

39 For the importance of egalitarianism in Yugoslav socialism, see Ivan Bernik, "Functions of Egalitarianism in Yugoslav Society," *Praxis International*, 9 (1989): 425–32; and Josip Županov, *Marginalije o društvenoj krizi* (Zagreb: Globus, 1983).

40 For the Hoxhists–Titoists division among Kosovo Albanians, see Shkelzen Maliqi: "A Demand for a New Status: The Albanian Movement in Kosova," in Thanos Veremis and Evangelis Kofos, eds., *Kosovo: Avoiding Another Balkan War* (Athens: Eliamep, 1998), 207–38.

41 Activities of the "critical intelligentsia" (i.e. "dissidents") in Yugoslavia were in fact tolerated (and sometimes even protected) by the elite when they limited their criticism to "Stalinism," without extending it to socialism in general. When criticising Stalinism (and also: unitarism, centralism, statism and bureaucratism) they were in fact on the same side with the elite itself. Closeness between the regime and intelligentsia was demonstrated, for example, in Croatia on the occasion of the "White Book" in 1984. On the other hand, those who attempted to criticize the Yugoslav elite by arguing that it had not abandoned all elements of Stalinism (for example: Milovan Djilas, or the Belgrade Six) were not tolerated but jailed.

42 Illustration of this could be found in Doder, 1978.

43 At first, the Yugoslav elite did not recognize the significance of the "Gorbachev factor." In 1985–1988 they welcomed his reforms as a "victory of the Yugoslav model," and failed to see the deeper consequences that this withdrawal of the main "Other" brought with it to Yugoslavia. For the reaction of the Yugoslav political elite to Gorbachev, see Raif Dizdarević, *Od smrti Tita do smrti Jugoslavije* (Sarajevo: Oko, 1999).

44 Famously, a public scandal broke out when the then Zagreb Television (now Croatian Television) reported that supporters of Milošević at a rally in Podgorica (then Titograd) in 1989 had demanded help from the Russians. Allegedly, they chanted: "We want the Russians" *(Hoćemo Ruse)*. The organizers denied this, saying that Milošević's supporters chanted *Hoćemo gusle* (not *Ruse*), i.e., "We want the *gusle*." To demand Russian support would have been totally unacceptable politically. For the importance of the gusle in the Yugoslav political tradition, see Maja Brkljačić's chapter 1 in this volume. The link between the Yugoslav and Soviet military elites at a time when the Yugoslav military elite was getting increasingly pro-Milošević has been documented in Veljko Kadijević's memoirs, *Moje vidjenje raspada* (Belgrade: Politika, 1993), and also in Borisav Jović's diary, *Poslednji dani SFRJ* (Belgrade: Politika, 1995).

45 Pro-Soviet views on the part of some Croatian separatists (especially regarding immigration) sometimes emerged. At its congress in London in 1980, the Croatian

National Council (HNV) declared: "Better divided by Russian occupation than united by American-supported Yugoslavia." See Raif Dizdarević, *Od smrti Tita do smrti Jugoslavije* (Sarajevo: Oko, 1999), 54. The strategic interests of the USSR were linked with access to the warm Mediterranean sea, the Adriatic included. This was potentially the main link between Croatian separatists and the USSR. Apart from this, some separatist groups among the Croatian diaspora promoted a revolutionary program, based on the notion of "self-determination."

46 For Titoists and Hoxhists within the Albanian nationalist movement, see Tim Judah, *Kosovo: War and Revenge* (New Haven: Yale University Press, 2000).

47 "It is beyond any doubt that Yugoslav society, all Yugoslav people and in all situations, will find enough strength to resist all disintegrating tendencies," claimed Kardelj in 1969. See Edvard Kardelj, "Yugoslavia—the socialist self-managing community of equal peoples" (speech given in 1969), in Edvard Kardelj, *The Nations and Socialism* (Belgrade: STP, 1980), 228.

48 A good illustration of this may be found by closer analysis of international proposals for Bosnia–Herzegovina. The model promoted by the high representative for this country is remarkably similar to that institutionalized by the 1974 constitution. Liberal notions of one-citizen–one-vote seem to be rejected as ill suited for Bosnian ethnic and political complexity. Nobody is treated as a "majority" and nobody as a "minority." This was the case in Tito's Yugoslavia too.

49 And they were not alone in this; the West could think of no good reason either. Respect for Tito and the assumption that Yugoslavia would continue was well expressed by the massive attendance of world leaders at his funeral in May 1980.

50 See Kardelj's speech at the 12th Session of the LCY Presidency, "Aktuelni problemi daljeg razvoja našeg političkog sistema," in Edvard Kardelj, *Izbor iz dela III: Politički sistem socijalističkog samoupravljanja* (Belgrade: Komunist, 1979), 259–83.

51 Vladimir Bakarić, "Unitarizam kao ideologija i ocjena nacionalizma u Hrvatskoj," speech at the Tenth Session of the Central Committee of the League of Communists of Croatia (15 January 1970), in Vladimir Bakarić, *Socijalistički samoupravni sistem i društvena reprodukcija* (Zagreb: Informator, 1974), 408–9.

LIST OF CONTRIBUTORS

John R. Lampe is Professor of History at the University of Maryland, College Park, and past Director of East European Studies at the Woodrow Wilson International Center for Scholars, Washington.

Constantin Iordachi completed his doctoral dissertation at the Central European University, Budapest; a study of the evolution of the concept of citizenship in Romania; he teaches at the University of Bucharest.

Mark Biondich completed his doctoral dissertation on Stjepan Radić and the Croatian Peasant Party in history at the University of Toronto and works for the Canadian Ministry of Justice in Ottawa.

Sandra Prlenda is a historian from Zagreb, affiliated with the Centre for Women's Studies in Zagreb, where she works on nationalism and religion in the nineteenth and twentieth centuries.

James Frusetta is a Ph.D. candidate in history at the University of Maryland, College Park; his doctoral dissertation is a study of intersections between Bulgarian and Macedonian identity. He has taught at the American University in Blagoevgrad, Bulgaria.

Andrew B. Wachtel is Professor of Slavic Language and Literature at Northwestern University, Department of Slavic Languages and Literature and Director of the Program in Comparative Literary Studies at Northwestern; his areas of interest include Russian and South Slavic literatures.

Ildiko Erdei is an anthropologist who teaches at the University of Belgrade, Department of Ethnology and Anthropology, and focuses mainly on the anthropology of political rituals and urban anthropology.

Maja Brkljačić is completing her doctoral dissertation in history at Central European University, Budapest; her main areas of interest are the history of Communism and the representation of history.

Rossitza Guentcheva completed her doctoral dissertation in history at Cambridge University and teaches at the University of Sofia; her research interests include the history of Communism and the history of perception.

Robert C. Austin is Project Coordinator at the Centre for Russian and East European Studies at the University of Toronto and a Consultant for Intermedia Global Research and Evaluation, Washington, DC.

Marko Bulatović is a Ph.D. candidate in history at the University of Toronto; his doctoral dissertation is a study of Yugoslavism in the interwar Kingdom of Yugoslavia.

Dejan Jović completed his doctoral dissertation at the London School of Economics and Political Science. He is a Lecturer in Politics at the University of Stirling, and a regular contributor to the *Economics Intelligence Unit* for the area of former Yugoslavia.

INDEX